Screwball Television

Television and Popular Culture
Robert J. Thompson, *Series Editor*

SELECT TITLES IN TELEVISION AND POPULAR CULTURE

Bigger than Ben-Hur: The Book, Its Adaptations, and Their Audiences
BARBARA RYAN and MILETTE SHAMIR, eds.

Black Male Frames: African Americans in a Century of Hollywood Cinema, 1903–2003
ROLAND LEANDER WILLIAMS JR.

Captain America, Masculinity, and Violence: The Evolution of a National Icon
J. RICHARD STEVENS

Inside the TV Writer's Room: Practical Advice for Succeeding in Television
LAWRENCE MEYERS, ed.

Reading Joss Whedon
RHONDA V. WILCOX, TANYA R. COCHRAN, CYNTHEA MASSON, and DAVID LAVERY, eds.

TV on Strike: Why Hollywood Went to War over the Internet
CYNTHIA LITTLETON

Watching TV: Eight Decades of American Television, Third Edition
HARRY CASTLEMAN and WALTER J. PODRAZIK

Watching TV with a Linguist
KRISTY BEERS FÄGERSTEN, ed.

Screwball Television

Critical Perspectives on Gilmore Girls

Edited by

David Scott Diffrient *with* David Lavery

SYRACUSE UNIVERSITY PRESS

Syracuse, New York 13244-5290

First Paperback Edition 2017

17 18 19 20 21 22 6 5 4 3 2 1

∞ The paper used in this publication meets the minimum requirements of the American National Standard for Information Sciences—Permanence of Paper for Printed Library Materials, ANSI Z39.48-1992.

For a listing of books published and distributed by Syracuse University Press, visit www.SyracuseUniversityPress.syr.edu.

ISBN: 978-0-8156-3239-9 (hardcover) 978-0-8156-3528-4 (paperback)
978-0-8156-5069-0 (e-book)

Library of Congress has cataloged the hardcover edition as follows:

Screwball television : critical perspectives on Gilmore girls / edited by David Scott Diffrient with David Lavery. — 1st ed.
p. cm. — (Television and popular culture)
Includes bibliographical references and index.
ISBN 978-0-8156-3239-9 (cloth : alk. paper)
1. Gilmore girls (Television program) I. Diffrient, David Scott, 1972–
II. Lavery, David, 1949–
PN1992.77.G54S34 2010
791.45'72—dc22 2010000442

Manufactured in the United States of America

Contents

Contributors

AMOR MUÑOZ BÉCARES earned a Ph.D. in journalism at Universidad CEU Cardenal Herrera in Valencia and has worked as professor of newspaper design and magazine design at Universidad CEU Cardenal Herrera in Valencia.

ALYSON R. BUCKMAN is associate professor of humanities and religious studies at California State University, Sacramento, where she teaches courses on film, popular culture, and American culture. Her work has appeared in journals and anthologies such as *Modern Fiction Studies, Exchanges, FEMSPEC,* the *Journal of American Culture,* and *Investigating Firefly and Serenity: Science Fiction on the Frontier* (2008). She has co-chaired the Science Fiction and Fantasy Area of the Southwest/Texas Popular Culture/American Culture Association. She believes that french fries are a gateway food, wishes she could be ice cream queen, and—like Rory—likes to carry a book with her always . . . just in case.

HYE SEUNG CHUNG is associate professor of film and media studies in the Department of Communication Studies at the Colorado State University. She is the author of *Hollywood Asian: Philip Ahn and the Politics of Cross-Ethnic Performance* (2006) and *Kim Ki-duk* (2014) as well as numerous articles on Korean cinema and Asian American cultural identities. She is currently writing a book, *Hollywood Diplomacy,* which explores the relationship between U.S. film regulation, foreign relations, and East Asian representations.

GIADA DA ROS is a law graduate and a journalist. She was a TV critic for an Italian weekly paper called *Il Popolo* for several years. She has published essays on *Buffy the Vampire Slayer* in *Slayage* and on *Queer as Folk, Lost,* and *The L Word* in *Ol3Media,* the official magazine of the Masters in Radio and Television of the Department of Communication and Show Business of the University of Roma 3. She has interviewed and written about TV writer Patrick Mulcahey on more than one occasion, including for the upcoming collection *The Survival of the Soap Opera: Strategies for a New Media Era* (2010). She might have followed Paris's studying regimen in the past, but—unlike her—she "deserves *General Hospital.*"

DAVID SCOTT DIFFRIENT is professor of film and media studies at Colorado State University. His essays have appeared in such journals and edited collections as *Cinema Journal*; *Film and History*; *Historical Journal of Film, Radio, and Television*; *Journal of Film and Video*; *Journal of Popular Film and Television*; *Post Script; New Korean Cinema* (2005); and *Reading "Deadwood": A Western to Swear By* (2006). He published a critical study of *M*A*S*H* as part of Wayne State University Press's "TV Milestones" series (2008) and is the author of *Omnibus Films: Theorizing Transauthorial Cinema* (2014). Like Lorelai, he believes that coffee is best brewed "one bag per cup of water."

JANE FEUER is professor of film studies in the English and Communication Departments at the University of Pittsburgh. Her main areas of interest are film, popular culture, television, and cultural studies. Her many publications include *The Hollywood Musical* (2nd ed., 1993) and *Seeing Through the Eighties: Television and Reaganism* (1995).

JOYCE GOGGIN is senior associate professor of literature, film, and new media at the University of Amsterdam. She has published numerous articles on the novel, Hollywood film, television, and computer games, as well as the history of money, gambling, finance, art history, and economics. Joyce fervently hopes that in the virtually inevitable *Gilmore Girls* movie, Lorelai will get married to Chris (again).

AMANDA R. KEELER is assistant professor of digital media and performing arts in the Diederich College of Communication at Marquette University. Her published work explores the history of using film, radio, and television for educational purposes. Her research interests include emergent media technologies, the television industry, and women's television.

DAVID LAVERY was director of Graduate Studies and professor of English at Middle Tennessee State University before his passing in September 2016. The author of more than one hundred published essays, chapters, and reviews, he was author, coauthor, editor, or coeditor of several published books, including *Late for the Sky: The Mentality of the Space Age* (1992), *Full of Secrets: Critical Approaches to "Twin Peaks"* (1994), *"Deny All Knowledge": Reading "The X-Files"* (1996), *Fighting the Forces: What's at Stake in "Buffy the Vampire Slayer"* (2002), *Teleparody: Predicting/Preventing the TV Discourse of Tomorrow* (2002), *Reading "The Sopranos": Hit TV from HBO* (2006), *"Lost"'s Buried Treasures* (2007), and *Finding "Battlestar Galactica"* (2008). The organizer of international conferences on *Buffy the Vampire Slayer* and *The Sopranos,* Lavery was a founding coeditor of the journals *Slayage: The Online International Journal of Buffy Studies* and *Critical Studies in Television.*

SARAH CAITLIN LAVERY is an assistant producer for WSMV (NBC) in Nashville.

A. ROCHELLE MABRY received her Ph.D. from the Film and Media Studies program at the University of Florida's Department of English. She is the author of several essays, including "About a Girl: Contemporary Popular Texts for Women."

JIMMIE MANNING is associate professor of communication at Northern Illinois University. His essays have appeared in such journals and edited collections as *Women and Language, Communication Currents, MP Journal, Grace under Pressure: "Grey's Anatomy"*

Uncovered (2008), and *Sexualized Bodies: Masculinity from Multiple Perspectives* (2009). He is the coauthor of *Researching Interpersonal Relationships: Qualitative Methods, Studies, and Analysis* (2014) and the coeditor of *Lucky Strikes and a Three Martini Lunch: Thinking about Television's Mad Men* (2015). He is still wondering whatever happened to Alex Lesman and how Taylor regained the position of town selectman from Jackson.

ANGEL CASTAÑOS MARTÍNEZ earned a Ph.D. in journalism at the Universidad Complutense de Madrid and is professor of newspaper design and news production at the Universidad CEU Cardenal Herrera in Valencia. Angel and colleague Amor Muñoz Bécares have published cowritten articles about the coverage of terrorist attacks in New York and Madrid.

LEAH E. MINTZ, M.D., is in private practice in Los Angeles, specializing in otolaryngology and head and neck surgery. She completed her residency training at UCLA in 2000, freeing up some time to appreciate Luke's curmudgeonly "Red meat kills—enjoy" in the pilot episode of *Gilmore Girls* a few months later.

SUSANNAH B. MINTZ, professor of English at Skidmore College in Saratoga Springs, New York, is the author of *Threshold Poetics: Milton and Intersubjectivity* (2003), *Unruly Bodies: Life Writing by Women with Disabilities* (2007), and *Hurt and Pain: Literature and the Suffering Body* (2014), as well as numerous articles on autobiography, disability representation, seventeenth-century literature, and creative nonfiction. She would never have heard about *Gilmore Girls* if it weren't for her sister Leah, her own "reigning Lorelai."

LAURA NATHAN is a freelance writer and editor, as well as a lecturer in the Sociology Department at the University of California, Berkeley. Her essays and articles have appeared in publications such as *Redbook*, *Cooking Light*, and the *Writer's Chronicle*. She previously taught women's studies and English at the State University of New York at Buffalo. Since *Gilmore Girls* went off the air, her Tuesday nights have felt a bit like Emily Gilmore's "half-empty box of Cheer" sitting alongside leftover dessert Lorelai brought to Friday-night dinner.

MATTHEW C. NELSON is assistant professor of English at Francis Marion University in Florence, South Carolina. His teaching and research interests focus on the relationships between high school and college writing pedagogy and assessment. His publications include "How Teachers' Professional Identities Position High Stakes Test Preparation in Their Classrooms." While he loves his job, he is holding out hope that Chilton Academy will come calling when Max Medina retires.

RADHA O'MEARA is lecturer in screenwriting in the School of Culture and Communication at the University of Melbourne. She has studied in Australia, the United States, and Germany and taught at universities in Australia and New Zealand. Radha has created fiction and nonfiction for film, video, television, and new media. Her critical research concentrates on serial narrative form in contemporary film and television. She has published on soap operas, superheroes, and cat videos. Like Finn, Radha is Australian and is partial to salt. However, she is keen to try Lorelai's invention of dessert sushi.

JUSTIN OWEN RAWLINS is assistant professor of communication and film studies at the University of Tulsa. He published an essay on John Wayne and *The Conqueror* in *Quarterly Review of Film and Video.* A historian trained in the study of disease, he was absolutely giddy at the revelation that Stars Hollow once had a street named "Sores and Boils" and that the Gilmores reside on said road.

ANNA VIOLA SBORGI completed a Ph.D. in comparative literature at the University of Genoa in 2007. Her research has focused on film and television and on the relationships between literary and visual culture. She has published journal articles and presented at conferences on different subjects, from British film of the 1980s and 1990s (in particular on Derek Jarman) to literary and visual portraiture in Anglo-American Modernism. After some years collaborating for research and teaching with the University of Genoa and working as an English language/culture teacher in Italian secondary schools, she went back to full-time research and is now a film studies graduate student at King's College London. Describing herself as the "thing that reads a lot," she could not help being "Gilmored" when she first encountered the lovely protagonist of the series, Rory.

Introduction

"You're about to Be Gilmored"

DAVID SCOTT DIFFRIENT

> "C'mon, c'mon, I want to get started!"
>
> —LORELAI GILMORE to her daughter, Rory, as they sit down at the breakfast table with the latter's application to Harvard in "Application Anxiety" (3.03)

> "Welcome to the S.H., bitch!"
>
> —ZACK VAN GERBIG to the "Korean Brad Pitt" in "Just Like Gwen and Gavin" (6.12)

The two above exclamations, taken from episodes of the critically acclaimed television series *Gilmore Girls* (WB/CW, 2000–2007), are not the kinds of hyperliterate lines of dialogue typically associated with the program. They do not express, as do many other spoken passages in the series, the protagonists' savvy ability to drop references to such disparate figures as Sun Tzu, P. G. Wodehouse, and Rick James into their caffeine-fueled conversations. But they effectively illustrate the need to establish a foundation for critical inquiry into the compulsive ways in which fans consume this most contradictory of TV shows, which has the capacity to both comfort and challenge viewers.

In "Application Anxiety," Rory (Alexis Bledel), the college-bound daughter of Lorelai Gilmore (Lauren Graham), receives an important-looking envelope from Harvard while watching *The Brady Bunch*

Variety Hour (1977), a song-and-dance-filled spin-off of the kitschy American sitcom that has inspired two feature-length parodies (*The Brady Bunch Movie* [1995] and *A Very Brady Sequel* [1996]) as well as a host of reunion specials, documentaries, and theatrical revivals. Described by the editors of *TV Guide* as one of "the fifty worst shows of all time," *The Brady Bunch Variety Hour* is in Rory's "top fifty *best*," something that might at first suggest a lack of sophistication on her part but is revealed to be an extension of her (and her mother's) penchant for undermining taste-based hierarchies and capsizing the status quo while proffering idiosyncratic preferences for the stinkiest of cheese. Yet Rory admits to feeling slightly ashamed that this most momentous of events—her receipt of the Harvard application form—should coincide with so guilty a pleasure, so ill-spent a pastime, as this.

The "anxiety" that Rory experiences upon receiving that envelope, exacerbated by her brief encounter with the Springsteen family (headed by Darren, a Harvard graduate of 1974 who gives her advice about the application process), may in fact spread beyond the confines of Stars Hollow and Hartford, Connecticut (the show's two main settings). Indeed, it may seep into the world of the spectator, who can be forgiven for feeling a similar sort of unease when confronted with so many allusions—cultural references (ranging from "high" to "low") that continuously test the audience's knowledge, much like Darren does to his teenage children (whom he quizzes on Shakespeare's plays and on the three subclasses of the Mesozoic era, while the Gilmore girls look on in amazement).

"These kids have no sense of history," complains Lane Kim (Keiko Agena), Rory's best friend who is flummoxed to discover that few teenagers today know that bassist Kim Deal used to be in the influential postpunk group the Pixies. This line, delivered by Lane during an earlier scene in "Application Anxiety," takes on deeper meaning when positioned next to the aforementioned moments, suggesting that in order to truly "get" *Gilmore Girls* one must have more than a passing familiarity with pop culture history; with the movies, TV shows, songs, and other artifacts created during this and previous centuries, be they Elizabethan sonnets or the trashy films of Elizabeth Berkeley. Indeed, viewers unfamiliar with *The O.C.* (2003–7) will likely not realize that Zack's above-cited verbal smackdown of Lane's young uncle (whom he mistakes as a rival suitor in the episode "Just Like Gwen and Gavin") is a parodic rewording of a line spoken by the character Luke Ward in that other WB series: "Welcome to the O.C., bitch!"

During its first two or three seasons, Amy Sherman-Palladino's show seemed to be engaging in a rather one-sided conversation with other cultural productions—television series as diverse as *The Donna Reed Show* (ABC, 1958–66) and *The O.C.* as well as motion pictures like *Gigi* (1958) and *Grey Gardens* (1975), which it habitually referenced. But now TV writers, directors, and producers are responding with their own references to *Gilmore Girls,* from jokes about wanting a similarly sisterly style of family relationship in *Joey* (NBC, 2004–6) to gender-bending admissions by male characters in *Scrubs* (NBC, 2001–) that Lorelai and Rory "speak so fast, but they speak so *true.*" In one episode of *The Ellen DeGeneres Show* (NBC, 2003–), the affable host took her studio audience to the Warner Bros. lot where the fictional town of Stars Hollows had been constructed from the material remnants of earlier films shot there (including *The Music Man* [1962]). A similar studio tour takes place in a Season Two episode of *Supernatural* (WB/CW, 2005–), in which the character Sam Winchester (played by Jared Padalecki, formerly Dean Forester in *Gilmore Girls*) is told by a tour guide to look at the set of Stars Hollow in hopes of spotting "one of the show's stars." Both *MADtv* (FOX, 1995–2009) and *Family Guy* (FOX, 1999–) have spoofed this most loquacious of TV series, giving us skits in which Lorelai and Rory (or, rather, comedians playing exaggerated versions of these characters) are shown talking nonstop for minutes on end. This particular element of *Gilmore Girls*—its emphasis on sped-up verbal discourse as a means of intergenerational communication—is highlighted by the title of the *MADtv* sketch: "Gabmore Girls."

Whether caricatured as "Gabmore Girls" or misnamed as "Calico Gals" (something Matthew Perry's character Matt does when speaking to Lauren Graham in an episode of the NBC series *Studio 60 on the Sunset Strip* [2006–7]), the titular protagonists were already two of the most memorable characters in American television history before the show ended its seven-year run, before *Gossip Girl* (2007–) supplanted *Gilmore Girls* as the CW's next big thing. This is owing not only to the increased proliferation of intertextual references in television shows ranging from *Six Feet Under* (HBO, 2001–5) to *Will & Grace* (NBC, 1998–2006) but also to the enduring, endearing relationship between Lorelai and Rory, which many female fans of the series—mothers and daughters who watch it together—strive to emulate. This book likewise strives to mimic the seemingly limitless locution of *Gilmore Girls,* giving the reader a string of critical commentaries about its significance as a televisual text unlike any other.

Accordingly, this volume brings together a group of unique perspectives on an equally unique American television series. Since its October 5, 2000, debut on the WB network, the quirky, family-friendly *Gilmore Girls,* created by writer and producer Amy Sherman-Palladino, built up a strong cult following and became an object of intense devotion among fans who flocked to their TV sets weekly, seeking comfort in the fictional hamlet of Stars Hollow. Although it is an ensemble series filled with several eccentric characters, *Gilmore Girls* centers on the sisterlike relationship between thirtysomething mother Lorelai and her teenage daughter, Rory. However, their special bond is only one of many notable aspects of the program. Indeed, as Justin Owen Rawlins argues in his contribution to this volume, the confluence of "*Gilmore*-isms" as a distinctive marker of cultural capital within the text "simply cannot be ignored, as they are vital to the show's identity and its discursive situation as a program of note," that is, as a "quality TV" program that attempts "to bridge the gaps of cultural knowledge" created by other critically esteemed shows.

Partially because of this "quality TV" designation, throughout its seven-year broadcast *Gilmore Girls* managed to pique the interest of media scholars and cultural critics who appreciate its sophisticated wordplay, in-jokes, cameo appearances, and willingness to "go deep" (in terms of references to high literature, serious philosophy, and obscure historical figures) while remaining "light" (as a buoyant "dramedy" filled with likable characters and emotionally involving narrative developments). A typical episode from Season Four, "Chicken or Beef?" (4.04), features a lengthy philosophical discussion about the nature of fate, filtered through a sarcastic lens, as well as a rumination on the role that historical preservation societies play in small-town communities, combined with copious references to movies such as *The Godfather* (1972) and *G.I. Jane* (1997), television shows such as *I Dream of Jeannie* (NBC, 1965–70) and *Queer Eye for the Straight Guy* (Bravo, 2003–7), fictional characters Gordon Gekko and Augustus Gloop, and rock groups Black Flag and Weezer.

Based on the enthusiastic responses that I have encountered at academic conferences in the United States and Great Britain, *Gilmore Girls* has already inspired professors and lecturers around the world to incorporate episodes of the series in their classrooms, as a means of covering a variety of subjects related to media studies, communication studies, cultural studies, women's studies, comparative literature, and American studies. This collection of essays seeks to bring *Gilmore Girls* more fully into academe not only as a topic worthy of critical scrutiny but also as an infinitely rewarding text capable of stimulating the imagination of students beyond the classroom.

Despite the fact that several articles about this television series have appeared in trade magazines, only two critical studies of *Gilmore Girls* have been published (compare this to the nearly two dozen published books that analyze—critically and theoretically—*Buffy the Vampire Slayer* [WB/UPN, 1997–2003]). One was published by McFarland in 2008, Ritch Calvin's slim edited collection, *"Gilmore Girls" and the Politics of Identity.* Although valuable as a source of information about the show's negotiation of gender and sexuality, it is much more narrowly focused than this volume and thus relatively limited in terms of its classroom applicability. Another recently published book is *Coffee at Luke's: An Unauthorized "Gilmore Girls" Gabfest,* a collection of highly readable yet somewhat lightweight essays edited by Jennifer Crusie and put out by BenBella Books (as part of their best-selling Smart Pop Series). Regardless of its shortcomings, however, the popular appeal of that book attests to the widespread interest in a television series whose most devoted fans form an interpretative community not unlike that surrounding other cult programs, such as *Charmed* (WB, 1998–2006), *Alias* (ABC, 2001–6), *Firefly* (FOX, 2002–4), and *Veronica Mars* (WB/CW, 2004–7). In the absence of much published material, *Gilmore Girl* fans (including their various subgroups, such as "Java Junkies," "Balcony Buddies," and "Chilton Chicas") have turned to the Internet as well as new media forms and digital technologies that facilitate communication and the sharing of knowledge across a variety of platforms.

In an effort to fill a substantial gap in the scholarship and literature surrounding *Gilmore Girls* (discounting the above-mentioned texts) and to elucidate just what kind of spectatorial demands this program makes, this volume brings together seventeen original essays written by scholars from around the world. The contributors take into consideration not only the show's unique wordplay and intense intertextuality but also such issues as gender, sexuality, feminism, masculinity, race, ethnicity, class, food consumption, and the question of "quality" alluded to earlier. It is in some ways similar to Rob Owen's *Gen X TV: "The Brady Bunch" to "Melrose Place"* as well as to Frances Early and Kathleen Kennedy's edited collection *Athena's Daughters: Television's New Women Warriors,* both published by Syracuse University Press. However, this volume is at once more focused than those significant studies, since it explores only one program in meticulous detail, and more wide reaching in terms of the broad range of theoretical paradigms and critical perspectives adopted by the contributors, who tackle such topics as serialized fiction, elite education, addiction as a social construct, food and the disciplining of bodies and desire, depictions of journalism in popular culture, the changing face of masculinity in twenty-first-century American society, liturgical and ritualistic structures in televisual narrative, Orientalism and Asian representations on American TV, Internet fan discourses and online "shipping," the production and consumption of Podcasts, and new genre theories sensitive to the landscape of twenty-first-century media convergence.

As such, *Screwball Television: Critical Perspectives on "Gilmore Girls"* is well placed to become an important study of a seminal television series, one whose social and cultural significance in the history of contemporary broadcasting as well as within media studies and other disciplines is made evident in the outstanding contributions that we have assembled. These essays provide a variety of insights gleaned from all 153 episodes of the TV series as well as from a voluminous amount of online material (fan forums, message boards, slash fiction, blogs, and the like).

The first section of this book provides an overview of the creation, strange evolution, conflicted meanings, and reception of *Gilmore Girls,* from its genesis as the first advertiser-advocated television show funded by the Family Friendly Programming Forum to its acceptance within a diverse set of critical communities on the left side of the sociopolitical spectrum. David Lavery kicks things off with an examination of Amy Sherman-Palladino's auteurist status and much publicized role in creating, producing, and writing for the series. Lavery also alludes to some of the many literary, televisual, and cinematic antecedents that influenced AS-P and the show's other producers, writers, and directors (including Helen Pai, Amy's husband, Daniel Palladino, final-season show runner David Rosenthal, and *Buffy* alums Jane Espenson and Rebecca Kirshner) over the course of its seven-year production.

Each subsequent chapter concentrates on a particular aspect of the *Gilmore Girls* phenomenon while exploring new avenues through which to write and think about television at large. In her essay on genre formations and the critical discourses surrounding *Gilmore Girls,* Amanda R. Keeler discusses the various ways in which the series has been "framed" or "branded" by writers for such trade magazines and periodicals as *Variety*, *Entertainment Weekly*, and *TV Guide.* Her overview of the critical reaction to *Gilmore Girls,* both before and after its premiere, emphasizes some of the conundrums of classification, which is a contentious activity insofar as "classically defined categories can mean the difference between winning and losing highly coveted television industry awards." Although never a big winner of Golden Globes or Emmys, and although it regularly ranked around 120 in the

Nielsen ratings (out of roughly 160 shows, making it one of the least-watched television series in North America), this series became a locus of critical commentary throughout its seven-year run. Also, in straddling the line between disparate typologies (family-friendly program, quirky dramedy, teen-centric show on the CW), it illustrates just how prone TV genres are to flux, to being "caught up in the shifting discourses surrounding new and earlier programs."

Similarly, Justin Owen Rawlins's contribution to this book is concerned with the critical discourses surrounding *Gilmore Girls*. However, he focuses not on the often conflicting commentaries offered by TV reviewers and industry insiders but rather on the scholarly interest in quality television as a site of meaning where cultural capital can be gained and exchanged. Rawlins argues that TV viewers engage quality texts "in an increasingly active manner" and thus need to be acknowledged as partial purveyors of the very rhetoric of exceptionalism being exploited by the networks. Indeed, a certain "pleasure in knowing" (or in understanding obscure references) informs the *Gilmore* universe (or what will hereafter be referred to as the "*Gilmore*verse"), suggesting that one's education and socioeconomic status can affect one's reception of a program celebrated for its literary qualities, which are highlighted as markers of "distinction" appealing to affluent consumers in the *Guide to Gilmore-isms* booklet included with the first few full-season DVD sets.

Bringing the first part of this book to a close is Giada Da Ros's examination of liturgical structures in *Gilmore Girls*, a program noted for its repeated scenarios and narrative schemas. Titled "TV 'Dramedy' and the Double-Sided 'Liturgy' of *Gilmore Girls*," this chapter—like Keeler's and Rawlins's before it—addresses the idea that drama and comedy combine to create a third term, a hybrid genre whose tonal shifts would be quite discombobulating for viewers were it not for the presence of narrative rituals (like Lorelai and her parents' Friday-night dinners). Such televisual liturgies, according to Da Ros, can bring consistency to a program while creating and sustaining "a sense of familial belonging, interpersonal relationships, and intimacy." But they might also remind us that the "contracts" between characters in the *Gilmore*verse (which stipulate certain terms of repeated contact) relate to the ways in which producers and audiences, creators and consumers, are bound by a mutual understanding of generic structures and formulas in this fictional world characterized by both enduring friendships and "unrestrained banter."

Just as individual episodes of *Gilmore Girls* flit between the generic thresholds and tonal registers of comedy and drama, so too does the entire series oscillate between a family-friendly type of programming suitable for all ages and a realistic worldview willing to incorporate risqué material and innuendo-filled dialogue, a program that remains largely free of dogmatic religious orthodoxy or morally responsible commentary about such topics as abstinence and sobriety. As one of the cohosts of the Unofficial Gilmore Girls Podcast states, it is "not the goody-two-shoes-type of family show" that *7th Heaven* (WB/CW, 1996–) is, and its honesty and openness not just about family relationships but also about sexual desire are what initially drew her and several other viewers to the series.

The second part shifts the focus from questions of authorship, genre, media literacy, and televisuality to observations about the ways in which communities—both real and imagined—are constructed inside and outside the series. In my contribution to the book, I explore the emergence of Podcasts as a new form of online programming and downloadable content that facilitates the free distribution of media files and the speedy construction of fan communities, composed of disparate individuals who contribute to a "cosmopedic" circulation of interpretations and—in the case of *Gilmore Girls* fandom—are asked to draw upon a wide array of pop culture references in order to articulate their passion for this particular TV series. With their emphasis on the spoken word, audio Podcasts serve as appropriate vehicles for delivering the listener into a more reflective, reflexive space that—however "virtual"—is rooted in very *real* encounters with television (in living rooms, bedrooms, and other spaces where talk is prone to flow freely). I furthermore argue that *Gilmore Girls* communicates the referential-tangential nature of adolescent conversation while gesturing toward the idea that *adults themselves* have been "taught" to talk that way by their kids. As such, we need to return to the televisual text to adduce just how often the traditional parent-child binary is collapsed in the series, particularly in episodes that either imply that level-headed Rory is more mature than her mother (something similarly suggested by the Susan-Julie relationship in *Desperate Housewives* [ABC, 2004–] and the Edina-Saffron relationship in *Absolutely Fabulous* [BBC, 1992–2005]) or simply put emphasis on teaching and learning as activities practiced by *everyone* regardless of age (as in "Lorelai's Graduation Day" [2.21] and "The Nanny and the Professor" [4.10]).

The tellingly titled "Teach Me Tonight" (2.19) is instructive here, since so much of this episode's running time is devoted to the education of its audience. Among the many intertextual allusions sprinkled throughout this particularly rich episode are the titles of more than two dozen films, including *The Yearling* (1946), *All about Eve* (1950), *What Ever Happened to Baby Jane?* (1962), *Sophie's Choice* (1982), *Crimes and Misdemeanors* (1989), and *Babe* (1995). These titles not only provide clues about the personalities and preoccupations of the main characters in *Gilmore Girls* (with *The Yearling* and *Babe*, for instance, reminding us of Rory's youthfulness, and *Crimes and Misdemeanors* being associated with Jess Mariano's [Milo Ventimiglia's] various "transgressions") but also hint at the potential reversibility of the parent-child binary. Moreover, the proliferation of such citations does much to destabilize the binaristic configuration of "high" and "low" cultures, as denoted by the fact that the great Japanese filmmaker Akira Kurosawa, director of *The Seven Samurai* (1954), could be confused with Asaad Kelada, the director of several episodes of *The Facts of Life* (NBC, 1979–88)—something Kirk Gleason (Sean Gunn) does at one point in "Teach Me Tonight."

Likewise concerned with those textual properties of *Gilmore Girls* that sustain the communities therein, Radha O'Meara's chapter makes a significant contribution to the study of larger issues pertaining to televisual narrativity. She sheds light on the series' complex negotiation of space through such strategies as crosscutting and intercutting, narrative devices that link the different social worlds inhabited by the main and supporting characters. O'Meara furthermore considers the deeper implications of the "two-worlds" schism so prevalent throughout the series, which presents us with ostensibly dissimilar environments marked by either class privilege (Hartford, Chilton, Yale) or egalitarian values (Stars Hollow) only to collapse those spaces through a proliferation of temporally "nonhierarchical" present tenses. This "nonhierarchical" notion is relevant insofar as the entire *Gilmore*verse seems to hinge on class distinctions, yet the series promotes a mode of middle-class consumption that is pro popular culture.

In their respective chapters on Stars Hollow as the embodiment of the American Dream and as a site where town meetings function to further mythologize the idyllic American small town, Alyson R. Buckman and Jane Feuer each bring historical insight and cultural-regional specificity to the study of the series. After analyzing the opening scenes of the pilot episode in detail and then linking the early history of Puritanism in America to the show's populist leanings and use of place as a means of invoking the nation's past, Buckman discusses the significance of town meetings as more than just a source of humor on the show. Indeed, as Feuer corroborates in her essay, Stars Hollow's distinctively New England style of town meeting evokes the promise of participatory democracy, something likewise conjured in another "quirky" TV series featuring a large ensemble cast spread across multiple, intersecting storylines, *Northern Exposure* (CBS, 1990–96). Just how far these two programs' utopian ideology and "nostalgically imbued idealism" extend beyond their diegetic communities (the "village of eccentrics" whose members engage in "face-to-face communal governance") and into the lives of TV viewers (who may in fact epitomize what Benedict Anderson has referred to as an "imagined community") is a question that is left tantalizingly open.

With the exception of tougher-than-nails Gypsy (Rose Abdoo), Stars Hollow's lone mechanic; Korean disciplinarian Mrs. Kim (Emily Kuroda), proprietor of Kim's Antiques; and Michel Gerard (Yanic Truesdale), Lorelai's style-conscious and snippy concierge at the Independence and Dragonfly Inns, racial and ethnic minorities are largely invisible in the series or simply confined to the background. It is ironic that two of the rudest characters in Stars Hollow, Michel and Mrs. Kim, work in industries dependent on customer relations, and that each provides a sometimes-caricatured counterpoint to Lorelai's relaxed attitude toward life. "I'm being discriminated against!" Michel complains in "Die, Jerk" (4.08), an exaggeration in the context of this episode (which shows him being sent away after sneezing near Sookie's [Melissa McCarthy's] baby), but one that speaks volumes about the very real prejudice sometimes faced by minorities in New England's small towns (something overtly referenced in "Face-Off" [3.15], when one of Taylor Doose's [Michael Winters]'s visiting relatives calls Michel "Frenchy" before saying that this graduate from the École Hôtelière de Genève "talks funny").

Hye Seung Chung addresses this often overlooked aspect of *Gilmore Girls* in her contribution to this book. Chung's article examines the portrayals of two Korean American characters (Lane and Mrs. Kim), thus providing important observations about racial discourses and ethnic representations. She argues that, in the Orientalist binary of the *Gilmore*verse, "Korea" is posited as an "other" place from which Lane—an all-American girl—must escape at all costs. Despite the show's liberal overtones, it is striking, then, that a foreign culture would be so grossly stereotyped for the sake of accentuating the meritocracy of small-town America and the superiority of egalitarian (white) parenthood therein. However, rather than attack the show's "racist" representations, Chung's essay carefully delineates the textual ruptures created by uplifting and nonstereotypical images of Asian Americans (Lane) and the outrageous caricatures associated with Mrs. Kim and her "Confucian entourage"—a contradiction compounded by the fact that the show's cocreator, Helen Pai, is Korean American.

Both Anna Viola Sborgi and Matthew C. Nelson engage the interrelated issues of class and education in their contributions to this volume. By spotlighting Rory's bibliophilia (her passion for reading and writing printed words), Sborgi—like the series itself—expands the horizon of expectations associated with teen television to accommodate images of young girls voraciously consuming books. Rory's bookwormish behavior confirms the underlying impulse toward educational achievement in the series, which is steeped in telltale literary allusions, among other types of intertextual references. As Sborgi states, the young protagonist "uses canonical examples of high literature to forge an identity and shape a world of her own, one that might seem detached from the more tangible world of face-to-face social relations." Yet, as Nelson argues in his chapter, *Gilmore Girls* puts forth contradictory messages about education and class, at once privileging elite forms of educational attainment in private schools and prestigious institutions of higher learning while promoting middle-class values that are not necessarily geared toward academic pursuits.

Bringing the third part to a close is an assessment of the series' connection to classic newspaper films and screwball comedies focusing on male and female journalists. Cowritten by Angel Castaños Martínez, Amor Muñoz Bécares, and Sarah Caitlin Lavery, this chapter situates *Gilmore Girls* in a genealogy of earlier cultural productions, from *His Girl Friday* (1940) to *All the President's Men* (1976), both of which are mentioned in several episodes. Like those and other Hollywood motion pictures, *Gilmore Girls* "presents a primarily positive view of journalism," however filled it may be with stereotypes about or simplifications of the profession. From its constant references to Bob Woodward and Carl Bernstein to its genuflectory celebration of all things Christiane Amanpour (a CNN reporter who actually appears in the final episode), the show reminds us that both Rory (who was initially told by a newspaper magnate that she doesn't have what it takes to be a journalist) and her verbal sparring partner Paris Gellar (Liza Weil) are overachievers who have a competitive, investigative drive to delve into the hows and whys of a story.

"The girl's got skills," Lorelai proudly proclaims during a Young Voices of Journalism panel in "Bridesmaids Revisited" (6.16), before remarking that Rory is "Anthony Michael Hall in *Breakfast Club* smart." With this in mind, one could argue that the program encourages the spectator to pay close attention to current events and adopt a similarly analytical perspective on pressing issues of the day. But *Gilmore Girls* might also lead young viewers to dig into the past, to seek out its cinematic antecedents—those screwball comedies of the 1930s and early 1940s that featured such luminaries of the silver screen as Katharine Hepburn, Myrna Loy, Carole Lombard, Claudette Colbert, and Rosalind Russell (the latter actress being famous for playing "Hildy" in the newspaper-themed *His Girl Friday*).

As the title of this book suggests, *Gilmore Girls* harks back to screwball-comedy films produced by Hollywood studios during and just after the Great Depression, a time when fast-talking heroines, sophisticated husbands and bachelors, and a host of eccentric characters were crawling out of the woodwork to inject levity into the beleaguered lives of moviegoers, thus providing temporary relief from the socioeconomic uncertainties of the era. In many of the classic examples of this subgenre, such as *It Happened One Night* (1934), *My Man Godfrey* (1936), *Holiday* (1938), and *The Lady Eve* (1941), gender inequalities could be remedied by spontaneous acts of sassiness or a well-timed witticism (or raspberry), just as class divisions could be bridged through romantic partnerships. Several other films, from *The Awful Truth* (1937) to *Bringing Up Baby* (1938), feature scenes set in the New England area, Connecticut in particular, where heiresses are able to relentlessly pursue their "prey" while retaining a certain "feminine allure"—an idiosyncratic attachment to both the finer and the most impractical things in life.

As one of the few contemporary American television series to combine sparkling repartee, intertextual references to earlier screwball comedies, farcical situations involving both the idle rich and common folk, and sometimes trenchant observations about class privilege, *Gilmore Girls* might seem out of step with the times. But, as many of the contributors to this volume make clear, the series is in line with those earlier motion pictures that capsized traditional gender roles and set the template for its own eccentricities as a text that transports the viewer to a simpler time and place. Sometimes its cinematic antecedents are directly mentioned, as in "The New and Improved Lorelai" (6.01), when Emily refers to her overly dramatic daughter as "Lorelai Barrymore," and in "Red Light on the Wedding Night" (2.03), which features a scene set in a drag club where cross-dressers mimic the look of Joan Crawford, Mae West, and other flamboyant stars of the studio-system era, or in "Say Something" (5.14), when

Lorelai tells boyfriend Luke Danes [Scott Patterson], "Man, they sure talked fast in those things," after watching the screwball comedy *My Man Godfrey.*

On other occasions, the references are more subtle. In "Lorelai Out of Water" (3.12), for instance, a scene in which Luke teaches Lorelai how to cast a reel in a kiddie pool (in preparation for her fishing date with temporary boyfriend Alex) is reminiscent of a similar moment in the screwball comedy *Libeled Lady* (1936), starring William Powell as an ex-journalist brought back into the fold so as to prevent a libel case from destroying his former newspaper employer. The film's famous crash-course-in-fishing scene is just one of the many moments in classic Hollywood motion pictures invoked by the writers and producers of *Gilmore Girls,* a series in which Lorelai is a modern-day Rosalind Russell (although she is frequently mistaken as Natalie Wood by Miss Celine in "Here Comes the Son" [3.21]), Luke seems like the now nearly forgotten character actor John Hubbard (a low-rent Ray Milland), Christopher is reminiscent of the characters played by Ralph Bellamy (destined to be romantic runners-up), Sherry comes across like Carol Landis with a touch of Paulette Goddard, Babette is a blonde version of comedic character actress Patsy Kelly, and even the town's traveling troubadour could be reasonably compared to the Charioteers, a group of musicians who function as a kind of Greek chorus in the Hal Roach comedy *Road Show* (1941).

The final part of the book consolidates a variety of perspectives on the show's emphasis on high-caloric food consumption and the potentially addictive behaviors expressed through similar acts of consumption online. Indeed, as A. Rochelle Mabry and Jimmie Manning argue in their individual contributions to this volume, it is on Internet Web sites where impassioned yet frequently peeved fans of *Gilmore Girls* articulate contradictory feelings of adoration and anger when writing about the show's heterosexual relationships. Focusing specifically on "shipping" (fan practices revealing an interest in the romantic relationships of fictional characters), Mabry argues that the "desires and anxieties expressed by shippers about their favorite couples" in the series "reflect concerns about gender, sexuality, and romance" in the culture at large. She illustrates this through references to online postings at TelevisionWithoutPity.com and FanFiction.net, where "fan-authored texts become laboratories for testing what romantic and sexual relationships can or should be after decades of questioning and redefining such concepts." Amplifying this idea, Manning's judicious deployment of interpersonal communication theories proves to be especially useful in charting out the complex relationships among the show's main characters, not to mention the values placed on those relationships by serious followers of *Gilmore Girls,* who go to great lengths to emphasize their desires for control over the series.

Susannah B. Mintz and Leah E. Mintz's chapter about the Gilmore girls' "perpetual hunger" lucidly identifies some of the problematic compulsions of the title characters, whose insatiable appetites and childish eating habits are displayed in several episodes. Such emphasis encourages us to see food as a multivalent metaphor in the series, one that touches on such themes as effective parenting, bodily control, and the managing of desire. As the authors point out, voracious eating represents sexual craving and gratification, but it also suggests "the intensity of Lorelai's need, physical and emotional, for caretaking." Thus, the dietary habits of both Lorelai and Rory are inextricably linked to their unique relationships with their mothers, who may unwittingly be leading these young women into potentially dangerous areas. Yet because the Pop-Tart-popping protagonists are able to be gluttonous without ever having to cope with the consequences of uninhibited eating (significant weight gain, health problems, high medical bills, and so forth), the series skirts issues related to body size and the denigration of overweight women in the United States.

In her wide-ranging essay on "addiction as a social construct in *Gilmore Girls,*" Joyce Goggin continues this investigation into food-related metaphors but shifts focus to acknowledge "the role that has been historically assigned to women as consumers" in Western societies. Linking Lorelai and her daughter "to a particular socioeconomic tradition of female food junkies," dating back to the eighteenth century, Goggin underlines the linkages between the serialized fiction of Charles Dickens and other nineteenth-century authors, the emergence of the modern market economy and the modern "consumer" (itself linked to imported commodities like coffee and tea), and the contemporary political context of the show's production (during which time U.S. congressional leaders declared that "all references to french fries and french toast on the menus of restaurants and snack bars run by the House of Representatives would be removed"). Goggin's ability to interweave such disparate things, including the history of addiction and the gendering of conspicuous consumption since the 1700s, with critical comments about recent political events and military decisions on the part of the U.S. government is especially praiseworthy. Such a perspective is absolutely *essential* to gaining a full understanding of the show's complex connections to world events (despite the fact that its producers present us with a seemingly hermetic social environment and close-knit community bearing little relation to the "real" world).

The final chapter, by Laura Nathan, explores the representation of men and the discourses of masculinity in *Gilmore Girls,* a series noted for its appeal to female audiences who respond favorably to the central mother-daughter relationship, but one that also offers compelling portraits of manhood that can be instructive for all viewers regardless of gender or sexual orientation. As Nathan argues, gender expectations are foisted on men as much as they are on women, expectations that may change over time and reflect their historical contexts but continuously delimit one's ability to "measure up" to the standards set by earlier images of masculinity. The successful negotiation of a masculinity crisis in the postmodern world therefore necessitates a willingness to look beyond traditional codes and conventions of manliness and acknowledge alternative ways to express "self" through romantic desire. Looking at each of Lorelai's and Rory's suitors (from the Proust-reading Max Medina [Scott Cohen] to the blue-collar Luke Danes, who at one point refers to Zima as "chick beer"), Nathan points out that the two main characters date modern men who allow for some degree of feminist freedom. But there are also times when the title characters seem to long for male partners who are throwbacks to earlier forms of masculinity, leaving their vulnerable suitors in a state of uncertainty as to how to properly "articulate their manhood."

Nathan's chapter, like the ones that precede it, indicates how uniquely suited and discursively situated *Gilmore Girls* is for this type of lengthy project, owing to the show's complexity and richness as a text that operates on multiple levels (televisual, virtual, literary, and so on). It is at once a kickier kind of screwball comedy and a kinder, gentler kind of cult-TV program.

Obviously, very few of the textual characteristics typically associated with cult TV can be found within *Gilmore Girls,* a lighthearted series lacking the sci-fi trappings and deep mythologies of *Babylon 5* (PTEN, 1994–98), *Firefly,* and other cult programs such as the many *Star Trek* spin-offs, which furthermore allow for alternate or mirror universes. There are no witches, warlocks, or vampires to be found in Stars Hollow, the show's nostalgically imbued main setting where comparatively inconsequential events and quotidian moments between friends and family members transpire. However, if one takes into consideration the ways in which the seriality of the program is linked to a preponderance of close relationships between male and female characters, it becomes apparent that *Gilmore Girls* flirts with cultdom by means of foregrounding what media scholar Matt Hills refers to as a "mutual sexual attraction that is never fully realized" or "which cannot progress beyond romance" (2004, 512), something likewise apparent in such shows as *Beauty and the Beast* (CBS, 1987–90), with Catherine and Vincent; *Star Trek: The Next Generation* (syndicated, 1987–94), with Picard and Crusher; *The X-Files* (FOX, 1993–2002), with Mulder and Scully; and *Farscape* (Sci-Fi Channel, 1999–2003), with Aeryun Sun and Crichton.

The central questions driving the plotlines each season have to do with both Lorelai's and Rory's romantic entanglements with members of the opposite sex. Although Lorelai had brief flings with Rory's Chilton High School teacher Max Medina in Season One and with her father's young business partner, Jason "Digger" Stiles (Chris Eigerman), in Season Four, the most vexing question running through the last three years was whether she would marry the rugged, baseball-cap-wearing diner owner Luke Danes or the father of her daughter, childhood sweetheart Christopher Hayden (David Sutcliffe). That question was answered during the November sweeps of its final season, when Christopher and Lorelai—after the latter's broken engagement with Luke—eloped while vacationing in Paris, although subsequent developments, including the breakup of the newlywed couple, gave new hope to the so-called Java Junkies (fans who wanted Luke and Lorelai to get back together).

Rory's long-term relationships have likewise been the subject of much online speculation and debate surrounding the feel-good series, which ushered in three significant male partners at various stages of her maturation from late adolescence to early adulthood. The introduction of Jess Mariano, Luke's rebellious nephew, in Season Two marked the beginning of Rory's "bad-boy phase," one that gave rise to the show's first love triangle (discounting her brief flirtation with Chilton classmate Tristan [Chad Michael Murray]) and resulted in her eventual breakup with kindhearted but dopey Dean Forester. Toward the end of the series, her initially rocky, then relatively stable relationship with Logan Huntzberger (Matt Czuchry), heir to the powerful Huntzberger Publishing Company, infused the unfolding narrative with another, more emotionally gratifying, level of seriality, one that not only provided interepisodic linkage, lending the previous two seasons a sense of direction and purpose, but also fed into audience expectations and hopes for the future. Only in the last two seasons did the show's producers venture into the arena of soap-opera theatrics, with unforeseen plot twists (like the sudden arrival of Luke's thirteen-year-old daughter, April Nardini [Vanessa Marano], or Rory and Logan's theft of a yacht) threatening to undermine the very things that made *Gilmore Girls* special. Before the fifth season, the program was at its best when it stuck to small moments and the day-to-day rituals and occurrences that resonated most deeply with the fans.

The "repetition, familiarity, and . . . iteration" that Matt Hills refers to as textual characteristics of cult television are thus pronounced elements in *Gilmore Girls,* which likewise hinges on a ritualistic deployment of narrative and thematic motifs (2004, 512). Throughout the series there are plot points or narrative elements that allude to previous episodes, encouraging spectatorial recognition for those who watch the series regularly. The prolonged conflict between Lorelai and her blue-blooded parents, spa-obsessed Emily and workaholic Richard (Edward Herrmann), adds necessary frisson to the series, which habitually highlights their different attitudes toward wealth, parenting, and etiquette while providing painful moments when the veil of social decorum drops to reveal deep-seated animosities and resentments. Lorelai and Rory's Friday-night dinners at Emily and Richard's palatial home in Hartford feed into the larger pattern of repetitions and structured familiarity, ensuring a certain number of arguments within the series and casting in relief the relative calm of Stars Hollow (a Capraesque community of locals and yokels safely removed from the outside world and located about thirty miles away from Hartford).

As in a number of the aforementioned cult-TV programs, there is a thematic emphasis in *Gilmore Girls* on couples as well as a close-knit, trusting community. Just as the officers of the USS *Enterprise* in *Star Trek,* the outlaw crew of the *Scorpio* in *Blakes 7* (BBC, 1978–81), and the "Scooby Gang" in *Buffy the Vampire Slayer* can be said to reflect the communal ethos of the fan cultures outside those texts, so too does the eclectic ensemble at the heart of *Gilmore Girls* suggest ways in which conflicts or disagreements within the imagined community of audience members can be peaceably resolved or at least managed through talk. Indeed, the recurring motif of town meetings, led by the tyrannical yet teddy bearish Taylor Doose, not only brings together many of the secondary characters embraced by the fans (such as Lorelai's best friend, chef Sookie St. James; Sookie's husband and vegetable supplier, Jackson Belleville [Jackson Douglas]; plus-size dance instructor Miss Patty [Liz Torres]; Lane's conservative mother Mrs. Kim; and Kirk Gleason, a man of many talents and jobs who is a bundle of neuroses) but also structures the series around a core community of quirky individuals who converse freely and seem more like family members than neighbors.

A few problems with the textually bound approach to studying cult television become apparent, insofar as several such programs (for instance, *The Prisoner* [ITV, 1967–68] and *Buffy*) have little in common with one another from either an industrial, stylistic, generic, or narrative point of view. Matt Hills acknowledges the inherent limitations of defining or ascertaining a television show's "cult-ness" through textual analysis alone. He directs our attention to "secondary texts" and asks that we look at such things as magazines, fanzines, newspapers, journalistic reviews, and publicity material, which not only convey reports dealing with forthcoming plot developments and cast changes but also delve into various programs' costs, ratings, and institutional contexts (2004, 515–16). Moreover, these secondary texts activate fan communities, stimulate consumer activism, and generate much of the qualitative discourse that feeds into the very language employed by readers who define themselves as cultural connoisseurs. While fanzines or magazines like the British publication *Cult Times* are not likely to feature articles on *Gilmore Girls,* given their "antimainstream" disposition and largely male readership, one can find an ample number of alternative sources or secondary texts paying respects to the series.

One can also find, at most major booksellers, a collection of officially licensed paperback novels, including Catherine Clark's *Like Mother, Like Daughter,* Cathy East Dubowski's *I Love You, You Idiot,* and producer Helen Pai's *Other Side of Summer,* as well as online teen magazines and indie fanzines whose contributors are able to see beyond the show's storybook setting and sentimental, almost sepia-toned opening credits (accompanied by Carole King's theme song "Where You Lead") and appreciate *Gilmore Girls* for what it really is: a snarky and sarcastic—or, to borrow Lorelai's word in "Always a Godmother, Never a God" (6.04), *snarkastic*—screwball series with traces of maternal melodrama and a high quotient of quirks, or what might be better termed "Kirks" (in recognition of the show's quirkiest character and ubiquitous juggler of odd jobs).

Finally, as Hills reminds us, one way to define a program's cult status is through an analysis of participatory fan practices—one that offers a bottom-to-top view illustrating how the grassroots campaigns and creative efforts of passionate fans in fact contribute to that status (2004, 517–18). This, I believe, is where emerging theories of fandom most productively intersect with a multidisciplinary study of

Gilmore Girls. As A. Rochelle Mabry argues in her chapter, fandom may act as a site of resistance or submission, but ultimately what matters most is that audiences are "responding to issues circulating in the larger culture" by way of media texts that, on the surface, appear to warrant little critical thought. Like Mabry, many of the contributors to this volume gesture toward fan practices, wherein audiences reorganize television shows into the category of "cult," not by passively consuming said programs but by actively producing their own work (creating fan fiction, for instance, which extends the already expansive narrative worlds). Moreover, as fans themselves, the contributors to this volume offer compelling evidence that what makes *Gilmore Girls* special are the very things that have not been (and perhaps cannot be) replicated elsewhere.

Only hard-core fans of *Gilmore Girls* would know that "Tookie Clothespin" is Lorelai's self-chosen alias (revealed in "Take the Deviled Eggs . . ." [3.06]). Ask those same individuals who "Picklepuss" and "Sauerkraut" are, and they will likely say "Emily" and "Richard" (the former were names used by Lorelai to describe her parents). *Gilmore Girls* fans will be the first to tell you that fuzzy Certs "taste like keys." They know their "Afterboom" from their "Copperboom." They are prone to pontificate on the relative merits of having too many poodles (Oy!) and can be counted on to offer seemingly meaningless words of wisdom at the most inappropriate of times, like those spoken by Lorelai in "Let the Games Begin" (3.08): "Sometimes eating a walnut is preferable to getting hacked to death." Yes, but only *sometimes.*

Part One

Authorship, Genre, Literacy, Televisuality

"Impossible Girl"

Amy Sherman-Palladino and Television Creativity

DAVID LAVERY

> Let's face it: I've peaked. This is it. It's all downhill for me or after this show. To be able to create a show that they let you do what you want to do, they let you write what you want to write, they let you put your crazy references in, to be able to work with really top-notch actors . . . it happens once. Once! Seriously. It's all over . . . It's just me under a bus after this.
>
> —AMY SHERMAN-PALLADINO ("Welcome to the *Gilmore Girls*," Season One DVD supplemental feature)

> Many people in the business will refer to a woman who did something or acted a certain way as "crazy." I then say, "You have to define what 'crazy' is." To me, crazy is not someone who has a creative vision and will fight for it.
>
> —AMY SHERMAN-PALLADINO, quoted in *Created by . . . : Inside the Minds of TV's Top Show Creators*, by Steven Priggé

> Is she Jewish or something?
>
> —T. J. (MICHAEL DELUISE), asking Luke (Scott Patterson) about Lorelai (Lauren Graham), in "The UnGraduate" (6.03)

During the second season of *Roseanne* (ABC, 1988–97)—a critically successful, long-running sitcom dealing with working-class issues and frequently labeled the "anti–*Cosby Show*"—a young writer named Joss

Whedon wrote several episodes (including "Little Sister" and "Brain-Dead Poets Society"). The movie version of his then already conceived script for *Buffy the Vampire Slayer* (1992) was still in his future, as were the three television series that would establish his reputation among cult fans of quality TV: *Buffy the Vampire Slayer* (WB/UPN, 1997–2003), *Angel* (WB, 1999–2004), and *Firefly* (FOX, 2002–4). The year after Whedon left the show a new member of the team, Amy Sherman-Palladino (hereafter referred to as "AS-P"), and her partner, Jennifer Heath, would be admitted to the *Roseanne* writers' room. Over the next four seasons (1990–94), she would author, both with Heath and on her own, more than a dozen episodes—stories in which Roseanne (Roseanne Barr) and Dan (John Goodman) shop for a new bed, Becky (Sarah Chalke) runs away from home and begins using birth control, a Halloween prank inspires revenge, and Roseanne deals with her father's death, meets his mistress, and gets breast-reduction surgery. In the fourth and sixth seasons, AS-P would have the honor of writing the season premieres.

Whedon and AS-P are both products of show-business families (her father was a Catskills and Borscht Belt "king of the cruise lines" [Heffernan 2005] comic);[1] for both, *Roseanne* was only a warm-up exercise, an apprenticeship. Her greatest creative achievement—the once-in-a-lifetime opportunity that would enable her to imaginatively rule over a "bizarro little niche" on television (Tobias 2005) but leave her with no alternative but to throw herself under a bus when it would come to an end—lay ahead of her.

1. Sherman-Palladino recalls, "Growing up, my father was, and still is, a professional comic. My mother was a professional dancer. So, I grew up in a show-business family that had the attitude, 'You want to go to college? What's that for?' I did take a lot of dance classes and acting classes. Many of my father's friends were comedians, and since they hung around our house, I was exposed to comedy at an early age, knew about Lenny Bruce when I was very, very young. I think that atmosphere really helped me with my writing" (Priggé 2005, 51). Whedon, of course, is perhaps the world's only third-generation television writer: both his father, Tom, and his grandfather John wrote for the small screen from the 1950s through the 1990s.

In "Twenty-one Is the Loneliest Number," a Season Six episode of *Gilmore Girls* (6.07) written by AS-P, a rare visit by Richard Gilmore to daughter Lorelai's Stars Hollow home leads to an argument between the two over Rory's future now that she has dropped out of Yale. When Richard's suggestion of bribing her to return to the university is summarily rejected, he exclaims, "Impossible girl," to which his daughter replies, with typical infuriating wit, "That was my Native American name." Lorelai Gilmore, made ingeniously real by Lauren Graham, is indeed an impossible girl, indefatigably her own person with her own tastes, her own eccentricities, her own style, her own mind, her own approach to mothering,[2] but *Gilmore Girls*' very *real*, original "impossible girl" is Amy Sherman-Palladino, the creator of both Lorelai and the series, and, for its first six seasons, its most prolific writer, its second-busiest director, and—more important—its show runner.

Understanding AS-P's "television creativity" is no easy task. The late scholar of the creative process Howard Gruber once observed that, historically speaking, creative individuals often "leave better traces." Indeed, "the making and leaving of tracks . . . is part and parcel of the process itself . . . a kind of activity characteristic of people doing creative work." "Wittingly or not," he notes, they "create the conditions under which we can study their development" (1985, 119). Gruber's observation holds true for many of the makers of television. Joss Whedon, David Milch (*NYPD Blue* [ABC, 1993–2005], *Deadwood* [HBO, 2004–6], and Ronald D. Moore (*Battlestar Galactica* [Sci-Fi, 2004–9]), for example—all frequent interviewees, bloggers, DVD commentators, or Podcasters—invite and reward investigation. By comparison, AS-P's trail is relatively cold.[3]

2. As AS-P admits to Steven Priggé, "The character of Lorelai in *Gilmore Girls* expresses a lot of my yapping and opinions. She is a nice vessel to use when I am angry at something and I want to get a point across" (2005, 108).

3. *Gilmore Girls* DVDs provide only one AS-P episode commentary (for "You Jump, I Jump, Jack" [5.07]—done with husband Daniel Palladino, who does much of the talking), and interviews, apart from the extensive online colloquy with Scott

A *Gilmore Girls* "Origin Myth"

Like many other successful television series, *Gilmore Girls* has an unusual origin myth. The idea that would eventually generate a seven-season, 153-episode, approximately 107-hour narrative had its origins in a requested meeting between AS-P, who had just completed a brief tenure on *Veronica's Closet* (NBC, 1997–2000), and WB head Susan Daniel. Daniel, it seems, had for some time been trying to wean AS-P away from the half-hour sitcom[4] and listened to a complicated pitch that day for a series about a Filipino girl, but it was a passing reference to another possibility, a show about "a mother and daughter who are best friends—more like real, genuine pals than mother and daughter," that caught Daniel's attention. Afterward, AS-P recalls, her satisfaction was tempered by the realization that she had "just sold a sentence, not a show" (Priggé 2005, 98–99), and knew next to nothing about her characters or setting. AS-P, we should note, has a complex theory about the pitch process, believing that, since no one is really listening, the pitcher is actually promoting herself: "You must walk into a room and essentially say through your pitch: 'Look how crazy, funny, and fun I am. If I'm this nuts, imagine what I can give you on paper.' . . . It's all about selling your confidence" (ibid., 120–21). Indeed, *Gilmore Girls was* crazy fun (and emotionally tumultuous) for seven years, the last of which, of course, was lamentably produced without its creator, but in the beginning the series she had successfully pitched was anything but fleshed out.

Soon after her meeting with Daniel, a New York vacation found AS-P and her husband, Dan, who would later become her inimitable collaborator on *Gilmore Girls,* visiting Connecticut for the first time

---

Tobias on the Onion AV Club, are few and far between. By far the best entry into AS-P's thinking is found in her generous and revealing responses to Steven Priggé's questions in *Created by . . . : Inside the Minds of TV's Top Show Creators* (2005).

4. Even after years on *Gilmore Girls,* AS-P would speak of her husband, Daniel Palladino, and herself as "sitcom refugees": "We'd love to return to sitcom, but I don't know where you go to do it" (Tobias 2005).

(in order to tour Mark Twain's house in Hartford). An "idyllic and perfect" stay in a charming inn, a burst of autumnal color, an everybody-knows-your name and pours-their-own-coffee diner—these all led Amy and Dan to pen some dialogue that would later end up in the show's pilot episode (ibid., 105). In two days, the idea of Stars Hollow as the girls' home; the epicenter of American insurance, Hartford, as Lorelai's parents' domain; and insurance as her father's business all fell into place. Stars Hollow was a bit of a reach for AS-P, a Jewish California-born "valley girl" who, by her own admission, didn't "know shit about small-town America"; she nevertheless drew inspiration from earlier days spent in an oddly similar Venice, California: "a funky, weird, closer community" where "a lot of odd, slightly damaged people . . . found a place to hang out and support each other" (Tobias 2005).

"Hats"

In control for the first time of a television series she had created, Sherman-Palladino would find herself in unfamiliar territory: an hour-long dramedy on a netlet (the WB) rather than a thirty-minute sitcom on a major network.[5] Moreover, she would be serving as both its show runner *and* its chief writer. Moreover, beginning with the Season One finale, "Love, Daisies, and Troubadours" (1.21), she would don an additional new hat—as director (by series end, only Jamie Babbit would helm more episodes). The terrain ahead may have been, at the outset, largely uncharted, but AS-P came equipped with maps drawn, lessons learned during her time at *Roseanne* ("I could not think of a better show to start my career on," she would tell Steven Priggé [2005,

5. "When you're on network television," AS-P would tell the Onion, "you've got advertisers and high expectations for ratings. I'm on the WB, and as long as they appeal to the demographics that mean the most to them, they're pretty happy. They're not as big as ABC. They're not even in as many markets as ABC. So they can't possibly compete on the same level that ABC does, because they're not even seen by as many people. It's not the same ball game" (Tobias 2005).

86]). *Gilmore Girls,* too, would prove to be an education. AS-P would become adept at wearing many hats—and with a style all her own.

When she worked on *Roseanne,* AS-P recalls, the show's star kept the suits from micromanaging: "The studio and network were banned from the set, because Roseanne had banned them. So I never saw the studio or network for four years. They didn't give notes on any of the scripts. I had no idea that the studio and network even came to the table." Their absence would leave a lasting impression. Later, as she would confess to the Onion AV Club, in the *Veronica's Closet* writers' room she "was left to wonder who all these fucking people were sitting around the table telling us what to do" (Tobias 2005). As *Girls'* show runner, she would continue to resent top-down interference with her show.

On *Roseanne,* under her acknowledged mentor Bob Myer, she would also acquire another skill essential to show running: story breaking. She would learn to lead by example, to be decisive, economical, and clearheaded, to plot the course ahead for the *Girls* narrative while setting the bar "very high" (Priggé 2005, 86). In the writers' room "a lot of hammering, a lot of work, a lot of sitting . . . , going, 'No, no, no, Lorelai *would* do this'" was the order of the day, as AS-P and Dan Palladino scrutinized every draft for "consistency of tone." "It's very important," she observed when *Girls* was still in its prime, "that it feel like the same show every week, because it is so verbal. It's not about car crashes or vampires or monsters or suspense" (Tobias 2005).

Early on, the WB was inclined to offer "On *Dawson's Creek* we do things this way" advice and object to her characterization of Lorelai, suggesting, as AS-P would tell Virginia Heffernan, that "'a mother wouldn't do this.' And I said: '*This* mother would. Because the relationship I'm doing here is not mother and daughter, it's best friends.'" AS-P won the majority of those skirmishes, and eventually she and the bosses argued almost exclusively about money. No one who has watched Lorelai go toe-to-toe with her mother, or Mitchum Huntzberger, or Taylor Doose will be shocked to hear AS-P's confession to Heffernan that, in doing the "big, big job" of show running, "I'm not a shrinking violet" (2005).

AS-P's show-running philosophy is clear and emphatic. Writing by committee never works: "You've got to have one or two clean, creative voices in charge, and there's got to be some faith by the studio and network in those people to make the right choices" (ibid.). The precedent, AS-P insists, is clear: "David Chase does not have 20 people telling him what to do on *The Sopranos*. Bright, Kauffman, and Crane did not have 20 people telling them what to do on *Friends*. David E. Kelley does not have anyone telling him what to do because no one can get into his office. . . . When you don't have a hundred people telling you what to do, it gives you the chance to do something good" (Priggé 2005, 147). Something more than quality control is at stake. The direction provided by one or two guiding voices and visions is absolutely essential to the long-term success of a show. "Keeping a show on the air goes back to the old saying, 'Too many chefs spoil the soup.' If you have too many chefs in the kitchen—too many people providing input—then it's hard to stay on the air and make a TV series last" (ibid.). Besides, no one external to the show can possible "know" it as well as its creator: "I definitely know when something doesn't work, and I don't need a network executive to call me and tell me that," an adamant Sherman-Palladino told Priggé. "No one is going to know what works and what doesn't work more quickly than I will. Also, no one is going to want to change it quicker than me. My name is on it and I want to make it good" (ibid., 199). Watching *Gilmore Girls* from beginning to end, all seven seasons, in a short period of time (one month), as I recently did, one is likely to be astonished at the continuity of style and tone, the quality control, maintained throughout its long run. The soup came out as satisfyingly as if Sookie had just brought it to the table fresh from the kitchen, handled by no one but her.

As a show runner, AS-P has very emphatic ideas concerning the real place of women in contemporary television. "You have to have thick, thick, thick skin," she tells Priggé. "You can't be a baby. Don't get upset when people do negative things to you because they know you're a woman. The only thing you can do about it is to just be better. Work harder and be better because, in the end the best script will get noticed. If your writing is too good for someone to ignore, then someone will want that product. Also, you have to fight for your vision and what you believe in." That fight is undertaken with absolutely no illusions—"Hands down, female show-runners do not get the respect or receive the good will that a male show-runner gets"—but with a postfeminist resolve: "I am a big girl and I can take it. You acknowledge it and keep moving forward, just put on another coat of lipstick and keep walking" (ibid., 192).

She recognizes, however, that there is a more practical, tactical response as well: to put herself in a position of power where she can make the decisions. *Gilmore Girls* demonstrates AS-P's commitment to changing women's place in television. Women writers ruled on the series and were responsible for 92 out of a total of 172 writing credits. AS-P herself authored or coauthored (with both her husband and others) no fewer than 46 of the series' 153 episodes. Former *Buffy* writer Rebecca Rand Kirshner wrote 8 episodes after joining the *Girls*' writers' room in Season Five, and Sheila Lawrence wrote 5 in Seasons Two, Three, and Four. No fewer than thirteen other women penned episodes, including Jennie Snyder (4), Joan Binder Weiss (4), Janet Leahy (3), Gayle Abrams (2), Elaine Arata (2), Gina Fattore (2), Whedonverse veteran Jane Espenson (2), Linda Loiselle Guzik (2), soon-to-be *Weeds* creator and show runner Jenji Kohan (1), Rina Mimoun (1), Jessica Queller (1), Lisa Randolph (1), and Joanne Waters (1). (By comparison, 62 of 203 writing credits on a landmark feminist show like *Buffy the Vampire Slayer* were credited to women.)

Perhaps even more impressively, given the relative paucity of female television directors, 67 episodes of AS-P's creation were directed by women. Jamie Babbit (18), AS-P herself (15), and Lee Shallat-Chemel (14, 12 of which were in the final season alone) were the go-to *Gilmore* helmers, each directing more episodes than Chris Long (13), the most often employed male director on the series. Other women responsible for more than episode included Gail Mancuso (5), *Twin Peaks* veteran Lesli Linka Glatter (4), and Bethany Rooney (3), while Arlene Sanford, Carla McCloskey, Joe Ann Fogle, Linda Mendoza, Marita Grabiak (another Whedonverse veteran), African American film director

Neema Barnette, indie director Nicole Holofcener (*Walking and Talking* [1996], *Lovely and Amazing* [2001], *Friends with Money* [2006]), and Sarah Pia Anderson all directed an episode. (Only 3 episodes of *Buffy* were directed by women.)

Acknowledging that her own particular approach to writing—more interested in character than in simply authoring joke after joke—was a good match for *Roseanne,* at least during her years there, her stint on the show, Sherman-Palladino suggests, may well have staved off a career move to Denny's. Unusual for its time, *Roseanne* was not primarily "joke-driven" but followed its own "mantra": "Make the big small, make the small big." Instead of "big stories," *Roseanne* "did tiny things, like Darlene getting her period" (Tobias 2005).

In much the same vein as *Seinfeld* (NBC, 1990–98), *Gilmore Girls* was often a "show about nothing"—albeit a "nothingness" nostalgically framed by a small-town New England setting rather than a metropolitan space like Manhattan. Taking its lead from AS-P, the *Gilmore* script template—described by director Glatter upon reading the pilot as "so articulate with . . . well-rounded characters and . . . the kind of verbal banter that reminded me of 40s movies" ("Welcome to the *Gilmore Girls*")—famously ran to eighty pages (the network norm for an hour show is around fifty to sixty). The humor was often black. Consider the Friday-evening dinner exchange between Lorelai and her mother (from AS-P's "Haunted Leg" [3.02]): Reading the paper at the table (a faux pas for which she is castigated by Emily), Lorelai discovers that a woman her mother characterizes as a "lovely girl . . . bright, cultured, well spoken," has pumped her philandering husband full of lead. Lorelai states, "Well, apparently this lovely girl came home to find her husband giving the nanny a nice little bonus package. And they say good help is hard to find. . . . The man was shot thirty-five times." As usual, appalled by her daughter's inappropriate humor, Emily asks for an end to the topic of conversation but manages to have the last word anyway in one of the great black humor when-will-you-get-married mother-daughter put-downs of all time: "At least she had a husband to kill." AS-P's scripts are full of such dark wit.

Grounded in the conviction that "audiences are as smart as you will allow them to be" ("I Jump, You Jump, Jack" [5.07] DVD commentary), *Gilmore Girls* was arguably the most literate show in television history as well, and its astronomical TV IQ has its genesis in AS-P's writing. In the *Gilmore*verse, Stars Hollow Elementary puts on a production of *Who's Afraid of Virginia Woolf?* ("The Breakup: Part 2" [1.17]), characters read Rainer Maria Rilke's *Letters to a Young Poet* ("Lost and Found" [2.15]), and Schopenhauer and Kierkegaard coasters prevent ugly circles from being left on fine furniture ("Written in the Stars" [5.03]). Although not herself college educated,[6] AS-P created a television text that challenges the most culturally literate college professor to annotate.

Actors, actresses, and performers past and present take the proverbial stage on a regular basis in Sherman-Palladino's own scripts (including Fred MacMurray [1.09], Barbara Stanwyck [1.09], Sally Field [2.01], Edgar Bergen and Charlie McCarthy [2.13], John Cleese [2.13], Lon Chaney Jr. [2.19], Jodie Foster [3.01], Judy Garland [3.01], Tommy Tune [3.07], Adrian Zmed [3.13], Daniel Day Lewis [3.16], Mary Martin [3.16], Dick Van Dyke [3.18], Johnny Depp [3.21], Olivia de Havilland [3.21], Audrey Hepburn [3.21], Ginger Rodgers [3.21], Jimmy Stewart [3.21], Natalie Wood [3.21], Eartha Kitt [4.09], Robert Downey Jr. [4.13], Francis Farmer [4.13], Adolphe Menjou [4.14], Shirley MacLaine [4.17], Al Gilbert [4.21], Farrah Fawcett [4.22], Hayley Mills [4.22], James Spader [4.22], Judi Dench [5.03], Ava Gardner [5.03], Giselle Bundchen [5.15], Julia Roberts [5.19], and Tom Sizemore [5.22]).

AS-P makes occasional mention of artists: photographers, painters, dancers, like Edgar Degas (3.02), Helmut Newton (3.02), Martha Graham (3.07), Titian (3.08), and Alfred Stieglitz (6.22), and of politics

6. Sherman-Palladino states, "One of my great regrets is that I didn't go to college. I had very little patience for school, and it was never stressed in my household. We were a showbiz family. You don't go to college when you're going to be in showbiz. Those are your good years. You're young and strong and your butt looks great. Why spend four years drinking away at a keg party?" (Heffernan 2005).

and politicians, historical figures, and current events: J. Edgar Hoover (2.01), Fidel Castro (2.02), the Unabomber (2.15), Hubert Humphrey (2.22), Woodward and Bernstein (3.01), Margaret Thatcher (3.02), Ted Bundy (3.07), Billy Carter (3.16), John D. Rockefeller (4.14), Bob Graham (5.10), and Joe Lieberman (5.15). Classic motion pictures and cult films as well as filmmakers are often alluded to, including: *Schindler's List* (1.02), *The Shining* (1.02), *The Fly* (1.06), *Freaky Friday* (1.06), *The Great Santini* (1.12), *Ishtar* (1.17), *Funny Girl* (2.01), *Girl, Interrupted* (2.01), Federico Fellini (2.05), *Boy in the Plastic Bubble* (2.13), *All About Eve* (2.19), Akira Kurosawa (2.19), *Nell* (3.01), *Shane* (3.02), *Blue Velvet* (3.07), *Boxing Helena* (3.07), *They Shoot Horses, Don't They?* (3.07), *Love Story* (3.08), *Brazil* (3.18), *Footloose* (3.20), Michael Moore (3.21), *Sabrina* (3.21), *Mommie Dearest* (4.03), *An Affair to Remember* (4.06), *Valley of the Dolls* (4.09), *Alive* (4.13), *Taxi Driver* (4.14), *American Splendor* (4.20), *Fatso* (4.20), *The Lords of Flatbush* (4.20), Blake Edwards (4.22), *Pretty in Pink* (4.22), *Jerry Maguire* (5.19), *The Elephant Man* (5.22), *Blue Lagoon* (6.01), *Bob and Carol and Ted and Alice* (6.01), *Mask* (6.09), Nora Ephron (6.13), *Driving Miss Daisy* (6.21), and *Misery* (6.21).

Characters of all kinds—from literature, television, and film—join the many characters of Stars Hollow, Hartford, Chilton, and Yale, becoming honorary members of the *Girls*' cast (from Andy Hardy [2.13] and Bobby Brady [3.07] to Daisy Miller [5.01] and Eve Harrington [2.19]). Troubadours stroll through the streets of Stars Hollow, and references to music and musicians snake through Sherman-Palladino's dialogue (examples include Yoko Ono [1.12], Cher and Greg Allman [2.01], the Damned [2.02], Sid and Nancy [2.05], the Shaggs [2.15], Marianne Faithful [2.19], Peaches and Herb [3.01], Gloria Estefan [3.08], George Michael [3.08], Don Ho [3.13], Jerome Robbins [3.16], Jim Morrison [4.01], "Sk8er Boi" [4.01], Jethro Tull [4.20], Roslyn Kind [4.22], the Polyphonic Spree [5.01], Wendy and Lisa [6.11], and Insane Clown Posse [6.22]).

Gilmore Girls might be the richest popular culture purveyor since *Buffy the Vampire Slayer,* and cultural ephemera, icons, and Americana are sprinkled liberally throughout AS-P's writing. The series has, at various times, referenced everyone from Dr. Laura (2.05) to Emily Post (1.09), from Anna Nicole Smith (4.17) to Annie Oakley (3.02), from Howard Stern (3.13) to John Hinckley (2.01), from Sunny von Bülow (3.01) to Stan Freeberg (2.19). Not surprisingly, television shows and TV personalities find themselves right at home in AS-P's television universe, with references to *The Waltons* (1.06), *The Donna Reed Show* (1.14), Marlin Perkins (1.14), Robin Leach (1.17), *Sesame Street* (1.17), Bob Vila (2.02), *Kung Fu* (2.15), Connie Chung (3.01), Señor Wences (3.07), *Quincy, M.E.* (3.13), Walter Cronkite (3.21), *Felicity* (3.21), *Daria* (4.01), Ted Koppel (4.09), *Reno 911* (6.13), Rowan and Martin (6.13), and Johnny Carson (6.22), among others, finding their way into her scripts.

Not surprisingly, AS-P (the show runner that reads) makes frequent mention of the world of books and writers in *Gilmore Girls* (including Jack Kerouac [1.01], Edith Wharton [1.06], Zelda Fitzgerald [2.01], Charles Dickens [2.05], Oscar Wilde [3.01], Graydon Carter [3.13], Gore Vidal [3.21], Hans Christian Andersen [4.06], Henry James [5.01], Alexander Pushkin [5.10], Dylan Thomas [6.01], and John Steinbeck [6.11]). "I've always felt," Sherman-Palladino would tell Virginia Heffernan, "that college is a wonderful privilege. To have four years where your only responsibility is to learn things! I'd give anything" (2005). In *Moby Dick,* which is mentioned in the *Gilmore Girls* pilot episode (during one of the first conversations between Rory and Dean), and which reappears in "Blame Booze and Melville" (5.21), a non-college-educated narrator, the hyperliterate Ishmael, explains that "a whale-ship was my Yale College and my Harvard" (Melville 2007, 128); *Gilmore Girls* was AS-P's Harvard and Yale.

"I want to speak visually, and writing is just a way of communicating visually. That's what it's all about," Joss Whedon has stated in an Onion AV Club interview, explaining how he became a television director. "But nobody would even consider me to direct. So I said, 'I'll create a television show, and I'll use it as a film school, and I'll teach myself to direct on TV.'" Sherman-Palladino's fellow *Roseanne* alum would indeed teach himself to direct on *Buffy the Vampire Slayer,* delivering some of the most innovative television episodes ever:

"Innocence" (2.14), "Hush" (4.10), "Restless" (4.22), "The Body" (5.16), and "Once More with Feeling" (6.07) on *Buffy;* and "Waiting in the Wings" (3.13) and "Spin the Bottle" (4.06) on *Angel.* "Objects in Space" (1.10) on *Firefly* greatly expanded the narrative and performative possibilities of the medium.

In both her ambitions as a director and her approach to the role, Sherman-Palladino differs markedly from Whedon. Wearing either of the two hats alone is very hard work, but authorship is "very solitary and directing is hanging out and interacting with a bunch of cool people." A writer can be threatened by solipsistic depression—"When you are alone in your room writing, you are saying things to yourself like, 'I suck. I have no talent.'" Directing, however, is a communal, collaborative pooling of talent. Troubled by "a feeling of combativeness between writers and directors that I feel is very harmful to the process," AS-P is nevertheless convinced that writers turn to directing primarily to protect their vision—"to see if it's possible to get something that I had envisioned written on paper exactly the same way on film" (Priggé 2005, 131).

She has learned that it is not possible. Directing her own scripts enables her to "go from 70% of the way you wanted the show to look to 90% . . . as close to the mark as it ever will be" (ibid.). The decision to assign herself "a couple of episodes a year where I know that if I don't get it, it wasn't going to work" instead of "killing myself" may seem hyperbolic, but it has a cinematic historical precedent: "You know, Billy Wilder considered himself first and foremost a writer—not to compare myself to Billy Wilder—and one of his big things was that he was just sick of people fucking up his scripts" (Tobias 2005).

Once AS-P began directing—"Love, Daisies, and Troubadours" (1.21) marked her debut in that capacity—she became an exemplary practitioner of the house style rather than an innovator. Her old-fashioned directorial aesthetic may not be in step with today's tendency toward a more cinematic televisuality, but it is appropriate for the sort of stories she wanted to tell. "My ideal show," she explains, "would have zero cuts in it. It would all be moving masters. There's an energy and style to our show that's very simple, in my mind. I think that sometimes directors err when they try to get too fancy. Like, 'Nice shot of a tree, but who gives a fuck? You've just missed four jokes!'" She remains convinced her show "needs to be shot like a play. That's how we get our pace, our energy, and our flow. Some directors love that, because it's something they don't get to do on other shows: Take a five, six, seven-page scene and try to do it without any cuts. That's a fun challenge. It's about choreography and movement. Our poor Steadicam guy goes home dead every night. He goes through four or five shirts a day" (ibid.). AS-P finds "television shows that have 14 shots of somebody looking at each other with the wind blowing through their hair" the stuff of madness. "Who's got that kind of time? We got that the girl was pretty when she walked in the door. Come on, somebody say something; let's go" (Heffernan 2005).

AS-P, AGG (After *Gilmore Girls*)

> *ENTERTAINMENT WEEKLY:* Are you ever going to tell us the ending you'd planned for *Gilmore*?
>
> AMY SHERMAN-PALLADINO: Not at the moment, but eventually. I'll be on top of a building, ready to jump, and I'll yell it to the world, and I'll plummet to my death.

Recalling Aaron Sorkin's insistence in a Charlie Rose interview that he would continue to watch his creation *The West Wing* (NBC, 1999–2006) after his departure, AS-P predicted a very different response to leaving her "baby": "Believe me, when I leave this show, I ain't watching. I'm sitting in a hole on Tuesday nights, sobbing and drunk for an hour. Jack Daniels. But hopefully, I'll be doing other things that I care about" (Tobias 2005). More than a year before Sherman-Palladino and her husband, Dan, would leave *Gilmore Girls* as the result of a contract dispute, she would, with characteristic wit, predict her departure, and explain the underlying causes, to the Onion AV Club:

> As a writer, you eventually have to move on. You can't do the same thing over and over again. This is also a very hard job. This has

> been five years of 24 hours a day, seven days a week. I've loved every minute of it, but there's got to be something else out there at some point. Your life as a writer in this town is actually not very long. It's short-term. When your heat is good, and people think you can do something, you've got to do it. Otherwise, you're sitting in the motion-picture home later on and someone's feeding you spinach, and then you die. So I'm learning to like spinach, because I know it is coming. Eventually, it's going to be time to move on and do something else. (ibid.)

Assuming Sherman-Palladino will not follow through on her playful threats to throw herself under a bus (or take a fatal leap), it is not easy to predict what the future holds for her. Her prediction that "it's going to be very different when I go out on the market . . . a whole new ball game" shows every sign of coming true (ibid.). AS-P had made her future ambitions very clear to Steven Priggé in 2005. "I want to write and direct a feature film in the next couple of years," she explained, but not to the exclusion of working in TV again: "I do want to keep my hand in TV. . . . I genuinely want sitcoms to come back very strong again. . . . I am also looking for a network to sell a new sitcom to—a network that will let my show breathe and thrive" (2005, 199).

True to her word, AS-P has worked on two appropriately "major" projects. The first is a sitcom titled *The Return of Jezebel James,* which debuted on FOX in 2008. It tells the story of estranged sisters, played by indie legend Parker Posey and *Six Feet Under*'s Lauren Ambrose, reunited when the former asks the latter to serve as surrogate mother to her baby. The second is an HBO movie, AS-P's debut as a feature-length film director, *The Late Bloomer's Revolution,* based on a novel by Amy Cohen and starring Sarah Jessica Parker as a woman-of-a-certain-age daughter who navigates the perils of dating in league with her newly widowed father.

"I'm going to keep creating new shows until the powers-that-be don't let me do it anymore" (ibid., 199–200), Sherman-Palladino promises. And she likes her odds: "Now that there's so much cable, so many different outlets to go to—FX, Showtime, HBO—it's becoming a different world, because there are so many levels on which to compete. . . . It's kind of an interesting time to be in TV, because if you have an idea you love and it's not right for a network, there's actually a place to take it now, and there didn't used to be" (Tobias 2005).

Early on, Amy Sherman-Palladino understood the deal: "To be really good, you have to be willing to have everybody in the world [of Hollywood] hate you" (ibid.); no doubt about it, she is really *that* good, so good in fact that *Gilmore Girls* fans will likely flock to all of her future projects regardless of critical reception or subject matter. In the words of Carole King and Toni Stern (the singer and lyricist, respectively, of the show's theme song, "Where You Lead"), "I will follow."

Branding the Family Drama

Genre Formations and Critical Perspectives on Gilmore Girls

AMANDA R. KEELER

Before its debut on October 5, 2000, *Gilmore Girls* had already made television history. According to an article published in *American Demographics* that year, *Gilmore Girls* was the "first advertiser advocated show" funded by the Family Friendly Programming Forum (FFPF), a group consisting of major U.S. corporations, who offered up a million dollars to "fund 'family-friendly' script development at the WB," the network that in 2006 partnered with UPN to become the CW ("Television" 2000). Taking into consideration other family-friendly dramatic television series aimed at multigenerational audiences on the CW, such as *7th Heaven* (1996–2007) and *Everwood* (2002–6), one might ask how a program about a single, never-married mom (until the final season), raising her daughter, could constitute family-friendly fare. What particular elements of this Amy Sherman-Palladino creation led the FFPF to fund its development? And is "family friendly" a viable genre label? In the context of television programming and criticism, does genre even matter anymore, considering the hybrid nature of most contemporary series?

In this chapter I will investigate what critics have written about *Gilmore Girls* and how the show has been linked to similar programs in terms of genre classification. My analysis will allude to other "family-friendly" CW programs that preceded the 2000 debut of *Gilmore Girls* as well as a host of others that followed over the course of its seven-season run. In this manner, the "family-friendly" classification can be investigated and formulated as part of the "discursive clusters" that surround *Gilmore Girls,* a program that falls between comedy and drama, teen and adult demographics, and family-oriented programming and left-leaning characters and situations.

What is it about *Gilmore Girls* that warrants such investigation? Simply put, this program contains a combination of elements that no other television program—currently or in the past—can boast: a mixture of strong female characters, with an emphasis on teenage and middle- and senior-aged adults' lives, and the show is quirky, populated by odd characters, all dealing with everyday problems, as well as some that most people will never face. The program was a triumph for the fledgling WB network almost immediately after its debut in 2000. It was one of the network's only programs to consistently score relatively high Nielsen ratings, particularly in relation to its Thursday-night competition on NBC, *Friends* (1994–2004). An hour-long drama/comedy shot on film and lacking a laugh track or live audience, *Gilmore Girls* was in many ways the anti-*Friends,* and perhaps for that reason drew viewers seeking something completely different. At the very least, the fact that this new, critically lauded program was earning high ratings on a minor network, despite competing against a mainstream major-network sitcom, begs further examination.

What, exactly, is this most unusual show all about? *Gilmore Girls* is an hour-long ensemble series centered on the lives of two Gilmore family members: sixteen-year-old Rory Gilmore and her mother, thirty-two-year-old Lorelai Gilmore. Their dynamic, sisterlike interactions and separate lives spent at school and work drive much of the comedy and drama of the show. Two other generations of Gilmore women are part of the narrative as well: Emily Gilmore, Rory's maternal grandmother, and Lorelai "Trix" Gilmore, Lorelai's paternal grandmother (also known as "Gran").

At the foundational level, the show is a family-centric dramedy featuring several concurrent storylines and an ensemble cast of characters who complement the eccentricities of these women and reside primarily in Stars Hollow, the fictional setting of *Gilmore Girls.* This formula is consistent over much of the show's seven seasons, with minor conflicts being resolved—usually within one or two episodes—through interpersonal discussions among the main and supporting characters. Larger conflicts, mostly family-related issues linked to Lorelai's tense relationship with her mother, Emily, and her father, Richard, ebb and flow season to season.

One notable aspect of *Gilmore Girls* is its generically hybrid nature, something frequently commented upon and debated by television critics and fans alike. To better understand how diverse groups of audiences have discussed and written about the show, I have looked to a number of sources with an eye to consolidating these various discourses. First, it should be noted that the least amount of writing available on the program is in scholarly books and journal articles. This discovery, in addition to my abiding interest in this particular television program, has led me to write this chapter to add to the existing literature and to better understand my own fascination and fandom.

The greatest amount of discourse available on *Gilmore Girls* can be found in trade magazines concerning industry discussions of the program, the CW network, and the show's stars. I culled this data primarily from *Variety* and *Entertainment Weekly*, both of which provide valuable insights into the program through the eyes of critics who work with one foot inside and one foot outside the television industry. The writers contributing pieces to these two publications are uniquely qualified and situated to speak to everyday viewers of television as well as industry professionals. Finally, I also examined as many accounts of the program that I could locate from local and national newspapers, "family-friendly" and parental guidance Web sites (such as the Parents Television Council [PTC] and the Family Friendly Programming Forum), online blogs, and critical assessments of other programs that make passing references to *Gilmore Girls*, itself one of the most reference-filled series on American television.

As this chapter primarily concerns the debates that surround the show in reference to its genre, it is important to first define what is meant by the term *genre* and how scholars have typically formulated opinions on this crucial matter of terminology. The television scholar whose work has proved to be the most illuminating in terms of classificatory status is Jason Mittell, author of *Genre and Television*. Mittell challenges existing conceptions of genre formation specifically relating to television programming. He writes, "Texts themselves are insufficient to understand how genres are created, merge, evolve, or disappear. We need to look outside of texts to locate the range of sites in which genres operate, change, proliferate, and die out" (2004, 9). In his formulation of genres as "cultural categories," Mittell repeatedly pushes for analyses that move outside of the television text and examine instead the "discursive formations," including factors such as audience reception, critical interpretations, and industry discussions, to name a few (ibid., 13, 18). This conceptualization of genre is born out of Michel Foucault's discourse analyses, where, by Mittell's assessment, genres "work as discursive clusters, with certain definitions, interpretations and evaluations coming together at any given time to suggest a coherent and clear" label (ibid., 17). What is most fascinating about Mittell's framework is his contention that genre study entails not just an analysis of one specific show but rather a cultural and historical examination over time through several related programs, as well as through critical, scholarly, and fan discussions. Relying on Mittell's methodology, this chapter will examine *Gilmore Girls* and the disparate genre assessments surrounding it from a multitude of sources, which define the program along a range of contrasting and complicating classifications, from "family friendly" to "dramedy."

"But I'm a Half-Hour Woman!"

In a 2002 interview series creator and executive producer Amy Sherman-Palladino stated that *Gilmore Girls* is "a family show, which means we write about real family life, and that encompasses deep emotional pain, awfulness and Prozac and hopefully therapy, and a lot of happy and funny stuff as well" (quoted in Zahed 2002). Here, Sherman-Palladino opts not to place the "family-friendly" tag firmly within the confines of traditional domestic dramas that involve married heterosexual couples, but rather puts drama within families, in whatever form that family takes. Alternately, Joy Press writes, "Sure, some of *90210*'s fans turned to *Dawson's Creek* and *Gilmore Girls,* but [these] wholesome series [lack] a certain glitz and tawdriness" that shows like *The O.C.,* on FOX, provide (2004, 49).

From this statement one can sense that *Gilmore Girls*' family friendliness stems not only from the content of the show but also from its relation to other programs. The television show that Press references, *The O.C.* (2003–7), starring former *Gilmore Girls* regular Adam Brody, also functions as a family drama of sorts, one whose storylines are spread among several families. Despite this moniker, *The O.C.* has been classified by the Parents Television Council as a red-light show that "may include gratuitous sex, explicit dialogue, violent content, or obscene language, and is unsuitable for children" ("Family Guide: *The O.C.*" n.d.). In relation to shows like *The O.C., Gilmore Girls* contains elements that usually denote "family-friendly" fare, such as the strong mother-daughter bond and the multigenerational emphasis. However, next to a more conservative program like *7th Heaven,* Amy Sherman-Palladino's snarky take on mother-daughter relations and New England eccentricity is a world apart. The Parents Television Council Web site classifies *7th Heaven* as a green-light program, a "family-friendly show promoting responsible themes and traditional values," while *Gilmore Girls* earns a yellow light, meaning that it is a show that "contains adult-oriented themes and dialogue that may be inappropriate for youngsters" ("Family Guide: *Gilmore Girls*" n.d.). Sherman-Palladino stated outright, before the program's debut in 2000, "It's not going to be *7th Heaven,*" meaning that the show would not succumb to the saccharine-sweetness of that "green light" show (quoted in Fretts 2000a, 80).

Amy Sherman-Palladino herself has made a point that the family-friendly assessment of *Gilmore Girls* is based less on plots and storylines than on the characters—quirky individuals who appeal to actual families viewing the program, a series whose attraction can be partly attributed to its multigenerational cast. This widens the appeal for several divergent family members rather than solely teenagers, differentiating it from other CW television programs like *One Tree Hill* (2003–). In an interview with *Entertainment Weekly,* FFPF member and corporate vice president for Johnson & Johnson Andrea Alstrup said, "We were looking for programming that wasn't what people typically thought of as family friendly. We needed to break that mold, to attract the broadest range of audience" (Weiner 2002, 66). What they attempted, and succeeded at, was creating a multigenerational ensemble cast to "skew older," a program that moved away from a singular appeal to teenagers toward a program that their parents could enjoy and approve of as well (Bergman 2000). The CW's Web site for *Gilmore Girls* adds the following statement, "The strong and loving mother-daughter relationship portrayed in *Gilmore Girls* reflects the growing reality of this new type of American family," presumably meaning nontraditional, single-parent households (CW Web site, www.CWTV.com).

From the beginning it was acknowledged that *Gilmore Girls* would not be a traditional "family-friendly" program, meaning that it would not exclusively focus on intact, married heterosexual families with children. When asked how the FFPF felt about Lorelai being an unwed mother, Alstrup replied, "There were discussions about that but we didn't feel that was a critical part of the story" (Weiner 2002, 66). To frame this differently, rather than consider *Gilmore Girls* unfamily friendly because of the unwed-teen pregnancy at the heart of the show's premise, the counterpoint to this plot is the program that wasn't produced: one that could have focused on a pregnant sixteen-year-old girl who has an abortion. Instead, the "family-friendly" element implicit in this formulation hinges on the presence of a young woman who—when forced to make a difficult decision—chose the "right" path, one that made her accountable for her youthful indiscretion. In the fifteen years between Rory's birth and the program's starting point, it is acknowledged that Lorelai has worked hard and is now a successful business owner, someone whose "accidental" daughter is the center of her sometimes difficult but satisfying life.

The series does not portray the "what if" factor: what if Rory had never been born? But the show is also quick to highlight Lorelai's missed opportunities and the consequences of her unplanned teen pregnancy, such as missing out on her cotillion and attending college, and the strained relationship with her mother. All of these factors are ushered forth not so much through Lorelai's character development but through Rory's, as their friends frequently make references to the things that the latter girl is able to do that her mother was not. All of the sacrifices Lorelai makes in her life are construed as opportunities for Rory and as lessons to prevent her from making a similar "mistake," to ensure that she will not follow the same path that Lorelai (accidentally) took. This is not to say that the program never focuses on regret, but Lorelai's accidental pregnancy is implicitly posited as a less than ideal condition for someone who aspires to do great things at an early age. It is this "less than ideal" status that underlines the relationship between mother and daughter. There are no regrets, but also no romanticizing of the difficulties and sacrifices endured by Lorelai to ensure that Rory will have the opportunities to fulfill her intellectual and educational goals.

Allison Weiner writes that many critics were initially "skeptical; most assumed the show was being used to advance a right-wing agenda," because of the initial funding it received from the FFPF (ibid.). This assumption is not entirely without merit. *Gilmore Girls,* like all televisual texts, is open to socially progressive or politically retrograde readings alike. Just as genre is prone to hybridity and at least partially predicated on a formulation of multiple sites of meaning, so too do televisual texts flit between several interpretations and therefore frustrate monolithic readings. With this freedom of personal interpretations people have claimed TV programs and films as representing precisely what another group may feel the same texts rally against. For example, depending on one's critical perspective, a program like *Buffy the Vampire Slayer* (WB/UPN, 1997–2003) can be understood as a family drama or as a horror and science fiction hybrid. In the first season, Buffy's family is made up of her blood relations (her mother, her absent father), but very quickly her family expands to include her friends Willow and Xander, and Giles, her "Watcher." Like *Gilmore Girls,* this Joss Whedon series has a multigenerational appeal with a diverse cast of characters that works on several levels for a variety of viewers and interpretations. Though "family oriented," *Buffy* is not without criticism, either. Many of the show's critics were concerned with the violence depicted on the program, as evidenced in Lisa Parks's essay "Brave New *Buffy:* Rethinking 'TV Violence" (2003). In that essay she convincingly argues that the violence in *Buffy* works on an allegorical, rather than literal, level. Parks, for one, points to the cultural scapegoating of *Buffy the Vampire Slayer* after the Columbine school shootings in 1999.

In this regard, any textual reading acts as a personal reflection within broader social and cultural issues at a particular moment in time. Rather than look at this program from my personal experience, I instead am interested in exploring genre by examining existing critical readings. Here, genre analysis is not a matter of adopting the preferences or prejudices of any one critic, but rather a means of looking at what several writers have expressed about *Gilmore Girls* and synthesizing their assessments. Many of these assessments were made near the beginning of the show's conception in 2000. But, as Jason Mittell writes, genre formation is a "fluid and active process" (2004, 16). In deference to the program's early "family-friendly" status, the Parents Television Council, years after the series premiered, gave it a yellow-light warning, noting that the program is "not very family-friendly" because of its "harsh language" and "casual treatment of sexual material" ("Family Guide: *Gilmore Girls*" n.d.). In 2003 *Entertainment Weekly* stamped a "Parental Warning" on the program due to Rory's relationship with then-boyfriend Jess Mariano, although these incessantly bickering characters do not engage in any explicit sexual experimentation (EW Web site, www.ew.com/ew/article/0,,411599_7,00.html). Despite these elements, not everyone agreed with the PTC's yellow-light warning: former child star Jerry Mathers, of *Leave It to Beaver* (ABC, 1957–63) fame, told an interviewer that he was turned on to *Gilmore Girls* by his daughter. He is quoted as saying, "*Gilmore Girls* is good. I just think there should be a few things kids could watch" (quoted in Wilonsky 2003). Executives at Disney seemed to agree with Mathers's assessment, as the ABC Family channel acquired the "exclusive off-network rights" to *Gilmore Girls* in 2003 (Grego 2003). As well, in 2001 the program won the Family Television Awards' "Best New Series" prize.

Within Mittell's formulation of genre are two questions in regard to *Gilmore Girls.* First, does "family friendly" constitute a viable genre according to Mittell's criteria? And second, does *Gilmore Girls* fit better within another, more classically defined, category, like comedy or drama? To help determine what genre a program belongs to or relies on, Mittell asks, "Does a given category circulate within the cultural spheres of audiences, press accounts, and industrial discourses?" (2004, 11). In terms of labeling the show "family friendly," a designation that is part of the industrial-critical discourses discussed above, it seems a viable option. But among audiences, I found little evidence of references to the program as "family friendly." What I did discover, however, was a curious inclusion of the program in the lexicon of fans and critics alike, with myriad groups of people, such as television critic Bill Frost, using the program to describe other shows that also seemingly fall outside classical genre delineations. Frost, for example, refers to the half-hour WB program *What I Like about You* (2002–6) as "*Gilmore Girls* in New York" (2002, 33). In an interview professional baker Jami Curl uses the program to describe her viewing tastes, saying, "I don't even watch *Sex and the City.* I'm more of a *Gilmore Girls* person" (Clarke 2005, 49). Joy Press of the *Village Voice* writes, "*Gilmore Girls* is still the sweetest show on TV. It's also one of the smartest, weighing in somewhere between *Buffy the Vampire Slayer* and *The Sopranos.*" Press goes on to write that Nancy, the pot-selling mom on Showtime's *Weeds* (2005–), "joins Lorelai Gilmore, the wisecracking mom of the *Gilmore Girls,* as one of the most flawed, fascinating women on TV, a giant fuck-you to the retro conservatism of Wisteria Lane," referring to the ABC television drama *Desperate Housewives* (2004–) (2004, 113). In a review for *Variety,* Michael Speier writes that *Everwood* (2002–6) is "a sound drama that does for father-son relationships what *Gilmore Girls* does for the women of the family" (2002). In describing a proposed reality show featuring the Gastineau family, *Variety* writer John Dempsey explains that the program will be *"Sex and the City* meets *Gilmore Girls"* (2004).

These and numerous other references made to the program and its characters by critics and viewers lack the phrase "family friendly," and illustrate how the program has become part of the descriptive language to reference other television programs that also frustrate easy categorization. By these accounts, then, "family friendly" may not qualify as a genre according to Mittell's conceptualization, despite the proliferation of the term among certain critics and organizations. There appear to be two reasons this term is not circulating among viewers and most critics. First, despite the show's origins as specifically "family friendly," overt labeling of the show as such might dissuade potential viewers from approaching it, given the usual connotations that accompany such fare. Thus, if this term were a larger part of the show's discourse, then it might risk self-selecting its audience, to the detriment of higher ratings and advertising dollars. Second, although there is evidence that actual families, like Jerry Mathers and his daughter, do watch the program together, *Gilmore Girls* aired on the CW, a fledgling network known for its large number of teen dramas. Although the network has been forthright in labeling *7th Heaven* as "family friendly," such a designation might have hindered *Gilmore Girls* from gaining popularity among teenagers, the primary demographic of CW viewers, and forever cast it as something uncool or unwatchable in the eyes of young audiences. In actuality, the show pains itself to sustain a high level of hipness through the characters' witty banter, their endless pop culture references, and Lane Kim's fetish for all things punk rock. *Gilmore Girls* relies on two generations of teenage rebellion to showcase its hipness, as witnessed through current teenagers Lane and Jess and former teenager Lorelai. Although the show profiles teenage rebellion on many levels, their rebellion is filtered and presented in a mostly benign, domesticated nature.

Although "family friendly" does not constitute a viable genre category, these references lead to the second part of my genre analysis, suggesting that the program can be situated within either the comedy or drama category. Again, Mittell writes that if either one of these terms is used to describe a program's genre, then it must circulate within "cultural spheres of audiences, press accounts, and industrial discourses" (2004, 11). By citing other programs to describe *Gilmore Girls,* TV critics avoid having to classify a program that does not fall purely into drama or comedy categories. Executive producer Sherman-Palladino writes, "There are these preconceived notions of what an hour-long show should or shouldn't do. . . . I'll let other people try to categorize it" (quoted in Zahed 2002). Here she is referring to the length of the program, an hour, which is generally associated with television dramas. By contrast, the half-hour show is usually associated with situation comedies. Mittell argues that, despite widely accepted practices of dictating genre by length of program or by time slot, such criteria might actually detract from our understanding of genre, especially insofar as a given program's hour-long length does not automatically make it a drama. Nor does *Gilmore Girls*' time slot (various weekday evenings at 8 p.m. eastern) necessarily denote prime-time comedy, although the show does have ties to that genre. Sherman-Palladino was previously a writer for *Roseanne* (ABC, 1988–97) and *Veronica's Closet* (NBC, 1997–2000), both half-hour-length sitcoms. When asked to create an hour-long program, she is reported to have said, "Are you on crack? I'm a half-hour woman!" thus complicating the genre labeling of *Gilmore Girls* even in the preproduction stages (Martin 2005).

But where does the program fit in this either-or configuration? The reasoning behind using existing television shows to describe "hybrid" programs like *Gilmore Girls* solves the problem of indistinguishable genre classification. Some critics have described the program as a straightforward drama. In 2000 Michael Schneider wrote that the WB network was adding "one new drama, the mom-daughter opus *Gilmore Girls*." According to Dan Jewel, the program is "a quietly intelligent, witty drama" (2002). *Gilmore Girls* is an "adroitly written, light drama," writes Ken Tucker of *Entertainment Weekly* (2000). These assessments of the program's drama categorization are really the exception rather than the rule. Indeed, many more critics refer to the program as a "dramedy," a hybrid genre mixing drama and comedy. Critic Michael Speier writes that *Gilmore Girls* and other shows like *Ally McBeal* (FOX, 1997–2002) and *Sex and the City* (HBO, 1998–2004) "fall into the mixed-bag mold. They're dramedies" (2002). Alison Weiner writes, "In one fell swoop, this dramedy about an unmarried mother and her teenage daughter has managed to get conservatives and liberals agreeing on fine family entertainment" (2002, 66). *Entertainment Weekly* critic Bruce Fretts writes that *Gilmore Girls* is "the WB's engaging family dramedy." Another *EW* critic writes that the program "is a pitch-perfect attempt at a young adult dramedy for the teencentric network" (Baldwin 2000).

In her book *Redesigning Women,* Amanda Lotz writes that, in the case of programs that straddle the line between comedy and drama like *Gilmore Girls* and *The Days and Nights of Molly Dodd* (NBC, 1987–91), the term "'comedic drama' replaces the increasingly common industrial term 'dramedy,' which has been used more frequently in response to a shift from traditional situation-comedy forms throughout the late 1990s, but lacks theoretical delimitation or precise use" (2006, 32–33). Most critics, however, have not taken up the language Lotz uses in her book. Industry writing repeatedly refers to the program as a "dramedy." Thus, there is a consensus among critics that the program is neither outright comedy nor purely drama but rather a combination of both. But if this is an industry term, what do audiences consider the program? And if audiences are not referring to *Gilmore Girls* as a dramedy, then does it too fail the genre classification set up by Mittell? By his accounting, the program is neither a drama nor a comedy, neither "family friendly" nor purely a program for teens or adults. If it is this difficult to classify a program, why, then, does genre matter at all?

Making Meaning of Genre

Genre delineations help periodicals such as *TV Guide* and *Entertainment Weekly* classify programs for the sake of readers' easy reference. By labeling a program a "drama," the audience knows immediately that it will likely be one hour long (counting commercial advertisements), occur during prime-time evening hours, and probably be more invested in character development than in zippy verbal and visual gags. Labeling a program a "comedy" means the likelihood that a program will air during prime time, will usually be thirty minutes in length, will often be a situation comedy, and will be accompanied by a laugh track or the presence of a live audience on set. These generic criteria are the foundational building blocks that allow critics and viewers to extrapolate additional characteristics of a program. Moreover, these simple determinations have accrued over time through popular discourses. When writers for *TV Guide* refer to a series as a comedy, they are adding that program to a lineage of other shows associated with that genre. This process, according to Mittell, is "fluid and active," with genres constantly and forever ebbing and flowing in different directions, mutating with each new program that emerges on the televisual landscape (2004, 16).

Within this dynamic process *Gilmore Girls* stands out as a new class of TV programming that occupies a relatively uncharted, undefined middle ground in terms of genre. Although this is not necessarily problematic on the surface, and while such matters do not detract from audiences' recognition, understanding, or appreciation of the show's textual parameters, the lack of language for such phenomena does impact the series in other ways. In an article titled "*Gilmore* Goes Laffer Route on Ballots," Geoffrey Berkshire writes that *Gilmore Girls* is "praised by critics and embraced by viewers but seemingly invisible to Emmy voters" (2002). In a *Variety* article titled "Dramedy Makers Need to Choose Sides: *Ed, Sex, Gilmore* Tough to Categorize," Michael Freeman writes, "Hour-long series such as the WB's *Gilmore Girls* . . . are submitted for Emmy consideration as comedy series, even though they really are dramedies" (2003). Berkshire agrees with this assessment, writing that "the blend of comedy and drama makes for a refreshing Emmy-worthy series but results in an Emmy quandary: Which of these series categories is a better fit?" (2002). Although the show has comedic moments, it is still sometimes heavily dramatic, such as the narrative developments that led to Rory's breakup with Dean and the ongoing frustrations surrounding Lorelai's relationship with her parents. Classification, then, proves to be problematic insofar as these classically defined categories can mean the difference between winning and losing highly coveted television industry awards.

To highlight the conundrum of classification, a quick glance at the awards for which the show has been nominated over its seven-year run might illustrate a similar schizophrenic differentiation. In 2001 and 2002 the Television Critics Association nominated *Gilmore Girls* for "Outstanding Achievement in Drama." Three years later, in 2005, it nominated the program for "Outstanding Achievement in Comedy." The Teen Choice Awards nominated the program for "Choice TV, Drama" in 2001 and 2002. In each of the next four years, however, the Teen Choice Awards nominated the program as "Choice TV, Comedy." The Satellite Awards deemed the program "Best Television Series, Comedy or Musical" in 2005, but that same year the People's Choice Awards nominated it as "Favorite Television Drama."

In 2002 Lauren Graham was recognized by the Hollywood Foreign Press Association (responsible for the Golden Globes) for her role as Lorelai and was nominated for "Best Performance by an Actress in a Television Series—Drama." That same year the Satellite Awards nominated her for "Best Performance by an Actress in a Series, Comedy or Musical." In 2002 the Television Critics Association nominated Graham for "Individual Achievement in Drama." Four years later it nominated her for "Outstanding Individual Achievement in Comedy." The Screen Actors Guild maintained its stance year to year by nominating Graham in both 2001 and 2002 for "Outstanding Performance by a Female Actor in a Drama Series." Alexis Bledel was nominated in 2001 and 2002 for "Best Performance in a TV Drama Series" by the Young Artist Awards. In 2002 the Satellite Awards nominated Bledel for "Best Performance by an Actress in a Series, Comedy or Musical." The Teen Choice Awards recognized Bledel several times over the course of the program, first as "Choice TV Actress, Drama," in 2001 and 2002, and later as "Choice TV Actress, Comedy," in 2004, 2005, and 2006.

As for the program being ignored by the Emmys, this anecdote was not entirely the case. In 2004 the show won its one and only Emmy, for Makeup. Interestingly, the one Emmy Award earned by the program was in a category that did not necessitate a genre differentiation.

In my attempt to begin unpacking the proposed genre term *dramedy,* one largely overlooked aspect makes itself felt, a curious sense that most of the shows labeled "dramedies" by critics are programs that center on female characters. Shows such as *Sex and the City, The Days and Nights of Molly Dodd, Ally McBeal, Gilmore Girls,* and *Buffy the Vampire Slayer* have all been coined "dramedies." Although, on the surface, this seems insignificant, it speaks to the ways in which female characters have been portrayed on contemporary network television. Though there has been a surge of female characters and female-protagonist-driven programs on American television in the past ten years, in a way the conflation of drama with comedy undercuts what appears, on the surface, to be gains for more female representation on television. When a female-centric dramatic program uses comedy to lighten the emotional load, it can be read as a displacement of seriousness. This means that, on one level, there is an inability to take female characters' emotional states and personal or professional challenges at face value, and thus comedy is added to them to make light of their true struggles. In this way *Gilmore Girls* mirrors the lack of seriousness afforded soap operas, which operate on different levels between viewer perceptions, from critics who belittle the programs to viewers who are willing to follow character and narrative arcs for decades.

Cable channels such as Lifetime have attempted, with great success, to fill a perceived programming gap by attracting women to television shows with an emphasis on drama and women's life stories. At issue, then, is whether women's dramas—and not dramedies—are to be found on network television, or only on select cable channels. Lifetime is able, as a cable channel, to narrowcast in order to fit the needs and wants of any demographic group of its choice. The five broadcast networks (ABC, NBC, CBS, FOX, and the CW) must provide as broad a range of options to attract the widest and most diverse audience for the sake of profits (derived through advertisement dollars). I am not condemning these dramedies; quite the opposite. But I do not want to dismiss the idea that these programs might mix comedy and drama in order to make them "watchable" for male viewers, in the process making serious "female" moments more easily digestible. But, as an aside, for as many ensemble shows featuring nearly all-male casts (such as *The West Wing* [NBC, 1999–2006]), where are the female-only ensemble dramas to counterbalance this trend? Why has gender gotten so tied up in these genre specifications?

In wrapping up this examination of *Gilmore Girls,* a brief discussion of the CW network aids in my assessment of genre formations. In 2001 Bruce Fretts wrote, "The WB has never appeared on the TV Academy's radar screen—witness the lack of nominations for *Buffy the Vampire Slayer* and *Felicity.* Maybe this exquisitely crafted family dramedy [*Gilmore Girls*] will break the jinx." As noted above, this has not been the case. *Buffy the Vampire Slayer* and *Felicity* (1998–2002) have both gone off the air. Original episodes of *Gilmore Girls* have left the airwaves and are in syndication, a shift that was precipitated one year prior to the show's conclusion by executive producer Amy Sherman-Palladino's exit from the series (at the end of the sixth season, in 2006). What is evident from the above quote is not only the nature of the CW but also that its programs have been overlooked. Although popular with audiences, a program like *Dawson's Creek* was never a favorite among critics, whereas viewers and critics alike lauded *Buffy the Vampire Slayer* and *Felicity,* both teen-friendly, female-centric ensemble series on the WB. The CW's fringe status, in conjunction with the somewhat lower status usually afforded television programs popular with teenagers, as well the marginality of programs with female protagonists all converge in the critical slighting of programs like *Gilmore Girls.* Though any of these reasons may have contributed to these programs' relative lack of Emmy nominations, they all follow a pattern and resonate with broader cultural attitudes and taste-based distinctions of television programming in the United States.

What, then, does an analysis of the dramedy form entail for future assessments of *Gilmore Girls*? Throughout this chapter I have raised several questions so as to emphasize that a multitude of impinging factors, critical judgments, and fan practices build on and play off one another. Any assessment of this show's generic affiliation, though, can never be final, as genre itself is always in flux, caught up in the shifting discourses surrounding new and earlier programs. Jason Mittell presents a formulation of genre that is nuanced and entirely appropriate, and I have adopted his model because it allows for the complications of many factors in determining the categorical affiliation of *Gilmore Girls*. Although there are elements that Mittell chooses not to include in his formulation, factors such as ideology and star status, his method provides a useful framework upon which to build more elaborate analyses of genre. Thus, I have attempted to locate *Gilmore Girls* within the discursive clusters that have led me to discuss its tenuous status as a "family-friendly" program, a "dramedy," and as a teen-centric show on the CW.

In the end, it is clear that, according to Mittell's reading protocol, the program does not fit conveniently or completely into any one of these categories. But perhaps that is the power of a program like *Gilmore Girls,* which moves the line between these disparate typologies that together prevent it from adoption by any one audience. Instead, it appeals to a variety of viewers. Though it might be perceived as a weakness that *Gilmore Girls* eludes any simple genre classification, this is also the program's strength, for it is able to fluidly cross boundaries within which other shows remain trapped.

3

Your Guide to the Girls

Gilmore-isms, Cultural Capital, and a Different Kind of Quality TV

JUSTIN OWEN RAWLINS

"Not the typical *Gilmore Girls* viewer." This is both the way in which I preface conversations with friends and associates about the television show and the thought transparent on the faces of fellow media scholars upon learning of my interest in a program on the CW network about the misadventures of a mother and daughter in a small Connecticut town. Although I do not fit within the targeted demographic for this program, which, according to a 2006 promotional agreement between the CW and American Eagle Outfitters, appears to include young women ages fifteen to twenty-five, I nonetheless have become an avid fan of the series. Just what attracts me to the show remains the operative question, and this ongoing internal interrogation rather easily bleeds into a larger question that consistently plagues academic pursuits, namely: Why does this matter? *Should* this matter?

Speaking personally, my own internal search to uncover the reasons I enjoy the series has in large part led me to realize why it is that *Gilmore Girls* demands critical analysis. After all, one's research agendas are fundamentally rooted in one's interests. To suggest otherwise would smack of the academy's historically problematic cloaking of subjectivity as disinterested judgment. What follows, therefore, is not merely an attempt to explain why it is that a twentysomething male enjoys watching a show on the CW network; rather, this analysis aims to outline those characteristics of the program that evoke viewing pleasure and to investigate the broader questions provoked in unpacking the term *quality TV.*

Although marketed toward a gender and age demographic substantially different from the audiences of other programs deemed to be exceptional (exemplified by HBO shows such as *The Sopranos* [1999–2007], *Six Feet Under* [2001–5], *Deadwood* [2004–6], *The Wire* [2002–8], and *Big Love* [2006–] and Showtime series such as *Dexter* [2006–] and *Weeds* [2005–]), *Gilmore Girls* nonetheless explicitly and repeatedly invites similar viewing strategies by relying upon what French sociologist Pierre Bourdieu has termed "cultural capital." Although other television series may appeal to this "capital" through particular narrative, episodic, or character sophistication, *Gilmore Girls* relies heavily on (and is epitomized by) a rich intertextual dialogue between the show's principal characters. Termed *"Gilmore-isms"* in both reception and production discourse (as evidenced by critical and popular responses, as well as the *Guide to Gilmore-isms* pamphlets accompanying Seasons Two, Three, and Four on DVD and available online for additional seasons), these often dense references to popular culture are central to the interactions between the protagonists and their idiosyncratic community of family and friends inside Stars Hollow, Connecticut, the fictional setting of the series. *Gilmore Girls* foregrounds this intertextual dialogue in such a way that the characters themselves are aware of it; references are often commented upon and frequently become the focus of conversation as well as a source of confusion for diegetic and extradiegetic witnesses.

In this way the program articulates what typically goes unsaid by other television programs, namely, that watching TV not only invites active participation but also makes serious demands of viewers. While other quality shows solicit and most often appeal to those viewers possessing cultural capital, those programs' intertextuality and prerequisite cultural knowledge often go unacknowledged within the diegesis and lead to a rigid divide between those "in the know" and those not. *Gilmore Girls,* on the other hand, openly discusses and questions the nature of cultural capital by repeatedly examining its relation to education and socioeconomic status. Indeed, the centrality of "*Gilmore*-isms" demonstrates the importance of the relationship between capital and class that makes *Gilmore Girls* distinctive in its reflexivity of what constitutes quality television. The show's emphasis on the exchange of cultural knowledge within the diegetic world of Stars Hollow further problematizes the confluence of education and cultural capital while promising to bridge the gaps in knowledge created by such shows.

This chapter, therefore, will engage some of the scholarly discourses surrounding the subject of quality television, looking both to those programs whose textual conventions and marketing strategies fall under this rubric and to the class implications of the rubric itself.[1] *Gilmore Girls* will be shown to largely conform to this concept through its formal conventions, its genealogy of production, and the discursive clusters in the mediasphere that situate it as a quality program. I will examine the critical and reception discourses concerning the signature "*Gilmore*-isms" deemed so essential to the show and elaborate Bourdieu's concept of cultural capital so as to trace its interconnections with education and class. The first three seasons of the series will also be investigated in the course of tracing this relationship, particularly as it pertains to the larger network of friends and family members who compose the *Gilmore Girls* universe (or "*Gilmore*verse") that surrounds the two protagonists and can be imaginatively "inhabited" by fans of the series. Through this

1. Attempting to address quality television as a contextually contingent cultural category situated in a variety of competing and complementary discourses understandably results in a rather large sample of "quality" shows. Indeed, this essay intends not to police the boundaries of taste (which are themselves areas of frequent contestation subject to synchronic and diachronic shifts) but rather to focus on a small group of programs that have been similarly labeled via their conventions and comparisons to *Gilmore Girls*. I am therefore less interested in gauging problematic notions of "good" and "bad" than I am in parsing out what makes *Gilmore Girls* distinctive as a show said to have "quality." Furthermore, the emphasis on the discursive construction of genres such as "quality television" is intended implicitly to suggest that scholars be cognizant of their role in contributing to value judgments and subsequent cultural policing of taste.

analysis I will demonstrate that, rather than couch itself within an invisible rhetoric of quality, *Gilmore Girls* overtly addresses notions of education and class and their various implications in the accretion (and subsequent display) of cultural capital, thereby remaking the relationship between the three and suggesting that they need not be so inextricably linked to one another. Although it may be easy to dismiss such a program for its melodramatic tinges and apparent bourgeois appeal, I offer an analysis that foregrounds the show's potential for expanding quality television beyond the intended demographics of age and gender as well as the horizon of expectations associated with education and class.

Although the idea of quality television may still ring oxymoronic in some circles, scholars have charted the emergence of a type of programming historically, culturally, and industrially shaped in the postnetwork era. Amanda Lotz provides a concise survey of the postnetwork era:

> By the late 1990s, the economy of the U.S. television industry had been significantly reconfigured from the fairly static relations that had characterized it from its 1950s origin to the mid-1980s. A variety of factors—including the success of cable and satellite transmission, the appearance of new broadcast networks, increased ownership conglomeration, decreased regulation, and the emergence of new technologies—combined to usher in a new era of industry competition, forcing adjustments by traditional broadcast networks. During the decade from approximately 1985 to 1995 these factors substantially altered the institutional environment of the U.S. television industry, a rupture commonly identified as the transition to a post network or neo-network era. (2004, 22)

Scholarship on quality television suggests that the genre's progenitors existed long before the sea changes of the postnetwork era. Jason Mittell argues that antecedents of the narratively complex programs of the past twenty years can be seen as early as the mid- to late 1970s, while David Marc points to the work of MTM productions in creating "literate speak" programs that defied genre specificity (Jancovich and Lyons 2003, 1).[2] Forced to compete for increasingly fragmented audiences brought about in large part by the industrial shifts noted by Lotz, television companies began to produce a greater number of programs that self-consciously engaged traditional conventions and chose to blend, subvert, or reject them in favor of creating a new kind of cultural production renowned for its quality. Whereas some scholars have argued that the heightened economic stakes (marked by dwindling audiences and skyrocketing production costs) have created a milieu of uniformity and timidity, John Caldwell sees this instead as an era marked by distinction and occasional risk taking.[3] This differentiation, epitomized by an "excess of style" that Caldwell terms "televisuality," lends itself to the economic crises noted by some to breed uniformity while also acknowledging an aesthetic or formal self-consciousness that becomes invaluable to our consideration of exceptional television (2000, 651).

It is here that Caldwell distinguishes the function of self-consciousness and intertextuality within the televisual medium. Rejecting the applicability of Fredric Jameson's notion of postmodernism to the televisual

2. Jancovich and Lyons (2003) point to shows such as *All in the Family* (CBS, 1971–79) and *M*A*S*H* (CBS, 1972–83) for their use of "literate speak" within the sitcom genre. They also look to MTM productions (*Lou Grant* [CBS, 1977–82], *Hill Street Blues* [NBC, 1981–87], *St. Elsewhere* [NBC, 1982–88]) and the work of MTM alumni (*Taxi* [ABC, 1978–83], *Cheers* [NBC, 1982–93], and *Northern Exposure* [1990–95]) in creating programs that transcend generic conventions and thus constitute a body of work deemed exceptional in its complexity.

3. Caldwell states that "televisuality cannot be theorized apart from the crisis that network television underwent after 1980," yet his conclusions regarding excess as distinction seem to suggest that uniformity is not an appropriate response to the postnetwork era (2000, 656). Christopher Anderson rightly points to the dilemma facing dramatic productions in the postnetwork era, performing a crude cost-benefit analysis of the television landscape and noting the high costs of production and the relative infrequency of success among new shows. As Anderson notes, episodic programs such as *Law and Order* (NBC, 1990–) are seen as good investments because they fare relatively well as repeats (thus maximizing the initial investment) and prove to be relatively safe shows to clone in lieu of reinventing the television drama (2005, 86).

medium, in his essay "Excessive Style: The Crisis of Network Television" Caldwell argues that television defies such periodization precisely because the medium has, since its inception, functioned as a pastiche of other established media forms. There can be no postmodern televisual era, therefore, because the medium itself is inherently postmodern. What is unique to this historical period (1980s–) is the degree to which the programs engage and acknowledge their intertextuality and the resulting effects such textual maneuvers have on viewing practices (2000, 653).

What has emerged during that time is, according to Jason Mittell, a new kind of narrative complexity that redefines "episodic frames under the influence of serial narration—not necessarily a complete merger of episodic and serial forms but a shifting balance" (2006, 32). Terming this period "television's second golden age," Robert Thompson claims that although terms of exceptionality may have originally been applied to unusually good shows, the "quality" in "quality TV" has come to refer to a generic style rather than to an aesthetic judgment (1996, 77). Thompson's comment echoes that of Caldwell in its observation of the medium's investment in the performance of style more than a particular look (Caldwell 2000, 651). This "style" for Mittell, Caldwell, and Thompson also marks the increased presence of Hollywood talent who seek to capitalize on the long-form capabilities of the medium.

Mittell's comments regarding television's potentialities suggest other characteristics of quality both implicitly and explicitly articulated in scholarly discourse. The potential for longer narratives provides greater opportunities for character development, the exploration of interpersonal relationships, and the creation of vast diegetic universes. Of crucial importance here too is the idea that exceptional shows make certain demands of audiences. The "Viewers for Quality Television" nonprofit organization defines a quality series analogously, saying that it "enlightens, enriches, challenges, involves, and confronts. It dares to take risks, it's honest and illuminating, it appeals to the intellect and touches the emotions. It requires concentration and attention, and it provokes thought" (quoted in Thompson 1996, 77).

The influx of Hollywood show runners in the 1990s, documented by Mittell, Caldwell, and Thompson, suggests a greater interaction between producers and fan communities, one that, along with the widespread circulation of VHS tapes and the subsequent emergence of DVDs, has encouraged both the growth of these communities and a greater means of engagement with the program. This interaction is a locus, Craig Jacobsen (2006) argues, around which production in the postnetwork era orients itself as it seeks to challenge the viewer while not asking too much from them.

Attributing notions of quality to discursive formations mobilized by viewers places a remarkable degree of importance on the relationships between the audience and the text. Shows must attempt to gauge the demands they make on audiences, for as Mittell states, viewers engage these texts in an increasingly active manner, moving beyond mere observance of the narratives to actually deconstruct them. This complex relationship suggests, at its core, that reception strategies speak to a pleasure in knowing. Furthermore, it suggests that such knowledge is deeply embedded in the convergence of education and socioeconomic status. As Mark Jancovich and James Lyons argue, "The compulsiveness of 'must see' television is designed to appeal to affluent, highly educated consumers who value the literary quality of these programs, and they are used by the networks to hook this valuable cohort of viewers into their schedules" (2003, 63).

Education, Class, and Leisure

In his 1979 study of taste cultures, French sociologist Pierre Bourdieu attempts to trace the corollaries between education, class, and cultural capital. For Bourdieu, "economic power is first and foremost a power to keep economic necessity at arm's length." He adds that "material or symbolic consumption of works of art constitutes one of the supreme manifestations of *ease,* in the sense of both objective leisure and subjective facility" (1984, 55). The type of engagement that quality television demands, I would argue, relies on this ease, this ability to invest considerable time in charting the mythologies and universes of these narratively complex programs. "Getting" the rich intertextuality of programs reflects an apt demonstration of cultural capital at work, a reflection of Jancovich and Lyons's observation that socioeconomic status lies at the heart of the target demographic for quality television producers in the postnetwork era of niche audiences and narrowcasting. Cultural capital, the knowledge of and ability to "play" with culture, is strongly influenced by both education and, as mentioned earlier, the "ease" that accompanies a particular socioeconomic status. Bourdieu argues that "the more the competences measured are recognized by the school system, and the more 'academic' the techniques used to measure them, the stronger is the relation between performance and educational qualification. . . . [T]he latter, as a more or less adequate indicator of the number of years of scholastic inculcation, guarantees cultural capital more or less completely, depending on whether it is inherited from the family or acquired at school" (ibid., 13). Along with socioeconomic status, then, the capital attained through education guarantees access to knowledge about culture.

It is worth noting here that although quality shows consistently make demands of viewers, and thereby call upon their cultural capital, these demands are rarely, if ever, explicitly acknowledged within the narrative. Programs such as *Twin Peaks* (ABC, 1990–91), *Northern Exposure* (CBS, 1990–95), *The X-Files* (FOX, 1993–2002), *Buffy the Vampire Slayer* (WB/UPN, 1997–2003), and *Angel* (WB, 1999–2004) ask that audiences involve themselves with those characteristics that mark the respective programs as exceptional. *Buffy* and *Angel* require viewer familiarity with supernatural mythologies surrounding vampires, while *The X-Files* demands that audiences follow complex narrative twists and turns around a clandestine government conspiracy. *Twin Peaks* asks that viewers accompany FBI Agent Dale Cooper in navigating the dark underworld of creator David Lynch's fragmented narrative to find Laura Palmer's killer. *Northern Exposure* invites audiences to follow the culture clashes between Joel Fleishman's urban lifestyle and the extreme ruralism and nativism of Cicely, Alaska, through varied literary parallels and existential themes.

All television shows ask that viewers understand the larger diegetic universes and become familiar with the dynamic interpersonal relationships formed through the cast of idiosyncratic characters that inhabit the particular space. They do not, however, explicitly foreground this required information. Knowing is therefore demanded and rewarded in relative silence as each of these shows' narratives plays out, and there is no attempt to fill in those gaps where viewer comprehension may prove inadequate. As it remains unacknowledged, the cultural capital necessary to enjoy these programs is kept invisible and subsequently reinforced as a privilege available to those viewers with the means to learn and accumulate. This point, I assert, is where *Gilmore Girls* distinguishes itself, because its fundamental characteristic, the "*Gilmore*-ism," is identified from various discursive sites as a marker of quality and is actively engaged by both producers and consumers in an effort to dispense and mobilize knowledge. To understand this idea more clearly, I turn to additional discourses surrounding *Gilmore Girls* to understand how this show differs in its explicit awareness of its quality status.

"Not a Typical WB Show": Reception and Production Discourse

Although scholarly discourse is no doubt important to the project of situating *Gilmore Girls* as a quality TV series, it is equally vital to outline the ways in which fans position it vis-à-vis other cultural productions. A glance at fan summaries posted on the Internet Movie Database provides a glimpse of how certain audiences make sense of the show. "Gregorybnyc" (2004) claims to fall outside of the target demographic, identifying himself as a middle-aged man, yet states that "I think this is the best series on TV, a thoughtful, funny, beautifully written and well observed show about the relationship between a loving mother and daughter. At the same time, it features the quirks and tics of a fictional town with the kind of appeal that is unrealistic, but makes us nostalgic for a sweet and picturesque hamlet that has taken the two formerly outsider main characters and claimed them as one of their own."

Fan discourse also identifies the component that most distinguishes the program, namely, its witty "*Gilmore*-isms." "Natan62's" post (2003) similarly points to the generic conventions of the program that mark it as quality: "The writing and acting are both superb. The familiar setting of the small, quirky town allows for the use of many inventive plot devices, like 24-hour dance marathons, picnic basket bachelorette auctions, and vagrants who apply to become the 'official town troubadour.' You can even throw in a smart-mouthed kid from New York to see how he fares (maybe a tribute to *Northern Exposure???*)." This post not only outlines the conventions but draws links to other series such as *Northern Exposure,* a program often identified as exceptional and prominently featured in Jason Mittell's exploration of television genre.[4] "Natan62" also draws literary parallels, arguing that "if Jane Austen were alive today, she'd be writing this show. It's a great show, first and foremost, because it treats the viewer as an intelligent person and requires one to pay attention. The rewards for doing so are the dozens of subtle jokes and pop references contained in the torrents of conversation that issue from the characters' mouths—(*Gilmore Girls* must have the highest words-spoken-per-minute ratio in the history of TV.)." "Natan62's" final comment points to the most discussed aspect of the show, the intertextual "*Gilmore*-isms," which emerge in the motormouthed characters' conversations and permeate the various discursive formations of quality surrounding *Gilmore Girls.* "Mercy Bell" (2002) likewise confesses in her post that "I was surprised by the quality of the series, considering it's on the

4. Mittell begins the introduction to his book *Genre and Television* anecdotally with a debate between him and a fellow viewer of *Northern Exposure* over the program's generic classification. Mittell claimed that the program's formal qualities (its one-hour duration, lack of laugh track, dramatic story arcs, and cinematic aesthetic style) warranted identity as a drama, while his friend claimed that it was a comedy because it made her laugh. Such a seemingly irreconcilable difference prompts Mittell's investigation into television genres as cultural categories constructed through discursive clusters.

WB.[5] It's intelligent, creative, and sophisticated in an everyday way." "Stillbits12" (2004) identifies *Gilmore Girls* as an "intelligent show with quick, witty dialogue that often refers to literature, music, movies, and pop culture. It's just one smart joke after another. Definitely not a typical WB show." These comments recall the scholarly discourses concerning similar programs that point to rich intertextuality, idiosyncratic communities, and a balance of episodic and serial narratives. They also attempt to differentiate the show as something unique by placing *Gilmore*-isms at the heart of the program's dialogue and subsequent identity.

Critical voices similarly attempt to position the show as both quality and distinct. During the first season, *New York Times* reviewer Caryn James lamented the show's position on Thursday night, a time that put the program in direct competition with *Survivor* (CBS, 2000–) and *Friends* (NBC, 1994–2004). Although both programs enjoy viewership that dwarfs the audience of any program on the WB (now CW) network, James's article clearly argues that audiences tuning into the latter two shows are engaging with an inferior product. "[*Gilmore Girls*] is redefining family in a realistic, entertaining way for today's audience," she writes, "all the while managing to avoid the sappiness that makes sophisticated viewers run from anything labeled a 'family show'" (2001). Numerous articles citing the program's quality have been published more recently, a reaction largely sparked by the exit of series show runner Amy Sherman-Palladino before Season Seven and an overwhelming concern about the show's alleged degradation under different creative leadership. Whether to praise or pan, critical discourse frequently coalesces around a sense of quality at the core of the show's identity.

The forces of production provide an equally significant contribution to the formation of exceptionalism, both through the DVD sets and the genealogy that highlights the producers' own ties to a

5. *Gilmore Girls* aired for all but its final season on the WB network. It was one of several programs to move to the newly formed CW network, where its final season aired.

lineage of acclaimed programming outlined by Mittell, Caldwell, and Thompson. The DVD sets foreground quality through the inclusion of favorable quotes from journalists and interviews with cast and crew that emphasize the program's extraordinary production value and content. Season One provides a montage of memorable "*Gilmore-*isms" while also including a featurette in which the show's stars and producers comment on the complexity of the show's dialogue and their own struggles with its intertextuality. Seasons One and Two also include special episodes with on-screen guides to explain many of the show's dense references. Season Three curiously lacks such features, and though it does include a *Guide to Gilmore-isms* pamphlet, its inclusion of a featurette on "Our Favorite '80s-Era Dance Moves" is an indirect acknowledgment of popular culture in line with the logic of the show's intertextual dialogue.

A genealogy of production is also conducive to understanding the show's alignment with quality, as many of the show's writers and producers came to *Gilmore Girls* from other celebrated programs commonly aligned with exceptionality in the postnetwork era. Series creator, writer, producer, and director Amy Sherman-Palladino and her partner, Daniel Palladino, worked as producers on *Roseanne* (ABC, 1988–97). Rebecca Rand Kirshner worked as a writer for *Buffy* and *Freaks and Geeks* (NBC, 1999–2000). Jane Espenson was a writer and producer on *Buffy* and *Angel*. Tracing the previous work of the creative forces behind *Gilmore Girls* might seem rather innocuous, yet this genealogy of production is frequently invoked by viewers and is a common means of illustrating that one is "in the know" regarding the auteurs that circulate in the world of television production. While staking claims to auteur status might prove more difficult because of the collaborative nature of production, viewer discussions of show runners, auteurs, and creative teams are a logical extension of the Hollywood-cum–television talent traced in the above analyses of postnetwork television provided by Mittell, Caldwell, and Thompson. Journalist Jaime Weinman calls on such knowledge in her discussion of the *Gilmore Girls*' show-runner change: "For six seasons, the WB's comedy-drama was run by the husband-and-wife team of Amy

Sherman-Palladino and Daniel Palladino. Now they've left the show, to be replaced by a staff writer, David Rosenthal—and fans are talking as if this could literally be the end of the show. What that reaction comes from is the fans' increasing knowledge of how a show's voice, its uniqueness, is a product of the person who runs it" (2006).

The question of genre has occasionally permeated this analysis, and this is certainly not by accident. Rather, it suggests that, as both Caldwell and Thompson have stated, quality has become a sort of "genre" instead of a mere barometer for measuring aesthetic worth or cultural legitimacy. Mittell argues that "television genres matter as *cultural categories*," and too often the text is privileged in the construction of categories, producing irreconcilable conflicts (2004, xi; emphasis in the original). Genre should instead be analyzed, he argues, as a product of discursive clusters, of competing conceptions that situate it from all aspects of production, exhibition, and reception. "Genres work within nearly every facet of television," Mittell adds, identifying these discursive clusters as "corporate organizations, policy decisions, critical discourses, audience practices, production techniques, textual aesthetics, and historical trends" (ibid.). My concern here is not to perform a genre analysis or investigate the larger ideological implications that categorization might suggest, but rather to attempt to make sense of the ways in which *Gilmore Girls* is constituted as *quality* through the multisited discourses that collectively construct the program as such. This practice is certainly not apolitical, yet it rightly points to scholars' (and other audiences') participation in, rather than sole creation of, categories of quality.

Although Mittell argues that examinations of genre should seek to decenter the text in favor of the larger discursive formations that shape these cultural categories, he accedes that the text still matters. This point is certainly true in the case of the *Gilmore Girls*. In the course of our introduction to the lives of thirty-two-year-old Lorelai and her teenage daughter, Rory, it becomes clear that their relationships (and the show's identity, according to fans and critics) are inextricably linked to the rich exchange of intertextual dialogue. In other words, although the show is situated alongside other programs, the

"*Gilmore*-isms" prominently featured within the text itself become the principal markers of the show's identity. The text cannot therefore be extricated from the discursive cluster of quality. Far from extraneous, it is central to our consideration of the show's alleged exceptionality and the manner in which *Gilmore Girls* distinguishes itself from its brethren.

The frequency of these intertextual *Gilmore*-isms within each episode certainly suggests their vitality to the program's particularity. Furthermore, the *Guide to Gilmore-isms* pamphlet included with the DVD sets demonstrates a concerted effort among production and marketing personnel to facilitate audience understanding of and interaction with the show at one of its core identificatory levels. This effort to expand fan knowledge and grant access to additional cultural capital promises an alternative kind of quality television that defies to varying degrees the links to education and class. Such facilitation operates in a twofold way: first, it makes explicit the demands of the program that mark it as quality (*Gilmore*-isms), and, second, it attempts to meet those demands through the bestowment of an encyclopedia of terms. The show therefore both emphasizes the constitutive components of its exceptionality and offers audiences the tools with which to unpack those items, fill in the gaps, and be "in the know." Whereas the production economy of *Gilmore Girls* foregrounds intertextual dialogue and facilitates viewer understanding, it is necessary to explore how the narrative of the show consistently addresses the relationship of class, education, and the display of cultural capital.

Often predicated on the interplay of class dynamics, education, and the use of *Gilmore*-isms, the diegetic world of the Gilmores witnesses repeated articulations of an idea made evident in the prior discussion, namely, the possibility that cultural capital may be available to everyone. In the final episode of Season Three ("Those Are Strings, Pinocchio" [3.22]), Rory delivers the commencement speech as the valedictorian of Chilton Academy. Although her speech includes the expected platitudes to the burgeoning relationship with grandparents Richard and Emily Gilmore as well as extended thoughts on her best friend and mother-daughter relationship with Lorelai, Rory interestingly comments that “I live in two worlds.” Although Rory alludes here to the literary-academic and real-quotidian worlds that she inhabits, this idea of two contrasting yet overlapping spheres is quite significant in respect to the dialectic between Stars Hollow and the world outside (something that Radha O’Meara similarly notes in her contribution to this book). A survey of the show’s first three seasons bears this two-world dichotomy out; interpersonal relationships and their subsequent exchange of dialogue seem predicated on the world they inhabit. What emerges here is, on the one hand, a world marked by class difference and the overt display of cultural capital, the world *outside* Stars Hollow (namely, Hartford, location of both Chilton Academy and Richard and Emily Gilmore’s palatial mansion). The world *of* Stars Hollow, on the other hand, is home to the everyday display of cultural capital. In the end it is the presence and circulation of *Gilmore*-isms that mark the greatest distinction between these two universes.

Within Stars Hollow, characters of various socioeconomic backgrounds and with varying degrees of educational capital routinely engage in the exchange of intertextual banter. An argument in the Season Two episode “A-Tisket, a-Tasket” (2.13) between Jess and Dean typifies this proclivity to engage in cultural allusions, as it is marked by references to Edger Bergen and Charlie McCarthy, the Vietnam War, Lenny Bruce, “the Minister of Silly Walks” (a sketch in *Monty Python’s Flying Circus* [BBC, 1969–74]), and John Cleese. Both characters engage in this heated exchange, and both clearly understand the references. Neither character is noted to possess much educational capital, however. Jess routinely skips school and will never graduate, whereas Dean is an average student at Stars Hollow High (earning Bs and Cs on his report cards, as he explains to an unimpressed Richard in “Sadie, Sadie” [2.01]). Moreover, neither Jess’s nomadic status (the “kid from New York” referenced in the post by “Natan62”) nor Dean’s parents’ occupations (stereo salesman and medical transcriber) suggest any notable level of socioeconomic status. Lane Kim, Rory’s best friend, is likewise imputed to be an average high school student who nonetheless frequently engages in dense intertextual exchanges (most often music oriented). Dialogue between Rory and Dean is largely relegated to the world of mainstream American and British popular culture (BattleBots, *Lord of the Rings,* and so on).

It is Rory's dialogue with Jess, however, that suggests the greatest separation of cultural and educational capital. Although he comes from an unstable family, is soon to drop out of school, and is without any stable financial base, Jess appears to possess the most cultural capital in Stars Hollow. His breadth of knowledge is surpassed only by his disdain for the institutions of education and class distinction that seem to exist in Stars Hollow only as interventions from the outside world.[6] Although Jess is criticized by others in the community for his rebelliousness, he repeatedly foregrounds the separation of cultural knowledge from the conventional institutions that work to shape it.

Like Rory, Lorelai also engages in such exchanges of *Gilmore*-isms with the residents of Stars Hollow. Whether it is with Luke (a blue-collar diner owner), Sookie (a bed-and-breakfast chef), or her overachieving daughter, dense intertextual references are volleyed back and forth without consideration for the educational capital or socioeconomic status necessary to participate. Although neither Sookie's nor Luke's educational background is discussed (it is known that Luke attended Stars Hollow High, and it is inferred that Sookie attended culinary school), both are frequently juxtaposed with the upper crust of the outside world, epitomized by Richard and Emily.[7]

6. Their respective treatment of books might help to clarify this further. Whereas Rory's books are often pristine hardcover editions (meticulously categorized in an unconventional manner, as pointed out by Richard in "Richard in Stars Hollow" [2.12]), Jess often carries dog-eared paperback copies in his back pocket. This difference hints at a class distinction and foreshadows the further stratification brought about by Rory's enrollment in Yale, yet their respective treatment of books also metaphorically encapsulates their respective relationships to the very structures that attempt to disseminate and control knowledge.

7. Luke is more frequently juxtaposed with the upper class than Sookie, both indirectly in his dress and directly in his matter-of-fact demeanor (as opposed to Richard and Emily's emotional repression). This tendency becomes even more pronounced in subsequent seasons when the relationship between Lorelai and Luke

Although Lorelai's past points to a life of socioeconomic privilege and access to elite educational institutions (it is hinted that she temporarily attended a prep school), her pregnancy at age sixteen and her subsequent estrangement from her disappointed parents cast her in a different light. Her relocation to Stars Hollow, a safe haven for the outcasts of the "other world," is therefore a symbolic move to a recuperative space where neither class nor educational capital prevents one from accessing and—perhaps most important—*playing with* culture.[8]

Interactions involving Richard and Emily epitomize the tenuous conflation of education, class, and cultural capital that the show attempts to undermine. Although the occasional intertextual reference does occur, most often in dialogue between Richard and Rory about literature, these infrequent displays of cultural capital are rarely linked with class or education (and rather resemble Rory's conversations with Jess). Class distinctions are conflated with education in the universe outside of Stars Hollow, particularly in conversation regarding Rory. A frequent source of conflict between the two worlds, Richard and Emily's desire to inject Rory into the prestigious institutions (Chilton, then Yale) prefigures their efforts to reclaim the upper-class dignity of the Gilmore name that they perceived to be tarnished with Lorelai's adolescent indiscretions. While Lorelai desires similar educational goals for her daughter, she dismisses the grandparents' utopian conflation of knowledge, education, and class in favor of the literary role models gained through Rory's early introduction to cultural capital (the literary half of Rory's "two worlds" dichotomy). Education for Lorelai is not a means of class distinction but rather an accentuation of Rory's existing cultural consciousness.

---

becomes romantic and various Stars Hollow outsiders (Christopher Hayden and Richard's business partner, Jason Stiles) enter the Gilmore universe.

8. Lorelai's pregnancy provides a symbolic break from her privileged life, one that denies her a high school diploma and Ivy League education that Richard and Emily periodically mention she possessed the potential to achieve. Lorelai does graduate with a business degree from a Hartford-area community college in Season Two, suggesting that she had at some point earned her GED.

The knowledge that Emily and Richard conflate with education and class is therefore not valued in the *Gilmore Girls* universe. This knowledge rarely enters the diegesis and is often situated as banal information, as part of a perceived joyless existence that typifies the members of the show's wealthier contingent.

The incongruity between these two spheres is reinforced in other ways as well. Richard and Emily's icy reception of Dean in the above-mentioned episode "Sadie, Sadie," during which the increasingly irate grandfather grills the young man on his school grades and career ambitions, epitomizes the distinction between Stars Hollow and everywhere else. Indeed, Richard's conclusion regarding Dean's inadequacy as a partner for Rory appears to stem solely from the teenage boy's admission that he is an average student. The absurdity of his rationale is made evident again when Richard is forced to grudgingly admit later, in "Richard in Stars Hollow," that he knows nothing about Rory's suitor. The elder Gilmores are also contrasted against Stars Hollow in the urban-rural dialectic that plays out in conversations about and encounters with the town's idiosyncratic elements. Their frequent willingness to dismiss such people and events as rustic or irrelevant highlights their problematic conflation of knowledge, education, and class status and their inability to grasp the town's isolation not as a source of socioeconomic pathology but rather as a constitutive element of its exceptionality. Stars Hollow may in fact be simple (even Rory calls it a "crazy doofus town" in "The Festival of Living Art" [4.07]), but its sophistication serves as a testament to the circulation of knowledge outside of those institutions upon which Richard, Emily, and the outside world rely.[9]

9. Although she and other outsiders attempt to expose the seedy underbelly of Stars Hollow, Paris Geller eventually concludes that it is annoyingly simple. In typical Paris fashion, she concludes that "this town would make Frank Capra throw up" ("Richard in Stars Hollow"). Her convictions regarding the dark side of suburbia evoke a Lynchian aesthetic familiar to anyone who has seen *Blue Velvet* (1986) and *Twin Peaks* (ABC, 1990–91) and are likely a subtle homage to one of the show's numerous quality progenitors.

The first three seasons of *Gilmore Girls* therefore draw a rather strict delineation between Stars Hollow and the universe that surrounds it. The outside world is characterized by a convergence of class, education, and cultural capital that stratifies society, yet Stars Hollow provides a utopian sphere where everyone engages in the ceaseless flow of knowledge and exchange of culture, regardless of their socioeconomic status or educational capital. Such an environment offers the possibility that "atypical" TV audiences may engage in the pleasure in knowing without requiring or having access to, as other quality shows do, the institutions demanded by the outside world.

Although this chapter has focused specifically on the first three seasons of the show, subsequent seasons have complicated this "two-world" paradigm by attempting to situate Rory firmly in both Stars Hollow and the world outside. No longer considered a true resident by some in the community (as evidenced in the first episode of Season Four, "Ballrooms and Biscotti" [4.01]), Rory's tenure at Yale is marked by a continued negotiation of class, education, and cultural capital. The introduction of Logan Huntzberger and his family contrasts Rory with members of the upper class (Richard and Emily make explicit how much wealthier the Huntzbergers are than the Gilmores), while her relationships with both Yale and Logan demonstrate her flirtation with the upper crust. Indeed, Jess's timely revelation upon meeting Rory again that "she has changed" ("Let Me Hear Your Balalaikas Ringing Out" [6.08]) suggests a tumultuous relationship between this prodigy of Stars Hollow and her hometown, a relationship that through the course of Season Six witnesses both her temporary estrangement from Lorelai and her decision to leave Yale.

Although the relationships to mother and school are soon mended, Rory's ability to exist in both worlds remains tenuous, fraught with complications. By Season Seven, Rory's class ascension is formally acknowledged by Logan, who comments (in "Introducing Lorelai Planetarium" [7.08]) that she has become one of "those" people she formerly viewed from an outsider's perspective. Ultimately, however, Rory's decision in the series' penultimate episode ("Unto the Breach" [7.21]) to reject Logan's marriage proposal indicates a fundamental unease with the class dynamics brought to bear on the *Gilmore Girls* universe by Huntzberger and his ilk. At the same time she remains somewhat aloof from Stars Hollow; indeed, her new vocation as campaign reporter for an online publication overtly reinforces her nomadic, liminal status that has, since the show's pilot episode, increasingly placed her both *within* and *without* the charming Connecticut hamlet.

Lorelai has encountered sea changes as well, as her love life has foregrounded a symbolic oscillation between Stars Hollow and the outside world. The series' long-deferred romance with Luke Danes temporarily fades owing in part to tensions between Luke's class standing and the socioeconomic baggage of the Gilmore name. Lorelai's marriage to Christopher Hayden, Rory's father and a newly minted millionaire, quickly crumbles under the weight of class difference and tension between the respective worlds of the newlyweds. The most overt of Luke's symbolic expressions in the episode "Bon Voyage" (7.22), his organization of the community to honor Rory's graduation, suggests that the inevitability of Luke and Lorelai's romance owes as much to their mutual connection to Stars Hollow as it does to his facilitation of her substantial coffee addiction.

The very reason that they belong together has long explained why Lorelai's other romantic relationships were doomed to fail; Lorelai has proved less adept than Rory at "walking in both worlds" and cannot find happiness outside the confines of what has become a utopian space both professionally and personally. Despite various indications that such a binary may collapse in the show's final four seasons, *Gilmore Girls* remains true to the thematic contrast between Stars Hollow and everywhere else. This contrast situates the community as an idyllic sphere where cultural capital need not be linked to class and education and creates in the process a diegetic locale that viewers may imaginatively inhabit and where they may exchange cultural knowledge free of the institutions that attempt to exert authority over them.

"Quality television" is a rather broad discursive classification that, I have argued, is constructed by a plethora of voices in production, exhibition, and reception. *Gilmore Girls,* I demonstrate, belongs in this category, for the discursive formation constituted by such voices has assigned it within the paradigm. This categorization is not enough, however, as the show's fundamental components, *Gilmore*-isms, become a means of engaging in an explicit discussion of cultural capital that other quality programs fail to foreground in their interaction with viewers. The explicit acknowledgments of *Gilmore*-isms within fan, critical, and industrial channels articulate the investment of producers and consumers in clarifying the vocabulary of the show. It reflects a concerted effort to enhance the understanding and the pleasure in knowing at the heart of the quality viewing experience. As *Gilmore*-isms make for a highly intertextual language among producers and audiences, the diegetic universe of *Gilmore Girls* provides a utopian realm in which this vocabulary can be deployed and made intelligible by anyone.

This collaboration certainly does not explode notions of class, as television programming, collectible media such as DVD sets, and the Internet remain inaccessible to many people. *Gilmore Girls* does not eliminate class considerations altogether; rather, it opens up a dialogue about quality television in ways that other programs have not regarding the relationship of class, education, and cultural knowledge. By suggesting that cultural capital need not necessarily be inextricably linked to education and socioeconomic status, and providing the means by which viewers may better locate themselves "in the know," *Gilmore Girls* offers a perspective on cultural knowledge that promises to let new and different audiences partake in and enjoy a new and different kind of quality television.

TV "Dramedy" and the Double-Sided "Liturgy" of *Gilmore Girls*

GIADA DA ROS

As a television series that combines levity and gravity, sparkle and depth, *Gilmore Girls* epitomizes the hybridized genre of "dramedy." As a drama, the program tackles a variety of serious themes regarding family relationships (parenthood and motherhood in particular), friendship, love, generational schisms, cultural affinities, independence and dependency, mistakes and remedies, personal goals and career objectives. However, as a comedy, it revels in jokes, rapid-fire dialogue, unrestrained banter, flippant cultural references, sarcasm, irony, hyperbolic situations, the exaggeration of eccentric supporting characters, and narrative events that are one step short of farce. So, yes, *Gilmore Girls* is indeed a dramedy. However, it does not merely position these two generic impulses as separate or competing tendencies of televisual narrative; rather, it allows for generic interpenetration, providing a space for comedy and drama to coexist in the same context. More than one rhetorical device is put into action to achieve this effect. The show's setting—a picture-perfect, almost fairy-tale-like place—facilitates the verisimilar use of narrative filters, intertextual allusions, witticisms, behavioral self-consciousness, and caustic comments, which all pervade the textual universe (or "*Gilmore*verse"), providing the base upon which a dialectical tension is played out. Indeed, the extreme, even absurd, seriousness of the comical characters complements the occasional frivolousness of the serious characters.

The most emphatic way in which *Gilmore Girls* links dramatic and comic aspects, though, is through liturgical structure, that is, via narrative ritual. Audiences know that weekly broadcast television programs depend on repetition, for seriality ensures the gratifications associated with one's textual expectations, allowing the audience to enjoy a new storyline or development while being reassured by the promise of return. Furthermore, spectatorial enjoyment is derived from the knowledge and recognition of serial mechanisms that link plot elements and facilitate the detection of variations, which, as Aldo Grasso and Massimo Scaglioni state, "mask the return of the identical" (2003, 133).[1] These words shall serve as a frame of reference for my ensuing discussion of televisual liturgy, which is not merely a form of repetition but a celebration of shared meanings and values through ritual behaviors. According to Paolo Taggi, televisual liturgy is "the acquirement of a ritual dimension of some recurring behaviors" (1997, 82). Notably, Taggi, in elaborating this concept, does not refer specifically to fictional narratives. However, since all TV dramas and sitcoms are engaged in the process of telling stories, liturgy should not be separated from story-driven programs. Liturgy as ritual—as established actions to which a symbolic value is attributed—constitutes a unique ceremonial form, but it is also steeped in amplified emotional and communicational elements. It furthermore requires the complicity of the audience. *Gilmore Girls* relies heavily on liturgical structures, using them to create both "drama" and "comedy." It stages emotionally absorbing ceremonies and, with the participation of the viewer, generates two different effects, binding together seemingly opposite generic impulses. Precisely how liturgy is used is what I will investigate. In doing so, I may at times stretch the concept to its limits.

Part One: The Dramatic Side of the Series

From a dramatic point of view, liturgy can create and sustain a sense of familial belonging, interpersonal relationships, and intimacy. These

1. This and all subsequent Italian-language quotes are translated by the author.

concepts are at the core of the *Gilmore*verse. The reiteration of pattern-situations, lived as a rite from the diegetic and extradiegetic points of view, is what constructs these concepts. The connection between the formal (the rite) and the substantial (the evocation of "family," "intimacy," "desire," and so forth) is so strong that where there is a disruption of liturgy, there is at the same time a disruption of the above concepts. We can observe this through an analysis of some pattern-situations typically found in *Gilmore Girls:* Friday nights at Richard and Emily's (family), Lorelai and Rory's video-viewing and junk-food rituals (family, personal relationship), and Lorelai's visits to Luke's diner (personal relationship, intimacy).

Friday Nights at Richard and Emily's

Let us begin with the pilot episode (1.01). In it, Lorelai turns to her parents, with whom she has had only sporadic contact and from whom she has moved away, in order to ask them for help in financing their granddaughter's education in a prestigious school, Chilton. Richard and Emily accept immediately, but the latter sets one condition: "I want to be actively involved in your life." This statement translates into: "I want a weekly dinner." As Emily states, "Friday nights, you and Rory will have dinner here." From the start, a meaningful link is created between the act of seeing one another with constancy and the idea of being involved in each other's lives, between partaking in a ritual and being members of a family.

It is not the occasional visit that makes a family. A "true" sense of family emerges from meals shared together around a table, an iconographic image pervasive in American popular culture and portrayed in everything from Norman Rockwell's paintings to TV shows such as *The Brady Bunch* (ABC, 1969–74) and *Eight Is Enough* (ABC, 1977–81). For example, in *Party of Five* (FOX, 1994–2000), the Salinger siblings try to remain a family after their parents' premature deaths by reserving some time each week for a communal meal. The last image of the program's opening credits reminds us of it, but the audience is not invited into that privileged space. Here, in the *Gilmore*verse, we are.

The image of Lorelai and Rory at the family home is ritualistically deployed throughout the series, thereby assuming the form of a liturgy. It happens at regular intervals (on Friday nights) and has the purpose of reinforcing bonds and values (being part of a family). It requires appropriate attire and food prepared with care (the refined menus Emily is so proud of). Regarding Friday night, Emily "has her Vulcan death grip on that one," a line uttered by Lorelai in "Rory's Birthday Parties" (1.06). Emily even demands that there be a serious reason for not participating, saying, "I just don't think that Rory should miss our dinners for something other than sickness or emergencies" (in "It Should've Been Lorelai" [2.14]). Of course, special permission to skip is sometimes granted, as in "That Damn Donna Reed" (1.14), when Rory misses dinner because of her three-month anniversary with boyfriend Dean.

We can observe these occurrences as a structured order of events. First, Lorelai and Rory are seen in front of the closed front door of the Gilmore mansion. There is a moment of waiting, almost of meditation or of stopping to exchange thoughts before partaking in the event. Second, they ring the bell, and someone comes to the door (Emily, or—more often—the maid). Third, they are ushered into the living room, where they have a drink and chat idly, perhaps about Rory's school activities. Then, in the dining room, they eat dinner, commenting on the food and on personal issues. Finally, the ceremony ends, Lorelai and Rory leave, free from their duty, sometimes making remarks on what has just taken place. Although not every episode shows all of the steps in this liturgical occurrence, it is evident that, in the constant repetition that dictates *Gilmore Girls,* a very recognizable structure begins to emerge. That it is included in the pilot episode is significant. Being the "business card" of a new TV series, a pilot is a declaration of its producers' intent. Moreover, François Jost has suggested that we define genre as a contract, a promise, between authors and viewers (in Grasso and Scaglioni 2003, 95). With this notion in mind, what dialogically follows, episode to episode, must be measured on the cornerstone that is the pilot. In the case of *Gilmore Girls,* this contract between the audience and the creators is all the more relevant as a metaphor for making sense of the family's Friday-night dinners, the outcome of an arrangement between Lorelai and her parents.

I wish to dwell momentarily on this specific liturgical occurrence in *Gilmore Girls* because it is the foundational structure of the show. It is the fundamental one, the strongest and most explicit in the sense of foregrounding the audience's own contractual relationship with the show's producers. This point is even parodied by the series itself through "a film by Kirk," an amateur production that shows the title character meeting the parents of his girlfriend and having dinner (in "Teach Me Tonight" [2.19]). To be included in the process of liturgical meaning-making translates as being included in a family, and vice versa. To alter it in any way without justifiable reasons means also to change the meaning of what liturgy establishes: the very concept of family.

In "Christopher Returns" (1.15), Rory's father is invited to Friday-night dinner. As a parent, he also is part of the family, albeit not the one that has been constructed liturgically. Nevertheless, there he is, waiting with Lorelai and Rory, in front of the door of the Gilmore mansion. The camera frames them from behind, gazing with them at the closed door. We take that first step of the ceremony with them. Rather than knock, Lorelai uses her key to open the door, to Emily's disappointment (for there has been an alteration of the structured order of events). Christopher's parents have been invited to that dinner, too. Like their son, Straub and Francine are strangers or outsiders, so for them the steps involved in partaking of the ritual do not have any intrinsic meaning. The idea, though, is to get reacquainted with Richard and Emily, and they are thus involved in the rite.

Unfortunately, while having a drink in the living room, a heated argument breaks out concerning the perceived poor life choices made by Lorelai, choices that crushed the parents' aspirations, resulting in their humiliation. Straub and Francine are asked to leave and to abandon the ritual. Lorelai thanks her dad, who defended her. He justifies having asked them to leave with the fact that his family had been attacked (and therefore he excludes them from a possible inclusion in the family circle). This statement comes from a man who believes in the need for "proper procedure to be followed" (said in relation to his will that Lorelai marry Christopher when she discovered she was pregnant with Rory). The idea of "family" that they have tried to build and sustain through liturgical events and inclusion has failed, just as liturgy itself has been disrupted. Emily and Rory end up eating leftovers in the kitchen, and Lorelai ends up kissing Christopher out on the balcony.

In "Star-Crossed Lovers and Other Strangers" (1.16), Emily wants Lorelai to date a "quality man," as she calls him, and invites the suitably affluent suitor—a man working in the actuarial business named Chase Bradford—to dinner. Lorelai, forced to participate, breaks the liturgical bonds by escaping through the window and fleeing the premises, with the consent of her father on both fronts. When it later becomes clear that Luke is a permanent fixture in Lorelai's life, Emily demands that she bring him to dinner (in "You Jump, I Jump, Jack" [5.07]). In "Sadie, Sadie" (2.01), Rory is invited by her grandparents to bring a guest. She brings Dean. The opening of the door is seen from Emily's perspective. Noticeably, there is an expression of disappointment at the participation of this boy in the weekly function, because she disapproves of him for Rory. The same is true for Richard, who grills him on his studying habits and job plans. The strong hostility directed toward Dean (substantial departure) prompts him, Rory, and Lorelai to leave the dinner sooner than expected. Rory's boyfriend remains seated, though, until dessert is served, because partaking in that ritual has meant being momentarily part of that family. Indeed, at the end of the evening Lorelai comments, "Dean, tonight you officially became a Gilmore," and then explains Richard's behavior to Rory.

The important point here is that Lorelai and Rory are not alone. The audience, too, participates in the show's liturgical processes that extend and expand the definition of "family" to encompass geographically dispersed viewers bound by their common knowledge and acceptance of said processes. However, those processes begin to break down at various junctures throughout the series. Trix imposes her presence ("The Third Lorelai" [1.18]), Rory brings Jess to her grandparents' house for dinner ("Swan Song" [3.14]), Richard and Emily separate and try to keep it from being discovered (the final episodes of Season Four), and Logan is invited ("How Many Kropogs to Cape Cod?" [5.20]). In the gap between repetition and variation, the audience is allowed the opportunity to measure the emotions brought about by any potentially disruptive moment. "Drama" thus becomes most pronounced when liturgy is disrupted for emotional affect, when our expectations of reassurance and a return to the status quo are challenged.

Lifestyle or Religion? Video-Viewing and Junk-Food Rituals

Throughout *Gilmore Girls,* rituals are endowed with a sense of obligation (or, as Lorelai calls it in the pilot episode, "flagellation"). But they also promise and provide rewards. Lorelai may try to flee from Richard and Emily's constrictive clutches, but not from the concept of ritual itself. Just as a ritual may be rigid, formal, and cold, so too can it be casual, informal, and warm. This flip side is exemplified during Rory's sixteenth birthday (1.06), which illustrates a different approach to building a family, one shaped by an unusual mother-daughter relationship that is itself dependent upon a different concept of liturgy. Longtime viewers of the series know that Lorelai and Rory are friends and accomplices. They talk and share life experiences, primarily during their video-viewing and junk-food rituals, which are intellectually stimulating, if not always physically nourishing. Such rituals allow the two to comment on and take part in the same fantasies (in contrast to Lane and Mrs. Kim) while watching television programs over and over (repetition) and decoding texts through often elliptical forms of communication. Their understanding of the world and appreciation of one another are anchored to these rituals. Only after "outsiders" have been introduced to the rituals can they begin to enter more fully these young women's lives.

For example, in "Kiss and Tell" (1.07), when Lorelai discovers that her daughter has kissed Dean, she immediately decides to include him in the ritual of their collective television consumption. Accepting him in that way is, for Lorelai, a means to bring him more fully into Rory's life, even if the latter is opposed to it at first. When Dean and Rory later break up, he is excluded from the mother's and daughter's binges in front of the TV, but as soon as they are back together (in "Sadie, Sadie"), participation in the ritual resumes. The teaser of "That Damn Donna Reed" is topical in the sense that it is the perfect example of how the girls relate to one another: through repeated viewings of TV they have created shared values that do not need to be explained between themselves, only to people on the outside. References to other texts provide an exemplification of their stand on various topics.

This form of communication permeates the entire series. Lorelai and Rory's discussions in front of the TV point out their modus operandi to an outsider. It is the liturgical apotheosis of the show's intertextuality in the sense that it shows their relationship with another text and provides a commentary on said text. At the beginning of "That Damn Donna Reed," Dean arrives bearing pizza (appropriate food for the ceremony) and salad (which the girls eye with suspicion). He is allowed to participate but remains outside the mother-daughter bond (he chooses salad). Moreover, it soon becomes clear that he is not familiar with *The Donna Reed Show* (ABC, 1958–66), which they are not just watching but worshiping. "So, it's a show?" inquires Dean, to which Rory responds, "It's a lifestyle," and Lorelai pipes in, "It's a religion." They then proceed to dissect the episode while commenting on their favorite moments in the series. They mock particular scenes and redub them as they please, saying that the main character "is medicated" and "acting from a script" that was "written by a man." To Dean, who defends the show's conservative and patriarchal representations, Lorelai's and Rory's behavior seems downright odd.

Later in the episode, *The Donna Reed Show* is once again invoked during a confrontation between Dean and Rory, who analyzes its significance ("She represented millions of women that were real and did have to dress and act like that"). To please Dean and provide him, if only momentarily, with a fantasy setting and a traditional image of femininity, Rory pretends to be Donna Reed, wearing a dress from the 1950s and a string of pearls. Even at this early point in its first season, *Gilmore Girls*' intertextuality is pronounced. Borrowing terms put forth by John Fiske (1987), we might say that the program in general and this episode in particular provide us with both *horizontal* intertextuality (indirect links to other texts on the basis of genre, characters, or content) and *vertical* intertextuality (explicit references to another text). Also, whereas the primary text is the program we watch and the secondary text is another text alluded to by that program, a tertiary text might be composed of the various comments (including gossip) circulating around that program. Here, in *Gilmore Girls,* the tertiary text (opinions formed about a program) is diegetically imbedded, becoming a central part of the primary text as it is included in the narrative, a narrative whose subtext (or implied meanings) becomes a kind of metatext (a text that reflexively "talks about" or helps to explain the program we are watching).

Throughout the series *Gilmore Girls*' narrative universe hinges on strong intertextual presuppositions, which contribute to the building of the central mother-daughter relationship. When possible, Lorelai and Rory choose their liturgy and *live it* with the same go-for-broke attitude that permanently bonds them and is steeped in equal parts reverence and irreverence, gratitude and independence. At the beginning of Season Four, Rory goes to Yale. The night before she leaves (4.01), Lorelai has a list of planned activities. Her plans fall through, but they do not want to renounce their tradition of "video and junk food" consumption, even if it means they have to sit through ballroom-dancing videos over biscotti at Emily's house. The episode's last image shows mother and daughter together on the couch united in the act of nighttime viewing. Throughout the whole episode they try to preserve the liturgy that unites them and is bound to be broken once Rory leaves for Yale. Indeed, the first half of the sixth season witnesses them separated (emotionally and physically). In "Always a Godmother, Never a God" (6.04), a videotape that Lorelai used to watch with Rory prompts her to call her daughter and leads to her discovery that Rory has changed her cell phone number. Their broken bond is symbolized by Lorelai's solitary TV viewing.

"Don't Read Anything into It": Lorelai and Coffee at Luke's

According to Taggi, liturgy gives solemnity to a program and is nourished by gestures and facts that can even be trite figures of speech, totally banal (1997). The very first scene of *Gilmore Girls* (1.01) is bracing in its simplicity, banality, and directness, showing Lorelai entering Luke's to drink some coffee. That same episode closes with the Gilmore girls back at his place, inscribing the idea that Lorelai and Luke belong together, because he—like Rory—is an integral part of her daily rituals. Rory is prophetic when she says, "If you date him, you'll break up and we'll never be able to eat there again" (1.02). Sookie likewise understands their relationship, even if Lorelai denies it, saying, "So now the fact that I suggested painting Luke's diner also means that I wanted to get him in bed" (1.14). Lorelai's repeated visits to Luke's to satisfy her coffee addiction are a constant component of their developing relationship, which later blossoms into a full-blown romance.

Lorelai's later breakup with Luke corresponds to deeper narrative rifts—breaks in the liturgical emphasis on her going to his place repeatedly. When Rory ends up in the hospital with her arm in a cast because of Jess's reckless driving (in "Teach Me Tonight" [2.19]), Lorelai blames Luke, resulting in a caustic row. The day after, Rory wants to know how things are between him and her mother. She asks questions that are increasingly specific regarding their going to Luke's place: "Are we on our way there?" "When we get there, will we get in?" "We'll get served?" "We'll get coffee?" "Refills?" "Free refills?" Once they get there, much to their surprise and the shock of the whole town, Luke's Diner is closed. A sign indicates that he has gone fishing, something that has apparently never happened prior to this point. "Don't read anything into it," Lorelai hurries to tell her daughter. But, of course, they *do* read something into it, and thus can be said to grasp the significance of liturgical structures in their own lives.

To create "drama," formal and substantial aspects have to be disrupted. When Luke reopens his diner, the two characters have not made peace yet. Lorelai's ritual of going to Luke's cannot resume until their personal relationship is mended. So, in "Lorelai's Graduation

Day" (2.21), she eats breakfast at Sookie's house. Earlier, after twenty minutes spent walking back and forth in front of the diner (while Rory and Dean, whose relationship with Luke is intact, are inside), Lorelai decides to apologize and make amends with the place and its owner. Luke is still cold, and she exits his place without touching the coffee and doughnut she was served at the counter (at this point, the relationship cannot be quickly mended, thus the ritual cannot resume).

In the first episode of Season Three ("Those Lazy-Hazy-Crazy Days" [3.01]), Lorelai goes back to Sookie's for breakfast. That same evening she enters Luke's place again for a second attempt to make peace. She confides in him and drinks coffee. He offers her a doughnut: she has been forgiven, and liturgy is recomposed. Soon thereafter, Lorelai resumes going regularly to Luke's. From these few scenes, scattered across several episodes, the correspondence between personal and liturgical relationships is crystal clear. Lorelai's official first date with Luke leads to her "indecent" exposure in front of the diner customers when she steps out only half-dressed to get coffee the morning after their upstairs fling ("Written in the Stars" [5.03]). After a breakup, Lorelai reenters the diner only once she has gotten back with Luke (in "Pulp Friction" [5.17]). Then, throughout much of Season Six, Luke keeps Lorelai away from April, his long-lost daughter, and—by extension—away from the place that has given her so much emotional, psychological, and caloric nourishment. Here, as in the mother-daughter relationship, there are recurring behavioral patterns that assume an almost "sacred" dimension for the characters, as well as for viewers of the series. That is, the audience's complicity is not merely linked to the formal expectation of anticipated moments that repeat themselves and are wholly predictable. Rather, it lies in spectatorial expectations linked to the show's deep structure and extendable content—its *substantial liturgy.*

Part Two: The Comedic Side of the Series

Turning now to the comedic side of the series, we see that liturgy is the foundation of the Stars Hollow community, with its many festivals, community rites, and bizarre characters. As with the aforementioned dramatic elements, the reiteration of pattern-situations contributes to the concepts that it gives shape, and these situations are lived as a rite from the diegetic and extradiegetic points of view. The Autumn Festival (1.07), the anniversary of the legendary Battle of Stars Hollow (1.08), the annual charity picnic-basket auction (2.13), the Annual End of Summer Madness Festival (3.01), the Dance Marathon (3.07), the High Winter Carnival (3.10), the Festival of Living Art (4.07), the annual Firelight Festival (4.13)—these and other social events abound in Stars Hollow. It is not simply the fact that they are community-based rituals in *form* that makes them liturgical for the viewer. They need to be a ritual for us, the audience members, as well, if they are to become a liturgy. We need to partake in the expectation of a celebration, not just see it represented. As for the characters, *our* ritual involves waiting—a rite of rites, so to speak. This metatextual foregrounding of rituality makes *Gilmore Girls* especially intriguing and distinct as an episodic yet serial television program.

The significance of such narrative components underlines the program's ability to establish a liturgical structure. Part of the pleasure presumably experienced by viewers relates to the "wait-and-see" formula of the series, the sense that some new occasion will be celebrated each week and that some new set of decorations will festoon the town as part of the festivities. This anticipated reiteration is what ensures the comical effect. Contrary to what transpires on the dramatic side of the series, here it is not the disruption but the *reconfirmation* of liturgical elements that provides the basis for amusement. An obvious example is the constant firing of waitresses and housekeepers by Emily, resulting in the presence of different workers each week, performing the same tasks at the Gilmore mansion (a metaliturgy, perhaps, contained within yet also containing the Friday-night dinners).

In the Season One episode "Kill Me Now" (1.03), Emily's discontent for her servants is addressed. Anton, Sophia, Trina, and Heidi are mentioned as the latest recipients of the pink slip. From that episode forward, part of the audience's enjoyment lies in seeing, once we have stepped inside the Gilmore mansion, who the newly hired help will be and what her personality is like. In this sense, an event—however apparently trivial—awaits us. Only visual confirmation—the actual witnessing of the expected event—ensures the comical effect. To amplify this effect, *Gilmore Girls* emphasizes the *sensation* of repetition, even in those instances when, in fact, the audience has not really witnessed earlier recurrences of the event. Lorelai complains about Taylor's choice for the Movie in the Square Night (2.19), which has been *The Yearling* (1946) for three years in a row (something viewers have not seen). Taylor leaves her with the responsibility of picking this year's film screening. From the list of titles she has been provided, the most appropriate film is *The Yearling,* which indeed is chosen for the fourth time in a row.

Similarly, at a Christmas recital in "Forgiveness and Stuff" (1.10), Rory says that the baby Jesus doll is missing its arm, "again," the latter word being significant, as it presents us with the idea that something is being repeated, even if we have not seen or experienced it directly. Significantly, Rory suggests that the doll be replaced with a new one, but Taylor replies that such a request is impossible, as that doll has been used since 1965. A comical effect is created through the confirmation of anticipated manifestations of liturgy. The final sections of this chapter will provide an analysis of some pattern-situations typical of *Gilmore Girls,* looking specifically at the town meetings as well as the supporting characters, including Kirk Gleason, who are so popular with fans of the series.

"Do We Have to Go Through This Every Damn Year?": Town Meetings

It is worth pointing out that, etymologically, the word *liturgy* comes from the Greek *leitourgia*, meaning "public work." The town meetings summoned by Taylor Doose provide much of the humor in *Gilmore Girls,* although they have neither the philosophical undertones of similarly constructed meetings in *Northern Exposure* (CBS, 1990–96) nor the moral implications of the meetings in *Picket Fences* (CBS, 1992–96). They do, however, contribute to the liturgy so intrinsic to life in Stars Hollow and provide a parody of social rites that gives rise to often absurd narrative situations. When Lorelai arrives late to a meeting already in progress (in "There's the Rub" [2.16]), the following exchange takes place:

TAYLOR: "Late again, are we?"
LORELAI: "Yes. I hope I'm not pregnant."

Here, in typical Gilmore fashion, Lorelai undermines Taylor's authority by cracking a joke. She is aware that everybody in the community knows her story, so she recalibrates the sense and value of punctuality and repetition, linking the reproach to the very personal element of menstruation with the effect of female empowerment. The joke might have worked in another context, but here it functions to parody the seriousness of town meetings while acknowledging the ritualistic limitations placed on such events (including Taylor's managerial attention to punctuality—the kind of attention that leads Babette to call him a "big anal creep" in "Say Something" [5.14]). It also reminds viewers that what we expect to see, moment to moment, is in fact the parody of a serious event: the Taylor-Luke rows (which could be considered a separate liturgy themselves, so strong and recurrent are they) and the town gossip (the "Jess situation" [2.08], the effects on the town of the Lorelai-Luke love story [5.03], and the absurd town issues like troubadour trouble [1.21] and the stink caused by the derailment of a train with a load of pickles [7.05]). But we also expect to hear the humorous comments of Lorelai and Rory on the event, sometimes delivered while chewing on a snack (cookies, for instance, consumed while Luke and Taylor quarrel in "Ballrooms and Biscotti" [4.01]).

The key to interpreting these meetings is given to us during the reenactment of the legendary Battle of Stars Hollow, which happened 224 years ago (1.08). Luke deems it stupid because it only consists of twelve men who stand outside all night in the snow. Lorelai and Rory comment on Luke's fidgety gestures, as he sits and tries to restrain himself, until he explodes, "Do we have to go through this every damn year?" and the Gilmore girls, satisfied with his anticipated outburst, shriek, "Yessss!" Liturgy is thus confirmed. On the discussion that follows, Lorelai sarcastically comments, "A sense of community is so important, isn't it?" to which Rory adds, "It's what made our country great." And when the citizens ask Taylor to explain what sounds like a repetition in the "cart, kiosk, cart/kiosk" line from "Dead Uncles and Vegetables" (2.17), in the context of a discussion about proper business permits for vegetable venders, the girls remark to one another:

LORELAI: "It's repetitive. And redundant."
RORY: "It's repetitive. And redundant."
LORELAI: "We certainly are entertaining, Mac."
RORY: "Indubitably, Tosh."

"Glad You Could Join Us": The Show's Supporting Characters

Invited to Stars Hollow one evening (in the aforementioned "Teach Me Tonight"), Christopher observes, "This town is like one big outpatient mental institution." Lorelai retorts, "Glad you could join us!" In Stars Hollow supporting characters are eccentric and grotesquely serious in their quirkiness. *Gilmore Girls* creates a kind of centrifuge effect: the more its supporting characters are removed from the dramatic reality of the main characters, the battier they appear. The moment they get near the emotional core of the show, they lose part of their eccentricity. This unique textual maneuver of the series enlarges the sense of community, in ways opposite to *Ally McBeal* (FOX, 1997–2002), where the main characters are the weird ones, while the supporting characters keep the proceedings grounded in reality, with the effect of insulating the protagonists. In *Gilmore Girls* the community is involved, and some of the characters have paroxysmal behaviors linked to specific ways of conducting themselves. Examples include Taylor, who is fixated on committees and rules, and Mrs. Kim, who is rigid, controlling, and unsociable. Michel is a snob, full of himself (and a misanthrope as well). These supporting characters all act in an exasperated manner, and their repeated behavioral patterns create a comical effect.

Here is where we need to stretch the concept of liturgy to its limits. Multidimensional characters do not only behave according to a few basic characteristics that have been attributed to them. They are far more complex and highlight how, as audience members, *we* live liturgically (according to expected, ritualistic modes). However, they have a compulsive drive toward a bidimensionality that, only when it is reached, becomes the basis for liturgy and the confirmation of a stereotype. Although it may sound absurd to call bidimensionality an asset in any narrative, it is here desirable inasmuch as it allows the characters to become "ideals," abstract icons. Religious icons in their bidimensionality of representation reach an absoluteness and atemporality. So too do these characters. When they abandon stereotype altogether, their behavior stops being the basis for liturgy. To ensure the presence of liturgical structures, therefore, their behaviors need to be extreme. Moreover, in this process we observe what might be called a "cultural synecdoche" at work, a trait thought of as specific to a given culture and made incarnate through national stereotypes (Michel = French = snob, Mrs. Kim = Korean = rigid, and so forth). The effect, though, is that the stereotype, through hyperbolic expression and excessive deployment, implodes, provoking the kind of laughter or bemused detachment that has the paradoxical effect of destroying the stereotype.

"Fifteen Thousand Jobs": Kirk and the Awareness of Liturgy

Finally we arrive at a more abstract, but no less important, form of liturgy. Through the oddball character Kirk, audiences are able to become attuned to the program's comical effects as well as its awareness of liturgy as a structural element. He has a different job in practically every episode, and the series retains memory of those occupations (a metatextual maneuver that foregrounds the variation-repetitiveness pattern in television). I might note here that in nearly every episode of the action-adventure series *The Fall Guy* (ABC, 1981–86), Howie Munson (Douglas Barr), cousin of the protagonist, says that he has attended some new class, which he doesn't complete but which has given him some expertise in a variety of fields. This far-fetched scenario is funny, but in its absurdity there is a margin of reasonableness that such an improbable thing could in fact happen. The principle is the same, but in *Gilmore Girls* such reasonableness is abandoned. Each time we see him, Kirk has a new job, and only after watching several episodes do we begin to notice the full extent of his engagements.

Appearing for the first time with a different name ("The Lorelais' First Day at Chilton" [1.02]) and then without one ("Kill Me Now" [1.03]), Kirk officially becomes "himself" when we discover that he is an assistant manager at Doose's Market ("The Deer Hunters" [1.04]). At the end of Season One he is a flower delivery man ("Love, Daisies, and Troubadours" [1.21]). In Season Two he is a photographer ("Red Light on the Wedding Night" [2.03]), a mechanic ("Like Mother, Like Daughter" [2.07]), a termite inspector ("Secrets and Loans" [2.11]), a video rental clerk ("Richard in Stars Hollow" [2.12]), and a movie director as well as actor ("Teach Me Tonight" [2.19]). In Season Three he becomes a bath-and-body-products entrepreneur ("Those Lazy-Hazy-Crazy Days" [3.01]), a hockey-game announcer ("Face-Off" [3.15]), a mailman ("The Big One" [3.16]), and a T-shirt salesman ("A Tale of Poes and Fire" [3.17]). In Season Four we see him as a promotional parachutist ("Ballrooms and Biscotti" [4.01]), a dog walker ("Scene in a Mall" [4.15]), a pedicab driver ("Girls in Bikinis, Boys Doin' the Twist" [4.17]), and a checkout clerk ("Last Week Fights, This Week Tights" [4.21]). In Season Five he is a pollster ("Tippecanoe and Taylor, Too" [5.04]), a movie theater usher ("We Got Us a Pippi Virgin" [5.05]), a walking hot-dog billboard ("Norman Mailer, I'm Pregnant!" [5.06]), a souvenir salesman ("To Live and Let Diorama" [5.18]), and a tow truck driver ("A House Is Not a Home" [5.22]). In Season Six he becomes a catering manager ("I Get a Sidekick Out of You" [6.19]), and in Season Seven he opens an outdoor diner ("That's What You Get, Folks, for Makin' Whoopee" [7.02]). At times he holds more than one job per episode (as in the aforementioned "Ballrooms and Biscotti").

Working the light booth at Miss Patty's one-woman show (in "Swan Song"), he dares to improvise an inappropriate effect: "I'm trying to subvert expectation," he explains. But, alas, he cannot. For Kirk, while prone to change jobs week to week, is a slave to ritual, trapped in his own situation-comedy schema. What contributes to the humor of his situation is the confirmation that comes with seeing him in a new job. The abstract quality of this liturgical form can be attributed to the fact that the rite the audience waits for—the sight of Kirk in some new professional endeavor or situational context—is in fact something that is always different, and thus indicative of the variation-repetitiveness relationship that animates this TV series and a few others. The producers of *Gilmore Girls* thus gratify those viewers who are able to recognize television mechanisms and appreciate cultural references through an awareness of metatextual liturgy. Taggi reminds us, "For a liturgy to be in place there must be in a certain measure a conspiratorial overestimation by the two partners . . . of television. If you think: 'After all it's only a show,' then liturgy is only the parody of a rite" (1997, 83). But there is no parody here. There is, however, conspiratorial overestimation in believing that Kirk cannot *reasonably* change professions every week. The producers count on this certainty of ours to make us laugh.

In "Blame Booze and Melville" (5.21) we discover, with surprise, that Kirk is rich. He tells Luke, "I've been working for eleven years, [and] I've had fifteen thousand jobs. I've saved every dollar I've ever made. That and the miracle of compound interest has created a bounty of a quarter of a million dollars. Again, just under. I don't want to brag." Fifteen thousand jobs. The show's liturgical use of Kirk's paratactic professionalism—and, by extension, other aforementioned textual elements—is verbally confirmed.

Liturgy keeps viewers tuned in more than cliffhangers do. But, as I have attempted to illustrate, this fundamental component of *Gilmore Girls* is delicately deployed for the purposes of strengthening the comedic-dramatic dialectic. For the six of the series' seven total seasons that they served as creative leads, Amy Sherman-Palladino and Daniel Palladino built liturgies like spider webs: transparent, but very strong. They and the show's other writers were able to buttress narrative events through ritualistic occurrences and repeated actions that did not tax the audience's patience but instead contributed to the immense outpouring of support among fans for the program. Through an analysis of the liturgical structures underlining *Gilmore Girls*' textual universe, we can begin assessing how the extension of the series' structural elements might facilitate an understanding of the extratextual discourses surrounding the program, which frequently engages in a dialectic of confirmed (comedy) and nonconfirmed (drama) expectations. Furthermore, we might also adopt new perspectives on the ways in which *Gilmore Girls* manages to effortlessly mesh the warmth associated with the family drama and the complexity of relationships therein with its farcical and hyperbolic—yet relentlessly believable—comedic components.

Part Two

Real and Imagined Communities (in Town and Online)

5

The Gift of *Gilmore Girls'* Gab

Fan Podcasts and the Task of "Talking Back" to TV

DAVID SCOTT DIFFRIENT

> Young people have the advantage of not being constantly astounded by the nature of the ever-expanding textual universe in which they find their bearings; their teachers and other interested adults must make conscious efforts to keep up.
>
> —MARGARET MACKEY, "Television and the Teenage Literate: Discourses of *Felicity*"

> Went straight over my head.
>
> —RICHARD GILMORE, after Lorelai shares one of her "funny jokes," in "The Bracebridge Dinner" (2.10)

Over the past ten years, television critics have become increasingly vocal in their admiration and support of Amy Sherman-Palladino's *Gilmore Girls* (2000–2007), a WB/CW series set in the fictional hamlet of Stars Hollow, Connecticut, and centered on the sisterlike relationship between thirtysomething mother Lorelai and her teenage (then twentysomething) daughter, Rory. One of the most frequently highlighted features of this program is its precise yet seemingly stream-of-consciousness dialogue, fueled by several cups of coffee, delivered with the assurance and speed associated with Hollywood's screwball comedies of the 1930s and peppered with the kinds of pop culture references that would make fans of the equally cultish *Mystery Science Theater*

3000 (*MST3K*) (1988–99) take notice.[1] Although many of the town's denizens contribute to the witty banter, most notably Rory's loquacious best friend, Lane Kim (whose encyclopedic knowledge of pop, rock and roll, punk, and alternative music runs "from Abba to Zappa" and rivals that of any writer for *Rolling Stone*), it is principally within the central mother-daughter dynamic where one finds the most unexpected allusions and in-jokes (or what are commonly referred to by fans as "Gilmore-isms").[2]

Gleefully mixing in references to everyone from Oscar Levant to Marcel Proust, from Friedrich Nietzsche to Pepé le Pew, from P. J. Harvey to H. L. Mencken, *Gilmore Girls* demands a certain degree of cultural literacy on the part of its viewers. Although it is safe to assume that the primary audience for the series consists of teenage girls and women in their twenties to thirties, that target demographic has increasingly widened to include male viewers, many of whom are perhaps too young to fully appreciate references to such classic or campy films as *Gaslight* (1944) and *Queen of Outer Space* (1958) but are nevertheless drawn to the unusual yet realistic relationship between the titular twosome, as well as the sheer velocity of the show's verbosity.

1. A much loved if little-seen (by the mainstream) cult television series that foregrounds the spoken word as a vehicle for appropriation, negotiation, and opposition, *Mystery Science Theater 3000* is strangely similar to *Gilmore Girls*. Each of this series' 198 episodes (telecast on Comedy Central and the Sci-Fi Channel over the course of eleven seasons) revolves around a cheesy B movie, shown in its entirety (with only slight editing) by way of a metatextual framing device in which the show's three protagonists—Joel (later replaced by Mike) and his robot companions, Tom Servo and Crow—sit before a giant screen and engage in all manner of verbal mockery. Like *Gilmore Girls, MST3K* mobilizes signifying codes in an ironic mode, inviting audiences to talk back to the screen just as the protagonists do when confronted with wooden acting, cheap special effects, impoverished mise-en-scène, and clunky dialogue.

2. "From Abba to Zappa" is a phrase borrowed from the episode "Norman Mailer, I'm Pregnant!" (5.06), in which an illegal music downloader explains to Rory (who is doing research for a *Yale Daily* newspaper story) that he can access practically any song by any artist thanks to the Internet.

Significantly, that intense verbosity, that densely intertextual array of citations that characterizes the show's dialogue, has seeped into the extradiegetic world of *Gilmore Girls,* a kinder, gentler kind of cult TV series whose most devoted fans form an interpretative community, one that has been sustained by the Internet as well as new media forms and digital technologies that facilitate communication and the sharing of knowledge across a variety of platforms. Indeed, fans of the program participate in a broad range of online activities, from posting messages on any of the many Web forums devoted to the show and downloading cast photos to participating in trivia quizzes and writing slash fiction.

One of the most recent outgrowths of this phenomenon—the consuming of fan-produced audio Podcasts—is particularly interesting for the ways in which devotees of the series are able to literally *voice* their opinions on everything from casting decisions to the plotlines and thematic content of particular episodes. Moreover, the experience of listening to *Stars Hollow Podcast* and *The Unofficial "Gilmore Girls" Podcast* (two long-running programs that consistently ranked among the top downloads at iTunes between 2005 and 2007) can be likened to watching an episode of the TV series, so filled are they with intertextual references to films, plays, novels, and other television programs.

In this chapter, I hope to show that *Gilmore Girls,* perhaps more than any other contemporary American television series, evokes the "ever-expanding textual universe" in which today's teenagers and young adults are immersed. Like Margaret Mackey in her study of another WB series, creator J. J. Abrams's *Felicity* (1998–2002), I am interested in the ways in which "the literate practices of the characters within the world of the story" correlate with "the external but connected texts" generated by fans (2003, 391). I intend to expand Mackey's conception of television's "new literacies," however, so as to illustrate that *Gilmore Girls* literally communicates the referential-tangential nature of adolescent conversation while simultaneously gesturing toward the idea that *adults themselves* have been "taught" to talk that way by their kids. In fact, the series presents us with a number of inversions that collapse the traditional parent-child binary, resulting in a further destabilization of the cultural norms related to teaching and intergenerational communication.

Perhaps more important, it also presents us with diegetically embedded "instructional models" or "tutorial tools" for consuming television, a favorite pastime for Lorelai and Rory, who see it as a means of stimulating, rather than shutting down, dialogue and, by extension, engaging in a kind of critical hermeneutics that is both celebratory and skeptical of the medium as a potentially retrograde, politically conservative guide for living. Moreover, the emphasis on both "pop pedagogy" and participatory or resistant televiewing habits in several spotlighted episodes (such as "That Damn Donna Reed" [1.14], "Red Light on the Wedding Night" [2.03], "Teach Me Tonight" [2.19], and "We Got Us a Pippi Virgin" [5.05]) relates to the ways in which *Gilmore Girls*' fans likewise gain a somewhat circumspect approach to media as well as an apprenticeship or education in the fine art of citation thanks to the two aforementioned Podcast programs.

Before proceeding to an exploration of those Podcasts, which have given both casual media consumers and hard-core fans the chance to talk about a show that is itself largely *about talk,* it is important to momentarily reflect on some of the textual as well as extratextual aspects of the series outlined in the introduction of this volume, aspects that connect *Gilmore Girls* to other cult television programs and distinguish it from more mainstream fare. Although not a sci-fi, fantasy, or horror series, *Gilmore Girls* can be considered a cult television show, albeit a rather unconventional one. This status is due not only to its complex interweaving of episodic and serial plotlines within a self-contained textual universe (the "*Gilmore*verse"), its compelling character arcs, its occasional use of dream sequences, its foregrounding of the act of TV viewing, and its willingness to depart from traditional genre formulas, but also to the depth and breadth of its fandom. Thus, the series not only serves as a convenient case study for ascertaining the ways in which consumption patterns and fan cultures have changed in recent years because of the increased viability of Podcasts as both method and content of multimedia delivery but also provides scholars an opportunity to test, challenge, and expand conventional definitions of "cult TV" and see beyond its typically male-defined parameters.

Limited space prevents me from unpacking the various ways in which questions of race, ethnicity, class, gender, sexuality, friendship, and parenting inform this incredibly rich series and figure within the participatory communities of fans who actively contribute to the show's cultivation, to its legitimization inside and outside academe. Nevertheless, I will at least gesture toward the somewhat paradoxical idea that male viewers of the series constitute a shadow demographic whose online contributions and listener feedback to the aforementioned Podcast programs play a pivotal role not only in recuperating otherwise submerged or sublimated subject positions but also in diversifying its fandom and highlighting how the discourses of "quality" and "cultness" impact one another. In fact, these qualitative terms commingle within the series itself, or, more specifically, within the small, tightly knit community of eccentrics who populate Stars Hollow, an imaginary space—ostensibly no more "real" than the virtual sanctuaries where fans reside—made all the more desirable and "cultish" by the quality of life there.

Borrowing Cassandra Amesley's notion of proprietary audiences (1989), who borrow, appropriate, or rewrite elements from fictional narratives while engaged in the very *real,* rather than *virtual,* act of TV viewing, I argue that the creators of and contributors to *Stars Hollow Podcast* and *The Unofficial "Gilmore Girls" Podcast* are changing the face of possessory fandom through both recorded and real-time commentary, spoken into telephones (old technology) or computer mics (new technology) and piped into the earphones and speakers of MP3 owners throughout the world. Simply put, the Podcast as a postmodern yet strangely old-fashioned media platform and cultural expression has helped to bring back a semblance of the "real" to online communities, the members of which can now take their downloaded talk "offline," out into the world both as mobile, rather than stationary, consumers and as "collectors" of verbal, rather than virtual, texts.

Moreover, as a form of fandom tied to both ephemeral content and material culture (with portable listening devices like iPods and other MP3 players becoming ever more collectible with the advent of glitzier or kitschier accessories), the Podcast can be understood as an aural object that invites consumers to acknowledge the socioeconomic disparity between insiders/owners and outsiders/nonowners. It also encourages those same listeners to adopt a more receptive, if also objective, attitude toward cross-cultural communication (since several Podcast callers and listeners from non-English-speaking countries are forced to articulate their thoughts and hear the comments of others in a language that, to them, is foreign).

Indeed, because fan-produced audio Podcasts not only put emphasis on the hosts' spoken words but also frequently feature listener call-in segments, articulation is very much a central component of these programs, shifting focus from the *content* to the *delivery* of their messages. How does their delivery stack up against the performance of the TV show's principal cast members, the spectacularly talented Lauren Graham and Alexis Bledel, actresses who were asked to speak more words per minute than any other performer on contemporary television?[3] What does the spoken voice reveal that would otherwise be at least partially masked online, where fan forums perhaps allow for a greater degree of anonymity, if also a more introspective search for personal meaning in written postings? How do Podcast producers and subscribers participate in the collective conversation that is online fandom while also expanding its discursive formations to allow for textual anomalies as well as the kind of rever-

3. As a hyperliterate televisual text, *Gilmore Girls* openly acknowledges the demands placed on the actresses in the series, whose fast-paced delivery of dialogue is self-consciously alluded to, whether through intertextual references to Hollywood's classic screwball comedies such as *Bringing Up Baby* (1938) and *His Girl Friday* (1940) or through the actual comments of the characters. For instance, in "It Should've Been Lorelai" (2.14), a competitive Paris informs Rory that her WPM (words per minute) could stand further improvement in preparation for a forthcoming debate concerning doctor-assisted suicide (Paris's WPM is 178, much higher than Rory's 135 WPM).

sals and inversions found within *Gilmore Girls,* a show whose title characters *talk back to their TV,* share a secret language that sounds foreign to outsiders, and have an equally unorthodox relationship to one another?

I explore these and other questions in the following pages, which are concerned first with the content and form of the actual Podcasts themselves (as both aural objects and imaginary "online-offline" spaces), and then with the deeper implications of dialogic communication, the very thing that drives these multiuser, tangent-prone amateur programs and reminds audiences of *Gilmore Girls'* self-reflexivity and constructedness as a talk-filled TV show *about* TV and talk. In this way, *Gilmore Girls* not only provides a new pedagogical model for "teaching television" but also inspires viewers to become speakers themselves, that is, to shuck their identity as passive receivers and become discriminating, *speaking* subjects willing to vocalize their support as well as criticism of the show. These interrelated aspects, in the final analysis, are what make the fan cultures surrounding Amy Sherman-Palladino's creation so vital for media scholars and cultural critics in this new millennium of "meaningful minutia."

Meaningful Minutia: Talking Trivia and Forming Communities Through Podcasts

> Go on a Web site, okay, because there are thousands, no, *millions* of your kind out there, debating all the minutia of not just this *Star Wars* movie, but *every Star Wars* movie.
>
> —LORELAI to Luke, in "Fight Face" (6.02)

> I mean, look at *Star Trek.* People have been talking about that for forty years. Why can't people talk about *Gilmore Girls* for forty years . . . except we don't have a secret Klingon language. . . . Maybe we should start a *Gilmore Girls* convention, and you could dress up as your favorite *Gilmore Girls* character.
>
> —SARA, one of the cohosts of the *"Gilmore Girls" Recap Podcast*

> It's just a hobby. We're not Trekkies!
>
> —A GUEST at the Independence Inn, in town for the Poe Admiration Society, in "A Tale of Poes and Fire" (3.17)

Like the most fervent followers of all things *Star Wars* (who, apparently unbeknownst to Luke, are notorious for scavenging through thickets of Web-based information for the latest bit of trivia), *Gilmore Girls* fans have a vast array of digital enclaves at their disposal, online spaces in which to stake out claims and shore up a sense of community through the reciprocal exchange of ideas. Besides the CW's official Web page and the countless personal and community blogs devoted to the program, such fan sites as www.gilmoregirlsnews.com and www.gilmoregirls.org provide the kinds of information that many viewers cannot find elsewhere and underscore Henry Jenkins's argument that "meaning is a shared and constantly renewable resource" online (2002, 160). The latter Web site contains bios of the cast members, a complete episode guide complemented by transcripts and screencaps, a news page where recent developments are put into narrative and institutional contexts, a spoilers page where fans can read about upcoming plotlines, an archive of photos and videos, a mailing list, a real-time chat room, and a message board. As of June 24, 2007 (nearly six weeks after the May 15 broadcast of the series finale, "Bon Voyage" [7.22]), there were 280,090 separate postings in the "Main Discussion" forum at www.gilmoregirls.org, more than one half of that number (149,816) found within the "Fun and Games" folder (or, rather, clickable coffeepot), which includes such threads as "The World Series of Gilmore Culture," "This or That," and "Hangman." These posts are in addition to another 16,715 within the "Episode Discussion" forum (broken into seven internal forums, coinciding with the series' seven seasons), and 17,977 additional posts within a "Community Center, Announcements, and Closed Topic" folder.

In addition to these Web sites are a number of audio Podcasts created by fans and made available for download through free subscriptions to RSS feeds at such places as iTunes and PodcastAlley.com.

Although most of these fan-produced shows, such as *The TV Addict Podcast, Pop Culture Shock, Frame of Reference,* and Shannon Kay's *Fangirl,* are not exclusively devoted to *Gilmore Girls,* several of their episodes feature in-depth explorations of the show's themes, plotlines, and character arcs. An iTunes search in the fall of 2007 revealed that there were roughly a dozen such amateur shows touching on some aspects of *Gilmore Girls,* but only four of them were devoted Podcasts. Two of them—*Stars Hollow Podcast* and *The Unofficial "Gilmore Girls" Podcast*—combine for a total of 101 episodes, each averaging forty-five minutes in length (roughly the time it takes to watch an episode of the television series, sans commercials). Because these two constitute the most sustained—if also tangent-filled—interrogations of the program in Podcast form, they serve as convenient case studies for illuminating the interactive and participatory nature of new media as well as the diminishing boundaries among producers, consumers, and critics.

They do so by leveling the playing field for everyone involved (amateurs and professionals alike) and by foregrounding a simultaneously digressive and dialogic type of communication that is patterned after normal everyday speech as well as the polished wordplay of Lorelai and Rory, pop culture connoisseurs whose witty living-room conversations provide the impetus for fans to "talk back" to the TV (a medium traditionally criticized for being mind-numbing, advertiser driven, and catering to the "lowest common denominator" of consumers). However, just as "the spirit of critical inquiry that dominates many of the online responses" to *Felicity* "is often shallow," according to Margaret Mackey (2003, 407), so too do the audio Podcasts produced by *Gilmore Girls* fans frequently descend into idle gossip lacking "serious reflection" and comments about the relative "hunkiness" of Logan or Dean, a deficiency or shortcoming that not only casts in relief the professionalism of the WB/CW series but also ironically proves advantageous and instrumental in strengthening the personal bonds among amateur Podcasters and their long-distance listeners.

From its inception in October 2005 until the airing of a batch of "highlight" episodes two years later, *Stars Hollow Podcast* consistently ranked among the top downloads in the "TV and Film" category at iTunes, alongside *The "Lost Podcast" with Jay and Jack,* the Parsec Award–winning *10th Wonder Podcast* (for fans of NBC's *Heroes* [2006–]), and *The Signal* (devoted to Joss Whedon's *Firefly* [FOX, 2002–3] and *Serenity* [2005]). Created by married couple Jon and Cara (whose last name has been withheld), *Stars Hollow Podcast* is complemented by a Web site (www.starshollowpodcast.blogspot.com) that includes a message board, a discussion forum, and a photo of the hosts, as well as a listener map (provided by Google), with pins placed in such far-flung countries as Denmark, New Zealand, England, Venezuela, Chile, and the United States. The hosts themselves are originally from California but currently live in Wisconsin, where they record the program from their apartment. From the very beginning (episode #00), Jon has been more vocal than Cara, dominating—if not completely dictating—the conversation. He is the one who recaps the previous week's episode and ensures that they stay somewhat focused on *Gilmore Girls,* despite the many opportunities to indulge in private affairs and in-jokes. Frequent listeners to their program know that Jon and Cara may spend several minutes regaling the audience with stories about their life together (including references to their young son, Elijah, who can sometimes be heard in the background) before actually getting to the matter at hand.

Ostensibly, these bits of personal information (like Cara's love of kitties and Jon's love of Disney music) have no relationship to the television show. However, attentive listeners may begin to pick up on uncanny parallels and strange synchronicities that suggest that what they have to say about their own lives relates, however tangentially, to *Gilmore Girls.* In episode #57, recorded on February 10, 2007, Cara and Jon explain that they are in their seventh year of marriage, a number that coincides with the seven years that *Gilmore Girls* has been on the air. Quite frequently they express their love of coffee, a passion that reflects their own personal tastes but also the preferences of Lorelai and Rory, who have been known to throw back several cups of joe in the course of a single day. Their post-Christmas 2007 episode (#55) begins with a lengthy discussion of what they did over the holiday break, as well as a list of the gifts they received, including a full seven hours of Disney music on CDs (which Jon transferred to his iPod) and a twelve-cup programmable coffeemaker that would fit right in at Chez Gilmore. Like Lorelai and Rory in the episode "Santa's Secret Stuff" (7.11), Jon and Cara celebrated Christmas a bit late that year. Also, in episode #58, recorded February 27, 2007, Jon explains that his car ran out of gas a few days earlier, an unfortunate occurrence that eerily foreshadowed the opening scene in that week's episode of *Gilmore Girls* ("I'm a Kayak, Hear Me Roar" [7.15]), in which Lorelai and Rory experience the same setback on the road to Stars Hollow and are forced to walk to the nearest gas station. This anecdote comes after Jon has complained about Cara's bad "Doritos breath," a playfully mocking comment that sets the stage for their later imitation of Emily's new maid, a meek woman who speaks almost inaudibly beneath her breath.

Significantly, it is in this episode of *Stars Hollow Podcast* that Jon proclaims, "If I was a superhero, I would be Analogy Man," because of his deftness in making connections between seemingly unrelated things and events, not to mention his ability to poke fun at the people in *Gilmore Girls* who remind him of others (for example, Mitchum Huntzberger is compared to the Newsman Muppet). After stating, "I don't understand guys who watch sports" and then likening the viewing of past sporting events (which Richard Gilmore, a golf enthusiast, does) to watching reruns of lottery numbers, Jon compares this lackluster episode of *Gilmore Girls* to vanilla ice cream. Because vanilla lacks the intense flavor of pistachio or rocky road, it seems fitting as a metaphor of the anticlimactic way in which "I'm a Kayak, Hear Me Roar" ends.

Gilmore Girls fans know that food is central to the series, which foregrounds Lorelai and Rory's unhealthy dietary habits, their "penchant for cheeseburgers, Chinese food, and mystery bags from Al's House of Pancakes." As Susannah Mintz and Leah Mintz state in their contribution to this volume, the main characters' "flaunted proclivity for junk food . . . articulates a central problematic of mother-daughter relations," with Lorelai's childish eating habits presented as a defiant gesture against her own mother, Emily, while simultaneously strengthening the faux sisterhood between herself and her daughter, Rory. The two's unabashed intake of high-caloric food they know is bad for them, while never impacting the shape of their bodies, can be said to correlate with their eager consumption of trashy films and television shows, something that I will return to in the final section of this chapter.

Moreover, their ritual coffee drinking does not so much activate speech but rather puts it into overdrive, keeping them alive to the world and its other sources of instant gratification and indulgence, such as TV, which they often watch while eating, drinking, and—most important—talking. Not coincidentally, a listener's e-mail to *Stars Hollow Podcast,* read by Jon at the end of the aforementioned episode, states, "You guys are like coffee to me," connoting the growing addiction that she and other fans of both the television series and the Podcast program experience each week, and inspiring Cara to chime in, "That was a great *analogy*!"

In the opening minutes of their first episode, Jon throws down the gauntlet and challenges other men not just to watch *Gilmore Girls* but to *talk* about it as well (months later, in episode #51, he would argue that the TV series can teach guys "how to win a girl's heart"). This point was apparently taken up by several male listeners, who have contributed approximately half of the voice-mail comments. Some of these contributors to the Podcast are part of a larger online support group, the "Abused Male *Gilmore Girls* Fan Support Group," which allows men to freely discuss their favorite program without fear of censure or recrimination.[4] Significantly, the listener call-in section of

4. In episode #06 of *The Unofficial "Gilmore Girls" Podcast,* cohost David explains that he is often teased by other males for being a fan of the series but was recently surprised to learn that one of his older male coworkers (a man in his fifties) also likes the show. GilmoreGirls.org features a message board thread titled "Being a Gilmore Guy," a space that allows men to proclaim their interest in the program (and, in the case of many straight contributors, their attraction to Lauren Graham and Alexis Bledel). One contributor to the forum named "warmblanket"

episode #51 features a diverse cross-section of *both* male and female fans responding, in fairly negative ways, to recent developments in Season Seven, the first to be produced after the Palladinos' departure from the series.

Paul, an older male caller from a small town near Seattle, phones in a long message, emphasizing that he loves their Podcast (and finds Jon and Cara's imitation of T. J. and Babette especially hilarious) but has some ambivalent feelings about the series. "You guys keep me interested in the show," Paul states, before concluding, "If it weren't for *Stars Hollow Podcast,* I might not keep up with *Gilmore Girls.*" This particular caller's comment is representative and casts in relief the importance of Podcasts as a means of sustaining the fan community during creative lulls or reruns in the programming schedule. Mentioning that, with so little time to devote to television these days, he must rush off to watch his recently TIVO-ed episode of *Battlestar Galactica* (Sci-Fi Channel, 2004–), Paul also italicizes the temporal demands and constraints of televisual consumption while contextualizing *Gilmore Girls* within a larger sphere of quality TV production, diversified to the point where sci-fi dramas can coexist with intellectually engaging yet emotionally comforting family fare (something already diegetically embedded within the text: a reference to Cylons—

---

writes, "I'm a Gilmore guy and I'm not ashamed at all to say it. Sure the title implies this is a girly girly show, but it is so much more than that. It has excellent, witty dialogue, interesting storylines and great acting. I actually started watching this show because of my sister. I would always complain about how fast they talk and how girly the storyline must be, but after less than two weeks I was hooked and have been ever since. Cheers to ASP for this great show" (October 24, 2005). In response, "Copperboom!" writes, "Amen, brother. I think that its outlook on life is much more fundamental to its appeal (and to its writing) than the fact that its core relationship is between a mother and daughter (as lovable as they are!). I was wondering if I could ask of the other Gilmore Guys (and, of course, any interested Girls) what you think of the portrayal of our gender on the show? Accurate, stereotypical, idealized from a female perspective? Time to represent, ye of the Y chromosome" (October 25, 2005).

the metallic "baddies" of *Galactica*—in "Let Me Hear Your Balalaikas Ringing Out" [6.08]).

Immediately following Paul's recorded message is a series of random observations phoned in by a much younger caller named Hannah, from Denver, whose scattershot comments cover a wide variety of topics, from Jon and Cara's terrible imitations (a criticism that cancels out Paul's earlier celebration of their work) to her need for a complete set of "*Gilmore*-isms" and the guilt that Christopher might have experienced had he known the circumstances leading up to Lorelai's return at the end of Season Six. Like the Podcast hosts, Hannah frequently utters "I love you" in a seemingly arbitrary fashion, and she admits that Jon and Cara are "taking over [her] brain cells," so much so that she claims to hear their voices at night after putting her iPod to rest.

The outpouring of support for their program continues in the next message, delivered by another young female caller, Stephanie, from Indiana. Having stumbled upon their Podcast only two days earlier, Stephanie claims to be already hooked. "I don't think I've ever laughed so much," she says, in reference to Jon and Cara's recap of the previous episode. This call is followed by another young female caller, who leaves two voice messages complaining about the modest screen time given to the secondary characters on the series (beloved townsfolk like Miss Patty and Kirk). After another male listener leaves a message, the call-in portion of the program comes to an end with the comments of a very young female caller from Colorado named Benji, who says, "You guys rock, and the new director sucks, and that's basically it." Her reference to the "new director" (or, rather, show runner) David Rosenthal, while meant to bolster Jon and Cara's Internet reputation (or "netputation"), might remind audiences of *Gilmore Girls*' comparative professionalism at the technical level vis-à-vis the slapdash production values of the Podcasts.[5] Moreover, the intense admiration

5. Perhaps the most slapdash of all the *GG* Podcasts is *The "Gilmore Girls" Recap*, hosted by Jess and Sara (a.k.a. "The Babette and Miss Patty of Podcasting"), which has featured real-time experiments with live call-ins, padded with several trivia questions as well as moments of dead air.

expressed by call-in listeners (a response we might attribute to the low expectations held by people who consume Podcasts) ironically casts in relief the dissatisfaction felt by those same audience members who expect greater things from the television series (thus setting the bar impossibly high for Rosenthal and Co.).

Episode #51 is both remarkable and representative, highlighting the unique capabilities of Podcasts to facilitate communication while at the same time underlining some of the inherent limitations of the medium, in particular the somewhat superficial and reductive nature of statements that constitute its content and, at times, read like sound bites. This episode, like several others, begins with Jon calling attention to the fact that their voices are disembodied, that listening to Podcasts can be a very discarnate experience. "Oh, you can't see me," Jon remembers, before segueing into a lengthy discussion with Cara about the costumes they plan to wear for Halloween. More than ten minutes of idle chitchat elapse, during which time Cara states that she will be getting a cat (despite Jon's allergy to felines) and that she plans to name it "Darth Vader" if it is black (a comment that might remind us of Lorelai's unusual name for her pet dog, "Paul Anka"). Only after the ten-minute mark do they begin discussing the previous *Gilmore Girls* episode, "'S Wonderful, 'S Marvelous" (7.04).

Lengthy intros and recaps are repeated elements of their Podcast, suggesting that Jon and Cara are seeking some kind of structure that might lend an air of professionalism to their amateur production. Just as "repetition, familiarity, and . . . iteration" (Hills 2004, 512) are core components of *Gilmore Girls'* textual universe, so too does *Stars Hollow Podcast* mobilize repeated elements as a means of solidifying its status as the most professional yet, paradoxically, casually tossed off and glitch ridden of the two main programs, from Jon's habitual utterance of "I love you" each episode to his imitations of a cat's "meow" and their constant complaints about the winter weather in Wisconsin. In the aforementioned episode #51, they invite a frequent caller named Sarah—who has been having problems at work—to submit a weekly e-mail report of her office woes, describing in detail the latest foibles of her boss, who is referred to as the female

Michael Scott (the dim-witted character played by Steve Carrell in *The Office* [NBC, 2005–]). Finally, their search for a catchphrase that could be spoken each episode is further indication that repetition breeds familiarity. Such structural consistencies are likewise a part of another Podcast program, one equally deserving of critical attention given that its data feeds really do "feed" into the "contributory literacies of fan-speak" (to borrow Mackey's phrase) (2003, 399) and can be said to "nourish" audiences in the days and weeks between television episodes.

In many ways, the first episode of *The Unofficial "Gilmore Girls" Podcast*—made available for download beginning on January 10, 2006—set the template for subsequent installments. Accompanied by the sound of acoustic guitars being strummed ("Pod-safe" music provided by the all-female group Don't Harass Betty), cohost David introduces himself, as does wife Alicia after him. Together they explain that, although they have been watching *Gilmore Girls* for only a year, they are "already hooked." Alicia first saw it on ABC Family and began recording it on their DVR. David initially refused to view it, having already shot down the idea of watching *Days of Our Lives* (NBC, 1965–) and *Dawson's Creek* (WB, 1998–2003) because, in his words, these and other daytime and prime-time soap operas are too predictable, featuring characters that are "wafer thin and corny." Alicia persevered and finally introduced her husband to *Gilmore Girls*. It did not take long before David became a "closet fan" and eventually "came out" as a devoted follower of the program, eager to buy the previous seasons on DVD. In an effort to catch up with the entire series before the start of Season Six, David and Alicia eagerly consumed all of the episodes in marathon fashion, back to back, a practice they refer to as "the best way to watch it."

Interestingly, the *Gilmore Girls* episode referenced halfway through their own program, "A House Is Not a Home" (5.22), was the Season Five cliffhanger in which Lorelai made an impromptu marriage proposal to Luke. It correlates not only with Alicia and David's marriage of five years but also with her proposal that he watch the show, taking the initiative and asserting her agency in a relationship that—like Luke and Lorelai's—is built on mutual respect as well as a recognition of the fact that the female half of the couple has rhetorical skills (that is, she has a way with persuasive language) that perhaps surpass her partner's. Significantly, David's voice trembles a bit during the opening minutes of this first episode, whereas Alicia, who speaks with a slight southern accent (she is originally from Tennessee), seems surer in her delivery. Eventually, David (a fan of talk radio, someone who admits to listening to Rush Limbaugh's program) settles into a more comfortable rhythm, and their conversation soon kicks into high gear, the two of them trading quips with aplomb.

In addition to foregrounding their own inexperience and recent initiation into *Gilmore Girls* fandom, David and Alicia acknowledge the presence of another Podcast program about the show, Jon and Cara's *Stars Hollow Podcast.* Although, according to Alicia, *Gilmore Girls* is popular enough for two Podcasts to coexist, the logic of competition and product differentiation demands that they depart from the other couple's formula and offer a shorter, more streamlined program for listeners with less time to devote to Podcasts. Rather than provide a lengthy recap of each week's episode, they promise to devote roughly thirty minutes to a thematic assessment and narrative breakdown that dispenses with unnecessary plot points. Alicia will also provide details about forthcoming episodes, information that she has culled from various Internet sources (including TVGuide.com and SpoilerFix.com).

Significantly, just prior to their segue into a discussion of what will likely happen in the next episode ("The Perfect Dress" [6.11]), David and Alicia relate some of the reasons *Gilmore Girls* is itself so different from other television programs. In addition to the fast-paced dialogue, the absence of a laugh track, and the unpredictable ways in which screwball comedy morphs into maternal melodrama (and vice versa), the presence of characters "you really do care about" distinguishes the series, in their words, as does its producers' willingness to end episodes on a downbeat note, with lingering traces of sadness or melancholia. For David and Alicia, this factor contributes to the show's "realism," a word they invoke time and again, as do Jon and

Cara—the latter outright stating, in episode #55 of the *Stars Hollow Podcast,* "It's so like real life" (a comment uttered at a moment when she and Jon are explaining why Lorelai would behave with her blue-blooded parents in sometimes hostile ways).

Interestingly, both Podcast programs parlay their own verisimilitude, their own "reality effect," into a marker of authenticity and a validation of their place within the larger fan culture. Each episode of *Stars Hollow Podcast* is filled with awkward pauses, malapropisms, mistakes, and unexpected, unscripted occurrences, reminding listeners that the show is done on the fly, with little recourse to postproduction editing or tweaking. Indeed, gaffes and glitches are partially what make these shows so compelling as genuine expressions of fandom. When Cara's cell phone starts ringing in episode #51 (something that happens fairly regularly in another Podcast program, the *Official "Grey's Anatomy" Podcast* hosted by series creator Shondra Rhimes), it momentarily becomes an audible part of the background, which—while unseen—is enriched and endowed with 3-D acoustics or spatial "depth" by means of such devices. It is just one of the many sonic events that can transpire during the production of a fan Podcast, textual eruptions that ironically call attention to the *lack* of such "real-life" occurrences in the meticulously scripted world of *Gilmore Girls*—the centerpiece of which is Stars Hollow, an obviously "fake" town (created on a Warner Bros. studio back lot) whose quaintness is achieved through artificial means of reproduction and distillation.

Despite the artificial means by which the producers of *Gilmore Girls* sustain the illusion of small-town American life and cast a spell on the show's most passionate followers, David and Alicia habitually praise the show's "realism," a mode of verisimilitude that, for them, makes the series so compelling as a portrait of familial relations. "I thought my family was dysfunctional," says Alicia in episode #05, after reviewing "Friday Night's Alright for Fighting" (6.13) and before concluding, "Holy crap, the Gilmore family is dysfunctional!" However, after their first dozen episodes David and Alicia's earlier worship of the program modulates, effectively shading into objective criticism.

In episode #16 they begin to voice their increasing dissatisfaction with the program, arguing that Lorelai's expensive outfits are *not* "realistic," that the Korean exchange student Kyon speaks with an accent that sounds "forced . . . almost derogatory" to Asians, that the "Aerie Girls" interstitials (the CW's own attempt to "teach" viewers how to watch *Gilmore Girls*) are irritating and inauthentic as an expression of fan culture, and that the producers are capitulating to corporate culture by placing products within the show (such as a Smartphone) as well as making references to wireless services like T-Mobile.[6] This criticism runs parallel to the increasingly critical remarks by Jon and Cara on *Star Hollow Podcast,* with the latter at one point remarking (in episode #57), "These are fictional characters that [don't] seem so real to me anymore."

By the time their final five Podcast episodes were made available for download in October and November 2006, David and Alicia—while still fans of *Gilmore Girls*—had adopted a much more jaundiced view of the series, not only nitpicking about continuity errors but also lamenting the noticeable drop in script quality after the Palladinos' departure. "The new writers can't really get that flow," David explains in reference to both the scene-by-scene progression of recent episodes and the bipolar quality of Emily (who now goes from "nice to bitchy in 0 to 60"). Although they apologize for being a "Negative Nancy" and a "Negative Ned," the couple cannot help but voice

6. There is something slightly ironic about David and Alicia's comment that the producers of *Gilmore Girls* are "selling out," given that the two Podcasters can be said to "promote" certain products on their own program (as in the final episode [#38], when Alicia says that they each drink a Starbucks coffee before every Podcast). Moreover, between the #12 and #13 episodes of *The Unofficial "Gilmore Girls" Podcast,* the couple provided video access to a commercial for Apple's iBook, featuring Milo Ventimiglia, best known to *Gilmore Girls* fans as Jess Mariano (but more widely recognized today as Peter Petrelli in NBC's *Heroes*). Running approximately one minute, this ad shows him choosing a middle seat on an airplane so as to take full advantage of the drop-down trays, on which the technoliterate passenger sets up an array of gadgets, all hooked into his Mac and literalizing what Margaret Mackey refers to as media "entanglements" (2003, 404).

their concerns about the direction of the series, which now lacks the patented "back-and-forth" (a term Alicia uses to describe the banter between Lorelai and Rory) and, worst of all, is just plain "boring." "Right now I feel like I'm watching a bizarro *Gilmore Girls,*" she says in their final episode, a comment that no doubt resonated with many listeners and contributed to Alicia and David's decision to end their Podcast for good (a practice known as "Podfading").

In David and Alicia's penultimate episode (#37), they discuss "Go, Bulldogs!" (7.06), which—borrowing a phrase made famous by the Comic Book Guy from *The Simpsons* (FOX, 1989–)—is the "Worst. Episode. Ever." "How do I put it into words?" an audibly shocked David asks, groping for language that might adequately express just how bad the previous night's episode was. In a moment of self-reflection and critical scrutiny, the two argue that the producers are "slowly changing the format" of the show:

> DAVID: If you want to go back to . . . some of our first episodes . . . we talk about why we love the show. And one of the things I mentioned was: it's as *true* to life as TV is *ever* going to get.
> ALICIA: It's not like *7th Heaven* or *Full House* where they present the conflict at the beginning and people react to it, and then it is all fixed and everybody is happy again by the end of the hour.
> DAVID: Right. TV shows, traditional ones, have a flow of what they call "exposition, complication, climax, and resolution." So it's like a perfect formula.

David and Alicia are very attentive viewers, pointing out that Luke is wearing a new baseball cap ("It symbolizes that [the program] is over for good," Alicia says) and that Rory has a new cell phone. These comments, delivered in episode #34, assume additional hermeneutic significance after the Podcasters state that Lorelai has begun to "overanalyze her life." Indeed, while they refuse to provide a "blow-by-blow" reiteration of the previous week's narrative, David and Alicia may appear to be "overanalyzing" the TV series by highlighting minutia and focusing on camera angles and setups that make Season Seven visually different from preceding seasons. However, it is precisely this kind of attention to detail and cultural and media literacy that enhances narrative pleasure for fans seeking like-minded people in the blogosphere or via such online sites as PodcastAlley.com.

Just as individual episodes of *Gilmore Girls* flit between the generic thresholds and tonal registers of comedy and drama, so too does the entire series oscillate between a family-friendly type of programming suitable for all ages and a realistic worldview willing to incorporate risqué material and innuendo-filled dialogue, a series that remains largely free of dogmatic religious orthodoxy or morally responsible commentary about such topics as abstinence and sobriety. As Alicia states in an early episode of *The Unofficial "Gilmore Girls" Podcast,* it is "not the goody-two-shoes-type of family show" that *7th Heaven* is, and its honesty and openness not only about family relationships but also about sexual desire are what initially drew her to the series. For example, the precredit sequence in "We Got Us a Pippi Virgin" (5.05) features references to prostitutes and suicide, not the kind of subject matter typically found in family dramas. This lack of moralizing and speechifying is a sign of the program's "realism," so prized by the Podcasters who connect it to Amy Sherman-Palladino's stated refusal to "teach a lesson," to tell people how to lead their lives.

However, *Gilmore Girls* and the Podcasts surrounding it *do* teach audiences a very important lesson, albeit not the kind learned by Lorelai from the Molly Ringwald film *For Keeps* (which "taught" her how to raise Rory). No, the message here relates to what Margaret Mackey calls the "protocols of entanglement"—the "multiple, interlocking texts" embedded within and circulating outside the televisual apparatus (2003, 405). In fact, the lesson to be learned concerns nothing less than spectatorial agency and the role of audiences in keeping the collective conversation that is fandom fresh and meaningful for future generations, the young men and women who will no doubt "teach" their parents how to "speak," how to communicate in an increasingly media-rich environment (much like April, Luke's daughter, schools him in the ways of the world).

Gilmore Girls as a Televiewing "Tutorial"

> LORELAI: Don't speak!
> RORY: If only!
>
> —Dialogue in "You've Been Gilmored" (6.14)

The above exchange between mother and daughter is indicative of *Gilmore Girls*' reflexivity as a TV series that is primarily "about" talk, about the imperative to speak and be heard, even if that speaking drowns out the voices of others. The fact that Lorelai is *imitating* Helen Sinclair—Diane Wiest's flamboyant character in Woody Allen's equally loquacious *Bullets over Broadway* (1994)—is doubly ironic as a diegetically inscribed reference to this television program's indebtedness to earlier cultural productions, especially to those films that were made immediately after the arrival of "talkies" in the late 1920s (the setting of Allen's screwball comedy). In this Season Six episode, mother and daughter acknowledge their own proclivity to verbalize while voraciously consuming both food and TV. This latter object of their collective obsession is perhaps even more nourishing than food, given their tendency to eat snacks lacking the recommended daily allowance of protein and vitamins, and given the way that classic movies and television reruns resonate in these young women's lives, sustaining them through difficult times. Indeed, the TV set is frequently foregrounded throughout this series not only as an electronic hearth around which friends and family members gather but also as a restorative means of recharging their emotional batteries while activating speech in a dynamic way.

"You've Been Gilmored" was not the first *Gilmore Girls* episode to put a metatextual spin on the series' savvy use of spoken words and dialogic communication. Although, in "The Fundamental Things Apply" (4.05), Lorelai informs Luke that there will be "no talking during the movie" prior to their viewing of *Casablanca* (1942), she is herself prone to pontificate on all manner of minutia while watching films broadcast on television or shown at the Black, White, and Red

Movie Theater.[7] Like that Season Four episode, which is packed with allusions to such diverse motion pictures as *National Velvet* (1944), *The Treasure of the Sierra Madre* (1948), *Bonnie and Clyde* (1967), *Chinatown* (1974), *Grey Gardens* (1975), *Diner* (1982), *Cujo* (1983), and *Hardbodies* (1984), the Season Five episode "We Got Us a Pippi Virgin" shows Lorelai and Luke sitting down to watch a movie, only this time the couple is joined by the newly reunited Rory and Dean. Having taken their seats on "Big Red" (Lorelai's nickname of the sofa inside Stars Hollow's only movie theater, its screen not much bigger than a TV), the foursome prepares to see the 1967 prison drama *Cool Hand Luke* (itself a nickname given by Lorelai to Luke).[8] However, due to a technical mishap (the first reel was destroyed in a fire), this Paul Newman classic is replaced by another more garish but no less beloved film from the late 1960s: *Pippi Longstocking* (1969), a Swedish-language West German coproduction (dubbed in English) that Lorelai refers to (with only a hint of irony) as a "classic of surrealism."

Significantly, the two young women's own activity during the screening of *Pippi* would make surrealists and other avant-garde practitioners of the 1920s and 1930s proud, for their quip-filled commentary breaks up the film and shifts Luke's and Dean's focus (as well as our own) *away* from the screen, *toward* the talkers. "I always

7. Similarly, in "Bridesmaids Revisited" (6.16), Lorelai remarks to Gigi, who is sitting before the TV, "I don't like it when people talk to me when I'm watching TV either."

8. Longtime fans of *Gilmore Girls* know that nicknames proliferate throughout the series. Lorelai calls Jason "Digger," and he reciprocates by calling her "Umlauts." "Boyfriend" is the name given to Marty by his girlfriend Lucy, someone who is likewise referred to by fans of the series as "Short Skirt." One can find a number of nicknames at *Stars Hollow Podcast,* from the fan-created "Flathair Bill" (Rory's coworker at the *Yale Daily*) to the fan-directed "Cranky Juan" (cohosts Jon and Cara's name for a frequent caller to their show). Another listener from Tennessee makes the following observation in episode #55 of Jon and Cara's program: "I think we're compelled to call [Lucy] 'Short Skirt' because she and 'Art Girl' call everyone by the same kind of nicknames. We're compelled to mirror their behavior."

wanted to lift an immense quadruped over my head," Lorelai states in reaction to a shot of the improbably strong pigtailed character holding a horse in the air. Such comments, delivered by the main characters in response to something seen on television or in the movie theater, are not unusual in the *Gilmore*verse and can be found in the tellingly titled "Say Something" (5.14) and "A Deep-Fried Korean Thanksgiving" (3.09), the latter featuring yet another reference to Albert Maysles and David Maysles's *Grey Gardens* (a documentary film about an eccentric mother-daughter pair, "Big Edie" and "Little Edie" Bouvier Beale).

The Season Two episode "Red Light on the Wedding Night" (2.03), which partly concerns some of the changes coming to Stars Hollow (in the form of the town's first traffic light and crosswalk), is notable for the ways in which the themes of progress and nostalgia inform not only the townspeople's connection to place and space but also Lorelai's transformative relationship with Max Medina, Rory's high school teacher to whom Lorelai is betrothed and around whom the two women initially plan to "form a cult." This comment, made by Lorelai in response to Max's mad skills in her kitchen (as Rory states, "He has *much* knowledge"), feeds into the scene that immediately follows, with the trio moving into the living room and sitting down to watch a Vietnam War–era cult movie, *Billy Jack* (1971).[9]

Here, Max's considerable book smarts prove insufficient in sorting through the densely intertextual dialogue provided by Lorelai and Rory, who talk throughout the movie and "shush" their guest whenever he asks a question. "Who's this guy Billy Jack?" Max inquires, before an oblivious Lorelai enthuses, "Here comes my favorite and least-favorite line all rolled into one" (at this point, a character in the film says, "I'm gonna cut your bowels out"). Significantly, Lorelai's admiration of Max at the beginning of the episode, prior to this scene

9. In "Red Light on the Wedding Night" there are several references to cult movies and camp icons besides *Billy Jack* and its lead actor, including *Them!* (1954), *Monty Python and the Holy Grail* (1975), *Life of Brian* (1979), Joan Crawford, Mae West, and Elizabeth Taylor.

of televisual talk, gives way to reticence toward the end, after Luke has fought Taylor on the issue of change and given Lorelai a chuppah for the impending (but eventually canceled) wedding. In a way, the suitability of Lorelai and Rory's suitors is measured by their ability to grasp the significance of relatively obscure films like *Grey Gardens* and *Billy Jack* while keeping pace with these young women's pop culture commentary: to, in effect, become members of their tightly knit community of two and *talk back to the screen* (something Max soon gives up on, instead falling asleep on the sofa and leaving Lorelai and Rory—professed "cult" members—to their fanatical adoration of this most unconventional of texts).

On numerous instances, the people around Lorelai fail to grasp her references and jokes. For instance, Emily does not understand her comment about meeting George Michael in a bathroom, nor does Richard fathom the complexities of a Wile E. Coyote–Road Runner cartoon, which has to be explained to him by Lorelai in "Tick, Tick, Tick, Boom!" (4.18). Although well versed in Mencken's *Chrestomathy,* Lorelai's father knows little to nothing about popular music produced after Chuck Berry's time, misconstruing his daughter's reference to Christopher "cranking Metallica" in his new Volvo as a euphemism for doing drugs (in "It Should've Been Lorelai"). In "Ted Koppel's Big Night Out" (4.09), we learn that Lorelai is developing a fondness for Jason because "he keeps up," a sentiment echoed much later in the series when Lorelai—upon realizing that Luke "gets" her Little Rascals joke—remarks, "You know, you are the *perfect* man" ("The Party's Over" [5.08]). Here, "getting" Lorelai obviously carries a double meaning.

One of the first and most important instances of this metatextual foregrounding of televisual talk occurs in the Season One episode "That Damn Donna Reed" (1.14). It begins with a precredit scene at Lorelai's house, where she, Rory, and a dumbfounded Dean sit down to watch an episode of the classic situation comedy *The Donna Reed Show* (ABC, 1958–66). Starring Reed as Donna Stone, a middle-class housewife who deals with her two children's various problems while her pediatrician husband is at the office, this series is similar to yet different from *Gilmore Girls,* a contemporary yet slightly old-fashioned program about a single mother's dynamic relationship with her only child.[10] As they provide a kind of *MST3K* running commentary throughout this scene, Lorelai and Rory mercilessly mock a hopelessly dated TV show from the Eisenhower era (which they ironically refer to as both a "lifestyle" and a "religion"). In doing so they engage in a viewing practice that is at once critical and celebratory, attentive and distracted, focused and diffused, and thus indicative of the interpretative negotiations brought to bear on *Gilmore Girls* by Podcast producers and listeners—the kinds of dialogic negotiations necessary to distance oneself from the past while reconciling the appeal of Donna Reed among young women (like Rory, who discovers, after doing research, that the actress was a powerful figure in the entertainment industry) and young men (like Dean, who thinks that the idea of a wife cooking dinner for her husband and family is "nice").

Speaking Geek and Seeking a Community

> I don't speak geek.
>
> —LORELAI to Luke after he whips out an *Outer Limits* reference, in "It Should've Been Lorelai"

As suggested above, the emphasis on talk as a means of resolving conflicts and strengthening the community spills over into the surrounding discourses about *Gilmore Girls,* not only in the online forums (where debates still rage between "Java Junkies" and "Balcony Buddies," the latter term used to describe fans of the Lorelai-Christopher pairing) but also in the Podcast programs. This fact is acknowledged

10. *The Donna Reed Show* is one among many classic TV shows mentioned or shown in *Gilmore Girls,* which references everything from *The Honeymooners* ("Secrets and Loans" [2.11]) to *I Love Lucy* ("Jews and Chinese Food" [5.15]), *Leave It to Beaver* ("Run Away, Little Boy" [2.09]) to *Bewitched* ("Afterboom" [4.19]), and *I Dream of Jeannie* ("Dead Uncles and Vegetables" [2.17]) to *Bonanza* ("Tippecanoe and Taylor, Too" [5.04]).

in a recent episode of *Stars Hollow Podcast* when Cara, one of the cohosts, says that the best way for Luke and Christopher to overcome their hostilities is to "talk, communicate, sit down and talk"—a proposition that has already been adopted by fans who may disagree about certain points (in particular on the appropriate partner for Lorelai), who may in fact splinter into narrower interest groups, but who are nevertheless "held together," as Henry Jenkins states in an article on the "collective intelligence" of media consumers, "through the mutual production and reciprocal exchange of knowledge" (2006, 27).

In her illuminating essay "How to Watch *Star Trek,*" Cassandra Amesley describes the negotiations involved when proprietary audience members "appropriate the primary elements of a mass-mediated narrative and actively rewrite it." The first phase in this hijacking of elements and eventual redeployment of them is the act of TV viewing, which often takes place within a *real,* as opposed to a virtual or imagined, community, an immediate and *actual* interpretative community of other fans who watch episodes together and frequently comment to one another about such things as the plotline, the themes, the characters, and the qualitative worth (the "goodness" or "badness") of particular episodes. Thus, the act of viewing (whether in a family's living quarters, in a residence hall or dorm room, or in other less private settings) is itself a *text-making event* as well as a communication process through which members of a *real* community share a common language, a vocabulary or lexicon that is deployed ironically but in a loving way toward the episodes. The immediate interpretations that spring from such interpersonal encounters continually replenish the text, keeping it fresh for subsequent viewings, and furthermore reveal a unique sort of "implicature," wherein *Star Trek* fans and other cult audiences "are at the same time apologetic and slightly reticent about their activities" (1989, 328).[11]

11. There are several references to the original *Star Trek* scattered throughout the *Gilmore*verse, in episodes such as "Love and War and Snow" (1.08), "Concert Interruptus" (1.13), "The Ins and Outs of Inns" (2.08), "Richard in Stars Hollow" (2.12), "A Tale of Poes and Fire" (3.17), "Ballrooms and Biscotti" (4.01), "Norman

In addition to foregrounding the lexicon of stock phrases within the *Star Trek* universe, axioms that act like a collection of anchors for the audience (who expect the characters to talk and behave a certain way), Amesley promotes a spectatorial paradigm that she describes as "double viewing" (ibid., 332). Double viewing suggests the ability to engage with a televisual text by way of "two sets of interpretative rules," and basically involves balancing *identification* and *distanciation*—a balance that recalls the negotiated reading strategy introduced in Stuart Hall's essay "Encoding/Decoding" (1980), as well as an argument put forth in Henry Jenkins and John Tulloch's book *Science Fiction Audiences* (1995, 85). Like Amesley, Jenkins and Tulloch insist that the best approach to understanding the significance of *Star Trek* (or any other cult television series) is to move fluidly between critical distance and extreme proximity (ibid., 19). Distance allows one the necessary space to objectively analyze the ideological components of a program, and proximity allows one to benefit from the mutual knowledge shared by fans within the larger reception community—what critics sometimes refer to (in not altogether complimentary ways) as "hives" or "fanclaves."

Podcast producers and consumers occupy one such enclave and are able to fill up the "empty time" between regularly scheduled episodes of their favorite programs in ways that differ from other expressions of fandom (although, it should be pointed out, several weeks may elapse between Podcast installments, owing to personal issues, family crises, sicknesses, and so on). In the midst of convenience technologies that have "expanded asynchronicity" by allowing "viewers to archive, share, and review content," according to Amanda Lotz, Podcast programs can be said to promote a return to *synchronous* viewing, encouraging fans to discuss or listen to plot points not long after a television episode has aired (2007, 62). Moreover, the glitches and gaffes sprinkled throughout *Stars Hollow Podcast* and *The Unofficial "Gilmore Girls" Podcast,* not to mention the witty banter and casual conversations

Mailer, I'm Pregnant!" (5.06), "I'm OK, You're OK" (6.17), and "The Real Paul Anka" (6.18).

provided by Jon and Cara and David and Alicia, mark a return to the "realism" that early seasons of *Gilmore Girls* were famous for but was sorely missing (according to some audiences) during the final season. Over time, the fan-producers—Jon and Cara, David and Alicia—have become "characters" themselves, with discernible tics and tastes as well as with their own fans who follow their programs religiously and post positive feedback (in the form of star ratings) at iTunes.[12]

Has the fan-produced Podcast replaced the office water cooler as a site of impassioned conversations and, more often, idle chatter about the previous night's television programs? Probably not. Just as people still sit together before the electronic hearth and bask in the glow of their (increasingly large) TVs, so too do avid fans continue to feel the need to congregate in actual places and discuss the latest plot twists of programs like *Lost* and *Heroes.* However, as a multistage process through which audiovisual content can be captured, posted to a Web site through an online data feed, and automatically or manually downloaded into mobile listening devices, Podcasting is just one part of a larger mediascape that diminishes the distance among producers, distributors, and consumers. By encouraging viewers to adopt a more active relationship to their favorite media texts, this particular communication technology is a facilitator of sorts, not unlike other earlier means of creating and sustaining imagined communities, like fanzines and conventions. But by putting so much emphasis on the *spoken word,* Podcasts seem especially well suited (technologically) and situated (historically) to comment on and channel the conversational discourses generated within and around *Gilmore Girls.*

12. Alicia, the cohost of *The Unofficial "Gilmore Girls" Podcast,* has been known to swoon at the mere mention of Logan's name, so enamored is she of the actor who plays him (Matt Czuchry) that she states, in episode #16, that he is as central to the success of the show as the Palladinos. It is in that same Podcast episode that she and David announce the news of the Palladinos' imminent departure from the series. "*They* are the show," David states, departing from his wife's comment and drawing a tightly wound circle around the core contributors, which includes Lauren Graham and Alexis Bledel besides the producers.

6

"I Will Try Harder to Merge the Worlds"

Expanding Narrative and Navigating Spaces in Gilmore Girls

RADHA O'MEARA

> LORELAI: He's not in this world; he's in my other world.
> EMILY: You keep so much from me with these separate worlds of yours. It's not right.
> LORELAI: I will try harder to merge the worlds.
> —"You Jump, I Jump, Jack" (5.07)

Longtime viewers of *Gilmore Girls* know that there is a fundamental conflict at the heart of this most unusual television series, a tension between the *separation* and *integration* of particular spaces.[1] This tension plays out thematically through a division of the narrative universe (or "*Gilmore*verse") into two main settings, Stars Hollow and Hartford, Connecticut. Although these towns represent contrasting worlds separated by physical distance, they are constantly colliding in the lives of Lorelai Gilmore and her daughter, Rory, whose social and spatial mobility produces integration, something expressed in the mise-en-scène and narrative form of *Gilmore Girls.* As I hope to show, the dominant narrative strategy of crosscutting between different settings reinforces the complex relationship between separation and integration. This thematic and formal tension between spatial

1. Thanks to Andrew Saunders, Mark Nicholls, Angela Ndalianis, and Elizabeth Avram for their generous help in developing this chapter.

dislocation and fusion becomes increasingly complicated as the series progresses, most notably with Rory's move to college (Yale, located in New Haven). The college girl's growing independence at Yale expands the textual horizons and social networks of the series, creating several opportunities for narrative expansion and character development.

"Those Thirty Miles Act as a Buffer": Stars Hollow and Hartford

Although Stars Hollow and Hartford are often contrasted in the series, the literal and figurative mobility of the main characters works both to separate and to integrate these spaces, producing a palpable tension within *Gilmore Girls.* From the first episode forward, the producers, writers, and directors of the series (including Amy Sherman-Palladino, the show's creator) establish Stars Hollow as a homey if slightly hokey small town where everyone knows each other's names, where social engagement is constantly reinforced through quaint community celebrations, and where town meetings are curiously well attended. Stars Hollow, Connecticut (founded 1779, as noted on the sign in the town square), is not merely a bucolic, fanciful backdrop to the stories of Lorelai and Rory. Lorelai is vocal about her love for the community that has steadfastly supported her as a young mother, ever since she first arrived there after a falling-out with her blue-blooded parents, Richard and Emily, over her teenage pregnancy. The series makes an effort to include many minor and recurring characters, such as the fanatically Adventist Mrs. Kim, her oppressed rocker daughter Lane, clumsy chef Sookie, greengrocer Jackson, haughty French concierge Michel, career-challenged Kirk, plus-size dancer Miss Patty, neurotic local politician Taylor, and the unnamed town troubadour. Despite their secondary status, the folks of Stars Hollow are not merely supporting characters, as they supply a regular dose of the ensemble show's celebrated quirkiness while contributing to the strong communal ethos of the town.

The series begins when Lorelai's parents, the well-bred Emily and Richard Gilmore, breach their daughter's world after a long estrangement. Rory has been accepted to the prestigious Chilton Academy in Hartford, and when Lorelai asks her parents to pay for the expensive private school, they make the financial assistance conditional on weekly Friday-night dinners. This setup creates the kind of interpersonal conflict on which television dramas typically rely and could be read as the inciting incident of the unfolding story. More important, it extends the network of characters beyond TV melodrama's conventional geographically constrained community, as Lorelai's parents live in Hartford, a city located approximately a half hour away from the fictional hamlet of Stars Hollow. Despite its relative proximity to Stars Hollow, Hartford is presented to us in very different terms so as to reinforce how *different* it is, how far removed it is—culturally and socially—from the tightly knit community that Lorelai and Rory call home. As Lorelai explains to her daughter in "I'm OK, You're OK" (6.17), she specifically moved there at the age of sixteen so as to put a thirty-mile buffer zone between her and her demanding parents.

Stars Hollow and Hartford are frequently contrasted in *Gilmore Girls,* as the two worlds represent an array of binary values. For Lorelai, her parents' house in Hartford is coded as the past, and Stars Hollow symbolizes the present, a place she has chosen to be and where she will presumably stay. This point is strongly suggested in the early seasons: our first glimpse of the Gilmore's Xanadu-like mansion is in a photograph of Lorelai as a young child, which dissolves into contemporary action. Hartford represents staid tradition, rules, obligation, and confinement, whereas Stars Hollow represents active community engagement, choice, warmth, and freedom—particularly the freedom to be eccentric in the face of conformity. Hartford is depicted as homogenous, whereas Stars Hollow is floridly diverse. The juxtaposition between the urban, upper-crust world of Hartford and the rural, middle-class world of Stars Hollow is a strong current throughout the series and provides an unusually powerful commentary on class, something rarely seen in the context of American television fiction. The towns are further contrasted ontologically, as

Hartford is an actual city in Connecticut and Stars Hollow a fictional country idyll. The relationship between the main characters and the two principal settings is marked by tension: the Gilmore girls themselves both construct the separation of spaces *and* work to integrate them. On one hand, the girls frequently call for the division of these worlds. For example, Lorelai explains to her best friend, Sookie: "My whole life, my whole existence, my essence, my being, my ability to be this sparkling creature standing here before you, all of this depends on the complete and total separation of my life from my mother's life. That's how it works" ("The Fundamental Things Apply" [4.05]). On the other hand, Lorelai and Rory sometimes celebrate the freedom and value of their bifurcated social experiences. For example, in Rory's valedictory speech, she proudly declares: "I live in two worlds" ("Those Are Strings, Pinocchio" [3.22]). Although Lorelai clearly created this spatial tension when she moved away from her parents as a teen mother, she endeavors to "try harder to merge the worlds" for the sake of Rory as the series progresses.

Lorelai and Rory are the only ones to continually move between the two worlds of Stars Hollow and Hartford; all of the other characters in the show clearly belong to one world or the other, despite occasional forays into the contrasting space. Supporting characters, including Richard, Emily, Paris, Sookie, Luke, Dean, April, Lane, and Logan, will be only visitors in the other world. Indeed, a "fish out of water" scenario constitutes a story strand in several episodes of *Gilmore Girls:* Emily's tour of the quaint town leaves her feeling disconnected from her family ("Emily in Wonderland" [1.19]); Lane crowds Rory's roommates when she beds down at Yale ("The Incredible Shrinking Lorelais" [4.14]); Paris momentarily becomes a drunken bum on the streets of Stars Hollow ("To Live and Let Diorama" [5.18]). This repeated "fish out of water" motif reinforces the conflicts between the two worlds by showing people to be ill-prepared for the experiences to be had in spaces they would otherwise avoid.

In their constant struggles to reconcile their connections to Stars Hollow and Hartford, Lorelai and Rory are themselves sometimes "fish out of water," even in their chosen home. For example, Rory is aghast when she is hailed as a poster child for media censorship ("Richard in Stars Hollow" [2.12]), and Lorelai is angered by the local moral majority (represented by an outraged gaggle of PTA moms fit to be gagged) after her talk about independent business and teen pregnancy at Stars Hollow High ("One's Got Class and the Other One Dyes" [3.04]). The two are often flummoxed by the protocol and punctilios of Hartford, but they continually return to reclaim their site of origin. The frequent collision between the worlds of Stars Hollow and Hartford, which creates internal and interpersonal conflicts for Rory and Lorelai, appears to be inevitable and essential to the frisson of the series.

For the Gilmore girls, spatial and social mobility is coded as fundamental to their personal happiness and success. In this way, Lorelai and Rory function as forces of integration, as vehicles capable of bridging the considerable cultural gap between Stars Hollow and Hartford. This emphasis on integration is consistent with the dominant generic influences evident in the series, which are strongly melodramatic and romantic. Thomas Schatz's structuralist analysis of classical Hollywood genres describes melodrama and romance as rites of integration, which attempt to negotiate a resolution to the social and ideological conflicts they represent (1981, 24–36). However, there is an important point of difference here: in classic Hollywood cinema, the heterosexual couple conventionally resolves the wider community's social and ideological conflicts through the male and female partners' embrace (ibid., 29–30). *Gilmore Girls* revises this device to a degree, putting the problem of integration squarely on the shoulders of the mother and daughter. This feminist twist adds weight to Lorelai's and Rory's roles as whip-smart heroines and strengthens the central relationship. The continuous struggle to reconcile conflicting worlds is culturally resonant, but it is also imperative to the demands of a serial narrative. In order to continue generating and replenishing an ever-expanding narrative, these characters must be both socially *and* spatially mobile. The process of integration in this television series is ongoing; it is not determined by a classic Hollywood resolution.

"I'll Even Run Interference for You": Partnering Worlds Through Crosscutting

The thematic tension in *Gilmore Girls* between Stars Hollow and Hartford is supported at the formal level. The tone and texture of a television series hinge on particular strategies for interweaving various spaces, characters, stories, and climaxes into a satisfying whole. Like most television fiction, *Gilmore Girls* relies heavily on the strategy of crosscutting to move multiple narrative strands forward. Crosscutting refers to the alternation of scenes set in different places to form a sequence, with the presumption that the narrative events and situations transpire concurrently. Crosscutting is a subset of parallel montage, a dynamic form of editing often associated with emotional manipulation, which dates back to the films of D. W. Griffith, most notably such masterworks of American cinema as *Intolerance* (1916) and *Way Down East* (1920). In her analysis of television narrative, Sarah Kozloff declares that television, a "newer" medium compared to motion pictures, "has taken parallel montage to a high art" (1992, 85). As she and other media scholars have suggested, crosscutting—though born out of the dramaturgical necessities of cinematic praxis—not only facilitates television series' conventional multiprotagonist and multiplot structures but also dovetails with serial television's necessary textual gaps produced by commercial advertisements and episode breaks.

Crosscutting is established early in the first episode of *Gilmore Girls,* as scenes freely alternate between Lorelai in one location and Rory in another. This editing strategy implies simultaneity: we assume that Lorelai is working at the inn at the same time that Rory is attending classes at Stars Hollow High School ("Pilot" [1.01]). As Charlotte Brunsdon notes, "The different present tenses of the narrative co-exist, temporally un-hierarchised" (1991, 468). By the show's second episode, "The Lorelais' First Day at Chilton" (1.02), crosscutting has already become an entrenched feature, allowing for a textual oscillation between scenes of Lorelai in Stars Hollow and Rory in Hartford. The series' ritual of Friday-night dinners, which Giada Da Ros discusses at length elsewhere in this volume, sets up the regular interaction of characters from and within two separate worlds. The continuous oscillation between these two worlds is a major theme of the show, but it is also a formal structuring principle that organizes the array of characters and multiple plotlines. However, crosscutting is not the only strategy employed in *Gilmore Girls* to arrange scenes and propel the narrative. Scenes are often presented in a linear fashion, and are also occasionally emplotted in such a way as to emphasize ambiguous temporal and causal relationships, such as in dream sequences designed to illustrate the main characters' latent desires, subconscious yearnings, or as yet unspoken fears. Still, crosscutting is the overwhelmingly dominant strategy employed by the producers, directors, and writers of *Gilmore Girls.*

Although crosscutting may appear to follow the paths of individual characters, spatial location is fundamental to its logic, since the beginning of a new scene or narrative strand is marked by a shot in a new space. Film theorists from Christian Metz to David Bordwell have defined a scene as a unity of time, space, and action. Bordwell explains, "Hollywood narration usually defines its scenes by neoclassical criteria—unity of time (continuous or consistently intermittent duration), space (a definable locale), and action (a distinct cause-effect phase)" (1985, 158; see also Metz 1974, 108–46). *Gilmore Girls* episodes, indeed entire seasons of the series, progress based on principles of editorial juxtaposition, as the narration returns to the same spaces, characters, and storylines repeatedly. As in most television series, many sequences in *Gilmore Girls* rely on the presumption of simultaneity through crosscutting, implying the fusion of causality with succession. Greg M. Smith describes a multiplot social network as "a truly interdependent community of people whose destinies are interwoven through an alternative form of cause-and-effect" (1995, 89). In television fiction, crosscutting is therefore essential to the producers' attempt to continually propel the narrative while forming causal, social, and thematic connections between disparate scenes.

So as to illustrate the above principles, I shall briefly outline the pattern of narrative development in a relatively typical episode. There are three main storylines in "Kill Me Now" (1.03), which are all causally interconnected. In the primary storyline, Rory goes to a country club in Hartford with her grandfather Richard to learn golf, and Lorelai becomes jealous. In the second storyline, Lorelai hosts a wedding between two sets of twins at the Independence Inn in Stars Hollow. In the third storyline, Sookie and Jackson fight over fresh produce deliveries. The first four scenes take place in Richard and Emily's house at a regular Friday-night dinner. The scenes are defined by significant ellipses of time, yet collectively they form a linear temporal sequence. The substance of the episode (ten of twenty-one scenes) takes place in two settings simultaneously: scenes alternate between Rory playing golf at the country club and Lorelai preparing for the wedding at the Independence Inn. During this crosscut sequence, Lorelai twice mentions that her daughter is currently playing golf with her father, reinforcing the contemporaneous temporality. The broader framework of crosscutting between Stars Hollow and Hartford continues, but it is also put to use within one world. One scene shows Rory and Richard walking back from the golf course, the next scene shows Richard in the men's steam room, and the following scene shows Rory in the women's steam room. The sequentially emplotted steam-room scenes can be taken as instances of crosscut simultaneity.

The broader separation between Stars Hollow and Hartford helps to organize the different characters and storylines. The wedding storyline and the vegetable storyline both transpire entirely in Stars Hollow, the former at the inn. The greatest narrative significance and causal consequence is accorded to the primary storyline by the complexity of its character and setting. It is rooted largely in Hartford but develops outward from the Gilmore mansion to the country club and is later discussed back in Stars Hollow. The budding relationship between Sookie and Jackson appears only toward the beginning and end of this episode, but is pursued later in the season. The storylines and characters never separate neatly into groups from Hartford and groups from Stars Hollow, though the complex interweaving of scenes in distinct worlds helps the audience understand their causal significance. Further, this binary oscillation between spaces creates a never-ending pattern of narrative progression.

The use of crosscutting highlights *Gilmore Girls*' interesting twist on class commentary mentioned previously. The two-world schism so prevalent throughout the series presents us with ostensibly dissimilar environments marked by either class privilege (Hartford, Chilton, Yale) or egalitarian values (Stars Hollow) in regular and powerful contrast. However, this juxtaposition is complicated by the tension between spatial separation and integration. Although the basic plot of Lorelai rejecting her privileged upbringing in favor of Stars Hollow might appear to promote dangerous notions of class as individual choice, the importance of crosscutting produces a continual and dynamic interplay between different settings and social strata. The spaces of class difference contrast in some ways, but they are also connected and equally valued in the narrative through the "un-hierarchised" present tenses. In *Gilmore Girls,* class difference is regularly highlighted, and class boundaries are represented as the product of complex processes of social and cultural imbrication.

Gilmore Girls presents multiple characters in clustered networks, centered on family, workplace, and geography. These lines of demarcation for fictional social networks may have a lot in common with the way audiences' lived experiences are fragmented, split into distinct tasks that coincide with particular hours of the day, but they are also entrenched in the conventions of television fiction. Most television fiction series rely on one or two of these demarcations, which are strongly connected to genre conventions. For example, a daytime drama like *Days of Our Lives* (NBC, 1965–) draws a geographic boundary around the town of Salem and organizes characters into family groups within this circumscribed setting. Sitcoms ranging from *M*A*S*H* (CBS, 1972–83) to *Just Shoot Me* (CBS, 1997–2003) center on social networks within a single stratified workplace. Although we probably think about these character clusters or social networks as sites of interpersonal contact and communication, they are also spatial markers. Prime-time dramas from *Dallas* (CBS, 1978–91) to *The O.C.* (WB/FOX, 2003–7) are named after the cities or towns on which the action centers. Families are located in homes; colleagues are located in workplaces. The hybrid generic form of *Gilmore Girls,* which is both a family melodrama and a workplace comedy, is reflected in the diversity of character relationships and settings.

Gilmore Girls uses conventions from multiple generic registers and traditions to draw characters and their spaces together around family, workplace, and geography. Spatial demarcation is important for organizing social interaction, as well as for plotting out narrative developments. In *Gilmore Girls,* the geographic separation of characters into two distinct worlds allows for the crosscutting between several parallel stories, as well as for thematic reverberation and the elaboration of issues related to spatial and social mobility. In addition, the communities of *Gilmore Girls* are themselves made up of several inner spheres or substrata of social relations, which allow for patterns of crosscutting within each world. Within Stars Hollow there is a public sphere, centered on the town square and Luke's Diner; a professional sphere, consisting of the Independence Inn and then the Dragonfly Inn; and a private sphere, principally Lorelai's house. The oscillation between these interconnected contact zones (where friends and family members often congregate) organizes the multiple characters and storylines in each episode and drives the narrative forward.

In the early seasons of *Gilmore Girls,* there are two key spheres in Hartford: the private arena of the Gilmore mansion and the workplace areas found at Chilton. These two spheres are repeatedly linked to form a coherent world: when Rory and Lorelai are first seen at Chilton, Emily is already waiting in the office of her friend, Headmaster Charleston ("The Lorelais' First Day at Chilton"). In early episodes, Chilton and the Gilmore mansion tend to be featured only when stories directly affect Lorelai and Rory, indeed chiefly through the duo's presence there for school activities and Friday-night dinners, respectively. Chilton soon develops into another enclave filled with major-minor characters, including classmates Paris, Madeleine, Louise, and Tristan and teacher Max Medina, while the Gilmore mansion supplies only the running joke of a new maid every episode. In later seasons the world of Hartford is spatially and socially expanded through the addition of further settings, including the country club, Richard's insurance business, and the social events of Emily's beloved Daughters of the American Revolution (DAR). As the world of Hartford expands, so too does its close causal connection to Lorelai and Rory also begin to loosen, allowing Emily and Richard more independent storylines.

Within the distinct worlds of Stars Hollow and Hartford, social spheres divide the space further to promote crosscut storylines around work, school, family, and friends. The series maintains a focus on Stars Hollow by always locating at least one story strand per episode in the town, often focusing on the many local rituals and festivals, like the picnic-basket auction for charity ("A-Tisket, a-Tasket" [2.13]), the "Festival of Living Art" (4.07), the Easter-egg hunt ("Tick, Tick, Tick, Boom!" [4.18]), and Revolutionary War reenactments ("Love and War and Snow" [1.08] and "Women of Questionable Morals" [5.11]). The multiple, competing social spheres are especially highlighted when Rory and Lorelai are forced to take part in four Thanksgiving dinners: Mrs. Kim's, Luke's, Sookie's, and the elder Gilmores' ("A Deep-Fried Korean Thanksgiving" [3.09]).

The show's habitual recourse to crosscutting gains complexity season to season. Rory's move to college in Season Four is the impetus for a major change in the role of telecommunications, and the interplay of space, character and story in *Gilmore Girls.* Lorelai has a cell phone in the first season; it is a token of her physical and social mobility. Luke's prohibition on cell phone use in his diner is emblematic of his own contrasting immobility. When Rory moves to Yale in Season Four, Lorelai and Rory begin regular telephone conversations and within a few episodes these calls are mobile. Even Luke gets a cell phone immediately after his romantic relationship with Lorelai begins to bloom, though he still does not know how to use voice mail ("Pulp Friction" [5.17]). As Lorelai tells her techno-illiterate beau, "You have got to learn how to use this thing, because it is very powerful and wonderful, and it could change your life."

The representation of phone calls—cellular calls in particular—increases the use and intricacy of crosscutting in *Gilmore Girls.* Editing therefore becomes not just a means to juxtapose a number of scenes into compelling, dynamically composed storylines but also a strategy through which to organize individual shots within a scene. The more frequent representation of phone calls in *Gilmore Girls* from Season Four forward considerably increases the use of this editing strategy. Indeed, the iconographic foregrounding of cellular phones in contemporary dramas, sci-fi series, and action-adventure programs can be seen as a way to provide narrative motivation for the increased proliferation of intercut scenes and situations, something apparent in "high-tech" series like *The X-Files* (FOX, 1993–2002), *Alias* (ABC, 2001–6), and *24* (FOX, 2001–).

It is important to point out that intercutting complicates the practice of crosscutting: the simultaneous passing of time in two different places is not merely assumed but marked by common dialogue. Intercutting necessitates the revision of traditional definitions of basic terms like *scene* and *event,* as it becomes difficult to define the temporal and spatial continuity of each audiovisual "block" of narrative information. Although Bordwell's definition of a scene ostensibly allows for crosscutting ("consistently intermittent duration" [1985, 158]), the bounds of classic narrative form are challenged by serial television's excessive use of intercutting and crosscutting. This strategy is also prominent in the series *24,* which relies heavily on mobile phones to both actualize and legitimize an unusual real-time temporal setup. From the fourth season of *Gilmore Girls* forward, intercutting is frequently used to bridge the worlds of Stars Hollow and Hartford within a single scene, forming a new kind of narrative merger. A good example is the pre-title-sequence teaser scene in the episode "How Many Kropogs to Cape Cod?" (5.20). The shots flit between Rory sitting silently on the phone in her dorm room and Lorelai sitting silently in her kitchen, phone in hand, before wide shots reveal that they are both watching their Roombas (automatic vacuum-cleaning robots). Finally, Lorelai asks, "So is this more or less fun than watching the same TV show at the same time?" Although the space is rendered discontinuous through a dual presence, it seems to be one scene, with one conversation being shared by close yet physically distant speakers. Significantly, telephony is not a substitute for a genuine face-to-face relationship, as demonstrated when both mother and daughter break down after an entire episode of voice-mail and e-mail interaction ("The Incredible Shrinking Lorelais").

The fact that there is no neutral social space in *Gilmore Girls* sustains the idea of a binary geography and perpetual narrative cycle, propelled by crosscutting. All the settings represented throughout the series "belong" to one of the main characters. Characters possess space in the obvious and common sense of Lorelai owning a house and Luke owning a diner (a reconditioned hardware store that had belonged to his father). More important, however, is the metaphoric ownership of much larger spaces: Stars Hollow is Lorelai's space; Hartford is Richard and Emily's space. Lorelai is at home in her living room, at Luke's diner, or at the Black, White, and Red movie theater. The senior Gilmores seem to own most of Hartford, literally and metaphorically: Emily reminds a nurse at the Hartford hospital that her family portrait hangs in the lobby ("Forgiveness and Stuff" [1.10]). The narration alternates between these separate worlds, but it does not blur them. Discounting occasional excursions, everything in *Gilmore Girls* occurs either in the cozy, quirky world of Stars Hollow (with Kirk, Luke Taylor, Gypsy, Babette, and the other lovable "oddballs" in attendance) or in the affluent, rarefied world of Richard and Emily, the DAR, and the Huntzbergers. The main characters constantly move between these two zones, and crosscutting integrates the settings into a single textual universe (the above-mentioned "*Gilmore*verse"). As the series progresses, increased intercutting strengthens this motif and adds greater complexity. Representing two social and spatial worlds through such editing tactics ensures an infinitely replenishable narrative.

"Relationships Need Verbs": Giving the Gilmore Boys Their Due

This formal analysis of narrative construction is intended to contribute to a broader understanding of the central tension between spatial separation and integration at the heart of *Gilmore Girls.* This tension is played out chiefly through the peregrinations of Lorelai and Rory, but also through the movements of minor characters in the two communities. The girls' main squeezes are constantly challenged by their social and spatial mobility. Specifically, Lorelai and Rory repeatedly form relationships with men firmly rooted in their respective worlds (Stars Hollow or Hartford), and then disparage them for an inability to negotiate the other sphere of social contact. As Lorelai explains to Rory in "Scenes in a Mall" (4.15), "Relationships need verbs." The Gilmore girls' boys are expected to have not just verbs but also the implied action or motion associated with that kind of word. The girls thus require that the boys be every bit as socially and spatially mobile as they are.

Lorelai has a string of Hartford-based boyfriends, namely, Rory's father, Christopher; Rory's teacher Max Medina; and Richard's business partner, Jason Stiles. Each of these potentially lasting, eventually hamstrung, relationships fails because the men have trouble fitting in to Lorelai's beloved Stars Hollow. Lorelai wants her boyfriends to go places with her (Martha's Vineyard, Paris, and so forth), and notably hits the road when it does not work out with Max ("The Road Trip to Harvard" [2.04]). Rory's first boyfriend, Dean, bows out of the running for her affections by acknowledging his inability to survive socially in Hartford ("The Party's Over" [5.08]). Other minor characters are similarly challenged by the spatial negotiation that the Gilmore girls demand daily. For example, Richard and Emily are so challenged in this regard that they cannot even follow the instruction of their car's global positioning system and must call Lorelai for directions ("I'm OK, You're OK" [6.17]).

The immobility of Lorelai's main love interest, Luke, appears to be so deeply entrenched as to create a roadblock in their relationship. Luke was born in Stars Hollow, still lives there, and works in his father's old shop. Sookie quips that they will probably have to bury him in the diner ("Concert Interruptus" [1.13]). When Luke goes on a cruise with Nicole and comes back married, we never actually see it; we never even see him depart for vacation and arrive home ("Ballrooms and Biscotti" [4.01]). This point is significant because it distances the viewer from these story developments, and also because it represents Luke and Nicole's relationship as both secondary and ill-fated. Luke's stasis is a niggling issue in his relationship with Lorelai. For example, on their visit to Martha's Vineyard, Lorelai explains

Luke's uncomfortable behavior: "He's just not much of a traveler, so it's all kind of foreign to him" ("A Vineyard Valentine" [6.15]).

Significantly, Luke reluctantly becomes more mobile through his relationship with Lorelai. Immediately after Luke and Lorelai get together romantically, Luke is seen traveling with his sister Liz and the Renaissance Faire in Maine ("Say Goodbye to Daisy Miller" [5.01]). Luke's developing mobility shows character development and signifies greater success in the terms set by the Gilmore girls; however, it also threatens his relationship with Lorelai. When Luke's daughter, April, arrives on the scene in Season Six, he begins to visit her regularly in Woodbury and even travels to Philadelphia with her ("The Real Paul Anka" [6.18]). After Luke and Lorelai break up, Luke's sister Liz comments on the significant point that Luke and Lorelai never moved in together: "You were in two different places" ("That's What You Get, Folks, for Makin' Whoopee" [7.02]). Initially, Luke's immobility represents a lack of adjustment to Lorelai's lifestyle, but as Luke grows, his increasing mobility makes him more independent, alienating him from Lorelai. When Luke and Lorelai get back together at the end of the series, the issue of Luke's mobility is again raised by Caesar's suggestion that Luke may not be so firmly rooted in his diner after all.

Jess, Rory's boyfriend throughout much of Season Three, represents a special case in this scenario. Jess is chiefly shown in Stars Hollow, though he repeatedly asserts his rejection of the small town, and his repudiation of Hartford is equally emphatic. In truth, Jess does not fit in anywhere, save for an independent bookshop or a park bench in Manhattan, and in the tradition of Nicholas Ray's classic tale of teenage angst, *Rebel Without a Cause* (1955), he does not want to. As the outsider, Jess harks back to the conventional figure of mediation from Hollywood's earlier rites of order, such as the western and gangster genres (Schatz 1981, 34–35). However, since the Gilmore girls play the role of the integrative couple themselves, Jess's outsider status does not fulfill the conventional cultural functions associated with those genres. Moreover, Jess effectively highlights the duality and limits of the Gilmore girls' spatial mobility: they are only *really* mobile between a few predictable spaces. In the early seasons, Jess is actually seen in places farther afield than any other character: the camera intermittently cuts to him in New York City ("Lorelai's Graduation Day" [2.21]) and Venice Beach, California ("Here Comes the Son" [3.21]). Jess seems to be able to make a home anywhere, but his lack of roots is ultimately a stumbling block for his relationship with Rory. When Jess finally proclaims his love for Rory ("Last Week Fights, This Week Tights" [4.21]), she rejects him specifically because (as she later tells Lane) he could not offer her a stable, alternative space ("Raincoats and Recipes" [4.22]).

Within this context of social and spatial mobility, the depiction of travel in *Gilmore Girls* reveals the complexity of spatial representation, narrative organization, and audience engagement. The constant alternation between scenes in Stars Hollow and Hartford means that we seldom see spaces beyond these two worlds, and many settings outside Connecticut exist only as places evoked in dialogue rather than through visual depiction. For example, we never see Lane's summer vacation in South Korea ("Sadie, Sadie" [2.01]), nor do we witness any highlights from Richard and Emily's trip to Switzerland ("The Nanny and the Professor" [4.10]). Rory and Lorelai's much discussed birthday celebration in Atlantic City is noticeably absent ("The Perfect Dress" [6.11]). Surely, this limitation in visualizing trips outside the hermetically enclosed spaces of *Gilmore Girls* is because of budgetary constraints, as the representation of unfamiliar places becomes more frequent and adventurous toward the end of the series (when a slightly larger budget allowed for the depiction of Paris and other sites of interest). However, this absence is significant because it denies the viewer direct engagement with particular story developments.

On the other hand, we do see Rory, Lorelai, and Paris go to New York for the Bangles concert ("Concert Interruptus"), Rory spending a portion of the summer in Washington, D.C., with Paris ("Those Lazy-Hazy-Crazy Days" [3.01]), and Lorelai's trip to France with Christopher ("French Twist" [7.07]). All of these travels allow for present-tense storylines (as opposed to flashbacks), with crosscutting between Stars Hollow and the new "other" space exacerbating the either-or tension of the series. Once again, this point is important because it connects the thematic significance of events with their narrative and spatial construction. Yet the representation of other settings is inconsistent. For example, when Rory and Lorelai spend the summer in Europe, the only thing we see is the airport shuttle outside their home in Stars Hollow, but when Rory and Emily go to Europe, we see them in hotel rooms and cafés, making small talk with Italian men. This inconsistency pinpoints a crucial connection: the series' thematic treatment of space is influenced by the formal construction of story and space. Social and spatial mobility thus "means more" in the narrative when it affects the way we, the audience, engage with the characters.

On the surface, Logan, Rory's boyfriend from Season Five onward, seems to contrast her former beaus Dean and Jess. Logan apparently represents a highly mobile lifestyle. As an ultrarich playboy, he has unparalleled access to transportation: he loans Rory a car and driver ("Say Something" [5.14]) and flits around in a private helicopter ("I'd Rather Be in Philadelphia" [7.13]). However, Logan's mobility is more notional than actual, as it is rarely realized on-screen. We never see his boys-only jaunts to Costa Rica ("Super Cool Party People" [6.20]) and Las Vegas ("Will You Be My Lorelai Gilmore?" [7.16]), though he is sometimes seen living and working in London, New York, and California. Logan seems more comfortable with his girlfriend's social and spatial mobility than previous partner Dean, though he still enters into conflict with Rory when he wants her to settle down with him. Logan's mobility is largely illusory, and his acceptance of Rory's mobility is ultimately limited and self-serving. Like other minor characters in *Gilmore Girls,* Logan both supports the core spatial tension and highlights Rory's and Lorelai's exceptional mobility.

"Do the 'Going-Off-to-College Walk'": Expanding Narrative Worlds

Thematically, *Gilmore Girls* ratchets the tension between spatial separation and integration through the developing lives of two women. This tension is formally reinforced by a narrative strategy of crosscutting, which, as argued earlier, structures every episode. In the first three seasons, *Gilmore Girls* is chiefly about Lorelai trying to reconcile her place between two worlds: her past and her present, her actual family and her chosen family. There is a significant change in the series when Rory moves from Stars Hollow to college at the beginning of the fourth season. Taylor, Stars Hollow town selectman, anticipates the change that this departure signals: "I should have figured that once you got into Yale, everything would be different. . . . You're no longer our little Stars Hollow Rory Gilmore. You belong to the Ivy Leagues right now. It's time to cut those small-town ties and go off and do something important" ("Ballrooms and Biscotti"). With Rory's move to Yale, the show gradually shifts to focus more heavily on Rory's struggle to reconcile her liminal place between Stars Hollow and Hartford. In this sense, *Gilmore Girls* becomes a more conventional coming-of-age tale. Rory's move to college is a logical development of the central theme of dislocation established in early seasons. It also extends the spatial and social networks of the series significantly, producing further narrative progression and expansion.

Rory's move from Stars Hollow to Yale is interesting within the context of teen TV. When young characters graduate from high school, teenage-centered television programs often take a precarious narrative turn. A study of recent television dramas reveals two trends for handling young characters' tumultuous transition from high school to college. First, most series practice harm minimization by incorporating college within the established setting. In this case, characters inevitably give up their Ivy-League dreams and usually choose to continue living at home (unlike in most teen films, which focus on the emancipatory aspects of leaving the nest). For example, the major characters in *Beverly Hills 90210* (FOX, 1990–2000) all wind up at California University, the same institutional destination for the characters in *Saved by the Bell: The College Years* (NBC, 1993–94). Similarly, most of the main characters in *Buffy the Vampire Slayer* enroll at the local college, UC Sunnydale, after their high school graduation in the same small town, and most characters gradually move back home to the houses they formerly inhabited. Second, some teen-centered television series use the move to college to motivate a major change in the direction of the unfolding narrative, introducing a raft of new settings, characters, relationships, and storylines. For example, in the *Cosby* spin-off *A Different World* (NBC, 1987–93) and the *Degrassi High* telemovie *School's Out* (1992), high school graduation inspires radical changes in the diegesis. *Dawson's Creek* (WB, 1998–2003) sends major characters to opposite coasts, which is just the beginning of the changes that ensue.

Within the context of these two different trends, *Gilmore Girls* negotiates the transition to college in an unusual way. In fact, Rory's move to college in Season Four has more in common with Meadow's complex negotiation of place and identity in Season Three of *The Sopranos* (HBO, 1999–2007) onward, when the teenage girl moves from her family home in suburban New Jersey to Columbia University. As is the case with so many teen TV characters, Rory gives up her dream college, Harvard, in favor of one closer to home. However, unlike most TV freshman, Rory attends not a fictional college but the real university of Yale. This transition is more complex than what viewers witness in conventional teen TV, since Rory has well-established connections in two worlds. Yale is located in New Haven, around 40 miles from the real city of Hartford and fictionally 22.8 miles from Stars Hollow, as Jess reported he discovered on Yahoo! ("Happy Birthday, Baby" [3.18]). So, technically, while living at Yale Rory is geographically closer to her mother in Stars Hollow than her grandparents in Hartford. However, the university's reputation as an old, moneyed institution associates it generally with the senior Gilmores of Hartford, and this specific connection is drawn through Rory's grandfather Richard, a proud Yale alumnus. In fact, Yale draws on other elements of the preestablished Hartford world, as Rory's high school friend Paris conveniently turns up as Rory's dorm roommate. In addition, Rory brings characters from Stars Hollow to Yale with her, if only temporarily: Lorelai stays the first night in her dorm with Rory, and best friend Lane stays for a few weeks, bringing the feeling of Stars Hollow with her. Therefore, Yale might be seen as a newly developed world, drawing on elements of both previous worlds.

The setting of Yale develops its own network of spaces, including the dorm suite, classrooms, the dining hall, coffee carts, the newsroom, and later Paris's dilapidated apartment, Logan's posh apartment, and the bar. Around these specific settings, networks of characters emerge: Rory's roommates and friends, like Janet, Tanna, and Marty, converge around the dorm; Rory's colleagues at the *Yale Daily News,* including Doyle, Glenn, and Logan, assemble in the newsroom; Logan and his friends Colin and Finn later gather in his apartment and the bar. In this way, the setting of Yale develops a social and spatial complexity rivaled in the series only by Stars Hollow. Hartford, on the other hand, is so centered on the Gilmore mansion that it has not developed such complexity, even after the later addition of a pool house. In effect, Yale develops its own social microcosm composed of characters of different types (friends, love interests, light comic relief). Yale thus extends the *Gilmore*verse with new settings, characters, and storylines, adding narrative energy to the well-established patterns of the series.

Given this complexity, Yale may be seen as a third space, expanding the world of *Gilmore Girls* beyond its formerly dyadic geography. Indeed, Yale does break down some of the binary oppositions represented by the two worlds of Stars Hollow and Hartford. If Hartford represents the past and Stars Hollow the present, then Yale would thus seem to represent the future: it is the scene of Rory's coming of age, her maturation into a young woman. While moving into her dorm suite, Rory declares it "my own space" ("The Lorelais' First Day at Yale" [4.02]). However, as suggested above, in some ways Yale is simply an extension of Hartford. The relationship between Richard and Yale is reinforced and brought into the present when Rory attends his lectures in economics in Season Seven ("To Whom It May Concern" [7.12]). The social circles also intermingle through Logan, who goes to Yale with Rory and knows the Gilmores through the Hartford upper class. Of course, her rivalry and growing friendship with Paris retain the connection to Chilton, as do storylines about the school paper. In a sense, the world of Hartford has simply expanded, colonizing new narrative spaces. Perhaps Yale is merely a replacement of Chilton in the world of Hartford, just as the Dragonfly is simply a replacement of the Independence Inn in the world of Stars Hollow. Ultimately, Yale represents both tradition and choice, a university Rory eventually chose over her long-cherished dream of Harvard precisely because she wanted to maintain her family connections. In this way, Yale pushes the established boundaries of the series but does not radically break with the dyadic geography of its earlier seasons.

As Rory struggles to find her place in this complex geography, she is briefly swallowed whole by Hartford in Season Six. Emily—whose nickname among society matrons (we learn in "Eight O'Clock at the Oasis" [3.05]) is "the Cobra"—perversely seizes the opportunity of Rory's arrest and conflict with her mother to arrange for her to be gradually absorbed into the world of Hartford. First she moves into the pool house, then into the main mansion (in the span of episodes between "A House Is Not a Home" [5.22] and "Let Me Hear Your Balalaikas Ringing Out" [6.08]). She is further embedded in Emily's social world when she takes a part-time job organizing fund-raisers for the DAR ("We've Got Magic to Do" [6.05]). Interestingly, while Rory and Lorelai are estranged, this promotes a convenient structure for crosscutting regularly between each Gilmore girl in her respective town. However, it is difficult to sustain crosscutting between characters and plots without causal connections between the story strands, so each Gilmore girl maintains some relationships with characters in both worlds. When Rory finally emerges, Alice-like, from the long, dark rabbit hole of Hartford, she reenrolls at Yale and eagerly reconnects with her mother. Rory's brief experience within the nucleus of Hartford, and her return to Yale, reaffirms that this space is, indeed, her own.

The tension between spatial separation and integration continues throughout the *Gilmore Girls*. Like a narrative frontier, the progression of the series seems tied to the expansion of its community of characters beyond Stars Hollow. This expansion initially incorporates the world of Hartford into the lives of the Gilmore girls, and after three seasons it mutates to also include the world of Yale. The central thematic concern with the colliding worlds of Stars Hollow and

Hartford is reflected in the corresponding narrative form, particularly in the spatial tension inherent in a narrative driven by crosscutting. The thematic focus on the integration of separate worlds develops and changes through the progression of the series, becoming more complicated and ambiguous with Rory's move to college. Ultimately, Rory's spatial mobility develops beyond her mother's two worlds, as the former builds complex, independent relationships with new spaces and characters beyond the latter's gravitational pull.

The final season reinforces the close relationship between Lorelai and Rory, as well as their differences in terms of emerging character identity, spatial mobility, and narrative drive. The limitation of Lorelai's spatial and social mobility is confirmed when her Jeep breaks down: Lorelai is advised to buy a new car, and even goes car shopping with Luke, but finally spends just as much money fixing the old Jeep ("It's Just Like Riding a Bike" [7.19]). This decision highlights the way that Lorelai ensures that her spatial and social mobility does not extend beyond her comfort zone. Meanwhile, Rory's fate in the final episodes launches her on an adventurously mobile course: "The planes, the buses, the whole deal," as she states in "Bon Voyage" (7.22). Rory refuses to be tied down by Logan and the diamond ring and avocado tree he offers her, opting instead for a writing job, which promises to take her around the country following the presidential campaign of Barack Obama. This move at once fulfills the ambitiously mobile trajectory Rory has been following from the first episode and sets her on a new path, leading outside her two cherished worlds and making her even less dependent on her family. Unfortunately, this promise of mobility is not fulfilled for the audience, who leave the girls at the end of the series in the same place they started: Luke's Diner.

"You've Always Been the Head Pilgrim Girl"

Stars Hollow as the Embodiment of the American Dream

ALYSON R. BUCKMAN

In the series finale of *Gilmore Girls,* town selectman Taylor Doose states—in a nausea-provoking analogy that goes into excruciating detail—that Stars Hollow has "birthed" Rory Gilmore and is now sending the young woman on her way into the world, just as we, the viewers, must let go of our girls.[1] Disturbing though Taylor's analogy might be for many viewers, it is an apt one. Stars Hollow *has* functioned as a womblike environment for Lorelai Gilmore and her daughter, Rory, one that has sustained yet also sheltered the series' protagonists for several years. Raised in Hartford, Connecticut, and giving birth to Rory there, Lorelai rejected her family's aristocratic heritage and expectations in favor of this small hamlet located some thirty miles away, a community of eccentric characters that took in the sixteen-year-old single mother and her infant daughter and fostered the duo's own eccentricities. Although viewers were privy to only the last seven years of Lorelai and Rory's development (discounting

1. Taylor rhapsodizes, "We are gathered here on this glorious spring day pregnant with pride and anticipation. Preparing to birth you from our collective womb, fully gestated, and nourished, and so we breathe deep and with these last painful contractions, we push you out into the world, spank your bottom, and wipe the amniotic fluid from your eyes, as you issue your first independent breath." This description rivals the one that occurs in "Let the Games Begin" (3.08), when a discombobulated Kirk says he is "shaking like a spastic colon" after losing his dance trophy.

the occasional flashback episode, such as "Dear Emily and Richard" [3.13]), the town of Stars Hollow beckoned to us as well.

I am not alone among *Gilmore Girls* fans when I say that, throughout much of the show's broadcast history, I wanted to live in Stars Hollow. And why not? After all, it had everything: beautiful landscapes, charming buildings, quirky townspeople, a sense of community, an intelligent populace that valued education and small businesses over monolithic box stores and sewage-treatment plants, and a predilection for pedestrian rather than automotive traffic. The names of such disparate authors as Dylan Thomas, Jane Austin, and Jack Kerouac are dropped into everyday conversations with the expectation that both community members and TV viewers will know who they are. Like Senator Barbara Boxer before her ("Those Lazy-Hazy-Crazy Days," 3.01), former U.S. Secretary of State Madeleine Albright has passed through town, albeit in spectral form, as Rory's dream incarnation of Lorelai in "Twenty-one Is the Loneliest Number" (6.07). A very real flesh-and-blood Norman Mailer visits the Dragonfly, just long enough for Sookie to scare him off ("Norman Mailer, I'm Pregnant!" [5.06]). Men are judged—and sometimes found wanting—according to their quickness of wit and their ability to make sense of pop culture and literary references, whether they are to the aforementioned Beat poet Kerouac, Hollywood writer and actress Ruth Gordon, Charles Dickens's character the Artful Dodger, Rod Serling's *Twilight Zone* (CBS, 1959–64), British alternative rocker P. J. Harvey, or that staple of Eisenhower-era domesticity, Donna Reed.

Pedestrian traffic also is valued in Stars Hollow. Almost everything is within walking distance in Stars Hollow—everything except for Richard and Emily Gilmore's palatial home, Chilton Academy, and the university that Rory eventually chooses, Yale. Unlike these latter comparatively distant spaces, Stars Hollow feels like a cherished home; it is friendly, supportive, community oriented, personality enriched, tolerant, and agreeable to the eye.[2]

2. Jill Winters likens Stars Hollow to a snow globe, arguing that the community is static and content to remain as it is; with the exception of Lorelai and Rory, the townspeople are "contented snowflakes" (2007, 103).

It is also rooted in place, deriving meaning from its material and social existence.[3] Its history, geography, educational system, and political forms; its proximity to larger towns, such as New York and Boston, and Ivy League schools; its position on the East Coast; its demographics; and its status as small town rather than suburb all create a very specific tenor for the town, one that, in combination with other narrative elements, results in a very particular enunciation of the American Dream. Although other fictional settings have also functioned as symbolic embodiments of said dream,[4] Stars Hollow's relationship with that dream is rooted specifically in the history and culture of New England.[5] In addition to positioning the town within a larger New England setting, the creators of the show also took pains to create a sense of place for Stars Hollow beyond the geographic, historical, and cultural imaginary. Amy Sherman-Palladino and Dan Palladino created a sense of rootedness and attachment to the place among the various characters, a sense of belonging that extends to the audience as well.

Place is not only an object, a specific space in which one finds oneself and others; it also informs the ways in which we look at the world and conceive of our identities. Place connotes geographic location, material

3. Although Amy Sherman-Palladino originally got the idea for the setting of Stars Hollow from Washington Depot, Connecticut, ironically enough the locale in which the pilot episode was shot is not in New England, nor even in the United States. The pilot was filmed on Main Street in Unionville, Ontario, Canada. However, the way the town is conceived, populated, and historicized marks it as distinctively "New England."

4. This symbolism is true, for example, of many of Frank Capra's films. For an excellent analysis of the contours of this representation in one classic example (*It's a Wonderful Life* [1946]), see Costello 1999.

5. Jim Cullen points out that there are several American Dreams, from the dream of religious tolerance of the Puritans in the seventeenth century to the dreams of civil rights and unabated consumption in the twentieth century. Stars Hollow's American Dream is linked to material success, although one might also discuss Rory's dreams of leaving the Hollow, a dream that depends on gains in rights for women. However, clearly the show is not depicting anything close to a dream of racial equality. Instead, we are presented with a very white, middle-class American Dream.

and social existence, attachment, rootedness, the accretion of time, and the relationships among the humans who occupy it (Cresswell 2004, 7, 21–22). Place may also be conceived in relationship to consciousness; one's subjectivity is tied to one's place in the world, including social and economic standing as well as geographic location. It involves taking time to rest, to pause, to belong (Tuan 2001, 149). It is through place and our situated relatedness to others that we are able to comprehend the world (Cresswell 2004, 11, 12). All of these dimensions of the meaning of place are present in the construction of Stars Hollow as setting.

The opening shot of *Gilmore Girls* goes a long way toward establishing Stars Hollow as not only place but as integral character. We start off with an aerial view of a church steeple, then the camera pans vertically past the skyline (with yet another church in view) until our vision is taken to street level. We see a boy on a skateboard and several people walking, one of whom is a woman. The frame of the mobile image shifts left at street level to show the town sign: "Stars Hollow, founded 1779." At this point, the woman walks out of the frame to the right. The only clue that she, rather than the town itself, might be the focal point in this scene is the song "There She Goes," which begins as a black card announces the title of the show.

The camera soon follows this as yet unnamed brunette, crossing the street behind her and following her into Luke's Diner. At this point, we quickly learn not only about this character but also about the place she inhabits. Lorelai is a caffeine junkie who carries enough flavored lip gloss to stop a truck in its tracks, steals her daughter's CDs, and is attractive to young men who find it unbelievable that this lovely creature is Rory's mother as well. Gruffly tolerant of his customer, Luke treats Lorelai as most in this town do: like a stray cat they've taken in and learned to love. (Lorelai would no doubt hate this comparison.)

In this brief yet telling opening sequence, we learn that this place is a small town where everyone seems to know their neighbors, where Lorelai and her daughter feel comfortable and loved, and where an array of eccentric personalities also reside. In addition to Luke's Diner and the main drag of the hamlet that is visible from its windows, we are soon introduced to Lorelai's house, her place of employment (the Independence Inn), and her parents' residence in Hartford. However, this main street is where the audience will spend most of its time in Stars Hollow, especially throughout the first five seasons. A fundamentally important aspect of this opening sequence is that the main character is placed within a community: we see Stars Hollow first and then see Lorelai in relationship to the town—to its streets and then to the diner, a hub of the community. We focus not on meaningless space but rather on an individual situated within a meaningful place. This focus is true for the credits as well, which begin with an even higher aerial view of a quaint New England church and steeple situated in the autumn foliage for which New England is known and then cut to scenes of the main characters in *Gilmore Girls*. Character and place are thus constructed from the very beginning of the show as interdependent.

Stars Hollow thus functions as a meaningful place both to those characters who inhabit it and to the viewers who enter it through the mobile gaze of the camera. We seem to be within Stars Hollow, personally encountering not only the characters but also the places deemed important by the narrative economy. The camera creates the appearance of intimate spaces and groupings; we generally experience a personal proxemic with Lorelai, Rory, and many of the other townsfolk through medium shots, meaning that extradiegetic audiences are positioned diegetically, as if they could talk with the characters themselves from a distance of a few feet. Often, characters are clustered in twos and threes, allowing us to feel as if we are gathered around a table or bellied up to the counter at Luke's Diner or sitting on the couch or at the kitchen table with Lorelai and Rory. Conversely, we find ourselves more frequently at a social proxemic in the Gilmore residence, with the camera keeping Richard and Emily at a distance from us just as they are distant from Lorelai.[6] The editing functions to

6. For instance, the director of the pilot episode, Lesli Linka Glatter, notes that she purposely kept the camera fluid and energetic for the Stars Hollow scenes while reverting to a more static and "presentational" look for the scenes shot in

create meaning within place as well. Cutting back and forth between characters with a shot–reverse shot structure, a technique that creates division among characters, dominates within the Gilmore parents' home while the visual rhetoric of Stars Hollow tends to include two or three characters within a single shot, creating a sense of unity. Although we are generally positioned inside buildings (settings that enable these intimate tête-à-têtes), when the camera goes outside it generally puts us on the streets of Stars Hollow, greeting passersby, witnessing eccentric behavior, or getting an earful of gossip from Babette, Miss Patty, or both (though it often comes secondhand from Eastside Tillie).

The community is thus constructed as of paramount importance visually and narratively. Indeed, part of the fun associated with Stars Hollow is the sense that one really "knows" the locals. This list includes Patty, the fun-loving and flirtatious dance teacher, and Babette, the slightly ditzy cat lover who lives next door to Lorelai with her oh-so-cool musician husband (Morey, who puts his boots in the washing machine and, modeling himself on saxophone artist Charlie Parker, can't seem to arrive at places late enough, as in "The Bracebridge Dinner" [2.10]). There is Kirk, who has worked at every conceivable business in Stars Hollow, still lives with his mother (his bedroom, we learn, is a refurnished bomb shelter), and owns an attack cat named Kirk; Taylor, a cardigan-wearing neofascist town selectman on a quest to find a tourist-appropriate holiday for every month; Sookie, an accident-prone chef; Jackson, a farmer who sleeps with his zucchini and accidentally winds up with an acre of marijuana ("Driving Miss Gilmore" [6.21]); Mrs. Kim, a Korean Seventh-Day Adventist who loves flaxseed and believes that french fries are "the devil's starchy fingers" ("The Party's Over" [5.08]); and Lane, a closeted drummer who hides CDs from her mother under her floorboards. Despite its title, *Gilmore Girls* does not simply revolve around a single

---

Richard and Emily Gilmore's home ("Welcome to the *Gilmore Girls*" Season One bonus material, part of the DVD set).

family or romantic couples; Stars Hollow is bigger than the Gilmores, the marriage plot, and teen love, and its resonance as a *place* relies on the wacky interactions among the show's many characters. One sign of Season Seven's less than stellar reception was the fact that this much loved social interaction disappeared for several episodes; the troubadour, for instance, simply vanished after he had returned from opening for Neil Young, and the town meetings occurred far less frequently.

This emphasis on community and place in *Gilmore Girls* ties into the construction of Stars Hollow as an embodiment or expression of the American Dream. In addition to recognizing the show's visual rhetoric and narrative economy, which emphasize interpersonal relationships and bucolic environs, we need to also take into consideration the unique sociohistorical geography of Stars Hollow, one that promotes the many cultural aspirations that have surfaced over the past four hundred years and are in some ways specific to the New England area.[7] Jim Cullen discusses the multiple variations of the American Dream, beginning with the Puritans' reliance on religious vision, from which it has morphed multiple times and become much more secular over the years. The American dreams of independence, upward mobility, civil rights, and home ownership (among other things) have taken the place of Puritan dreams, and we see this history in *Gilmore Girls.* The slender thread joining all of these variations upon the Dream is a desire for acquiring more. As Jim Cullen states, "The American dream was never meant to be a zero-sum solution: the goal has always been to end up with more than you started with" (2003, 159). Laurence Shames (2005) concurs, arguing that "the more factor," which is also the title of his essay, is central to American ideals.

The Puritan dream was a dream of building a godly city, one that provided religious freedom to those individuals who believed that the Church of England was corrupt and that a stricter devotional form (in Calvinism) was necessary to worship God. It was not a dream of

7. Stephanie Rowe states, "One of my favorite things about watching *Gilmore Girls* is that it's chock-full of so many reminders of New England" (2007, 107).

generalized religious freedom but a desire for greater religious freedom for *themselves.* They were a chosen people, seeing themselves as analogous to the Israelites, and sought to create a New Eden in the New World. In 1620 Puritan Separatists (Pilgrims) obtained a charter from England granting them the right to settle on land owned by the Virginia Company of London. English investors agreed to finance the trip in return for the shipment of furs, fish, and minerals back to England. Thus, the immigration to the New World by Puritans was marked by religious goals, economic initiatives, and colonization from the beginning. Sixty-five days after leaving England, they sighted land off the coast of Cape Cod, Massachusetts, and—weak from the journey and fearful of a sea voyage on the Atlantic in winter—they disembarked in New England. To bring an end to arguments that their rules for government were void because their charter applied only in Virginia, the Pilgrims created the Mayflower Compact, the first effort to establish formal self-government in the New World. John Winthrop and the Massachusetts Bay Colony followed ten years later, beginning the largest exodus of Puritans to the New World and establishing the center of government at Boston.[8]

A central tenet of Puritan ideology in their move across the Atlantic was that of the covenant. In addition to the covenant into which they had entered with God, they had entered into a covenant with each other. John Winthrop emphasized the need to "be knit together in this work as one man" (2003, 104). Thus, community was a central tenet of their society; although said emphasis also makes practical sense when one considers the conditions in which they found themselves in 1630, the covenant emphasized the community that they formed before God, one that would serve as an example to all other Christians: "For we must consider that we shall be as a city upon a hill. The eyes of

8. *Puritan* refers to those individuals who believed that the Church of England had not cleansed itself enough of its association with Catholicism; further reform was necessary beyond substituting king for pope. Pilgrims went further than those Puritans who believed the church could be purified from within; the former believed that complete separation from the Church of England was necessary.

all people are upon us" (ibid., 105). This covenant found expression in the ways in which they designed their towns, a design that Stars Hollow replicates; the presence of the church and school on Stars Hollow's green is in keeping with its (fictional) history, for instance.

In colonial New England, townships were created in approximately thirty-acre-square lots with a green at the center. New Haven, Connecticut, is the oldest formally planned community in America and is in fairly close proximity to Stars Hollow. A nine-square grid covering a half-mile square, the original settlement of 1641 gave each family in a single-family house its own lot, which was set well back from its boundaries on what would eventually become a lawn. Whereas the eight surrounding squares were divided into house lots, the center square was reserved for the green, upon which the first meetinghouse (the symbolic and literal center of the community), cemetery, town's watch house, jail, and school were placed; it also functioned as a trade center and town square. This schema relied as well on the notion of a contract for godly behavior among the town's citizens; one had to be ever vigilant of one's own conduct and the behavior of others, for if one was not, then God's wrath would be felt. The remaining land was divided so that everyone received portions of land equitable in quality. New inhabitants to the area had to be approved by town authorities, and land could not be sold or rented to someone who had not gone through the approval process. Land distribution was based consciously on the precept of nurturing the community (Simpson 1999, 49; Mackin 2006, 32).

As the developing colonies matured, however, secular life became more important, planting the seeds for a hearty individualism that was nevertheless linked to the ways in which Puritans faced God—and judgment—alone, taking a journey toward justification that often left them with a sense of their isolation in the world. The Puritan American Dream would gradually manifest itself in the myth of hearty individualism, the myth of meritocracy, Manifest Destiny, and other American ideals.[9]

9. Lorelai even drives a Jeep, a brand of vehicle often represented in American popular culture as a rugged form of automobility capable of the feats of Manifest Destiny: control of the terrain through the assertion of skill and will.

Significantly, it is also a very racially constricted dream, an idea that—although beyond the scope of this chapter—is reflected in the pervasive whiteness of Stars Hollow and the producers' use of a few ethnic minorities as exotic "seasoning" for an otherwise racially homogenous town.

Both Puritan and Revolutionary histories are relevant to Stars Hollow in its geography as well as its depiction of an interdependent community that is also watchful of its members, with Taylor playing the role of William Bradford or John Winthrop. Not only does the town's Revolution-era founding—not to mention the appropriately named and doubly signifying Independence Inn, at which Lorelai works prior to her founding of the Dragonfly—mirror our heroine's declaration of independence from her parents, but the history of the town is important in capturing tourist dollars. A tourist's dream, Stars Hollow is home to several antique shops. Thus, the symbolic economy of the town as a tourist destination (and as narrative setting) relies on *selling history*.

Street names as well as the types of stores and products that are made available mostly depend on a specifically Puritan and Revolutionary history or, at least, a sense of nostalgia for a bygone era; these historical aspects interact with the lives of the characters, helping to shape them, to provide humor for the audience, and to situate Stars Hollow as a true place, one that is not only American but specifically New England. Rory plays the head Pilgrim girl at Thanksgiving and participates in the Christmas pageant, citizens engage in knitathons and dance marathons to help pay for the renovation and covering of bridges, and there is a town celebration for every month, even the "lazy-hazy-crazy days" of summer. Such historicity is reinforced by Emily Gilmore's participation in the Daughters of the American Revolution (DAR), her leadership of which helps to provide the elder Gilmore with additional social status.[10] Stars Hollow's symbolic roots

10. It also serves as an organization for which Rory can work during Season Six. In order to be a member of the DAR, one must have documentation that one's ancestor(s) fought in the Revolution; we also know that one of Rory's ancestors came over on the *Mayflower*.

are in the soil that John Winthrop, George Washington, Thomas Jefferson, and Benjamin Franklin tended. It is here where George Washington apparently stopped long enough to blow his nose, as Lorelai reminds Taylor in "Chicken or Beef?" (4.04), adding "the whole town is a historical building."[11]

Community, Geography, Historicity

> TAYLOR: Really, you should try to be more punctual, Lorelai. I banged the meeting in a half hour ago.
>
> —Dialogue in "Dead Uncles and Vegetables" (2.17)

One aspect of the Hollow's reliance on history (whether real or fictional) is the representation of the continuing practice of the town meeting, a centuries-old practice now in danger because of suburbanization and population growth (Nordell 1999, 12; Nifong 1996). As Jane Feuer also argues in this volume, the town meetings mark Stars Hollow as distinctively New England, enabling the sense of covenant first inscribed by Winthrop and Bradford, though under much different terms. In addition to being representative of the American Dream's emphasis on equality and democracy, it is also the source of

11. One might also perceive a critique within the text of the show of Stars Hollow's emphasis on the past. In "Love and War and Snow" (1.08) and "Welcome to the Dollhouse" (6.06), the town is represented as misguided in its celebration of a Revolutionary War that enabled the further decimation of Native Americans and the town's minimal role in said Revolution; the reversion to colonial street names, such as Sores and Boils Alley, which glorify the pain of the past solely to promote tourism; and Taylor's decision to reenact the Boston Tea Party, for which they are still paying fines imposed by the Environmental Protection Agency. Significantly, Rory is leaving Stars Hollow (and has been since she began attending Chilton) for her big future; the American Dream seems to be an excellent place to be nurtured, but one must leave it behind to be successful. There seems to be more than a hint that the Hollow cannot provide what she wants out of life. Dean notes this point when he says to Luke that Stars Hollow is not enough for Lorelai and Rory in "To Live and Let Diorama" (5.18).

much humor in the show. Although actual town meetings in communities occur less frequently than what is depicted in *Gilmore Girls,* the practice itself has been around for so long (dating back more than 375 years) that it seems to be an intrinsic part of New England American life. According to John Nordell, "For hundreds of years New Englanders have gathered in open town meetings . . . debating issues large and small—sometimes with rancor—thereby participating in a direct form of democratic government practically unique to these former colonies" (1999, 12). The Massachusetts Bay Colony was home to the first town meetings circa 1629, since the citizens needed to make decisions related to survival as well as the establishment of church meetings (ibid.). One could argue that the first New England town meeting occurred even earlier, since passengers on the Mayflower met to create the Mayflower Compact (1620), the first effort to establish formal self-government in the New World.

As local citizens Steve Jeffrey and Laurie Berkenkamp respectively argue in John Nordell's article, not only is the town meeting "the lifeblood of local government" and "a chance to be heard on equal ground," but it also is significantly about community. As Berkenkamp states, "It's great to see everyone after a long winter. It's a great community gathering" (ibid.). Perhaps the Sherman-Palladino team decided to use the town meeting in the show because it provides an antidote to the increasing pace of modern society and facilitates a representation of the American Dream that is tied to the construction of nostalgia, upon which so many fantasies of place reside. Andrew Ferguson of *Time* derides the town meeting, seeing it as a form of "mobocracy," but his strongest criticism of it (that it rewards "the fellow with the loudest voice—the crank with the thickest sheaf of mimeographed papers under his arm") reveals the foundation for some of the humor of the show (1998, 88); the arguments that occur in the town meeting entertain Lorelai, Rory, and the audience. Taylor's attempts to silence Lorelai or Luke, Kirk's odd interjections, Miss Patty's rationality against Taylor's despotism, Babette's husky-voiced comments, and general arguments over whether, for instance, there should be a town troubadour or whether Luke and Lorelai should date provide both humor and a sense of community within this specific (and specifically historic) yet imaginatively constructed place.

The businesses that dot the main drag of Stars Hollow provide additional support to the geography and historicity of Stars Hollow as exemplar of the dream. Echoing the dream's gradual secularization, Stars Hollow no longer sees the church as the center of the community. Notably, the central locations, other than Lorelai's home, are sites of commerce. Instead of coming together over prayer (although there is still the occasional funeral, wedding, or baptism attended by the citizens of the town), the community of Stars Hollow converges most frequently over coffee at Luke's—hence the difficulties that arise when Lorelai and Luke are separated.[12] The diner is where we most frequently witness the banter between Luke and Lorelai and the exchange of information (read: gossip) among townsfolk.

Meetings also occur at Doose's Market. For example, it is where Rory has her first kiss (and has her first quasi date arranged for her), where Lorelai and Rory stock up for their calorie-laden movie nights, and where Luke temporarily breaks up with Lorelai. Miss Patty's dance studio is the site of a few of Rory's transgressions as a young woman (for instance, bedding down with Dean after losing her virginity), and it is here where the town meetings are frequently held. Another small business in town, the Independence Inn, provides Lorelai with her first job (as a maid), promotion, and the training necessary to become a small business owner in her own right. Significantly, in accordance with conventional notions of the American Dream, all of these businesses are independently and locally owned operations (although Mia, the owner of the Independence Inn, has moved to California by the beginning of the narrative).

12. Luke has such a strong sentimental attachment to place and his father's memory that he transforms his father's hardware store (while still keeping the sign, a marker of the past) into something that reflects his skills: a diner. He even lives above the workplace, at one time struggling to exert parental authority over his nephew and then his daughter there.

In another move toward nostalgia, there are no big box stores or chains in Stars Hollow, although Richard attempts to get Luke to start a chain of diners in order to make the latter more respectable (according to the senior Gilmores' entrenched notions of such things). Significantly, Luke refuses to follow this advice. Throughout the seven seasons of *Gilmore Girls,* small businesses and their owners are central. The attempt to acquire a business—not just a room—of one's own is a dramatic touchstone for Lorelai in the first four seasons of the show.

Obviously, Stars Hollow's downtown area is not facing the same sorts of economic difficulties as many other downtowns across America. All the stores seem to be successful, even Le Chat Club. Perhaps this prosperity is due to the "Hello Kitty" allegedly stamped on all of the town's products ("Ballrooms and Biscotti" [4.01]).[13] Such success also reveals a connection between Stars Hollow's American Dream and the dream of the Puritans. For the latter, material success was often read as a sign of one's election, or one's predestined path toward heaven. Although good works could not contribute to one's salvation for the Puritans, living right, working hard, and being successful were all signs that God was smiling on one. By the time Ben Franklin arrived on the scene more than one hundred years later, this vision was becoming secularized; Franklin emphasized good works as a means to good citizenship and morality in his autobiography, and Stars Hollow seems to have taken this advice to heart.

Both of these visions are a part of the Stars Hollow experience. The town's denizens have all, to varying degrees, succeeded, in part through owning their own businesses and taking civic life seriously. Although, in "Take the Deviled Eggs . . ." (3.06), Luke jokes that Jess is "like the all-American boy" upon discovering that his nephew is working at Wal-Mart, when Jess later (in "Say Goodnight, Gracie" [3.20]) snidely quips that it's no worse than working at a diner, his uncle yells, "I *own*

13. Sara Morrison argues that most of the businesses in Stars Hollow would have a slim chance of succeeding at best (2007, 85–96).

this business, kid. I built it; this is mine. I'm not at the mercy of some boss, waiting and hoping to be chosen Employee of the Month for a couple extra hundred bucks and a plaque. I'm always employee of the month. I'm employee of the year. Of the century! Of the universe! You should be so lucky to have a job like mine!" Being a small business owner is clearly privileged (at least by Luke) over working for someone else, which is completely in keeping with the American Dream.[14]

Lorelai's and Rory's dreams of success are also rooted in the myth of meritocracy, reflecting the values of hard work, persistence, and merit. Neither person works hard and fails, perhaps because each is linked to a supportive community. Lorelai asks her parents for money in securing Rory's education, asks them to cosign a loan to rid her home of termites, and borrows money from Luke in order to open the Dragonfly. Rory, in turn, asks her grandparents (and then her father) to finance her education at Yale.[15] While the former moments provide a further excuse for Friday-night dinners, emphasis remains placed on the hard work of these women. Even though Lorelai has a reserve of financial credit and security that most Americans do not, she is also able to criticize

14. Jess offers the potential for another reading of the show, one that sees a far more critical perspective on the dream. When he exits the bus in "Nick & Nora/Sid & Nancy" (2.05), Elvis Costello's "This Is Hell" plays while the camera pans from Jess's point of view across Prozac-inspired long shots of Stars Hollow citizens, including a mother and daughter wearing identical Laura Ashley–style clothing. Looking at Stars Hollow through the eyes of Jess, an already cynical youth, Stars Hollow begins to look like a reincarnation of *The Stepford Wives*' main setting. Later, after he publishes his own novel and becomes a partner in the small press that printed his book, his success in following his own path will serve as a wake-up call for Rory to get back on track at Yale and in life. Though Jess often functions as a James Dean wannabe, he also provides a different perspective on Stars Hollow, potentially suggesting that it offers little more than a stultifying life. From Jess's perspective—and perhaps even from Rory's—people who are hip, creative, and have a future *leave* Stars Hollow.

15. This simultaneous attraction to and rejection of the world of Richard and Emily adds another site for a potential critique of the American Dream as realized in the show. Lorelai and Rory, no matter how hard they work or how smart they are, cannot quite make it on their own. They need outside help in order to realize their dreams, perhaps suggesting the limits of the myth of meritocracy.

the world of Richard and Emily, a world of largesse and privilege that stands in stark contrast to Stars Hollow. The narcissism, sense of entitlement, emphasis on bloodlines, and stress on social commitments (not out of a sense of civic duty per se but from a sense of noblesse oblige and desire for standing in the community) drive the world of Richard and Emily and provide a foil for the development of Stars Hollow as a more authentic community.[16] Although the Daughters of the American Revolution is filled with women like Emily Gilmore, ironically enough they seem to represent the world against which the Revolutionaries rebelled in favor of a world like Stars Hollow.

"Place Ballet": Between Mobility and Rootedness

> This is a very small, weird place you've moved to.
> —LORELAI to Dean, in "Kiss and Tell" (1.07)

In Season Seven, some of Stars Hollow's allure, a bit of its dynamic, was beginning to diminish. Perhaps it was because of the loss of the community of eccentric townspeople who had made visiting it each week such a joyous experience. Although Lorelai and Rory continued to be dominant presences—albeit with a little less of the snappy patter[17]—viewers were also confronted by the diminished presence of characters like Sookie, Miss Patty, Babette, Morey, Michel, Kirk, Taylor, Luke, and even the town troubadour. Though most of these characters did appear, for several episodes they simply did not function as they once had. Instead, there are all too fleeting glimpses of them.

16. Stephanie Rowe also rightly recognizes the way in which the interaction between Old Money and New Money is specifically tied to East Coast history; there is not enough history in, for instance, California, for there to be the sort of established Old Money and the sort of entrenched history and bloodlines of the East (2007, 112–13).

17. According to star Lauren Graham, Season Seven "was strange sometimes because I had a lot less to say, and that was really weird. For some people I'm sure that was great, but I would find myself in long scenes where I was not rattling on, and it was just really weird to me" (quoted in Ausiello 2007).

Replacing their presence as helping hands, gossips, nuisances, best friends, and Greek choruses were Logan and Christopher, bland lovers stuck in adolescence. Community was replaced by an overemphasis on romance that, for many viewers, was unfulfilling. We were less often put on the streets of Stars Hollow and more often situated in placeless locations, such as Christopher's apartment, a remote field, or a jail somewhere.

Lorelai's relationship to the town as place is essential. Her ribbing of Taylor, the great girlfriend vibe she shares with Sookie, and the eccentricities of Michel, Miss Patty, and Babette (which are made all the more bizarre in Lorelai's presence) are essential parts of the series' construction of place. Indeed, we might call their interactions with place a "place-ballet," to borrow a term from David Seamon (quoted in Cresswell 2004, 34) that refers to the way in which the various characters move through places preconsciously (for instance, heading to Luke's each morning without thought). In Season Seven, this "place-ballet" began to falter, as the audience was no longer privy to the community interacting in Luke's Diner, Taylor's market and soda shop, the gazebo, and Miss Patty's dance studio or with the troubadour on the corner. Food culture was also less conspicuous. Although Chris occasionally indulged Lorelai's sweet tooth with Red Vines and popcorn at the movies, gone were the lengthy exchanges about food at Luke's and the downright hedonistic diving into sweets by Lorelai and Rory; there were no more movie nights with towers of Oreos, greasy pizza, and take-out Chinese from Al's Pancake World.

Significantly and satisfactorily, though, the series ended with the old community back in place. Lane's baby shower, the hay maze, Karaoke Night, and Rory's graduation and postgraduation party returned the mother and daughter, as well as the show's longtime viewers, to the womblike environment of the community (to continue Taylor's analogy) and its construction of place.[18] Saying bon voyage to Rory as

18. The construction of Stars Hollow as metaphorical womb suggests that one must leave one's origins—and perhaps even the mythos of the American Dream—behind in order to become a fully functioning adult or even to survive: in the literal

she heads off to cover Barack Obama's presidential bid on the campaign trail, the community that had nurtured our girls once again came out in droves, making clear the attachment and rootedness of a true place. Finding success at last (albeit not as a reporter for the *New York Times*), Rory went forth into the world—but not without one last stop at Luke's Diner. In a shot identical to the last shot of the pilot episode (1.01), the camera dollies back from the main characters through the window as Luke puts on a pot of coffee and cooks them breakfast.[19] Fittingly, our girls appear to have achieved their very American dreams. Lorelai has achieved ownership of her own business and the successful resolution of her romance with Luke even as Rory ventures forth to a life that will emphasize mobility (the campaign trail) rather than rootedness, perhaps reinforcing the generational divide between these women and within the audience itself.

---

womb, one must be born in order to avoid death. Perhaps Stars Hollow is only a starting point rather than a destination.

19. This return to the pilot scene potentially reinforces the stasis represented by Stars Hollow and the American Dream: we visually end in the same place we began seven years previous. It also works as wonderful visual closure to the series.

Town Meetings of the Imagination

Gilmore Girls and *Northern Exposure*

JANE FEUER

A mythology of the idyllic American small town has long permeated American literature, film, and television. Thornton Wilder set his iconic 1938 play *Our Town* in Grovers Corners, New Hampshire; the speech patterns and accents localize the imaginary town in northern New England (Bryan 2004, 36n37).[1] Indeed, New England has provided the iconography for the look we all imagine such a town to have, and so compelling has the small-town set become that we can scarcely sense much difference between the vaguely located Carvel of the Andy Hardy film series (M-G-M, 1937–47) and the quite specifically located village of Stars Hollow, only a stone's throw from both Hartford and New Haven, Connecticut.[2] Of course, both Carvel and Stars Hollow are imaginary utopian villages. To a nonfan viewer of *Gilmore Girls,* Stars Hollow looks like just what it is: the most obvious of studio sets. Yet to fans of the show, years of narrative pleasure have imbued it with the patina of a real place. Luke's Diner, Doose's store, the Gilmore girls' house, the town square, and Miss Patty's dance studio (which converts to the town hall) have

1. Frank M. Bryan quotes Perry Westbrook (1982, 215) on this point.

2. *Gilmore Girls* was filmed on the back lot at Warner Brothers Studios in Burbank, California. The entire town of Stars Hollow was on the set called "Midwest Street," which was built after World War II for the Warner Bros. film *Saratoga Trunk* (1946).

been given meaning by the narratives that have occurred there during *Gilmore Girls*' seven seasons.

When, in his critique of nationalism, Benedict Anderson defines a nation as an "imagined political community," he is getting at something that is relevant to a discussion of the utopian small town. According to Anderson, the nation is *imagined* "because even the members of the smallest nation will never know most of their fellow-members, meet them, or even hear of them, yet in the mind of each lives the image of their communion. . . . [I]n fact all communities larger than primordial villages of face-to-face contact (and perhaps even these) are imagined. Communities are to be distinguished, not by their falsity/genuineness, but by the style in which they are imagined" (2006, 6). In this way Stars Hollow—or, for that matter, Carvel or Cicely, Alaska (the latter the setting of another important dramedy, *Northern Exposure* [CBS, 1990–96])—is no more and no less ideologically tainted than other less utopian communities in which popular narratives unfold, no less imaginary either than, say, New York and Miami, as they are represented in countless television series. All American towns may be mythical, but the New England town bears a set of meanings that link it to other larger American mythoi. Through historical and ideological references to the New England town meeting, long a symbol of American participatory democracy at its best, the Connecticut town takes on an added link to Anderson's (imagined) primordial villages. In a fascinating if perhaps overly zealous microstudy of actual New England town meetings, Frank M. Bryan argues in favor of participatory over representative forms of government, the former embodied to this day in the town meeting in which each citizen represents her- or himself. Bryan states that "except for some townships in Minnesota, the New England town is the only place in America where general-purpose governments render binding collective action decisions (laws) in small face-to-face assemblies of common citizens" (2004, xii).

In the fictional universes of television, the New England town meeting need not take place in New England. For example, in the aforementioned *Northern Exposure,* Cicely represents the New England village. The run-down, real-life setting of Roslyn, Washington (where the CBS series was filmed), would seem a far cry from the charming studio-set Americana of M-G-M and Warner Bros. back lots, and indeed the place functioned partly as a critique of that whitewashing of the reality of rural American life.[3] Moreover, *Northern Exposure*'s symbolization of its townspeople would seem to have derived more from the western genre than from something so eastern as the New England village. Yet the sense of community and of participatory democracy that Cicely ultimately came to represent is very close to that which the Stars Hollow of *Gilmore Girls* would later epitomize.

More significantly, representations of town meetings lifted from New England folklore permeated *Northern Exposure* from its beginnings. In "All Is Vanity" (2.03), we see the town functioning as a unit when an unidentified dead body is discovered around the same time that Holling wishes to be circumcised. Dr. Joel Fleischman hosts a town meeting to decide whether to move the body to Juneau, but his fellow Cicelians decide to keep it. In a speech to the townspeople, Joel refers to Cicely as a town of 850 people, just about the size of many New England towns in which all citizens are invited to meetings (of course, not all people actually participate).

Presumably, the extras on the show are meant to represent the entire population of Cicely. Certainly, they are meant to signify a broad range of social types and seem to have been cast with, to use Richard Dyer's term, "ordinariness" in mind (2003, 152). Both *Northern Exposure* and *Gilmore Girls* highlight the ordinariness of their extras-townsfolk by showing their faces to a far greater extent than would be strictly necessary to establish them as a crowd. In fact, the regular viewer comes to recognize certain faces in the crowd (the faces of Caesar and Morey, for example) in a manner that goes against the meaning of the term *extra* and veers in the direction of a term like *citizen*.

At the town meetings in Cicely, all populations appear to be represented: rednecks, Native Americans, white settlers. Toward the end of

3. Yet thousands of fans made pilgrimages to Roslyn (this author included).

"All Is Vanity," Chris does the funeral eulogy for the dead man, who is wrapped in an Indian blanket in the presence of the entire community. In a shot that is characteristic in the series, the camera pans the faces of the townsfolk—an image accompanied by Chris's voice. Meanwhile, Holling has a wide-angle nightmare in which the entire town witnesses his circumcision; in reality, the whole town knows about it anyway, even to the point that allusion to it is made at the funeral ceremony ("all is vanity"). In this and other early episodes of *Northern Exposure,* the actual locale for the meetings shifts from the town hall to Ruth Anne's store to the Brick saloon and to various outdoor ceremonies connecting Cicely to its natural surroundings.

In the episode "What I Did for Love" (2.04), Chris practices his Founders Day sermon on a church set that also serves as the town hall, complete with U.S. and Alaskan flags. The run-down interior of the church and hall features a cookstove, hand-lettered posters and notices, but also church pews. Curiously, there is a stock establishing shot of a white clapboard New England–style church in this episode, one that is never shown again in the series. I mention this arcane detail because it speaks to the iconographic links to the New England town that I believe *Northern Exposure* invokes indirectly (while directly citing western and northwestern geography).[4] The Founders Day town meeting is similar to the one in the previous episode—and to ones that take place in *Gilmore Girls*—in that very personal matters (a premonition that Joel will die in a plane crash) are discussed with the same seriousness and fervor as are more ceremonial or legal matters. The town takes a plebiscite on the show's storylines, acting as a kind of authorial Greek chorus. It is almost as if the metaphor of participatory democracy extends to the creation of the show itself.

4. Both the primitive western settlement and the New England village provide powerful iconic representations of participatory democracy that can be invoked by television. For example, the recently produced reality program *Kid Nation* (CBS, 2007–8) sends forty children to form a utopian community in a western ghost town.

As does *Gilmore Girls, Northern Exposure* makes direct references to the process of adjudicating town matters such as elections, where to locate stop signs and garbage dumps, and other issues traditionally discussed at actual New England town meetings. One episode in particular, "Democracy in America" (3.15), deals explicitly with the ideology of participatory civic engagement, so explicitly in fact that it seems to be a little lesson in American democracy for the viewers, with its citations of Alexis de Tocqueville, Abraham Lincoln, Henry David Thoreau, and Walt Whitman. In a "grudge match over a stop sign," Edna Hancock challenges Holling in Cicely's mayoral election. The extremes of idealism and pragmatism are represented by Chris and Joel, respectively. Joel, who did not even know that Holling was the mayor, refers to Cicely as the "Brigadoon of electoral politics." Meanwhile, Chris waxes eloquent on the subject of American democracy, referring to it as a "sacred rite," and even broadcasts a little history lesson that echoes historical defenses of the New England town meeting as exemplar of American democracy at its best:

> Friends, Romans, registered voters, lend me your ears. Holling Vincoeur has picked up the gauntlet thrown down by Edna Hancock. We have a mayoralty race, folks, to which I can only add, *alea jacta est,* the die is cast, the battle is joined, hold on to your hats, Cicely. We're about to bear witness to that sacred rite when each and every one of us become acolytes before the altar of the ballot box, our secular shrine. Fellow Cicelians, my heart is pounding, dancing to the drum of a free people, a city on a hill, *E Pluribus Unum*. I feel at one with Whitman, shepherd of the great unwashed. . . . O Democracy! Near at hand to you a throat is now inflating itself and joyfully singing. My friends, today when I look out over Cicely, I see not a town, but a nation's history written in miniature, inscribed in the cracked pavement, reverberating from every passing flatbed. Today, every runny nose I see says "America" to me. We were outcasts, scum, the wretched debris of a hostile, aging world. But we came here, we paved roads, we built industries, powerful institutions. Of course, along the way we exterminated untold indigenous cultures and enslaved generations of Africans. We basically stained our Star

> Spangled Banner with a host of sins that can never be washed clean. But today, we're here to celebrate the glorious aspects of our past.

I have quoted this text at length because I want to illustrate the way in which *Northern Exposure* both accesses the most celebrated texts praising American democracy and critiques that celebration. Particularly ironic is the fact that Chris, a convicted felon, is not himself eligible to vote. As a visionary propagandist and artist, Chris by no means acts as the voice of Cicely, and, by the time this episode originally aired, audiences were becoming well aware that he represented the extreme idealistic pole in philosophical debates. Similarly, we know that Joel's urban cynicism is typically tempered by his encounters with the enactment of participatory democracy that Cicely has come to represent. Moreover, since *Northern Exposure* features a large ensemble cast spread across multiple storylines, many other positions find expression in this episode as well, especially in the election debate that Joel and Maggie cosponsor at the town hall.

Producer David Chase (who subsequently helmed *The Sopranos* [HBO, 1999–2007]) has stated that even a quality show like *Northern Exposure* was "propaganda for the corporate state. . . . [I]t was ramming home every week the message that life was nothing but great and that heartfelt emotions and sharing conquers everything" (quoted in O'Brien 2007, 20). Although there is little doubt that Chris and his glorification of democracy exert ideological sway in the episode, to say that it and thereby the entire series is propaganda for "feel-good" capitalism would be, I believe, an oversimplification of the viewing positions that *Northern Exposure* actually allows for its audience.

Throughout its seven seasons, *Gilmore Girls,* like *Northern Exposure* before it, used actual portrayals of town meetings to convey its utopian ideology. Both the literal meetings and the events taking place on the town square grew into an expected part of the contemporary folklore propagated by the show, and dedicated viewers would not have been surprised to discover that the final scenes of the last episode were set at Rory's going-away party on that very town square. Although most critics locate the popularity of the show in the mother-daughter relationship, I believe that an equally compelling locus for viewer pleasure is the "village of eccentrics" milieu that structures the show's main ideological oppositions: Stars Hollow versus Hartford, egalitarian versus class stratified, quirky and spontaneous versus rule abiding—basically all those qualities that separate Lorelai Gilmore from her family of origin.

Structurally, the quirkiness of Stars Hollow is remarkably similar to the eccentricity of Cicely. Both towns represent those places that people can presumably go to when they need to escape contemporary American life in order to dwell in an imaginary past that still holds up powerfully well as an enduring myth. And in each case, the town meeting comes to represent the kind of face-to-face communal governance that today's politicians seek to invoke when they hold their own televised "town meetings." None of these phenomena are "propaganda for the corporate state," strictly speaking. All represent a subtle critique of the corporate state whose representatives always reside in each town: Maurice Minnifield, the capitalist prince of Cicely; Taylor Doose, business magnate and self-proclaimed leader; and the Gilmore parents—Richard (an insurance executive) and wife Emily, who together reside in übercorporate Hartford and are members of America's ruling class. *Gilmore Girls* attempts to visualize a type of town—located ideologically in the past but culturally in the present—in which the playing field between the rulers and the common folk is leveled through the device of the town meeting. In these meetings, presided over but not ruled over by Taylor Doose, the quirky, the whimsical, and the populist voices are not just heard. They triumph.

For example, in "Love, Daisies, and Troubadours" (1.21), Rory defends the guitar-strumming troubadour (at a town meeting in which he is accused by curmudgeons Taylor and Luke of loitering) on the grounds that Stars Hollow needs an official singer-songwriter whose only motivation is to express himself through music. Five years later, in the episode "Partings" (6.22), Stars Hollow is overrun with troubadours when the original musician is "discovered." But at this point in the series, Taylor's efforts to rid the town of busloads full of bad folksingers are portrayed as ludicrous: he cannot even motivate the community's one pubescent police officer to unload them. No town meeting is necessary. Both episodes serve as meaningful finales of their respective seasons (One and Six), hinting that defending the civil rights of a wandering minstrel has some ultimate thematic significance for the show as a whole.[5] Perhaps it takes a troubadour to punctuate the two storylines that dominate these season finales (that is, Lorelai's and Rory's romances). In the Season One finale, a troubadour is needed to celebrate Rory's reconciliation with Dean and Lorelai's commitment to Max. It seems important to sing of "this little corner of the world" when the mother and daughter embrace in the town square as the camera cranes away from them. Conversely, at the end of Season Six, we need a sad song to mark Logan's departure for London and Lorelai's ultimatum to Luke.

In what kind of universe are the celebration of lovers coming together and the threat of their parting a matter for business at a town meeting? *Northern Exposure* poses this question, but *Gilmore Girls* makes it thematically central. In "Written in the Stars" (5.03), the town has discovered that Lorelai and Luke have spent the night together. At the ensuing town meeting, Taylor uses maps, graphs, and pie charts to show how economically disastrous a breakup between these two residents of the community would be for Stars Hollow. When the couple later has a rift ("Say Something" [5.14]), Taylor forces the entire town to take sides by choosing either pink or blue ribbons. Although at the level of character motivation Luke's protest that their relationship is none of the town's business may seem valid, according to the contextual "logic" of Stars Hollow (which fans by now have come to accept) it seems completely appropriate for the town to adjudicate Luke and Lorelai's romance, just as it seems right for the community to vote on guilt in traffic accidents. The only court in Stars Hollow is the court of public opinion, but for a utopia such as this one, it could be enough.

5. It does not seem coincidental that this time span encompassed Amy Sherman-Palladino's reign as chief "troubadour" for the show itself.

Stars Hollow is not just a site for participatory democracy. It is also a locale for all manner of bizarre town rituals, reenactments and celebrations, from the annual Stars Hollow charity picnic-basket lunch auction to the town square knitathon. In the former event ("A-Tisket, a-Tasket" [2.13]), there is more than a bit of an echo of the musical *Oklahoma!* as the men's bidding on the women's picnic baskets causes all kinds of trouble for the town. Why make such a lighthearted yet pointed reference to a canonical text dealing with the formation of a community in the American West? Perhaps it is because, as Rick Altman (1987) has argued, in the "folk" musical, the fate of the couple runs parallel to the formation of a civilized community. Although perhaps not so obviously as the Rodgers and Hammerstein classic, *Gilmore Girls* is centrally concerned with the way that the fates of multiple sets of couples intersect, with the possibility of Stars Hollow fulfilling its utopian potential. We know that Connecticut is a state, but is it the kind of state we want to live in, one that has a future? Or is it threatened by the ossification of ruling-class ideology at Yale and in the Gilmore mansion in Hartford? Should America as a whole turn its back on Hartford and turn its attention to a land where capitalism is still at a primitive stage of development and the only government needed is an occasional coming together of all the town's citizens? It seems to me that *Gilmore Girls* is primarily concerned with asking these questions. No matter how light or facetious the show's tone may be, there is an underlying seriousness that it shares with all great comedy.

Repeatedly, we are taught that neither Taylor Doose nor his "henchman" of sorts, Kirk Gleason, will be permitted to abuse power. This point is rendered clear in *Gilmore Girls*' own "Democracy in America" episode, aptly titled "Tippecanoe and Taylor, Too" (5.04). It seems that Taylor has gone too far in his autocratic reign as town selectman. Just as Holling had been forever mayor of Cicely prior to Edna's arrival on the scene, Taylor's power is challenged when Sookie's husband, Jackson, decides to oppose the never-opposed officeholder. As with the stop-sign grudge match, the issue is that Taylor has gone too far in enforcing zoning technicalities, now requiring Jackson to move his greenhouse a few feet in order to comply with the law. At the same time, he has angered Lorelai by turning down her request for parking spaces at the inn because she did not sign her middle name on the forms. Doose's crime is thus not just authoritarianism but also a severe lack of imagination, spontaneity, and adaptability, qualities cherished by the Gilmore girls and enshrined in their quick-witted mother-daughter relationship. Soon Luke's Diner has become Jackson's campaign headquarters, and Kirk—in his chameleon-like fashion—has morphed into a campaign pollster. Jokes about campaign lore ("that's very *Manchurian Candidate*") start to emerge from Lorelai's mouth. Getting into the fantasy role-playing aspect of the event, Sookie goes to the polls in a candidate's wife's pink wool suit.

But just at the point where it has all become a fun game, and after it is revealed that no one in town plans to vote for Taylor, Lorelai starts to feel sorry for him and attempts to get him a few votes. Meanwhile, Jackson gets cold feet and tries to withdraw from the race, but the townspeople will not let him. Miss Patty announces the vote of 1,113 for Jackson, but she does not announce Doose's total. Taylor gives a seemingly noble concession speech in which—while praising democracy in America—he actually asks for a recall. Unlike the "Democracy in America" episode of *Northern Exposure,* which makes a grand (and grandiloquent) statement about the subject of social equality and the roles of elected representatives, *Gilmore Girls* takes a cynical and comical view of the governance of Stars Hollow.

What the town does take seriously, however, are the ludicrous celebrations and local enactments that run throughout the television series' seven seasons and in which the entire community appears to participate: a wake for Babette's cat, various birthday parties,[6] the Founders' Firelight Festival, the Stars Hollow Charity Rummage Sale, Lorelai and Max's engagement party, the aforementioned picnic-basket lunch, a farmers' market, Luke's uncle's funeral, "Movie

6. Very early in the series ("Rory's Birthday Parties" [1.06]), the stodgy event given by Emily is contrasted with the typically fun Stars Hollow celebration.

in the Square Night," the First Annual Stars Hollow End-of-Summer Madness Festival, the Stars Hollow Dance Marathon, the Stars Hollow High Winter Carnival, the baking of the world's largest pizza for Lorelai's birthday, the Stars Hollow ice cream queen crowning, the annual Revolutionary War reenactment, the Festival of Living Art, the Easter-egg hunt on the town square, Liz's Renaissance wedding on the town square, the town knitathon, Lane's baby shower, the Spring Fling festival featuring the hay-bale maze,[7] and Rory's bon voyage party. The town as a whole gathers not just to commemorate weddings, funerals, the births of babies, and arrivals and departures but also to enact seemingly ancient seasonal rituals, to remember New England history, and—this notion covers a lot of events—to have wacky, irrational fun together.

My aim in compiling such a list is to demonstrate just how many of these events the show has featured and just how varied they are. Yet few occupy the narrative center of an entire episode; most of these events are woven among other more character-driven storylines and dramatic arcs. Still, these ceremonial events seem central to life in Stars Hollow and always justify Lorelai's choice to run away from home. These ceremonial events stand in direct contrast to other equally ceremonial social rituals—the ones that Emily Gilmore tends to organize in Hartford and even the ones that Rory enjoys at Yale. They also differ from the moments in episodes when a character from the Hartford world—Richard, Emily, Logan, and even Christopher—is given a guided tour of Stars Hollow and fails to take in its charms.

In the aptly titled first-season episode "Emily in Wonderland" (1.19), Rory takes her grandmother on a tour of the significant locations of the girls' early life in Stars Hollow. Although Emily is pleased by her encounters with Michel and Mrs. Kim, she becomes horrified

7. This final-season episode ("Hay Bale Maze" [7.18]) seems to rehash the Stars Hollow dynamics that have structured previous seasons, as Taylor angers the entire town by spending all the money for the Spring Fling festival on an enormous hay-bale maze and Rory introduces Logan to the town.

by the sight of the potting shed that served as Lorelai and Rory's first home after their departure from Hartford. Later, in a fight with Lorelai, she tells her daughter how appalled she is that Lorelai left her family to live like "a hobo." Much later, after she impulsively marries Christopher, Lorelai realizes she has made a mistake when he is unable to fit in with the rituals of Stars Hollow life. In this regard Rory's estrangement from her mother in Season Six and her subsequent identity crisis take the form of a rejection of all things Stars Hollow, something furthermore highlighted when she immerses herself in the Daughters of the American Revolution—the group most unlikely to hold its charity events in the Star Hollow town square. Rory's initial discomfort with Logan is revealed by her inability to enjoy any of the social events in which he and his friends participate. In this way, even after she departs for Yale, the show is successful at keeping in our minds one of its central premises: Rory is the daughter of Stars Hollow, and in many respects she was raised and nurtured by the entire town. For this reason it seems more than fitting that the series should end with the town celebrating Rory's graduation and departure into the world, a real world that includes Christiane Amanpour and Barack Obama but whose satisfactions will likely be less profound than the comforts of Stars Hollow.

So far I have analyzed *Gilmore Girls* as an extended text that encompasses and works through a number of significant ideological oppositions in relation to town meetings in many senses of the term, referring to the New England town meeting in particular, to places where citizens and ideas truly meet each other, and to the intermingling of certain binaries that structure the show thematically. I have not attempted to capture the surface appeals of the show: its look, its wit, its brilliant dialogue, its interwoven storylines, its development of characters. I have taken these components for granted in my attempt to show the way in which *Gilmore Girls* extends the metaphor of the town meeting beyond what was established by *Northern Exposure,* in a manner perhaps belied by the "quirky" and "whimsical" tone of the program.

Indeed, both programs could be encompassed under the genre label "quirky TV," a designation that spans drama and comedy and includes some of the most notable "quality TV" programs of the 1990s and beyond, from network series like *Twin Peaks* (ABC, 1990–91) and *Ally McBeal* (FOX, 1997–2002) to premium cable shows like *Six Feet Under* (HBO, 2001–5) and *Weeds* (Showtime, 2005–). The term *quirky* is used by industry insiders (writers, producers, executives) to indicate a show whose characters do not conform to television's stock-character stereotypes. It is used descriptively but also qualitatively. When *quirky* and *whimsical* are used by critics, however, a disparaging note sometimes slips in, the implication being that such TV shows cannot be taken as serious artworks, because art simply is not whimsical or quirky. It should be pointed out, though, that *quirky* has long been a term used to describe a kind of Yankee eccentricity and individualism perfectly attuned to the ideals of the town meeting. It is precisely because New Englanders are thought to be "quirky" that the gathering of unique individuals is considered a preferred form of governance. Resistant to authority, New England citizens would seem better suited for participatory rather than representative democracy. Thus, the town meeting syncs with the kind of extreme individualism that characterizes these programs. To return to Benedict Anderson's earlier formulation, the style in which these communities are imagined has deep roots not only in American populist ideology but also in a history of more utopian thinking about television as a form of mass communication—not as a "vast wasteland" but rather as a "town meeting of the nation."

I do not believe that this nostalgically imbued idealism is necessarily conservative or antiprogressive. A television series, even "quality" ones like the two discussed here, can reach large audiences, many of whom are not professional intellectuals. Perhaps the idea of looking back in order to look forward is not such a bad ideology for a television show to offer its audience. As with many long-running and much loved TV series, both *Northern Exposure* and *Gilmore Girls* ended their broadcast runs on an elegiac note. But these particular programs culminated with the message that it was the towns and their inhabitants that audiences would most miss. If all is well in Cicely or Stars Hollow, it does not mean that all is well in the corporate state. Just as the town meeting represents an alternative to the corporate state, so too do *Northern Exposure* and *Gilmore Girls* offer alternatives to the brutal contemporary society portrayed on other television series.

Part Three

Race, Class, Education, Profession

Escaping from Korea

Cultural Authenticity and Asian American Identities in Gilmore Girls

HYE SEUNG CHUNG

> Inside every gook there is an American trying to get out.
> —POGUE COLONEL (BRUCE BOA), in Stanley Kubrick's *Full Metal Jacket* (1987)

> When are you going to let your parents know that you listen to evil rock music? You are an American teenager, for God's sake!
> —RORY addressing her best friend, Lane, in the pilot episode of *Gilmore Girls*

This chapter opens with quotes that are derived from two cultural productions that could not be more different from one another. It may seem antithetical to compare two things that are about as similar as "hammers and veils," "raincoats and recipes," or "ballrooms and biscotti" (paired objects that provide the titles of three *Gilmore Girls* episodes). After all, *Full Metal Jacket* is a testosterone-filled antiwar film set partially in a U.S. Marine boot camp and in wartime Vietnam, while *Gilmore Girls* is a female-centered, lighthearted television dramedy set in the small town of Stars Hollow, Connecticut. Yet each text ushers in dialogue that conjures the interwoven tropes of duality and passing, two recurring motifs superimposed atop the contested terrain of Asian and Asian American identity formation.

In a patriotic lecture delivered to Private Joker (Matthew Modine), a cynical war correspondent who wears a peace-sign button along with a helmet bearing the inscription "Born to Kill" to represent the "duality of man" metaphor he so frequently invokes, Pogue Colonel justifies U.S. intervention in the Vietnam War as a benevolent attempt to Americanize willing imperial subjects in the Third World. Joker's Jungian conception of man as both pacifist and militant, internally withdrawn and outwardly aggressive, when joined to the colonel's Manichaean bifurcation of Asian identities (as would-be Americans trapped in Asian bodies), is related to the way in which the character Lane Kim is first introduced to audiences of *Gilmore Girls.* Lane, like the South Vietnamese in *Full Metal Jacket,* is *dualistic:* a rock-obsessed, all-American teenager who has to pass as an obedient "Korean" daughter in the presence of her hymn-loving, Bible-toting parents (or rather, parent, as Mr. Kim—like Kirk's mother—never appears in the *Gilmore*verse despite numerous references to his existence).[1] Significantly, in the episode "Face-Off" (3.15), Lane's mother, Mrs. Kim, is compared to the drill instructor in *Full Metal Jacket* (by her future son-in-law Zach), an assessment that not only conjures the unyielding nature of this woman (who is known to wield a mean cricket bat) but also says much about the continued applicability of that film as a cultural touchstone evoking the harshness of stoic Asian "others."

From the moment Lane makes her first appearance, she is codified as someone who *passes.*[2] Walking toward the front gate outside Stars

1. Throughout the seven-year broadcast of *Gilmore Girls,* these allusions to the offscreen presence of Lane's father led to the rise of "Kim spotters," a subset of *GG* fans who watch intently for any hint of their favorite character's perpetually absent papa. Unfortunately for these audience members, Mr. Kim is nowhere to be seen in the series, not even at his own daughter's wedding (in the Season Six episode "I Get a Sidekick Out of You" [6.19]). In a way, his conspicuous absence paves the way for another more problematic omission in the series' finale: Mrs. Kim, who is not there in the town square to tell Rory good-bye.

2. In "Those Lazy-Hazy-Crazy Days" (3.01), other characters are jokingly (self-)identified as passers of religious and sexual identities. For example, Lorelai, after tasting kosher bacon, tells Sookie, "I am so Jewish." Later, informing his wife

Hollow High with her schoolmate Rory (who will soon transfer to Chilton High), she puts on a colorful pullover with the "Woodstock" logo atop a plain pink T-shirt. Responding to Rory's question quoted above, the Korean American teen girl reasons, "If my parents still get upset over the obscene portion size of American food, I seriously doubt I'm going to make any inroads with Eminem." Then, Lane informs Rory that she will go on a hayride, a town event held for local teens, and that her partner on the outing will be the sixteen-year-old son of her parents' business associate (a boy, Mrs. Kim is proud to say, who already has plans to become a doctor after college). When Rory makes light of the Kims' matchmaking mentality, stating, "He's going to be a doctor in a hundred years . . . you're kidding," Lane half-jokingly replies, "My parents like to plan ahead. . . . Koreans never joke about future doctors!"

This scene occurs before the first ten-minute mark of the episode, and by this time the unusually strong bond between the titular mother-daughter—the backbone of the whole series—has already become apparent to viewers. During the precredit sequence set in Luke's Diner, Lorelai and Rory are seen sharing not only morning coffee but also personal items, including lip gloss and CDs. After futile attempts to hit on both, a stranger at the diner is stunned to learn that the sisterly duo is in fact mother and daughter. In the scene that then follows, Rory makes an impromptu after-school stop at her mother's workplace, the Independence Inn, where she picks up a free book of stamps and asks Michel Gerard, her mother's sarcastic French assistant, to check the grammar of her French homework. Thus, the first two scenes of the pilot episode effectively establish the harmoni-

---

that he likes flowers and ruffles, Jackson declares, "I'm very, very gay." According to Sookie, who is shopping for "manly" items in the antiques store, Mrs. Kim "would make a great nun." However, the most notable passer of them all is Michel, whose latent homosexuality is never explicitly mentioned throughout the series (much like in classic screwball comedies produced under the watchful eyes of Hollywood's homophobic censors).

ous tone, egalitarian values, and reciprocally nurturing relationship between Rory and Lorelai.

Lane's relationship with her Korean mother is not mutually enriching in the least; indeed, it is presented as the exact opposite of the connection between our two heroines. As the owner of an antique shop stocked with overpriced furniture, Mrs. Kim is first introduced as a disciplinarian linked to "old-fashioned values" yet also someone who is greedy with money (later, in the Season Three episode "A Deep-Fried Korean Thanksgiving" [3.09], she even charges invited family members a slightly discounted price for any household items broken in the course of the celebration). In the pilot episode, the ever-vigilant mother sternly demands that Lane tell her if any of the girls in Stars Hollow High have gotten pregnant, and then orders her to drink tea with no dairy or sugar added. In lieu of sugary cookies or carb-filled brownies, a meager portion of healthy muffins is made available to Lane by her mother, who has used wheat so fiber rich that the hardened clumps of baked goods (or, rather "bads") need to be dampened first to make them chewably soft. Mrs. Kim's unappetizing muffins, like the tofurky she serves to Lorelai and Rory in the Thanksgiving episode (not to mention the homemade granola, wheatgrass juice, and soy-chicken tacos that constitute her basket for auction in "A-Tisket, a-Tasket" [2.13] as well as multigrain soy pudding that she brings her estranged daughter as a conciliatory gift in "Last Week Fights, This Week Tights" [4.21]), contrast sharply with the sweets, junk food, and caffeine indulgences that Lorelai allows Rory to enjoy.

As an orthodox member of the Seventh-Day Adventists, Mrs. Kim resents Lorelai for having given birth to and raised Rory as a single woman (an animosity that is softened in Lane's words, "[My mother] doesn't trust unmarried women"). The Korean mother is no more accommodating to her daughter's dearest friend; for example, she coldly responds to Rory's casual joke with a stoic look, saying, "Boys don't like funny girls," and goes so far as to call the teenage girl a "carrier" before attacking her with a water hose when the Gilmore residence develops a termite problem (the insects later infest the front porch of Lorelai and Sookie's soon-to-be-renovated Dragonfly Inn).

Before moving out of her parents' house in Season Four, Lane is seen leading a double life. Her true self is literally "closeted" in her secret stash of contraband music CDs, posters, and books hidden under the baseboard of her bedroom floor. Lane is a spiritual nomad who feels free to express herself only outside the suffocating space of house and home, dominated by her tyrannical, control-freak mother. In "Cinnamon's Wake," (1.05), for example, the would-be John Bonham is seen dancing wildly to the upbeat music of Rancid in Rory's room (the same image is shown during the credit sequence to introduce actress Keiko Agena). When asked by Lorelai where her mother thinks she is, the Korean American teen replies, "On a park bench, contemplating the reunification of the two Koreas."

Throughout the series, Lane shares her deepest emotions—her joys and bitter disappointments—with Rory and Lorelai at their house, in Luke's Diner, and in the town square. Lorelai and Rory lend more than a sympathetic ear to Lane; they contribute significantly to the realization of her dream of becoming a musician, something begun in Season Two, when they allow her to use their telephone to interview potential bandmates, and continued later, in the Season Three episode "Lorelai Out of Water" (3.12), when they clear out a garage full of boxed junk to give the fledgling rockers (Lane, Dave, Gil, Zach, and Brian) a suitable place to rehearse their music.

In the second episode of Season One, "The Lorelais' First Day at Chilton," while enjoying a predinner snack of pizza and coffee with her favorite Gilmore girls sheltered from the watchful eyes of Mrs. Kim, Lane complains about her mother's recent bulk purchase of tofu, a trademark of Asian cuisine, which apparently does not suit her Americanized palette. Lorelai expresses sympathy, saying, "Honey, your life is scary." A recapitulation of this food motif occurs in "The Fundamental Things Apply" (4.05), when Lane dashes in to Lorelai's house for a quick bite of recently delivered pizza, saying, "My mom ordered all the okra in the Western Hemisphere. She got a great deal, and I'm starving to death." These examples attest to the fact that Lane is most decidedly an *American* girl—a "Connecticut Yankee" as she describes herself in "Hammers and Veils" (2.02)—trying to get out of her "gook" lifestyle (to paraphrase the above-cited colonel in *Full Metal Jacket*), a "coming-out" that is possible only when she is around the Gilmores (her surrogate family), not the Kims (her biological family).

Tied to the Statue of Liberty

> Welcome to America. . . . It's a whole new world!
>
> —LANE to a recently arrived Korean exchange student, Kyon, who has just discovered the magic of french fries

In the first two episodes of Season Two, Lane's impending trip to South Korea provides a pivotal point of personal crisis mirroring Lorelai's own emotional roller-coaster ride as her wedding with Rory's high school English teacher, Max Medina, is fast approaching. The second-generation Korean American's loyalty to the United States (as opposed to Korea) is made apparent as this dramatic subplot thickens. Instead of being excited about visiting her parental homeland for the first time, Lane flips out when she learns that her mother is sending her to South Korea for the summer, with a one-way plane ticket and no set return date. In "Sadie, Sadie" (2.01), she confides her worst fears to Rory, saying, "It's going to be just like that Sally Field movie [*Not Without My Daughter* (1991)] where the husband took them [his wife and daughter] to Iran and wouldn't let them come back. Except that I won't have to keep my head covered." Lane also asks Rory if she could pronounce Hyun-kyung—her Korean name—to make a point about how it fails to convey her all-American identity.

In the episode that immediately follows, "Hammers and Veils," the Asian American teenager has cobbled together a "Lane Kim retrieval kit," which consists of the phone number and map of her cousin's house in South Korea (where she will be staying), a current photo of herself and a mock-up picture showing how she will likely look in six months (thinner, to denote a state of malnutrition), the contact information of the American Consulate, and several Korean phrases written out phonetically (such as "Help," "Have you seen this girl?" and "Come for money"). As a fail-safe device designed to rescue the fearful teenager from the direst situation imaginable (a kind of purgatory to be spent in a distant, "third world" country with little food and no alternative rock bands in sight), Lane's "retrieval kit" is a visible sign of her neuroses and frustrations, her inability to wrest control of her destiny away from her mother.

Yet, for all of the comical intent of the scene, the underlying assumptions here are problematic, since Lane imagines her familial homeland—a high-tech, democratic nation and the eleventh-largest economy in the world—as a backward and underdeveloped country, a land of chaos and calamities where she might experience starvation and kidnapping. It is, to borrow her words in a later episode ("Lorelai Out of Water"), "the Old Country," a place so out of step with contemporary standards of marriage and romance that eligible daughters are sent to the United States to wed Korean American bachelors sight unseen (a feudal practice that might have happened with frequency during the Chosun dynasty period [1392–1910] but is unlikely to transpire today). Rather than trusting the Korean relatives with whom she will spend the summer, Lane opts to depend on the American Consulate, an overseas agency of the State Department, to which she makes an international phone call.

Audiences anxious to discover what transpired during Lane's indefinite exile in South Korea had to wait only two weeks before learning, in "The Road Trip to Harvard" (2.04), that her apprehensions were in fact groundless. Toward the end of this episode, she is reunited with Rory in the town square, after the latter has just returned from an impromptu road trip with Lorelai to Harvard. The first words out of the ecstatic teenager's mouth are, "Rory, I'm back! Did you ever think this day would come? I escaped from Korea. I'm home." We, like the young girls, may be swept up by the emotional cadences of the homecoming, but the moment, which attempts to conceal but actually *reveals* the ideological mechanisms at play behind an "us-them," "self-other" dichotomy, subtly displays the kind of cultural anxieties that would not seem out of place in a cold war–era fiction while assuming deeper connotations in the current political climate (this episode, after all, was broadcast six weeks after 9/11).

Here, "Korea" signifies an *other* place. It is a foreign land—apparently not that different from Afghanistan, Iraq, or Iran—from which one must escape in order to return "home," a word that connotes comfort, safety, and familiarity. This conception runs counter to the logic of nostalgia and the emotional yearning for a lost homeland found in postcolonial literature and diasporic narratives (such as Theresa Hak-kyung Cha's *Dictée* [1982] and Mira Nair's *Namesake* [2006]), which conceive of such spaces as more accommodating and restorative sites of memory and belonging than what are provided by the inhospitable host country. Lane's prejudiced view of her ancestral homeland is once again evoked when Rory recites, from memory, the first letter she received from South Korea: "The one that said, 'Korea equals death,' with a bunch of exclamation points and [Lane's] very sad face cut up and plastered all over it."

However, Lane makes a startling admission, surprising both Lorelai and Rory when she relays information about some of the good things to come out of her cross-Pacific visit. Not only did she sample a lot of the local food and get better acquainted with her Korean cousins, but—best of all—she bought several hard-to-find bootleg albums featuring the likes of Elvis Costello, Nico, and Iggy Pop, icons of 1970s punk rock whose vinyl recordings somehow found their way to a black market in Seoul. "How did you get them past customs?" Rory asks. Lane responds, "I strapped them to my body like in *Midnight Express*"—a comment that forges a connection between this episode and a later one ("Ballrooms and Biscotti" [4.01]), which alludes to the horrors of a Turkish prison after Lorelai and Rory's return from their European trip. Although she acknowledges some of the positive aspects of her vacation, Lane ultimately remains unchanged (as a small-town American girl), with no traces of cultural enlightenment or reconnection to her heritage. Although she may have enjoyed authentic Korean cuisine and may have derived some pleasure from meeting her relatives, the best thing about Seoul, for her, was its diverse selection of rare American music.

Apparently oblivious to the *reasons* American popular culture pervades South Korea, a country where the United States has maintained a hegemonic presence (militarily, economically, and culturally) since its occupation south of the thirty-eighth parallel (1945–48) and its involvement in the Korean War (1950–53), Lane wholeheartedly celebrates the symptoms of U.S. neocolonial domination and displays no interest whatsoever in indigenous musical traditions or trends. As Rory jokingly puts it, Lane would have done "everything but tie a string with [her] at one end and to the Statue of Liberty at the other" to avoid going to Korea. This comment vividly underscores a lack of physical and emotional attachment between the American-born Korean and her parental homeland.

Subservience and Subterfuge: The Dialectical Dilemmas of Being Korean American (on Television)

> LANE TO RORY: Dave has a natural gift for subterfuge.
> DAVE: Wow, a compliment from the master.
> —Dialogue in "Face-Off"

The running joke about Mrs. Kim, at least throughout the first three seasons, is her single-minded quest to marry her daughter off to a prospective Korean doctor. As mentioned earlier, in the pilot episode Lane gently pokes fun at her mother's grand ambition, a design for living linked to many Korean immigrant moms who stake their hopes of a better future for their American-born children by encouraging them to become doctors or lawyers or to seek such professionals as their potential spouses.[3] Nazli Kibria's ethnographic research of second-generation Chinese and Korean American informants shows that first-generation immigrant parents tend to pressure their children to "compensate for

3. Another televisual example of obsessive "doctor-in-law" hunting can be found in the character of Katherine Kim (Jodi Long), the mother of the title character, Margaret (Margaret Cho), in the short-lived TV series *All-American Girl* (ABC, 1994–95).

the disadvantages of their racial identity by being 'twice as good,' outshining their peers in their achievements." As Kibria states, "Doing well at school was presented as an effective means to achieve socioeconomic status and rewards in the United States and to overcome the racial barriers to such achievement" (2002, 53).

Korean immigrant parents' obsession with doctors or lawyers as the most favored vocations for their own children as well as potential in-laws, as well as their educational zeal and pride in sending their kids to Ivy League schools like Harvard, Princeton, and Yale, should thus be understood in the context of a diasporic culture that puts "messages of race" (or, as Kibria puts it "lessons and ideas about how to deal with the experience of racialized exclusion") at the foundational level of the immigrant experience (ibid., 63).[4] In an odd reversal of stereotypes, throughout the run of *Gilmore Girls* it is a Caucasian American mother, Lorelai, who steadfastly nurtures the tunnel-vision ideal of her daughter attending Harvard, ever since Rory first started to speak. Significantly, this long-cherished dream is not shared by Mrs. Kim, who is more inclined to send her daughter to a strict Seventh-Day Adventist school. Lorelai's usurpation of what is an integral part of Korean immigrant parents' American Dream is further indication that the series seeks to provide ongoing parallels and mirroring scenes between the two mother-daughter pairs.

This doubling structure is perhaps most apparent when the two mothers are forced to contend with the potentially negative influence of teenage boys on their daughters halfway through Season Two. Beginning with Jess Mariano's arrival in "Nick & Nora/Sid & Nancy" (2.05), Lorelai becomes increasingly concerned about Rory's interest in this unruly nephew of Luke, a rebellious teenager whose black-sheep status in his own family only further differentiates him from everyone else in Stars Hollow, a town he incredulously gazes upon as

4. The linkage between the immigrant experience and the educational zeal to send kids to Ivy League schools is gestured toward in "Application Anxiety" (3.03), an episode in which Lorelai expresses anger that teenagers from China and India are traveling to the United States to attend Harvard.

either an anachronistic remnant of the past (right out of a Frank Capra film) or a Disneyfied portal into a parallel universe. Eventually, Jess's less than stellar track record with the town's police and the school's principal runs the gamut from petty crimes like vandalism and minor theft to academic offenses such as unexcused absences and fights with fellow students.

While Lorelai is busy consulting Dean, Rory's initially unsuspecting boyfriend, in "A-Tisket, a-Tasket," Mrs. Kim mistakenly suspects that Lane is dating an American boy behind her back, when in fact the young girl's love interest is Rory's overachieving Korean American schoolmate at Chilton, Henry Cho. Afraid of her mother's opposition, Lane has been clandestinely communicating with Henry through the help of Rory, who, in "Run Away, Little Boy" (2.09), calls her friend first so as to circumvent Mrs. Kim's censors and then relays the line to Henry, who has been waiting in the wings. This sneaky three-way phone call foreshadows another elaborate ruse in "It Should've Been Lorelai" (2.14), when Rory masterminds and stages a mission to deliver a new Belle and Sebastian CD to Lane. On Rory's cue, the chameleon-like Kirk tails Mrs. Kim, who is accompanied by her daughter and dressed for Sunday-morning church service. He then distracts the woman with questions about her store hours. Posing as a jogger, Michel passes by Lane and skillfully drops the contraband disc into her open bag, an amateur act of espionage that goes unnoticed by Mrs. Kim, still busy talking to Kirk. This scene and many others like it are indicative of the fact that a strange mix of subservience and subterfuge defines Lane's relationship to her mother, distinguishing it from the sorority-like support between Lorelai and Rory.

In "A-Tisket, a-Tasket," both mothers confront their daughters with maternal misgivings. Jess outbids Dean in the annual Stars Hollow picnic-basket auction, winning the basket of food that Rory put together as well as her companionship for the afternoon. Linked by their appreciation and love of literature, Rory and Jess not only share a basketful of snacks but also indulge in a postpicnic outing to the pizza parlor and bookstore. This incident triggers Lorelai's protective-mother mode, and her prejudice against Jess later upsets Rory.

Lane, meanwhile, is heartbroken to learn that Henry—frustrated by his inability to date her openly—has invited another girl to the school prom. Noticing Lane's "postbreakup stress disorder," Mrs. Kim pressures her daughter to name the boy who has hurt her and, much to her dismay, realizes that the person in question fits all of the criteria she had set for a future son-in-law: a churchgoing would-be doctor who is Korean. Despite this apparent backfire of her strict parenting, the Korean immigrant woman refuses to budge an inch and does not soften her rigid exterior.

In the episode that immediately follows (the aforementioned, "It Should've Been Lorelai"), viewers learn that Lane has been harshly punished for her brief, unauthorized association with Henry. Sentenced to "the mother of all groundings"—two weeks of home schooling with a mere five minutes of phone time set aside each day (discounting the "Psalm-a-Day line" for which she has been granted unlimited use)—Lane temporarily becomes a home prisoner whose sole source of comfort and vicarious thrills is to watch for Rory from her bedroom window (with a telescope) and to call her for quick news updates. The Korean mother's oppressive disciplinary methods contrast sharply with Lorelai's egalitarian solution to her own teen daughter problem. After receiving old-school advice (from her uptight mother, Emily) that she should keep Rory from Jess by any means necessary ("change her curfew, lock her up, throw away the key," and so on), Lorelai does the exact opposite: she tells Rory that she trusts her judgment and allows her to befriend Jess on the condition that the teenage girl will exercise caution and be careful. Thus, she restores the "fabulous cool-mom clause" (to borrow Lorelai's own expression) of her sisterly pact with Rory, rather than turning into another Mrs. Kim or Emily Gilmore, someone who suffocates and alienates her daughter.

Prior to her gradual softening and show of support for Lane's career as a rock musician (from Season Five onward), Mrs. Kim is consistently portrayed as an authoritarian Christian fundamentalist (a comic version of Mrs. White [Piper Laurie] in Brian De Palma's *Carrie* [1976]) and as a miserly merchant who makes other stereotypically represented Korean shopkeepers—like Sonny Kim (Steve Park) in Spike Lee's *Do the Right Thing* (1989)—look like Good Samaritans in comparison. Although the Korean woman prides herself in having lived in the United States long enough (twenty years) to understand Lorelai's clever double entendre about James Madison's predilection for big knockers (in "Last Week Fights, This Week Tights"), Mrs. Kim—in a manner that recalls the titular character from Kazakhstan in the satiric film *Borat* (2006)—owes her prime-time existence to the kind of outrageous foreignness and social ineptitude that television so often mobilizes to please mainstream viewers.[5]

Gross caricatures of Mrs. Kim and her Confucian entourage (running the gamut from dutiful nephew David, handpicked by her to escort Lane on a picnic, to the emissary-like Aunt Jun, who is sent to Lane's new house down the street to announce an impending maternal visit) walk a fine line between gentle ridicule and outright insult for in-group audiences of Korean descent. However, rather than attempt to educate American viewers about "authentic" Korean culture and traditions, *Gilmore Girls* simply (mis)uses Mrs. Kim's otherness to further enrich its already complex narrative universe filled with parallels among the mothers and daughters of the Gilmore family. In other words, Mama Kim is constructed and situated as an extreme counterpoint to both Lorelai and Lane. She is exactly what they are not: an inept (if well-intentioned) mother, a fun-hating foreigner, a hawkish businesswoman, a religious fanatic, a stoic vegan, and a fashion philistine whose severe ways lead her usually obedient daughter to act out by dying her hair purple (in "One's Got Class and the Other One Dyes" [3.04]), only to revert back to its original color (out of both fear and scalp pain).[6] For Lane to be truly herself (a carefree

5. One marker of Mrs. Kim's foreignness is that nobody in Stars Hallow addresses the woman by her first name, Young-ja, which is mentioned only once in the series (notably, by Lane's Korean-speaking grandmother, who pays a rare visit to the town in "I Get a Sidekick Out of You").

6. After being forced to apply to Quaker and Amish colleges by her domineering mother, Lane explodes, "I spent my whole life compromising and being the good little girl, not doing what I want. Or doing what I want and feeling guilty for

American girl) means denouncing everything that Mrs. Kim stands for and emulating *another* (white) mother, Lorelai, who cares for the girl as if she were her own daughter. Inevitably, Lane is compelled to lift her mask as the filial, devout Korean daughter when Mrs. Kim discovers the hidden stash of countercultural consumer goods in the Season Four episode "In the Clamor and the Clangor" (4.11). Near the end of this episode, the Korean American youth bravely confronts her mother and discloses the origins of her secret defiance, dating back to the time when she was six and was told by Mrs. Kim that "the Cookie Monster was one of the seven deadly sins."

After enduring a painful "cold war" stage of separation (a cooling-off period during which the prodigal daughter pays a nocturnal visit to the Kim residence and gently kisses her sleeping mother on the forehead), Lane eventually reconciles with Mrs. Kim. Ironically, it is the disciplinarian's strong church connections that save Lane's struggling band, Hep Alien,[7] which ends up booking a two-month tour of the "entire east coast Seventh-Day Adventists entertainment circuit" in the episode "A House Is Not a Home" (5.22). Mrs. Kim's immersion into typically American ways of life is further evidenced in her acceptance of Lane's blond bandmate Zach as a son-in-law, but not before testing whether he is capable of writing a hit song and supporting his family (in "I'm OK, You're OK" [6.17]). The intersubjective reciprocity between the formerly feuding "Kim Girls" becomes salient in the episode devoted to Lane's wedding, "I Get a Sidekick Out of You": in a burst of cognizance, the second-generation daughter sees a mirroring image of herself in Mrs. Kim, who has been hiding the fact that she is a Seventh-Day Adventist from her own mother (a Buddhist

it, and I'm sick of it." This frustration leads to the teen's impromptu decision to dye her hair purple as a means to express her true identity. Intriguingly, Lane muses about "Vin Diesel's mysterious ethnicity" during the painful bleach session, as if envisioning her own hybridized appearance.

7. Lane's band, Hep Alien, is an anagram of Helen Pai, the Korean American executive producer of *Gilmore Girls* and longtime friend of the series' creator and writer, Amy Sherman-Palladino.

who bows repeatedly before the religious iconography hastily installed in their living room). In the villain-free, feel-good *Gilmore*verse, the Korean mother is yet another faux antagonist, in the vein of Emily, Paris, and Michel, whose harsh exterior and arrogance are mere shields concealing vulnerable, compassionate alter egos.

Sandra Oh Meets Mao Zedong: TV Orientalism, *Gilmore*-Style

> We gotta walk to China. Which way's China?
>
> —BABETTE expressing her need to walk off her Thanksgiving meal at Luke's, in "A Deep-Fried Korean Thanksgiving"

> LANE: I photograph so Asian.
>
> LORELAI: Ming Na has that same problem.
>
> —Conversation in "Bridesmaids Revisited" (6.16)

The Season Five episode "A Messenger, Nothing More" (5.02) includes a significant, reflexive bit of dialogue that sums up the producers' own attitudes toward Asian cultures. Responding to Rory's aversion to putting steak sauce on pizza, Lorelai reasons, "But this is America, where we unapologetically bastardize other countries' cultures in a gross quest for moral and military supremacy." Although applied to the ungodly mixing (the "miscegenation," if you will) of Italian and American cuisines (complete with "imperialistic condiments," according to Rory), Lorelai's comments tellingly evoke the two main institutions behind American Orientalism: the church and the U.S. military.

In an article titled "The Undoing of the Other Woman: Madame Butterfly in the Discourse of American Orientalism," film scholar Nick Browne identifies three dimensions of American Orientalism: (1) military and economic hegemony in Asia; (2) missionary discourses and agendas that stress "Christian re-education and spiritual conversion"; and (3) aesthetic tendencies among artists to objectify "the East's refinement and exoticism" (1996, 249). Post–World War II pro-

Japanese films, such as *Japanese War Bride* (1952), *The Teahouse of the August Moon* (1956), *Sayonara* (1957), and *The Barbarian and the Geisha* (1958), idealize U.S. military and economic occupation of the Far East through interracial romances between submissive Japanese geishas or war brides and patriarchal American military heroes. In marked contrast, a number of prewar and wartime Hollywood films express the America public's sympathy toward and fascination with China through religious narratives. For example, Frank Capra's *Bitter Tea of General Yen* (1932) explores the theme of spiritual conversion of the Oriental "heathen" against an exotic backdrop of war-torn China, affirming Browne's second taxonomy. John Stahl's religious drama *The Keys to the Kingdom* (1944) likewise translates the relation between West and East into a binaristic configuration in which paternalist Catholic priests and doctors act as spiritual guides for the primitive, childlike Orientals. The third category of American Orientalism—the aestheticization of the East—is a strong tendency of Hollywood's Orientalist productions, from the 1915 black-and-white silent film *The Cheat* (with expressionistic shots of shoji panels) to the Technicolor Cinemascope war romance *Sayonara* (with lengthy ethnographic scenes of Kabuki performances).

In the Season Seven episode "That's What You Get, Folks, for Makin' Whoopie" (7.02), our cinephilic heroine Lorelai (a not so thinly disguised surrogate for the show's creator, Amy Sherman-Palladino) playfully invokes the legacy of Hollywood Orientalism and has put together a miniature "Asia" to please Rory, whose planned trip across the Pacific has been aborted (due to her temporary falling-out with Logan). Presenting a kimono to "honorable Rory-san," Lorelai—adorned in an orange kimono and topped with chopstick hairpins (an image that harks back to her wearing a white shirt with a geisha-figure and sequin design in "Let the Games Begin" [3.08])—gives her impressed "guest" a tour of what she calls "an exact replica of Japan, China, Vietnam, Cambodia, Hong Kong, Korea . . . the old Asia . . . the prototype." Like the once-sepia-toned Dorothy, who steps into a Technicolor fantasy world in *The Wizard of Oz* (1939), a momentarily dumbstruck Rory admires a roomful of hodgepodge

Oriental objects, such as lanterns, masks, paper umbrellas, and "feng shuied" furniture covered with silk fabrics. But what most catches her attention are two prominent "billboards" hanging side by side on the wall running along the stairway: framed portraits of Mao Zedong and Sandra Oh (the latter referred to by Lorelai as a "goddess"). Like Lorelai's mishmash itinerary, which includes "[relaxing] with some tai chi in preparation for the Kabuki play" and back-to-back screenings of Bruce Lee's kung fu flick *Enter the Dragon* (1973) and the Audrey Hepburn romantic comedy *Breakfast at Tiffany's* (1961),[8] the jarring visual juxtaposition of the former Chinese Communist Party leader and the young Korean Canadian TV and film actress is whimsical yet problematic. This ethnic-national slippage between revolutionary China and diasporic Korea in the American living room's display of token Asian faces ironically reminds us of the show's cross-ethnic casting of two Japanese American actresses—Keiko Agena and Emily Kuroda—as Lane and Mrs. Kim.

Unlike contemporary ABC dramas that have initiated a "correct casting" approach to ethnic representations (with actual Koreans Kim Yunjin and Daniel Dae Kim playing a Korean-speaking couple in *Lost* [ABC, 2004–] and the aforementioned Sandra Oh as the sassy Korean Jewish American intern Christina Yang in *Grey's Anatomy* [ABC, 2005–]), *Gilmore Girls* regretfully shied away from an ever-expanding pool of Korean American talent despite the fact it was coproduced by Helen Pai (Amy Sherman-Palladino's best friend, a Korean American

8. When Rory is baffled by the selection of the 1961 Blake Edwards film *Breakfast at Tiffany's* as a part of an "educational video" about Asia, Lorelai elaborates, "Starring Mickey Rooney in his tour-de-force racist performance as Holly Golightly's Japanese landlord." It is perhaps not coincidental that this grotesque yellowface performance, historically linked to the civil rights era, was chosen for this most Orientalist of *Gilmore Girls* episodes, since it famously enraged Chinese American actor Bruce Lee upon its original theatrical release. Significantly, it is the iconic Hong Kong action star whose trademark shirtless fighting style Lorelai and Rory are shown watching in this scene. Besides *Breakfast at Tiffany's,* the other films that Lorelai lists are *Bridge on the River Kwai* (1957), *Karate Kid* (1984), *Shanghai Surprise* (1986), *Mr. Baseball* (1992), and *The Joy Luck Club* (1993).

after whom Lane's character is modeled). Undoubtedly, the casting of a Korean American actress in either role (particularly Mrs. Kim, who is supposed to be a native speaker of Korean)[9] would have exponentially increased the authenticity of the show's cultural representations—authenticity that is sadly lacking in the otherwise endearing narrative universe of the series. On the other hand, *Gilmore Girls* is not a show *about* Korea or Korean culture, and it *does* put forth positive, uplifting images of Asian Americans by portraying Lane Kim as a hip audiophile devoid of racial and ethnic stereotypes (even such "positive" stereotypes as the nerdy overachiever and the studious member of a model minority). As such, and bearing in mind that Stars Hollow is a fictional universe that misrepresents, exaggerates, and idealizes small-town American life, an important question arises: for diehard cult fans and mainstream lay audiences, does cultural authenticity (or lack thereof) in this television series or any other really matter?

In an attempt to begin unpacking this rhetorical inquiry, let us turn our attention to a pivotal yet curiously overlooked scene in the series, one that hinges on a Korean wedding. In the aforementioned episode "Lorelai Out of Water," Rory (an "honorary member of the [Kim] clan") is serving as a hairdresser and makeup artist for the bride of Lane's cousin. The Korean woman has been "shipped over from the Old Country . . . and doesn't speak a word of English." When the bride (played by Korean American actress Jessica Shim) speaks to Lane in her native language, saying, "I can't remember my husband's last name," the Korean American teen shares a perplexed look with her best friend (who expects her translation) and shrugs it off, musing, "Too much

9. Helen Pai's mother reportedly taught Korean to Japanese American actress Emily Kuroda, who groaned about it in an interview: "I had to speak a lot of Korean for the wedding episode. It was very stressful. My Korean is very bad. I warned them. But I tried my best." Pai's mother was often consulted by her daughter on those sections of scripts dealing with Korean subjects. Pai quoted her mother saying, "Helen, you have to be very careful, because you're representing the Korean community," although it is unclear how much the Korean woman actually contributed to improving the ethnic images in the series (Tseng 2006).

for me." Then Rory and Lane engage in gossipy girl talk while putting makeup on the confused bride, acting as if she were not there. After congratulating one another for making progress with their current love interests (guitar player Dave Rygalski and Jess, respectively), Lane and Rory reminiscence about the forty-six (!) Kim family weddings they have attended since elementary school years. When Rory remembers Lane's relative named Min-ja who married a mean Korean guy, Wan-nam, Lane lets her in on a scandalous family rumor:

> Min-ja put up with seven years of Wan-nam telling her she was stupid and ordering her to cook all his meals. Then one day he was in the kitchen looking for his lunch, and she just snapped. Took a carrot peeler and turned on him. . . . She just came at him and started peeling. The neighbors called the police, and Wan-nam just stood there, all peeled. He didn't press charges. But now he makes all his own meals, sleeps in a locked, separate room, and keeps the cutting board for protection. Still married, though. Everybody's still married; it's like a factory system here. They come to the weddings, find a spouse, get married, and stay that way until they die.

What is notable about this scene is that during Lane's nonstop babble, the camera cuts twice to a medium close-up of the muted bride's doll-like face (with sad, downcast eyes), as if implying that she will be the next Min-ja, an abused Korean wife who will one day snap and go mental. The Stepford Wife–to-be thus functions as a cautionary reminder for Lane that she should resist her mother's efforts to arrange a marriage between her and a prosperous yet patriarchal Korean man (such as Young-chui, a doctor's son, whom Mrs. Kim introduces to Lane as her approved prom date after the wedding).

Should American viewers seek evidence that Korean teenagers and twentysomethings are as cool and hip as Lane and Rory and bear no resemblance to the stereotypes of Korean cousins and relatives in *Gilmore Girls,* they need only skim through a few episodes of South Korea's recent batch of "trendy dramas" such as *Rooftop Room Cat* (MBC, 2003) and *My Lovely Sam-soon* (MBC, 2005). These television shows and others like them centering on the romances and career ambitions of young urban professionals showcase the country's cosmopolitan settings and a cell phone–based dating culture that is decidedly high-tech and illustrate that South Korea is not just "where you go to get kids" (Lane's deeply problematic comment to Rory in "Afterboom" [4.19]). According to coproducer Helen Pai (who, like Lane, grew up under the watchful eyes of Seventh-Day Adventist parents), "During the first season of *Gilmore Girls,* we had a panel, and there were a lot of questions about Mrs. Kim and Lane and the stereotypes. And, Amy would then explain, 'Listen, these are real stories. They're based on a real person.'" Pai's on-screen surrogate, Keiko Agena, has likewise defended the show's Korean representations by stating, "The intention is there to represent it well, but not necessarily 'accurately,' because, after all, it is a comedy. It's going to take elements of something and blow it up to the extreme" (Tseng 2006).

These points are all well taken. However, I am inclined to ask if it is too much to expect Lane to be a bit more thoughtful and inclusive of her cousin's alienated bride (rather than treating her like an invisible nonperson) on the latter's wedding day. Couldn't the producers of *Gilmore Girls* have been more culturally sensitive about their wardrobe choices and presented a piece of clothing that might actually pass as a traditional Korean wedding gown in the eyes of in-group audiences? At the very least, a classic white wedding dress (which modern Korean brides prefer to wear) would have been preferable over the costumelike Oriental garb and hair accessories that were used in "Lorelai Out of Water."[10]

As noted by Edward Said in his groundbreaking treatise on Orientalism, when assessing the images of the Orient in Western cultural

10. Thankfully, the producers did hire Korean consultants for another wedding episode ("I Get a Sidekick Out of You"), as attested in the aforementioned interview with Kuroda. The traditional gowns that Lane and Zack wear for the "Buddhist" ceremony in this episode are indeed authentic. However, Ralph Ahn (the youngest brother of famous Korean American actor Philip Ahn), who plays the monk presiding over the ceremony, has limited command of Korean, and his speech makes little sense to Korean-speaking audience members.

productions, "the things to look at are style, figures of speech, setting, narrative devices, historical and social circumstances, not the *correctness* of the representation nor its fidelity to some great original" (1979, 21). Said emphasizes the "*exteriority* of the representation," since Orientalism—as a structured set of Western *ideas* about the East—"has less do with the Orient than it does with 'our' world" (ibid., 12). These definitions, I believe, are useful in understanding the logic (or, rather, *illogic*) of Asian representations in *Gilmore Girls,* which frequently uses minority characters as mere window dressing or as silent witnesses to the main characters' quirks (as in "They Shoot Gilmores, Don't They?" [3.07], which shows Kirk entering a marathon dance contest with a mute Asian woman curiously named Donna Delain).

"Koreanness," in this context, can be defined as a set of ideas, values, and lifestyles that are in direct opposition to the ones denoting or connoting "Americanness." For Lane Kim to fully claim her American identity necessitates an escape from "Korea," something that she literally and figuratively does at various junctures throughout the series. The lingering question, though, is whether *all* audience members are expected to accompany Lane on that journey into "self" and in her escape from "otherness." If so, then cultural authenticity—to answer my earlier question—*does* matter. It matters precisely because Korean representations in *Gilmore Girls* have less to do with Korea (as an actual geopolitical site) than with the mythical ideals associated with small-town America and the meritocracy that such a utopian space promises (if not always provides) to *all* people regardless of their race, ethnicity, or nationality.

10

"The Thing That Reads a Lot"

Bibliophilia, College Life, and Literary Culture in Gilmore Girls

ANNA VIOLA SBORGI

> You don't have a tumor. You're reading too much. You're probably just losing your eyesight.
>
> —LORELAI to Rory in "That Damn Donna Reed" (1.14)

Because of the alternative family model that Lorelai Gilmore and her daughter, Rory, embody, as well as the show's frequent intertextual references to underground culture and the ironic tone permeating its 153 episodes, *Gilmore Girls* marks a significant, if not radical, departure from the prototypical American family comedy-drama. The strong opposition between the egalitarian Stars Hollow and the more socially rigid environment represented by Emily and Richard's posh circle and prestigious academic institutions such as Chilton and Yale further reinforces this interpretation. However, questions of class and heritage as well as the relation of the characters to conventional mainstream culture are not rendered binaristically or schematically in terms of acceptance or refusal. Rory Gilmore constructs her identity by negotiating different models of behavior, and what are typically conceived of as American values—self-reliance and competitiveness—make their way into spaces otherwise reserved for alternative taste cultures. Moreover, Lorelai's hopes and achievements can be said to reflect "the American Dream": she is a symbol of self-reliance and is determined to ensure that her daughter—with as little support from her own parents as possible—has educational and professional opportunities made available to her.

This complex relationship is made all the more evident by the way in which literature figures in the series. By devoting screen time to the experience of reading and the complex interaction between high and popular culture—much of which takes place in educational institutions—*Gilmore Girls* is unusual as a TV show whose priorities seem to lie in decidedly nontelevisual material. Rory immerses herself in a variety of textually rich cultural environments, from academe to the worlds of journalism and popular culture, and these experiences shape her interests and passions, which—prior to attending Yale—had been nurtured by her mother. This chapter will trace the contours of *Gilmore Girls*' cultural models, focusing in particular on the ways in which literary allusions, among the many other types of intertextual references, are deployed throughout the series.

Of Books and Bibliophilia

Rory's bibliophilia—her love of reading and writing printed words—is not likely to be found in other contemporary television series depicting teenage life. Rory's passion for books and literary culture is rendered imagistically throughout *Gilmore Girls*' seven seasons. This peculiar aspect of the girl's personality is made clear in the first episodes of Season One. For instance, in "The Deer Hunters" (1.04), when Rory comes back exhausted from carrying heavy bags to her mother's workplace after one of her first days at Chilton, Lorelai addresses her in an amiably ironic tone: "Oh, behold, in theaters now, the thing that reads a lot." Several other scenes confirm this impression. In "Like Mother, Like Daughter" (2.07), Rory attempts to cram a number of books into her backpack, substantial tomes that she intends to read during her bus trip to school and her lunch. When confronted by her skeptical (and slightly shocked) mother, who advises the teenager to take only the necessary schoolbooks, Rory explains, "No, the Millay is a biography, and sometimes if I'm on the bus and I pull out a biography and I think to myself, 'Well, I don't really feel like reading about a person's life right now,' and then I'll switch to the novel, and then sometimes if I'm not into the novel, I'll switch back." The following dialogue then takes place:

LORELAI: Hold on. What is the Gore Vidal?
RORY: Oh, that's my lunch book.
LORELAI: Uh-huh. So lose the Vidal or the Faulkner. You don't need two novels.
RORY: Vidal's is essays.
LORELAI: Uh-huh. But the Eudora Welty's not essays or a biography.
RORY: Right.
LORELAI: So it's another novel. Lose it!
RORY: Un-uh. It's short stories.
LORELAI: Ugh. This is a sickness.

Throughout the series, a significant amount of screen time and space is dedicated to the representation of places connected with reading: from Rory's bedroom at home, where books festoon the shelves and are piled under her bed, to classrooms and libraries, both at high school and at college. Libraries in particular seem to hold a great fascination in Rory's world. In "But Not as Cute as Pushkin" (5.10), for example, she has been asked to give Anna (a current Chilton student and prospective Yale undergraduate) a tour of the campus, and recounts the history of the university in detail. The seriousness with which Rory carries out her task is furthermore exemplified in a conversation she has with her grandfather Richard, someone who shares the young woman's bibliophilia. As Rory mentions all of the places she wants to take Anna to, Lorelai pokes fun at her daughter and father and suggests that the girl would be bored to death unless Rory shows her the less serious side of college life. But neither Rory nor Richard seems to take the slightest notice of Lorelai's comments. When Rory walks into the Sterling Memorial Library with Anna, she explains to the younger girl, "One of my favorite places on campus. It was built in 1930, and it houses over one-third of the university's ten million volumes. I love libraries. I just spend I can't tell you how many hours there." But the younger girl's attention wanders. Anna seems most interested by the fact that students at Yale do not have to wear uniforms. She also asks Rory how many boys the latter has dated since coming to college. Rory, still enraptured by the university's setting, takes little notice of her companion and goes on with her explanation: "Oh, well, none from Yale. Anyhow, the books—are you seeing the books? [She pulls an ancient-looking book off the shelf.] Everything you'd want to read is right here. Feel it. [She hands the book to Anna, and takes another one for herself.] Feels good, right? Now smell it. [Rory smells her book and sighs.] Nothing, nothing smells like that." At this point Logan Huntzberger (Rory's prospective boyfriend) interrupts her reverie, making fun of his girlfriend's almost fetishist sniffing of the book. Anna is predictably fascinated with Logan, whom she calls "cute," but Rory replies that he is "not as cute as Pushkin."

However fascinating a library might be to certain students, looking for an ideal place to read is not as easy as it might seem. Even at Yale, Rory struggles to find her own place to study without being disturbed by the outside world, as her tragicomic experience with her "study tree" illustrates in "An Affair to Remember" (4.06). Being disturbed by her roommates, who show no comprehension for her concentration problems, Rory finds a tree to sit under in the campus park. The tree suggests Rory's idea of perfect comfort, as she tells her mother on the phone, saying that it is "just far enough away from anything major so there's not a lot of noise but still not in Siberia." This comment reflects Rory's complex personality: for all her need for intimacy, she still rejects complete isolation; the perfect location for studying is at the same time detached and connected to the external world. As often happens in the series, the young woman's passion for studying seems almost excessive, but it is counterbalanced by comic aspects. When she loses her study tree because a boy is sitting in her place, she overreacts ("Yes, I will figure out what my alternate profession will be because now I can't study, I'm gonna flunk out of Yale, and I'm gonna have to give up all hope of being a foreign correspondent. This sucks"), and thereafter seeks refuge at her mother's house, only to find her room covered with broccoli tarts Sookie has made for a catering job at the elder Gilmores'. When Lorelai cools her down, Rory returns to Yale and finds her own solution: she bribes the boy with twenty dollars to get her place back. Her pragmatism and the comical tone of this scene mitigate the exaggeratedly serious attitude she had at the beginning of the episode.

Similar situations are sprinkled throughout the series, and—though all these images might contribute to form a somewhat rigid view of Rory's personality—ironic commentaries by other characters are often put forth to counterbalance this effect and to prevent her bookwormish behavior from becoming too humorless. Lorelai, who often adopts a more lighthearted approach to life than her daughter, takes up this counterbalancing role. It happens during their trip to Harvard (2.04), for instance, when Rory panics about her feelings of inadequacy in front of the colossal university library. Lorelai tries to comfort her and cheer her up by making jokes, effectively toning down her irrationally high expectations. Rory has convinced herself that she should read all of the library's volumes (thirteen million books) in order to be able to converse brilliantly with the students at Harvard.

This particular reference implies that Rory wants to raise herself up to a certain social standard—in the process acquiring refined conversational skills—which contrasts with the usual depiction of her interest in culture for the sake of itself while at the same time confirming the underlying impulse toward educational achievement in the series. Furthermore, Lorelai's suggestion to skip books that would fall outside the Western canon (*Tuesdays with Morrie*? *Who Moved My Cheese*?) is another example of the tension between opposing values underpinning the two women's relationship with culture. As often happens in *Gilmore Girls,* the possible social implications of the scene are softened by irony, which is obtained by the contrast between the characters in a verbal exchange: Rory is exaggeratedly serious, and Lorelai dismisses this seriousness, both comforting her and lovingly making fun of her. Although Rory does not normally change her mind at the end of these dialogue scenes, being able to express her feelings verbally—and not through written words—helps her to cope with her inner conflicts.

Rory's bibliophilia and passion for studying are peculiar to her, but the paradoxical tone of this dialogue prevents her character from becoming dull. She is also capable of self-irony and of recognizing a "real" bookworm when she sees one, something that happens when Stars Hollow hosts the Edgar Allan Poe Society convention in "A Tale of Poes and Fire" (3.17). At one point in this episode, several members of the society dressed as the nineteenth-century poet and short-story writer repeatedly give readings of "The Raven" and argue about who the "true" Poe among them is. The Gilmore girls sit in the audience, a diegetic inscription of our own spectatorship, and crack satirical jokes about them.

Comparing this scene to the Harvard episode, we can see a different modality of verbal exchange between mother and daughter. In this case Rory actively takes part in her mother's jokes, thus expressing a more relaxed side of her personality. This scene is also used to tone down the consequent pressure Rory is experiencing, as she is trying to decide which university to attend. Also, literary references interspersed in the scene and connected to the blending of fictional and real-life elements convey a symbolic value. Here, as in other episodes, the Gilmore girls pretend to oscillate between different spatiotemporal dimensions:

> LORELAI: If the Poes start fighting, does that punch a hole in the space-time continuum?
> RORY: And throw us into a universe where everything is the exact opposite of what it is here?
> LORELAI: Cool. There'll be funny sitcoms there.

Further highlighted by this scene's metatextual reference to sitcoms, the dichotomy between reality (the choice) and imagination (going to Harvard, what the young girl had always dreamed of) symbolically reinforces the importance of this decisive moment in Rory's life.

The experience of reading is a very private one for Rory, who uses canonical examples of high literature to forge an identity and shape a world of her own, one that might seem detached from the more tangible world of face-to-face social relations. However, this seemingly hermetic existence is "perforated" at various junctures throughout the series, and her personal day-to-day experiences come into contact with cultural attitudes associated with institutions of higher learning. Literary allusions and the experience of reading thus become vehicles for different social and cultural values. Rory is fascinated with prestigious universities such as Yale and Harvard because of her love of knowledge and because she hopes to pursue her dream of becoming a journalist through further acquisition of said knowledge. Yet, for all of her self-awareness, she does not always see the full range of social implications these institutions hold. The complexities involved in gaining cultural literacy and enjoying the benefits associated with being a college student come to the fore when she enters Logan's world, evoking the same milieu of upper-class families her grandparents belong to, a social environment in which sons and daughters are sent to prestigious educational institutions to follow in their parents' footsteps.

Rory does not seem to be fully attuned to the implications of her relationship to Logan until she experiences a double confrontation. The first event that makes her aware of the differences between them is a dinner with her boyfriend's family in "But I'm a Gilmore!" (5.19), where she is ostracized by his mother and father because of her determination to work and be independent, something that makes her unsuitable to become the wife of "the heir to the Huntzberger fortune," as Logan, with a note of both sarcasm and bitterness, labels himself. Later, in the Season Five episode "Blame Booze and Melville" (5.21), Logan's father, Mitchum—who is a press tycoon—has a role in demolishing the girl's hopes of a journalistic career. This episode acquires specific meaning in light of Mitchum's reappraisal of Rory in Season Seven, suggesting that his roadblocking of the young woman's intended career path was a way to prevent her from marrying his son. Significantly, the Huntzbergers' cold reception of Rory is not very different from the condescending attitude Richard Gilmore displays in his meeting with Dean earlier in the series. Actually, the elder Gilmores do not accept Rory's relationship with Dean for the same reason that the Huntzbergers express apprehensions about Logan's possible marriage with Rory, only this time the rationale is reversed. Precisely because she has cultural aspirations and wants to pursue a professional career of her own, Rory is deemed unsuitable for Logan (just as Dean had been deemed unsuitable for her). Eventually, much like Logan has to put up a facade with his family while struggling to gain his father's respect, Rory—although more unconditionally loved by her relatives—has to live up to her grandparents' expectations, as her mother explains to her: "You are the great white hope of the Gilmore clan. You are their angel sent from up above. You are the daughter they didn't have. I mean, you're gonna go to college. Hell, you're gonna graduate from high school."

The second moment in which Rory's and Logan's worlds come to a clash occurs when Jess visits Rory in "Let Me Hear Your Balalaikas Ringing Out" (6.08), during her break from collegiate life at Yale. The two young men are presented as opposing models of manhood and masculinity. Logan plays the prototypical rich and cheeky twentysomething who has little to no interest in bibliophilic culture. He makes sarcastic jokes about the length of books and mocks Jess's efforts as a fledgling writer. On the opposite end of the spectrum, Jess has grown more mature and has channeled his energies into writing, thus finding his place in life. Observing their stark behavioral contrast, and confronted by Jess's perplexity about how Rory is leading her life, the college dropout suddenly realizes that she has become a completely different person from the would-be journalist she had once embodied. This self-awareness leads her to overcome her existential crisis and return to Yale, full of vigor and a passion to read.

In a certain sense, Rory's relationship with Logan—while peppered with romantic and supportive moments—seems destined to fail. No matter how much Logan matures and shows respect toward his more academically driven girlfriend, being with him would likely mean having to comply with his lifestyle and values. This likelihood explains Logan's somewhat abrupt exit from the series in the penultimate episode ("Unto the Breach" [7.21]). Although Logan has problems in accepting his role as family heir and even manages to gain independence from his father, he is still too immersed in his environment and expresses quite traditional expectations about Rory's role in their relationship, which eventually fails in part because of these reasons (with Rory's refusal of his offer to marry him and move to San Francisco). Rory's attraction to and separation from Logan are part of her constant oscillation between different social and cultural worlds. What prevents *Gilmore Girls* from being identified with any one of these worlds is the characters' penchant for irony.

An important role in managing the series' ironic tone and complex rhetorical modes is given to Paris Geller, a character whose contrasting personality makes Rory seem less rigid. We might say that Paris represents Rory's alter ego, a more competitive overachiever at both Chilton and Yale who shares with the Gilmore girl a number of traits. Paris mirrors, in a much more neurotic way, Rory's own longing for success, which is combined with a desire to learn and make a good impression as a model student. Paris is determined to obtain stellar results for several reasons: for the sake of success in itself, because of her fear of failure, and owing to a need to comply with her family's expectations. As she states in "The Big One" (3.16), "Five generations of Gellers have gotten into Harvard. Even if I was the Billy Carter of the family, the name is still supposed to carry some weight."

Like Rory, Paris often uses literary quotations to underline pregnant moments. For example, she quotes Shakespeare on at least two occasions. The first occurs in "The Deer Hunters," when—in the early days of their acquaintance—she challenges Rory, showing her academic aggressiveness and whispering by heart the bard's Sonnet 116 into her companion's ear: "Let me not to the marriage of true minds admit impediments." This verse might seem to be an odd passage for Paris to quote, considering that it comes from a love sonnet. However, it can be seen as a symbolic reference to their love-hate relationship, something later emphasized in the spring-break episode "Girls in Bikinis, Boys Doin' the Twist" (4.17), when Paris plants an impetuous (yet nonsexual) kiss on Rory's mouth. At the same time, the allusion to perseverance might be a way to exacerbate the tension between the two, suggesting that Paris will be the one to endure the various trials and tribulations set before the young women on their career paths.

Second, the last words Paris utters in the series—after the tumultuous relationship between the two girls has been sorted out—are derived from Shakespeare's *Henry V.* The two girls are lining up at the graduation ceremony at Yale, and, just before taking the stage, Paris holds Rory's hand and exclaims, "Unto the breach!" (which is also the title of the episode), quoting a passage from the battle scene in Act 3, Scene 1: "Once more unto the breach, dear friends, once more." As this show is the penultimate episode of the series, these words are particularly resonant because they mark a watershed moment in the two girls' life together. Just before uttering these words, Paris expresses her feelings that they will be driven apart after graduation. A new world is waiting for them outside, there are many things to battle for, and—though Rory reassures Paris on this point—they might not be together in the fight. These lines symbolically highlight the culmination of a relationship developed during adolescence while at the same time suggesting that they are sharing a leap into the dark, into the unknown.

Whenever Rory experiences a meltdown, a *mid*midlife crisis, Paris acts as her counterpart, proving to be more determined, if sometimes more tunnel-visioned, than her friend. As a fictional character, Rory is much more realistic and well rounded and seems to view university life and educational attainment in general as opportunities for gaining self-realization, not merely résumé-building elements that will put her first in the race toward professional gold. Although faced with difficult challenges herself, Paris always maintains an energetic demeanor, a fierce determination, as in "To Whom It May Concern" (7.12), an episode in which she makes Rory participate in her frantic "Operation Finish Line" program (on a board in their room Paris has made a list of all the fellowships and jobs they both should apply for; she also tells a puzzled Rory that they should have weekly meetings to monitor their progress). This scene is a parody both of the character and of the competitiveness and pressure imposed by the educational system itself. Indeed, the absurd seriousness that characterizes Paris's personality is mirrored in the way that the administrators of institutions of higher learning sometimes see themselves.

This attitude is already evident in the pilot episode of the series (1.01), when Rory leaves Stars Hollow High and enters the upper-crust world of the Chilton prep school. In "The Lorelais' First Day at Chilton" (1.02), the easygoing look and style of both mother and daughter (especially Lorelai's totally "inappropriate" clothes) make a strong and hilarious contrast with the dull and austere atmosphere of the school. Lorelai's behavior and appearance help to throw in relief the differences between the world of wealth and affluence and the world of hip, yet grounded, personalities like herself. In later episodes Rory is shocked by the competitiveness and aggressiveness of the other students, and learns that failing in class means for them failing in life. Her occasional low grades (for instance, a D on a test) are a "cause for concern" to Paris, "a cry for help," and "a job application at McDonald's." The institution itself is partly responsible for stimulating these attitudes, as is shown by the heated dialogue between Lorelai and Headmaster Charleston when Rory accidentally fails to attend an important test in the aforementioned "The Deer Hunters." Lorelai accuses the headmaster of nurturing "horrible kids who treat each other like mortal enemies" and of setting "impossible standards that make normal people feel less than everyone else." Rory and Lorelai's private world apparently contrasts the establishment represented at different levels throughout the series—by the elder Gilmores or by academic institutions in this case—but at the same time it is important for Rory (and for Lorelai as well) to uphold certain standards.

As the above descriptions suggest, the literary references sprinkled throughout the show's episodes are drawn from a variety of sources. While tracing every single literary reference in the series would be a task best suited for a much longer essay (perhaps, fittingly, for an entire book), I will provide a handful of examples of texts that are cited and, more generally, outline the way literary allusions work. In the same way that other types of cultural references in the series range from high to popular culture (in the interconnected spheres of music, film, and television), Rory's readings range from alt-culture indie books to canonical works of literature. Still, the student's tastes in literature are sometimes opposed to Lorelai's, which are lighter, less bound to literary traditions (for instance, she is often shown reading women's magazines and "trashy" paperbacks like the Mötley Crüe biography, *The Dirt: Confessions of the World's Most Notorious Rock Band*).

Although Rory's interests are always diverse, references to books in the series gradually change, mirroring the development of her character. In the first seasons especially, the novels she reads are by female authors and portray strong-willed, witty, and independent women in the process of fashioning their own identity. From Jane Austen's heroines and Brontë's Jane Eyre to more contemporary figures such as Dorothy Parker, Sylvia Plath, and the aforementioned Edna St. Vincent Millay, different models of literary womanhood are presented, echoing Rory's own struggles in "writing" her own life narrative, as well as her attempts to relate to her real-life female models: her mother and the more conventional figure of femininity represented by her grandmother.

Although some of these writers, in very different ways, reflect the kind of irony that permeates the series, one—Plath—at first seems an odd choice for intertextual inclusion, given her famously tormented personality. In "Double Date" (1.12), Rory reads the *Unabridged Journals of Sylvia Plath* while waiting for Dean and sitting on a bench outside his school. Plath's own personality, as much as the depiction of her autobiographical heroine in *The Bell Jar* (1963) (a girl making her way in the male-dominated New York editing world), might create some meaningful connections (for instance, Plath, who suffered from serious depression, herself dropped out of Smith College for a whole semester, in 1953). There is, therefore, thematic overlap between this pioneering female author and the narrative developments in *Gilmore Girls,* with Rory's more positive, upbeat personality being reflected in Plath's own commitment to an academic career.

In a similar way, Dorothy Parker is quoted in "Rory's Dance" (1.09), after Dean discovers that Rory has taken *The Portable Dorothy Parker* to the Chilton Ball. Although they reference one of the wisecracking author's well-known poems ("Coda"), the intertextual allusion remains significant because it reflects an interest in Parker's journalist career, something Rory would like to pursue. But her writing is also emblematic both of the blending of popular culture and high culture and of the kind of New York witticisms that permeate the series (notably, *Gilmore Girls* was produced by Dorothy Parker Drank Here Productions). Sometimes the same bleak, nonsensical irony of Parker's work sprouts up in the nonstop verbal exchanges between mother and daughter.

References to classical works of literature appear with frequency throughout the first season. For example, in "Love and War and Snow" (1.08), Rory and Dean talk about Jane Austen, whose *Emma*—an 1816 novel concerning an intelligent and boisterous young matchmaker—Rory has convinced Dean to read. She would like him to move on to Charlotte Brontë upon completion of said text, while he advises her to read Hunter S. Thompson's "gonzo" brand of psychedelic fiction. In Season Two, another alternative cult book, J. D. Salinger's *Franny and Zooey,* makes its appearance via Rory's developing relationship with Jess, who shares the girl's passion for reading more actively than Dean, though he denies it with his typical understatement. Jess "steals" Rory's copy of the book just to add notes in the margins for her. The girl is quite surprised, as he had previously denied encountering that particular book and affirmed that he did not read much. When Rory points it out to him, he replies, rather philosophically, "Well, what is *much*?"—thus bringing forward concerns about culture that are very similar to the young woman's.

Literary references often accompany significant moments in Rory's life. For example, in "Application Anxiety" (3.03), the Gilmore girls are watching *The Brady Bunch Variety Hour* on TV when the official response to Rory's application to Harvard arrives. She worries about the fact that this important moment could be handed down to posterity in connection with such a trashy TV show. So Lorelai decides that they will tell people Rory was reading Gogol's 1842 Russian novel *Dead Souls,* which the girl had actually been reading just a few hours before. Here again the interplay between high and pop culture is skillfully mastered by the writers: Rory's tragicomic overreaction softens the contrast between the two different cultural levels and blends them.

Moreover, Rory refers to Melville's *Moby Dick* as "inspiration" in "Blame Booze and Melville" (5.21) before stealing the yacht with Logan, a moment representing a significant turning point in her life:

> RORY: You know the beginning of *Moby Dick,* when the narrator says that when he finds himself growing grim about the mouth and wanted to knock people's hats off, he takes to the sea?
> LOGAN: Yeah.
> RORY: Well, I feel like knocking people's hats off.
> LOGAN: So I guess we got to take to the sea.

Midway through the seven-season run of *Gilmore Girls,* Rory's interests decisively shifted to the world of journalism. Beyond its many references to literary texts, the series also gestures toward well-known journalists, so much so that it is entirely fitting that real-life news correspondent Christiane Amanpour (whom Rory has idolized for years) should make a cameo appearance in the series finale, wishing the young woman success in her future endeavors. Indeed, allusions to Rory's reading preferences gravitate more toward political editorials and hard-boiled journalism than toward canonical literary texts. For example, Mitchum Huntzberger advises Rory to read Philip Meyer's *Vanishing Newspaper* (2004) in one of the last episodes ("I'm a Kayak, Hear Me Roar" [7.15]), although, predictably, she has already read it. Moreover, the experience of writing at the *Yale Daily News* and in her different internships takes center stage.

In addition to the above-mentioned literary quotations and the representations of reading and writing thus far discussed, the entire structure of the series resembles the literary model of the bildungsroman. Single episodes are not to be understood independently; they are tied together into a larger coming-of-age narrative, one that encompasses not only Rory's interpersonal and academic experiences but also the experiences of her best friends, including Lane and Paris. Ever since her first steps into the series as a shy teenager focused mainly on her studies, Rory grows into a more mature person, struggling to break the standard models of behavior and molds of femininity she finds in the world around her. Moreover, titles of the episodes are often named after novels, short stories, and other literary genres. Although this fact does not necessarily mean that the series mirrors any of these forms, it certainly draws on them for inspiration. For example, the reference to Henry James in "Say Goodbye to Daisy Miller" (5.01), an episode in which Rory decides to travel to Europe with her grandmother Emily as a chaperone (after beginning an adulterous affair with married Dean), allows bibliophilic audiences to make comparisons between two heroines—one literary, the other televisual—similarly involved in a process of self-discovery and soul-searching. Rory herself acknowledges this connection, exclaiming to her mother, "So, what is this, a Henry James novel? The young lady acts up, and her family ships her off to Europe?" Although the reference is to Daisy Miller, because of Rory's difficult situation with Dean she ultimately turns into an Isabel Archer kind of character, eager to learn things about Europe and enjoy new experiences.

The typical structure of the bildungsroman involves personal loss or discontent or both, which the main character has to deal with and places her or him in the process of constructing her or his own identity in the face of external conflict and internal turmoil. Although this may not sound exactly like *Gilmore Girls,* the series does in fact hinge on the clash between one's goals and desires and the demands foisted on that person by the social environment. The tensions Rory experiences are mirrored by her mother's choices in life, the refusal of her social background, and the eventual necessity of returning to it. Furthermore, although Lorelai's drifting apart from her parents might not have been perceived as a tragic event in her daughter's life, because it happened at the time of her birth, she experiences it indirectly. Actually, although the main narrative thread in the series is the daughter's education and growth, a parallel thread involves Lorelai's own "coming-of-age" story, or rather her coming to terms with the lifestyle of her demanding parents. The two levels are connected by Rory's constant efforts to heal old wounds and bring family members together again. Eventually, the series culminates with the main and secondary narratives coming full circle.

If the series had begun with the almost impossible return of Emily and Richard into Lorelai's life, it ends with some sort of reconciliation, with a more balanced relationship among the three, and most important with the parents' recognition of her strength as a fiercely independent woman. Although Rory's equally independent future is set out, Richard and Emily finally recognize Lorelai too as an adult who, struggling for years, has achieved a great deal of professional success. As Richard himself says to her at the end: "It takes a r— [his voice breaks] a remarkable person to inspire all of this." Richard's comment highlights the important role Lorelai played in Rory's formation.

The choice of this moment to end the series seems quite appropriate. The end of the story coincides with the end of our heroine's formal and informal education. Rory is now an intellectual being, with her social role being quite clear, and, although we might want to look back with a nostalgic eye to the days of her daydreaming and clumsy bookwormish behavior (which we may find hard to recognize in this sometimes too perfect woman of the world, who has skillfully synthesized social models around her), we must acknowledge this result as the natural outcome of her growing-up process.

As we have seen, literary references and encounters (occasionally clashes) with diverse cultural worlds make *Gilmore Girls* especially rich at the textual level and are used throughout the series' seven seasons to mark important events in a girl's life. Also, the fictional characters in novels and other literary forms with whom Rory has lived for years have effectively merged into her personality, which, as in an actual novel, has been written out, page by page (or, rather, episode after episode). Rory's opportunity to realize her dream and pursue a career in journalism (she eventually gets a job as an online magazine correspondent for Barack Obama's campaign) is the predictable outcome of her years of reading experiences and writing apprenticeship, and offers her the most suitable means of expressing her full-grown personality and blending all the different cultural domains she has experienced.

11

Stars Hollow, Chilton, and the Politics of Education in *Gilmore Girls*

MATTHEW C. NELSON

> College is breaking my spirit. Every single day, telling me things I don't know, it's making me feel stupid.
>
> —MARTY speaking to Rory after a marathon study session, in "Emily Says Hello" (5.09)

In Lorelai Gilmore and the fictional town of Stars Hollow, Amy Sherman-Palladino created a character and place that represent a kind of middle-class American ideal. Lorelai is a smart, successful, fiercely independent woman who has made a comfortable life for herself and her daughter, and she has done it on her own. Lorelai's neighbors are, for the most part, like her: hardworking, community and family oriented, and self-made. Stars Hollow and its residents represent the meritocratic ideal; if you excel at what you do—make the best coffee, cook the best food, grow the best produce—you will be successful. The middle-class ideal exemplified by Lorelai's life in Stars Hollow is set against the upper-class community of her parents, Richard and Emily, in Hartford. This community is built on aristocratic rather than meritocratic ideals. If you are not from a family with a proper pedigree, you are unlikely to be fully accepted. And even if your family credentials are impeccable, they still may not be good enough for all members of this community, as we see when Rory is deemed "unsuitable" for Logan Huntzberger (having not been "bred" for it), even though, as she argues in "But I'm a Gilmore!" (5.19), her ancestors "came over on the *Mayflower*."

In the diegetic world of *Gilmore Girls,* these two communities exist as binary forces, and Rory is the only character who can effectively function in both. Other characters' attempts to cross the class-based boundaries are portrayed as "fish out of water" situations that are usually played for laughs. For example, in "Rory's Birthday Parties" (1.06), the audience is treated both to Lorelai's horror at the over-the-top extravagance of the titular shindig thrown by Emily as well as the latter's discomfort at drinking out of "Holiday Inn" wineglasses at Lorelai's party. Although humor is often derived from the differences between Hartford and Stars Hollow, Sherman-Palladino's juxtaposition of these two communities can be seen as a serious statement about class. And as the audience makes judgments about social relations and class mobility based on the ways they are presented in *Gilmore Girls,* the deck seems stacked in favor of Lorelai's middle-class life in Stars Hollow.

Indeed, the audience is invited to appreciate the eccentricities of the Stars Hollow residents and their rummage sales, knitting marathons, and Revolutionary War reenactments while finding amusement at the pretentiousness of Emily's inability to remember the names of her ever-changing household staff or her obsession with the personal lives of other members of Hartford's elite. Likewise, the spontaneity and independence of Lorelai's self-made life are portrayed to be more admirable than her parents' affluent but formal lifestyle. The upper-class characters on the show are generally snobby, condescending, and confrontational. We see examples in Emily's constant critique of Lorelai's table manners and fashion choices and in the way she disparages Luke's appearance when he accompanies Lorelai to the renewal of Richard and Emily's vows. We root for Lorelai to end up with the ever-present Luke instead of the irresponsible and undependable Christopher.

Likewise, Rory's Stars Hollow love interests have a likability and relatability that the would-be suitors from her grandparents' world do not. In the show's first season, Rory is pursued by Tristan, a classmate at Chilton. Tristan is a smarmy snob who refuses to call Rory by her name while intimating that she would be lucky to go out on a date with him. Meanwhile, Dean, Rory's boyfriend in Stars Hollow, is polite and hardworking. When Tristan and Dean confront one another at a school dance, Tristan insults Dean's clothing and provokes him into a fight. This incident leads the audience to believe that Dean is a good guy and that Tristan is not. In short, the upper-class characters in *Gilmore Girls* are, for the most part, arrogant, unlikable, and unpleasant people who seem more interested in their own status than anything else, and it is difficult to see how audience members are expected to find anything admirable about them beyond their wealth.

The privileging of Lorelai's life in Stars Hollow over the upper-class life her parents live in Hartford is almost certainly influenced by the fact that, as the show's central character, she is the person with whom viewers are likely to identify. Also, since most Americans would identify themselves as middle class, the audience is more likely to relate to Lorelai's life in Stars Hollow than her parents' life in Hartford. The series' apparent middle-class sympathies are confounded, however, when *Gilmore Girls* deals with education, particularly when Rory's academic pursuits (which provide the impetus for much of the conflict and plot development over the course of the series) become the focus. The young woman's educational accomplishments—her enrollment at Chilton, an elite private school in Hartford, and her graduation from Yale—serve as bookends for the series. And when it comes to education, Stars Hollow and Hartford still exist in a binary relationship. However, although middle-class Stars Hollow is typically portrayed more favorably than upper-class Hartford, in the case of education, it is the upper class—as represented by Rory's education at elite private schools, Chilton and Yale—that seems to be privileged over the middle class.

This comparison between the educational system in Stars Hollow and the elite training Rory receives at Chilton and Yale is actually invited by the series from its first episodes forward. A scene early in the pilot episode shows Rory sitting in a classroom while an offscreen teacher discusses an upcoming assignment on *Huckleberry Finn*. The classroom is dark and crowded. As the camera tracks down one of the many rows of desks, we see a group of girls ignoring the teacher and using a bottle of nail polish. The girls notice Rory, in the back seat of the row, scribbling in her notebook. One of them speculates that Rory is writing a love letter, another that she is completing an entry in her diary. Finally, a third girl looks over Rory's shoulder and states incredulously, "She's doing the assignment!"

The Stars Hollow students' lack of interest in academics and their rather depressing learning environment are set against the decidedly different school culture we see in the series' second episode, "The Lorelais' First Day at Chilton" (1.02). The classrooms are spacious, with hardwood floors, high ceilings, and large picture windows. Upon their arrival that first day, Lorelai and Rory go to see the school's imperious headmaster, Charleston. Headmaster Charleston first compliments Rory on her grades at Stars Hollow High, then warns, "You may have been the smartest girl at Stars Hollow, but this is a different place. The pressures are greater, the rules are stricter, and the expectations are higher." In subsequent episodes, as Rory attempts to adjust to life at Chilton, we see several permutations of the idea that Stars Hollow is indeed different from Chilton and that, as the headmaster suggested, Chilton is more difficult, but decidedly better. In another Season One episode, "The Deer Hunters" (1.04), Rory complains to her mother that she misses Stars Hollow because Chilton is so hard. Later in the episode, after receiving a D on her first English assignment at Chilton, Rory opines, "A D at Stars Hollow is like an F at Chilton. It's worse, like a G or a W."

In contrast to the rigorous assignments and expectations foisted upon Chilton students, Stars Hollow High seems to offer little of value to the students who go there. None of the characters who attend the high school finds any kind of personal or academic fulfillment by being there; rather, it seems as though the only way they can find satisfaction is by leaving. For example, Lane Kim, Rory's best friend in Stars Hollow, is bright (as evidenced by her extensive knowledge of rock music history and her ability to hold her own in the rapid-fire dialogue with Rory and Lorelai); however, she has no educational ambitions. She is bored in high school, and her only interest in school is related to participating in extracurricular activities like band and cheerleading. Lane's lack of interest in school carries over to college. Although she briefly attends a local Seventh-Day Adventist college after graduating from high school, she soon quits to pursue a career with her band. She is consumed with making her band successful, and it appears that her education, or lack thereof, will have little effect on her long-term success.

The only teenage character in Stars Hollow who shares Rory's love of books and learning and has the intellectual capacity to keep up with her is Jess Mariano. During his brief time in Stars Hollow, and even when he pops up in later seasons, Jess is constantly reading. In "Nick & Nora/Sid & Nancy" (2.05), after Jess returns a copy of Allen Ginsberg's *Howl* that he has stolen from Rory's room, Rory finds extensive notes in the margins. She states, "I thought you said you didn't read much," and Jess responds, "Well, what is much?" The episode concludes with Rory calling Jess, "Dodger," to which he responds with a burst of recognition, *"Oliver Twist!"*

So what becomes of this Stars Hollow intellectual? Jess skips class so that he can work extra shifts at the local Wal-Mart and eventually drops out of high school to move to California. When he reappears in Season Six, the once struggling wordsmith and rebellious teenager has become an author and the owner of an art-house bookstore. Jess's success in life, even a life dedicated to books, comes *in spite of* his education in Stars Hollow, not because of it. Even though he loves reading about and discussing new ideas, or perhaps *because* he does, Stars Hollow High School offers his inquisitive mind little of substantive value. This point reinforces the notion that the place has nothing to offer bright, intellectually curious teenagers. All of the characters that fit that description—Rory, Lane, and Jess—go to great lengths to leave the high school or simply bide their time until graduation.

The other school-age characters in Stars Hollow demonstrate little academic interest or ability. Dean, Rory's on-again, off-again boyfriend, is one of these people. When he meets Rory, he seems intimidated by her intellect and out of his depth when Rory discusses her work at Chilton with him. In the episode "Rory's Dance" (1.09), Dean reads

Anna Karenina at Rory's request and concludes, "Maybe Tolstoy's just over my head." The book is too "big" and "long" for Dean, but he slogs through it because it is one of his girlfriend's favorite texts. And although eventually, at Rory's urging, Dean gains admission to Southern Connecticut State University, he quickly drops out of school to work full-time in construction to support the wife he married shortly after graduating from high school. The other high school characters from Stars Hollow are even less intellectually inclined than Dean. Lindsay, Dean's wife, is portrayed as pleasant but vapid. Her only goal seems to be the creation of a household and marriage in the style of a 1950s sitcom. Zach and Brian, Lane's bandmates, are shown to be lazy and rather dim-witted. They spend most days playing video games and are unable to set up the computer they purchased; they are forced to ask Lane to do it.

In contrast, Rory's private school classmates are portrayed as bright, talented, and ambitious. Paris Geller, Rory's rival at Chilton and her eventual roommate and "best friend," is obsessed (to put it mildly) with academic and professional success. Like Rory, Paris dedicates her seemingly inexhaustible energies to gaining admission to Harvard, and her entire life seems to revolve around achieving that goal. She is the editor of the student papers at both Chilton and Yale. She is the president of the student council, the head of the debate team, and driven to be powerful and successful. Beyond Paris, even the "dumb" students at Chilton are successful academically. Paris's sidekicks at Chilton, Madeline and Louise, are portrayed throughout their run on the series as affluent, vapid party girls—Chilton's version of Paris Hilton and Nicole Ritchie. However, even they have academic ability. They both score higher than Rory on Rory's first English assignment at Chilton, and they both attend Tulane University.

Stars Hollow High and Chilton are also dissimilar in terms of what the students do while they are there. At Chilton, we see the students engaged in activities like staging productions of Shakespeare, running the student paper, holding debate competitions, and participating in an elaborate, cutthroat student government. Athletics are rarely mentioned. In fact, the only sports the audience sees being played at

Chilton are golf, which Rory learns from her grandfather, and a spirited fencing duel between Rory and Paris that takes place in a lavishly decorated, carpeted, and wood-paneled room. Conversely, nearly all of the extracurricular activities in Stars Hollow revolve around athletics. Luke is viewed as a town legend because of his exploits as a high school track star. We also see the town becoming obsessed with a hockey game against a rival school. Lane seeks to assimilate into the cultural life of the school by becoming a member of the marching band and later a cheerleader. The nonathletic activities at Stars Hollow are few. In fact, Lane tells Rory that after she left for Chilton, the Stars Hollow High School German Club had to disband because it had only three members, and two of them have moved away.

The portrayals of the parents from the two educational spaces also invite comparison. The Chilton parents are shown to be actively concerned with the academic performance and college preparedness of their children. In the first season, we see them grilling the school's English teacher about how effective the curriculum will be at preparing students for the AP exam. The one glimpse we get of parents in Stars Hollow occurs in the episode "One's Got Class and the Other One Dyes" (3.04), when a group of mothers confronts Lorelai after she discusses her teenage pregnancy during the school's career day. After Lorelai responds to students' questions about being pregnant while in high school, she is confronted in the town square by a group of angry moms who chastise her for "flaunting her mistakes" and say that she might as well have brought condoms into class if she was going to talk about her pregnancy. This scene suggests that the Stars Hollow parents are interested more in what their children *do not* learn than what they *do*.

Not only are the parents who confront Lorelai unconcerned about the academic success of their children, but there are no adults in Stars Hollow who are portrayed as having been academically successful. As far as the audience knows, not one of the adults in the town holds a bachelor's degree. Lorelai receives her associate's degree near the end of the second season, and we learn that Sookie, Lorelai's business partner, attended a culinary institute. We also know that Luke chose to stay in Stars Hollow rather than leave to go to college. Otherwise, the audience is given no information about the educational histories of the other townspeople. Stars Hollow is full of successful entrepreneurs and small business owners including Luke, Taylor, Jackson, Gypsy, Miss Patty, Mrs. Kim, Kirk, and, of course, Lorelai; however, none of them has the elite education that Rory pursues and eventually attains.

Although Lorelai's own relative lack of education identifies her squarely with the traditionally middle-class values of Stars Hollow, her attitude toward Rory's education complicates the view of Lorelai as a champion of the middle class. So much of what is appealing about her character—her unique relationship with her daughter, her independence, and her rejection of her parents' affluent but restrictive, aristocratic world—is complicated, and perhaps even undermined, when Lorelai deals with Rory's education. The nature of Lorelai's unique relationship with her daughter is evident starting with the first scenes of the pilot episode. The series opens with Rory and Lorelai eating breakfast at Luke's Diner, discussing makeup and music. The implication here is that their relationship is less a typical mother-daughter relationship and more like one between sisters or best friends. This point is highlighted when the young man who hits on Lorelai when she first enters the diner later hits on Rory. His shocked reaction that the two could possibly be mother and daughter gives voice to what the audience is meant to see as the unique nature of their relationship. Later in that same episode, Lorelai, speaking of her relationship with Rory, tells Sookie, "We don't fight. We never fight." Throughout the series, the notion that Lorelai and Rory have a bond that resembles one of best friends rather than parent and child is reinforced. They enjoy the same music, movies, and television shows, they talk to one another openly about their romantic relationships, and Lorelai constantly resists the urge to impose her will on Rory's life.

Significantly, the relationship between the two undergoes changes when they have disagreements about Rory's education. When Lorelai feels that her daughter might be putting her education at risk, and thereby waste her "special" ability, she takes on the more traditional maternal role that she otherwise tries to resist. In the pilot episode, Rory indicates that she does not want to go to Chilton, a reluctance that Lorelai attributes to her daughter's infatuation with Dean. At first, Lorelai approaches the situation by taking on the role of a friend, a tactic she uses in most of her interactions with Rory: "Listen, can we just start all over? Okay, you tell me all about the guy, and I promise not to let my head explode." When Rory fails to respond, Lorelai explicitly asserts her maternal voice, saying, "We always had a democracy in this house. We never did anything unless we agreed. But now I guess I'm going to have to play the 'mom card.' You are going to Chilton, whether you want to or not. Monday morning, you will be there. End of story." As Lorelai suggests, it is an atypical stance for her to assume, and it is the thought of Rory wasting her educational opportunities that leads her to take it.

Although their argument with one another is settled by the end of the first episode, Lorelai and Rory have other longer-lasting disagreements about the latter's education. Perhaps the most significant rift in their relationship comes at the end of Season Five, when Rory decides to quit Yale. When Rory breaks the news to her momentarily dumbstruck mother, Lorelai tells her that she is not dropping out of school, and says that, if Rory insists on leaving Yale, she should simply go to another elite university. Lorelai labels Rory's decision "immature," and when Rory refuses to change her mind, Lorelai breaks off contact with her, and they remain apart for several episodes (to many audience members' distress and deep dissatisfaction).

In the same way that Lorelai is defined by her close relationship with her daughter, she is also defined by the contentiousness of her relationship with her parents. Because of her parents' upper-class status, Lorelai's tense relationship with them, and her seeming rejection of their aristocratic lifestyles and values, bolsters her identity as a representative figure of the middle class. We learn early on that Lorelai became pregnant with Rory and left home to make it on her own at the age of sixteen. As the series begins, the point is made repeatedly that Lorelai and her parents rarely talk with one another. A running joke during the pilot episode is that Lorelai and Rory only visit the elder Gilmores on holidays. The difficult relationship between Lorelai and her parents provides one of the series' staples—the rapid-fire, sharp-tongued arguments between Lorelai and Emily. Although the show usually pits Lorelai and her parents as rivals with different agendas for Rory's future, their relationship is at its most constructive when they are discussing the teenage girl's education. Although Lorelai compares asking her parents for a loan to reenacting scenes from a horror novel, she seeks rapprochement with the elder Gilmores, and agrees to the weekly "Friday-night dinners" as a condition of the loan she receives to pay Rory's tuition at Chilton. And later, when Rory decides to take an indefinite break from Yale, Lorelai goes first to her parents to seek their support in convincing Rory to change her mind. A shared interest in Rory's education provides common ground for Lorelai, Richard, and Emily and changes the dynamics of their relationship (however briefly).

Perhaps even more than these relationships, Lorelai's independence and pride—traits that highlight her rejection of the privilege afforded by her family in favor of building her own life—are what truly define her. In a conversation with Emily during the series' first episode, Lorelai asserts the value of what she has done for herself: "I am living a lovely life right now. . . . I found a good job. . . . I worked my way up. I run the place now. I built a life on my own with no help from anyone." Lorelai's self-description is seconded by Emily when the latter ruefully agrees with her daughter's assertion that she never asked for financial assistance. However, the proud and independent Lorelai recedes when she talks about Rory's educational opportunities. When Lorelai learns that Rory's been accepted to Chilton, she exults, "This is it. She can finally go to Harvard like she's always wanted, and get the education that I never got, and get to do all the things that I never got to do. And then I can resent her for it, and we can finally have a normal mother-daughter relationship." Lorelai's dismay at missing out on an education by leaving home at such a young age resurfaces during the episode "The Road Trip to Harvard" (2.04). As she wanders through the hallway of a building at Harvard, Lorelai gazes wistfully, almost in tears, at the picture of the Harvard valedictorian from 1991, the year, we are to assume, that Lorelai would have graduated from college. This scene is followed by Lorelai watching as Rory discusses the philosophy of Stoicism with a Harvard professor. We see Rory's academic potential juxtaposed with Lorelai's regret.

Even when Lorelai graduates from community college near the end of Season Two, her focus is on the academic opportunity she missed: "I was supposed to graduate from high school. Go to Vassar. Marry a Yale man and get myself a proper nickname, like 'Babe' or 'Bunny' or 'Shih Tzu.' Instead, I got pregnant. I didn't finish high school. I didn't marry your father. And I ended up in a career that, apparently, Jessica Hahn would view as beneath her." Although this declaration, delivered in the episode "Lorelai's Graduation Day" (2.21), ends with a joke, the first two lines are delivered sincerely. The fierce independence and confidence that Lorelai so often exhibits have been replaced by an acknowledgment of the opportunities she missed.

Lorelai's attitude toward Stars Hollow itself also seems to change when the subject is Rory's education. Although it is clear that Lorelai loves her adopted town, in part because it is where she "grew up" as a young mother, she seems to think it is wholly unable to provide Rory what she needs to achieve success. When Rory suggests that it might be possible to get into Harvard by going to Stars Hollow, Lorelai dismisses it as "crazy talk" and tells Rory that staying in school in Stars Hollow would be like "throwing her life away." For Lorelai, there exists a clear connection between the education Rory receives in the elite private schools she attends and Rory's ability to pursue her career ambitions. In the episode "Friday Night's Alright for Fighting" (6.13), as Lorelai thanks her parents for paying Rory's tuition at Yale, she again suggests that remaining in Stars Hollow would have changed Rory's life drastically: "Rory and I are so grateful for everything you and Mom have done, all the help you've given her. I mean, she would not be at Yale right now if it weren't for you, and she would have never gone to Chilton. She would have graduated Stars Hollow High and then gone to community college and then beauty school." With this statement, Lorelai simultaneously suggests that extraordinary ability without an education that is just as exceptional is useless.

She also denigrates the career path that she and many of the other Stars Hollow residents have followed. Although she is quick to defend Stars Hollow and its residents when her mother disparages them, Lorelai herself provides the insults when it comes to Stars Hollow's educational system.

One reading that might result from my above comments is that the Stars Hollow education is inadequate for gifted students like Rory. Her unique ability is heralded by Lorelai and others. A typical discussion of Rory's intellect occurs in "We've Got Magic to Do" (6.05), when Richard tells Emily, "This girl could name the state capitals at three, recite the periodic table at four, discuss Schopenhauer's influence on Nietzsche when she was ten. She's read every book by every author with a Russian surname, and had a 4.2 grade point average at one of the toughest schools on the East Coast."

Perhaps it is her belief that Rory possesses unique academic gifts that causes Lorelai to act in ways that ironically subvert the identity established for her character. What emerges, then, is a view of education and class in *Gilmore Girls* that is complicated and troubling. Although it seems that the audience is invited to identify with Lorelai's middle-class life, they are sent several seemingly contradictory messages that the kind of education most accessible for people in the middle class has little value.

Put simply, this privileging of elite education in private schools over public education complicates the way in which social class is addressed in *Gilmore Girls,* because the type of academic pursuits that are valued by characters on the show corresponds to a narrowly defined, elitist notion of education. Furthermore, in much the same way as the portrayals of most of the upper-class characters seem designed to elicit an unfavorable reaction from the audience, when the subject is education, Stars Hollow becomes the object of ridicule. It also complicates the audience's view of Lorelai, as the audience is left to wonder precisely why the show's "middle-class hero" is the one most assertively leading the charge for elite education.

12

"You Don't Got It"

Becoming a Journalist in Gilmore Girls

ANGEL CASTAÑOS MARTÍNEZ, AMOR MUÑOZ BÉCARES, AND SARAH CAITLIN LAVERY

From the beginning, Rory's quest to become a journalist is a major ongoing storyline on *Gilmore Girls.* Since her first day at Chilton, we knew of her idolization of international reporter Christiane Amanpour. Rory's obvious dedication to her future career makes the viewer understand her mother's efforts to ask her parents for help in paying for a top prep school. How else, Lorelai wonders, can she ensure that her daughter will be accepted by the best universities in the young woman's bid for a brilliant career? And how else will Rory's professional aspirations be realized in an increasingly uncertain economic climate in which traditional newspaper reporting has given way to new means of delivering information to people on the go? These questions permeate the series, which is unique in its deployment of comedic modes and journalistic motifs that are beholden to films of the 1930s and 1940s, a period in American cultural life when the genre known as "screwball comedy" contributed to a progressive reconceptualization of the relationship between men and women, bosses and employees.

Of course, as illustrated throughout *Gilmore Girls,* it takes much more to break into the competitive world of journalism than an Ivy League degree and a private school pedigree. Historically, Americans have placed a great deal of emphasis on the university education of journalists, a practice not as common in other Western countries besides the United States. Rory, however, does not envision majoring in journalism at a reputable American university. From childhood on, she wants to attend Harvard, where, in the real world, journalism courses form only part of the continuing education program through the auspices of the prestigious Nieman Foundation. Rory's lifelong dream of Harvard does not come to fruition, of course: her grandfather, a domineering force on the show, changes her mind in favor of Yale, despite her non-university-educated mother's efforts. The rivalry between Harvard and Yale is suspiciously commercial (although not focused on in the show), but Rory's selection of Yale makes much more sense for an aspiring journalist. Unlike rival Harvard, Yale offers a journalism program for undergraduates, as well as the oldest (and one of the most highly respected) college daily papers in the world. Over the course of the series, audiences do not, however, see Rory attending specific journalism classes, and we even hear her say once that her major is English ("The Great Stink" [7.05]).

But her academic record means little when Rory starts dating publishing heir Logan Huntzberger. The viewer can easily begin to see her future determined by rubbing elbows with journalists and using her boyfriend's last name for career gain, exploiting personal ties to further ambition in a tried-and-true male fashion, not relying on her female intelligence and education. Despite her initial reticence, Rory accepts an internship at a small newspaper owned by Mitchum Huntzberger, reinforcing the idea that becoming a journalist has nothing to do with what is taught at the "best universities in the most powerful country in the world." Instead, it is all about who you know. The internship turns out to be devastating for Rory, however, causing her to temporarily abandon her ideals when Logan's father caustically tells her, "I've worked with a lot of young people over the years. Interns, new hires. I've got a pretty good gut sense for people's strengths and weaknesses. Whether they have that certain something to make it in journalism. It's a tough business. Lot of stress . . . And I have to tell you. You don't got it" ("Blame Booze and Melville" [5.21]). In the end, however, we see that Rory's familial influence is bigger than Logan's. Growing up watching her mother's unfailing independence makes her reject the impending nepotism implied by Huntzberger. She chooses to forgo marrying into an incredibly rich family to start a career. Without the help of the Huntzbergers, she starts from the bottom of the journalism career ladder, her own considerable capabilities being her only guarantee of success. Before examining further this complex dialectic of imagined failure and likely success, it will be helpful to reflect on the intertextual connections linking *Gilmore Girls* to the its cross-media antecedents: newspaper films and screwball comedies that similarly foreground determined young women striving for professional success and lasting personal relationships.

Gilmore Girls, Newspaper Films, and Screwball Comedy

If, as David Scott Diffrient suggests in the introduction of this collection, *Gilmore Girls* is an example of "screwball television," then journalism provides one of the most prominent links to that generic form and tradition. Late-silent-era and early-sound-era motion pictures about the newspaper business, including *The Power of the Press* (1928) and *It Happened One Night* (1934), established the popular profile of the journalist.[1] Frank Capra's movies were responsible for much of what Americans thought they knew about journalists in the twentieth century (Saltzman 2002, 54). Female reporters were put into action on the screen but in a quite unrealistic way: in real newsrooms around the 1920s and 1930s, women were scarce, their tasks limited to fashion, family, or style departments, their influence relegated to the society pages.[2]

1. The first American film featuring a reporter character was the silent movie *The Reform Candidate* (1914).

2. From the beginning of journalism's history there have been several important female reporters, albeit not on a big scale. In 1924 the *New York Tribune* under the vice presidency of Helen Rogers had the most women journalists, and in 1939 Eleanor Roosevelt accepted only female reporters at her press conferences, forcing newspapers to keep at least one woman in their newsrooms.

The prolificacy of screwball comedies about journalism, with storylines that "frequently mirrored the former occupations of the screenwriters" (Gehring 2004, 65), is not surprising. Several classic-film screenwriters worked as journalists prior to their careers in Hollywood (Bordwell, Staiger, and Thompson 2002, 165). Magazine writer Sonya Levien, for example, became one of Capra's writers and was perhaps responsible for some of the female journalists portrayed in his work. In these early films, women journalists had to go above and beyond societal expectations to prove that they were as capable as their male counterparts; they were always under careful scrutiny, and they tended to threaten disruption of the status quo, "throwing away" their family lives or potential marriages.

Screwball comedies about journalists understood and commented upon the sometimes misogynistic conditions in which female reporters worked. In Howard Hawks's *His Girl Friday* (1940), produced at Columbia Pictures (one of the major studios responsible for the surge of screwball comedies in the immediate prewar era), the male journalist and editor Walter Burns (Cary Grant) is responsible for a female journalist's career. Hildy Johnson (Rosalind Russell) arrives at the newspaper as a young student from a school of journalism, and when she decides to quit five years later, Walter reproaches her: "I made a great reporter out of you." In a comparable way, Mitchum Huntzberger suggests that he can make a journalist out of Rory. From that point forward, she will have to face battles similar to her cinematic forebears. Despite her intelligence, education, and talent, she is deemed not good enough to be a journalist, according to Mitchum's standards. Like *His Girl Friday*'s Walter, Mitchum reminds Rory that he has given her an opportunity and, because he has a "sixth sense" in evaluating journalistic potential, intuitively *knows* that she does not have what it takes to succeed in the high-stress world of journalism. In his opinion, she lacks initiative and an innate ability, and he does her the "big favor" of telling her this straightforwardly. Rory retorts that she has "always done what is asked of [her]," but, in Mitchum's mind, attitude, intelligence, and an Ivy League education mean little. In "Blame Booze and Melville," he states, "See, that's the thing, Rory. In the real world, it's not always enough to do just what is asked of you. Now, I'm not saying you're not competent. You're very smart and good at anticipating people's needs. You'd actually make someone a great assistant." Rory's innocence and polite demeanor make her not question Mitchum's words; also, he "happens to be the top newspaper guy in the country," and "if you're going to get one man's opinion, he's the one man you get" ("A House Is Not a Home" [5.22]). She is devastated, and this time her mother's advice means nothing to her. When she learns about the encounter later, Lorelai is certain that Mitchum's words about Rory's aptitude are driven by motives that have nothing to do with her daughter's abilities:

> LORELAI: This is the man who doesn't want you to marry Logan.
> RORY: That wasn't him. It was Logan's mother and his grandfather.
> LORELAI: And you really think he's okay with it? I mean, his whole family looks at you and sees Anna Nicole Smith, and they tell you that to your face, but he thinks you're swell and wants to pay for the honeymoon.
> RORY: That's not why he said what he said.

In some ways, Mitchum's role conjures movie images of "evil publishers [that] destroy the public trust and put their own political or financial gain above all else" (Saltzman 2002, 56). On the other hand, in a classic newspaper-fiction context, Mitchum's words may be sincere. He is the quintessential media tycoon who used to be the hard and cynical old-style journalist. He simply may not see once-valued journalistic attributes in Rory, who personifies calmness, civility, and steadfast dedication to larger causes.

Despite these initial setbacks and Mitchum's unfavorable opinion, Rory does eventually reenter the field of journalism. She regains her confidence and reclaims her dream. Indeed, the series ends with Rory getting a job as a political commentator for an online magazine following the campaign of Democratic presidential front-runner Barack Obama, showing the triumph of a new journalist profile (it has often been said that the future of journalism will be on the Internet). After nearly surrendering to Emily Gilmore's style of life, planning parties in lieu of pursuing a meaningful career and working for the Daughters of the American Revolution, Rory finally succeeds as an emerging "woman on top," determined, in true screwball heroine fashion, to achieve her goals using intelligence, determination, and hard work—attributes she showed before meeting the Huntzbergers. It could be argued that she is an example of the "standard college-educated yuppie journalist" (Hanson 1996, 47), with a perfect-on-paper past and a brilliant future based on high principles.

Gilmore Girls evokes screwball comedy not only in its allusions to classic movies and Rory's idealism but also in its small details and ostensibly tossed-off lines of dialogue, including references to a "scoop" and shots of Logan wearing a hat with a press sticker at the *Yale Daily News* office ("Norman Mailer, I'm Pregnant!" [5.06]). The show's witty, blitzkrieg-speed conversations; visual representation of Connecticut as the Green World (Frye 1991, 67); humorous look at marriage and politics; depiction of settled life represented via the insurance business (Lorelai's father and Hildy's fiancé, the latter being a character played to perfection by Ralph Bellamy in *His Girl Friday*); high-society rituals (debut balls, cotillions, alumni parties, and the eccentricities of secret societies); and love between men and women closer to companionship than idyllic romance: these semantic elements of *Gilmore Girls* provide links between the screwball newspaper films of the past and this most unusual of contemporary TV series.

His Girl Friday is mentioned explicitly on three occasions: Lorelai suggests that Luke see it in "The Fundamental Things Apply" (4.05), she calls Rory "Hildegaard" and greets her by saying "Hildy" in "Farewell, My Pet" (7.14), and Rory says her "blue coat would be too *His Girl Friday*" in "Hay Bale Maze" (7.18). Another screwball comedy with a journalistic focus, M-G-M's *Philadelphia Story* (1940), is a favorite of Luke's ("French Twist" [7.07]). Other nonscrewball movies that portray real or fictional journalism are equally omnipresent in *Gilmore Girls: Citizen Kane* (1941) is mentioned three times (in "Christopher Returns" [1.15], "The Fundamental Things Apply," and "An Affair to Remember" [4.06]); *All The President's Men* (1976) is referred to in "You Jump, I Jump, Jack" (5.07) and "It's Just Like Riding a Bike" (7.19); at one point in "Here Comes the Son" (3.21), Lorelai says Rory is like Holly Hunter in *Broadcast News* (1987); she thinks the outfit Rory is trying on is "Lois Lane style" ("French Twist"); and Logan compares Rory's appearance to Faye Dunaway in *Network* ("Bridesmaids Revisited" [6.16]).

Journalism in *Gilmore Girls*

> When you write for the *Yale Daily News,* you are a *real* journalist.
>
> —DOYLE to Rory (who has been struggling to write a compelling piece), in "Die, Jerk" (4.08)

The dominant impression the viewer gets of journalism in *Gilmore Girls,* however, comes from the ideas Rory has of the profession and from the journalists mentioned in the characters' dialogue. References to fictional and real journalists, columnists, and critics are made from the beginning: Susan Faludi ("Rory's Dance" [1.09]); A. J. Benza ("Hammers and Veils" [2.02]); Barbara Walters ("Nick & Nora/ Sid & Nancy" [2.05]); Paula Zahn and Pauline Kael ("Teach Me Tonight" [2.19]); Walter Cronkite ("Here Comes the Son"); Jason Blair and Stephen Glass ("The Reigning Lorelai" [4.16]); Hunter S. Thompson ("You Jump, I Jump, Jack"); Joseph Mitchell ("The Party's Over" [5.08]); Jimmy Breslin ("But I'm a Gilmore!" [5.19]); Ben Bradlee ("We've Got Magic to Do" [6.05]); and George Plimpton ("French Twist").

As already pointed out, *Gilmore Girls* presents a primarily positive view of journalism. The constant references to Bob Woodward and Carl Bernstein—two of the most admired and famous American reporters in recent history—evoke the idea of the press hero. Both journalists embody the ideal press professional and even become, literally, dream-worthy men representing investigative rigor: in "Those Lazy-Hazy-Crazy Days" (3.01), a talking-in-her-sleep Paris mutters, "Woodward, Bernstein." Doyle also cites Woodward as a top journalist

("Norman Mailer, I'm Pregnant!"); Rory mentions both reporters ("Jews and Chinese Food" [5.15]); and two of Logan's friends greet the *Yale Daily News* staff by exclaiming the duo's names ("It's Just Like Riding a Bike").

By way of contrast, in classic movie style, the villain is often the newspaper owner, embodied in *Gilmore Girls* in Mitchum Huntzberger and evoked in allusions to real media tycoons: William Randolph Hearst (in "Christopher Returns," "The Breakup: Part 2" [1.17], "Lost and Found" [2.15], and "Dead Uncles and Vegetables" [2.17]); Rupert Murdoch (in "I'm a Kayak, Hear Me Roar" [7.15]), and the Sulzbergers (in "Lorelai? Lorelai?" [7.20]).[3] Moreover, among the many references to journalists, we have to highlight CNN reporter Christiane Amanpour, who is mentioned in the first episode and makes a cameo appearance as a guest at the Dragonfly Inn in the series' finale. Amanpour is Rory's ultimate inspiration, as she explains to Headmaster Charleston in "The Lorelais' First Day at Chilton" (1.02):

> RORY: I want to go to Harvard and study journalism and political science.
> CHARLESTON: On your way to being . . . ?
> RORY: Christiane Amanpour.
> CHARLESTON: Really? . . . Why do you wish to be Christiane Amanpour?
> RORY: Well, I don't wish to be her, exactly. I just want to do what she does.

Rory reminds us of her esteem for Amanpour frequently, and in the very last episode of the series, she gets to express her admiration to CNN's chief international correspondent in person, saying, "You are so inspiring. Your reporting is so bold and moving and fascinating. . . . I just want to say thank you" ("Bon Voyage" [7.22]). In fact,

3. In some ways, Logan is portrayed as a future tycoon despite his best efforts to assert his individuality. He is able to satisfy his overbearing father by lackadaisically writing for the *Yale Daily News* and only for the occasional byline.

we should *all* thank Amanpour, as she embodies a spirit of journalism in *Gilmore Girls* that is far removed from the old-fashioned, unyielding style represented by Mitchum. Amanpour is able to succeed as a foreign correspondent while having a family life, as Rory explains to Dean ("Application Anxiety" [3.03]). She believes in hard work more than in "guts," and is even willing to help Rory (something, she says, that does not happen often), even expressing awe at her impressive résumé:

> AMANPOUR: Your mother says you have graduated at Yale. You are editor of the *Yale Daily News.* That's not bad.
> RORY: I want to pursue a career in journalism.
> AMANPOUR: Is that print you want, TV, CNN maybe?

When Rory says that, ideally, she wants to work at a major daily, or for "anyone that will take me," Amanpour responds, "That's the spirit. Get in there, do what you can, show them what you've got, and the rest will take care of itself." Just like the unfailingly independent Lorelai, this experienced journalist trusts that hard work will win out in the end.

Initially, Rory has not determined which avenue of journalism she most wants to pursue. In the end, she narrows in on print, but her early indecision seems to follow the example of recent films and series in which television newsrooms are more often the focus than newspapers. Rory explains her plans to Headmaster Charleston ("The Lorelais' First Day at Chilton"), and those aspirations have not changed by Season Two: "I'd rather know right now if I'll be working at CNN or carrying a basket around its offices with sandwiches in it" ("Presenting Lorelai Gilmore" [2.06]). In her daily life, Rory's references to television are, for the most part, negative. For example, she worries that she will be watching television when her Harvard application arrives, afraid that it will somehow undercut the seriousness of the Ivy League college ("Application Anxiety"). Despite the ideal set by Amanpour, Rory finally chooses a career in print journalism and, accordingly, is trained as a print journalist at the *Yale Daily News* and through her internship.

Newspapers are also the most common way that the characters in *Gilmore Girls* get informed. Despite its preponderance, we never see a TV set tuned to broadcast news, a programming form mentioned only twice throughout the entire series. But Rory, Lorelai, Emily, Richard, Logan, and Max Medina *do* read daily newspapers. In the show's first episode, we see Richard reading the paper, and this image becomes a motivic element in the series' credit sequence. In subsequent episodes, he can be seen reading in the sauna ("Kill Me Now" [1.03]); at home ("Love and War and Snow" [1.08], "Let the Games Begin" [3.08], "Dear Emily and Richard" [3.13], and "Bridesmaids Revisited"); in the hospital, where Rory reads the *Wall Street Journal* and the *Financial Times* aloud to him ("Forgiveness and Stuff" [1.10]); at a business meeting ("P.S. I Lo . . ." [1.20]); and at Lorelai's inn, where he prefers his newspaper to the books his daughter offers him ("Richard in Stars Hollow" [2.12]). As we shall discuss later, the scene in the first episode in which Richard hands Rory a newspaper represents his influence on his granddaughter, an influence that extends to her subsequent choice of college.

Throughout the series, businessmen are shown reading newspapers every day; they even "help them recover from illness" (according to Lorelai in the episode "Forgiveness and Stuff"). Teachers are also presented as newspaper dependent: we see dailies strewn over a table in Max's house ("Sadie, Sadie" [2.01]), and, in "Red Light on the Wedding Night" (2.03), Rory says he reads three papers every day (the *Hartford Courant, New York Times,* and *Wall Street Journal*). Luke, Max's romantic antithesis, complains about the waste of trees from reading so many papers, but jokes about newspapers usually come from women: Paris's gang at Chilton, Louise and Madeline, talk about newspapers in a derisive fashion while gossiping about Paris's parents' divorce ("Paris Is Burning" [1.11]), and Lane even jokes that she is not reading papers anymore ("Welcome to the Dollhouse" [6.06]). Of course, Lorelai does the most in terms of making journalism humorous: she creates a bridal veil from newspaper pages, and Rory starts perusing the articles while her mom tries it on ("Hammers and Veils"), and, although she is seen reading and buying newspapers,

Lorelai complains that they make her hands black ("Sadie, Sadie"). She prefers "soft" sections like style and entertainment ("Richard in Stars Hollow" and "Haunted Leg" [3.02]), uses newspapers to cut coupons ("The Festival of Living Art" [4.07]), and is always bound to turn something serious (like her daughter's future career) into a joke, as this exchange in the episode "Norman Mailer, I'm Pregnant!" makes clear:

> RORY: I'm really going to have to work—constantly. Maybe I'll have to look for something part-time at a local paper.
>
> LORELAI: Good, that's good. . . . Or you could work for a fishmonger.
>
> RORY: What?
>
> LORELAI: 'Cause there's lots of newspapers there.

In Season Five, we see Lorelai reading and buying newspapers more frequently. She becomes proficient enough to suggest Rory work at a reputable paper near Stars Hollow, such as the *New York Times, Boston Globe,* or *Hartford Courant.* References to and images of magazines are also frequent (the *New Yorker, New York Times Magazine, Cosmopolitan, Time*), but Rory eventually decides to start her career in the newest form of media: as a political reporter for an online magazine ("I'm a Kayak, Hear Me Roar"). She does not show any disappointment about this change in plans—she is only concerned that everything is happening so fast. In this new job, her salary is "next to nothing," but she is happy because she "will have credentials. Real press credentials" (as she states in "Bon Voyage"). Finally, she will be a "real" journalist.

Longtime viewers of *Gilmore Girls* are no doubt familiar with some of the myths about journalism presented within the series: that it implies travel and social respect, and that a war correspondent is the epitome of the profession. When Rory explains her aspirations to Headmaster Charleston, she says that she wants to "travel, see the world up close, report on what's really going on, be part of something big" ("The Lorelais' First Day at Chilton"). She continues, stating, "Being on TV has nothing to do with it. Maybe I'll be a journalist and write books and articles about what I see. I just want to make sure that I see . . . something." We also learn a bit about the current state of journalism, which adds verisimilitude to Rory's character.

Gilmore Girls shows just how difficult it is to find a position in journalism even with good references. What really seems to matter is having the right contacts and learning to live with a tiny salary. When Lorelai has trouble figuring out how to pay for Rory's Yale tuition, she jokingly tells her daughter to major in something that will guarantee a lot of money when she graduates, like "business or engineering." She knows that Rory will earn little money working as an intern for a magazine or a small-town newspaper ("Those Are Strings, Pinocchio" [3.22]).

Becoming a Journalist at Yale

As Rory agonizes over her college choice, Richard Gilmore worries because he thinks she will need help. He assumes that it will be easier if she applies to Yale, reminding Lorelai that, as an alumnus, he is better qualified in making decisions about his granddaughter's academic future and that his opinion on the subject should be taken seriously ("Richard in Stars Hollow" and "Let the Games Begin"). She responds, of course, with her usual wit:

> RICHARD: I paid Yale a great deal of money. Getting Rory in would be a breeze.
>
> LORELAI: We don't like breezes; they mess up our hair.

Despite her insistence that her daughter major in journalism—"You are not changing your major from journalism just because of my lack of money," she tells her ("Those Are Strings, Pinocchio")—her dream school does not offer a bachelor of arts in journalism. Finally, she opts for Yale, the university from which Bob Woodward graduated and the place where "new journalist" Tom Wolfe obtained his Ph.D., allowing her to remain close to home (thus fulfilling a narrative function: keeping the titular "girls" within driving distance of one another). After considering three options (Harvard, Yale, and Princeton all accept her), Rory sees that Yale's "pro" list is the longest (as highlighted in "A Tale of Poes and Fire" [3.17] and "Happy Birthday, Baby" [3.18]), explaining to then boyfriend Jess that it is near home, has good professors, and offers interesting classes. Yale provides Rory and "frenemy" (friend-enemy) Paris Geller the oldest college daily in the world, internships, and possibly participation in panels about journalism.[4] One wonders if the creators' and writers' interest in the school was owing in part to the Yale Journalism Initiative, a multimillion-dollar program that began in 2006 but originated with an advanced journalism seminar that started in 2001. According to spokespeople for the "real-life" Yale, "to be designated as Yale Journalism Scholars, students will have to complete certain courses, participate in a journalism internship, and edit or write for publications at Yale or elsewhere" ("Yale Launches" n.d.). Rory follows a strikingly similar path throughout the final seasons of the series.

Yale Daily News reporters are treated like "real" journalists, and it is through her work at the college paper that Rory proves her journalistic chops: she has to suffer harsh critiques from the then editor in chief about her lack of opinion ("The Nanny and the Professor" [4.10]), she joins debates about plagiarism and ethics ("The Reigning Lorelai"), and she learns just how hard it can be to find an original story or a new approach to an already visited one ("Norman Mailer, I'm Pregnant!"). From this college paper, as former editor in chief Doyle says, students can move on to the *New York Times,* the *Washington Post,* or *Time* ("The Nanny and the Professor"). Established

4. Paris's education as a journalist becomes a bit of a lost narrative thread on *Gilmore Girls.* Despite her initial interest in journalism—at Chilton she was the editor of the *Franklin,* whose former editors had won the Pulitzer Prize or became reporters at the best U.S. newspapers ("Nick & Nora/Sid & Nancy"), and compared the school newspaper with the best dailies ("Richard in Stars Hollow")—she ends up going to medical school, and her commitment at the *Yale Daily News* seems a bit wasted.

newspapers even print stories from college papers like the *Yale Daily News* from time to time.

Rory's internship with the *Stamford Eagle Gazette* does not come from her work at Yale or her excellent curriculum vitae. Instead, she gets the job through the father of her boyfriend. Rory accepts Mitchum's offer, and despite some original hesitation about his reasons for hiring her ("But I'm a Gilmore!"), she tries to be professional. Like any beginner, Rory is thrilled by small details like her first office ID card, and her first success at the *Gazette* is bringing the right type of coffee to Mitchum ("How Many Kropogs to Cape Cod?" [5.20]). Entering the profession through superficial ties, Rory could be compared to Helen Rogers, who became vice president of the *New York Tribune* in 1924 after marrying a member of the Reid family, the paper's editors ("American Women" n.d.; "Women's History" n.d.), or to Yale alumnus Agnes Wahl Nieman (wife of Lucius W. Nieman, founder of the *Milwaukee Journal*), who helped establish the aforementioned Nieman Foundation at Harvard in 1937 ("Nieman Foundation" n.d.). Might these precedents be indicative of Rory's future?

As alluded to earlier, Logan's family is governed by patriarchal authority and entrenched in conservative ideals related to gender and femininity. They disapprove of the couple from the beginning, worrying that Rory is too career focused. As Rory states in "But I'm a Gilmore!": "They went on and on about how I'm going to be a career woman, and, 'Logan, you don't want that, she won't understand our lifestyle or the demands, or, or the family responsibilities!'" When Mitchum discourages Rory from becoming a journalist, telling her that "she just doesn't have it," audiences may be unsure if he is being sincere or if he just wants Rory out of Logan's life. A dispute with Logan nevertheless becomes Rory's motivation to return to her ideals and pursue her professional goals. She goes back to the *Gazette* and essentially badgers the editor in chief into giving her a job. Despite Mitchum's negative proclamation, Rory eventually gets what she wants. She returns to Yale and to her mother ("The Prodigal Daughter Returns" [6.09]), and at the *Yale Daily News,* she is going to show Mitchum just how wrong he was.

In an attempt to regain Rory's favor, Logan's father tries to sway her back to journalism ("I'm a Kayak, Hear Me Roar"), saying, "It's an interesting time in journalism. I'll tell what our field needs: it's an infusion of bright, talented people like you, Rory. . . . I mean it." He even offers to take care of her in *Godfather* (1972) fashion, telling her, "We have newspapers all around the world. You can take your pick." She replies, "My pick? I seem to remember you saying I didn't have 'it.'" Mitchum responds, "Circumstances change." Ultimately, Rory paves her own path. She becomes a journalist and a fiercely independent woman in the process.

Ladies and Career Women

Marriage and family are still considered constraints on a woman's career, and *Gilmore Girls* makes reference to the dichotomy between a "lady" and a career woman. The first and most obvious example emerges during an exchange between Emily and Logan's family, who joke that "ladies need help for everything" or that, "at this rate, [Rory] is going to actually get a job and only marry once" ("Presenting Lorelai Gilmore"). Paris and Lorelai both joke about marriage being an option for noneducated women. When Rory receives her Harvard acceptance letter, Lorelai says, "A big envelope means she's in; a little envelope means she needs to marry rich" ("The Big One" [3.16]). Louise and Paris come to a similar conclusion, as illustrated by this exchange in "Hammers and Veils":

LOUISE: Princess Grace didn't go to college.
PARIS: Thank you for the history lesson, A. J. Benza.
LOUISE: Take a pill.
PARIS: Marry rich.

Rory's dedication to pursuing a career over finding a husband can be closely aligned with a stereotypically masculine attitude. Throughout the series, there are several references to Rory's "male" qualities versus her "female" ones. For example, Lorelai calls Rory "the kind of man she wants to be" ("The Third Lorelai" [1.18]). Perhaps more symbolically, she acts as her grandfather's best man at her grandparents' vow renewal ceremony, even dressing the part ("Wedding Bell Blues" [5.13]). Paris also proclaims, "I am the man!" after becoming editor in chief of the *Yale Daily News* ("Twenty-one Is the Loneliest Number" [6.07]).

But Rory's most important decisions about her future are always clouded by the presence of a man: she hesitates about attending Chilton after meeting Dean ("Pilot" [1.01]); her choice about Yale is based on her grandfather's advice and, partly, on the proximity to her then boyfriend, Jess; and, finally, Mitchum nearly ends her dream of becoming a journalist. In most cases, Rory looks to her mother for guidance, but she sometimes ignores Lorelai's opinions when they contradict the thoughts of the aforementioned men. This point not only serves to highlight Lorelai's independence but also helps viewers understand that when Rory does not follow her own initiative, she usually takes the wrong path.

The following exchange with her mother shows that the root of Rory's career crisis can be traced not only to Mitchum but also to her grandfather, a graduate of Yale whose long shadow occasionally threatens to darken Rory's path toward self-fulfillment:

> LORELAI: I know you're hurt and you're confused, but you're acting incredibly immature, and you need to snap out of it. This is too important. You've worked toward going to Yale your whole life!
> RORY: No. I was working toward Harvard my whole life.
> LORELAI: Then go to Harvard. That's cool.
> RORY: I don't want to go to Harvard!
> LORELAI: Then go to Princeton or Columbia.

Her grandfather is presented as Rory's intellectual pillar. Like Richard, she attends Yale, and in her second year she even lives in the same building he did ("Written in the Stars" [5.03]). But she feels the pressure of making him proud and expresses worry when she disappoints him: "I'm so sorry, Grandpa! I'm so sorry about everything! I just, I don't know what to do" ("A House Is Not a Home" [5.22]). In her crises, Rory often comes to realize that her mother was right. When she solely trusts men, either because she respects their opinions or because she relies on their comfort, she winds up being emotionally crushed. Finally, Rory is conscious that Lorelai protects her, and both come to implicitly agree that those men managed to manipulate Rory.

All of these tumultuous experiences make Rory realize that she cannot make her postgraduate decisions based on Logan's goals and desires. Choosing between a career or a relationship—"negotiation between female desire and the places 'offered' to women in patriarchal society, especially in terms of marriage and the family" (Neale and Krutnik 1995, 133)—is a prime feature of the classic romantic comedy. Despite loving Logan, Rory tells him, "There are just a lot of things in my life right now that are undecided, which used to scare me, but now I kind of like that it's all wide open. And if I married you, it just wouldn't be" ("It's Just Like Riding a Bike"). But Rory still feels unhappy: "It was supposed to be a happy day in my life [college graduation], and now every time I look back on it, I'm going to think of this horrible thing that happened" ("Unto the Breach" [7.21]).

Although the Gilmore girls are wonderful examples of female power, men still play a vital role in their achievements. Lorelai, who has attended business school, still needs Luke's help to start her own inn ("The Ins and Outs of Inns" [2.08]), and she often looks to him for guidance. And even though it is Rory who helps Jess study, he says that he feels able to help her become a foreign correspondent. Jess first makes her hesitate about her potential, telling her that it looks "too hard" (bombs, armies, foreign languages), though he eventually assures her that she will manage to achieve it. He nevertheless causes her to worry about her chances and wonder what she would do if she were to fail—as she does again in the final episode ("Bon Voyage") when she says, "What if I am a terrible reporter?" Male influences that make Rory feel unhappy and even incompetent seem to determine her attitude toward romance. Her boyfriends are always portrayed as the antithesis of her professional ambitions. Both of Rory's graduations end with a breakup (as depicted in "Those Are Strings, Pinocchio" and "Unto the Breach"). Boys not only are constraints to her career but also bring her misfortune—an accident with Jess ("Teach Me Tonight") and jail time with Logan ("Blame Booze and Melville"). Sex is even presented as a fault that needs punishment: when Paris fails to get into Harvard, she believes it is because she has slept with Jamie ("The Big One"):

> PARIS: I can't believe I slept with Jamie. I'm a slut.
> RORY: No, you're not. You love him.
> PARIS: What if he doesn't love me anymore? What if he doesn't think I'm special anymore? How am I going to tell him I didn't get into Harvard? What am I going to do?
> RORY: Paris, I don't know why you didn't get into Harvard. But you are smart and so special, and you'll see, everything's going to be fine.
> PARIS: Well, all I got to say is after all the trouble this sex thing has caused me, I better have been good.

Because of Paris's meltdown, Lorelai tells Rory that, "apparently, you are the biggest virgin in the world" when she is accepted into her three top-choice schools.

Roughly seventy years after screwball comedies revealed (and perhaps fostered) a reconceptualization of the relationship between men and women, both in love and in the workplace, Rory still has to fight to find her place in both arenas. Like an evil publisher in a classic newspaper movie from the 1930s, Mitchum tries to deter the female protagonist's dream of becoming a journalist. But Rory, like Hildy in *His Girl Friday,* becomes a heroine embodying intelligence and determination. She reclaims her dream, though her final decision to accept a job as a political reporter means that she must turn down Logan's marriage proposal.

Even though men are still often shown as believing themselves to be intellectually superior, twenty-first-century-female Rory ultimately discovers that she can be a reporter, follow the advice of a female journalist, and lead an independent life just like her mother. Lorelai embodies Rory's independent future, and we are furthermore shown that her family's influence is bigger than Logan's. Following her mother's model, Rory rejects nepotism and a rich marriage to start a career as a journalist, working from the bottom up through her own capabilities.

Part Four

Food, Addiction, Gender, Sexuality

13

Pass the Pop-Tarts

The Gilmore Girls' *Perpetual Hunger*

SUSANNAH B. MINTZ AND LEAH E. MINTZ, M.D.

> What are we if not world-champion eaters?
>
> —LORELAI to Rory in "A Deep-Fried Korean Thanksgiving" (3.09)

Some reference to food occurs in nearly every episode of *Gilmore Girls,* and most of the show's main characters have a direct connection to food or cooking. Beyond their ritual coffee drinking, Lorelai and Rory are infamous for their junk food habits, having a particular penchant for cheeseburgers, Chinese food, and mystery bags from Al's House of Pancakes. Luke, Lane, and Zach serve up french fries and pie with gruff but homey attentiveness. Sookie's artistry as a chef is legendary in Stars Hollow, and she wields as fierce a hand over her kitchen staff at the inn as Emily does over her bewildered parade of cooks. Mrs. Kim's strict dietary regime of tofu, flaxseed, and multigrain bread seems almost the most egregious of the many restrictions she imposes on her daughter. Jackson is the town's most industrious produce grower, and Taylor has a monopoly on ice cream and groceries.

This vocabulary of food in *Gilmore Girls* is more than mere character development or realistic texture. Interior shots of diners, kitchen nooks, dining rooms, and banquet halls depict eating as a class- and race-inflected activity. It makes sense, given the show's interest in probing the ways in which social milieu shapes identity; simply put, where and what one eats mark socioeconomic status. Lorelai's modest and notoriously underused kitchen, for example, clearly contrasts with her parents' stately dining room and the ritualized meals that take place there. Similarly, the down-home crowd at Luke's diner stands in opposition to the more homogenized, upper-crust demographic of the Yale dining hall. But more curiously, although food tends to be abundant, characters are rarely shown eating it. Even in scenes unrelated to meals, tables are often laden with food, as if to insist on the availability of nourishment yet also to withhold any direct representation of pleasure. This point is true even of Lorelai and Rory, whose junk food binges are only implied: we see the food they plan to eat or the aftermath of their eating, but their actual on-screen consumption is limited. These apparently rapacious eaters are hardly ever shown chowing down.

Something is at work here about the dangers of gratification. To the extent that both Lorelai and Rory are defined by their alternating immersion in and defiance of Gilmore wealth, a world in which food is always at the ready but only indirectly consumed, points to the difficulties they have in negotiating their proximity to, and their fear of, objects of desire. Lorelai in particular knows that she could obtain nearly anything from her parents if she were willing to ask—but to do so would be to capitulate to their expectations and demands (such as the Friday-night dinners in exchange for Rory's Chilton tuition). To emancipate herself from parental influence, Lorelai must maintain a steadfast resilience toward the pressure of her own wishes, stalwartly denying herself easy pleasure in favor of independence and individuality. Lorelai *does* grant Rory the kind of superabundance that she prevents her own parents from offering, in the form of junk food in greasy takeout bags rather than lavish spreads of French pastry or filet mignon on Spode china, but she walks a thin line between thumbing her nose at the Gilmores' economic advantage and actually imitating the structure of that privilege. In its habit of rarely portraying Lorelai and Rory actually eating, the series suggests that no matter what the Gilmore girls might crave, consumption is fraught with risk. The excessiveness of their desire seems to be inevitable, and just as surely must be curtailed, particularly in the pursuit of an autonomous identity.

In a related way, food foregrounds a central problem of mother-daughter relations in *Gilmore Girls.* It is not surprising that Lorelai's food habits seem childish; she is still her parents' defiant teenager, more often a sister figure to Rory than a mother. The fact that she feeds Rory in so lax a manner suggests an ongoing tension between her status as the rebellious sixteen year old who ruins her parents' hopes for her and the self-aware grownup who raises a poised and accomplished daughter. The leaning-in to adolescent sexual desire that, quite literally, produces Rory as well as the rupture between Lorelai and her parents becomes, in adulthood, the leaning-in to junk food that holds Lorelai and Rory in a uniquely intense bond and demonstrates Lorelai's capacity for emotional generosity. Lorelai *can,* as Emily cannot, love her daughter in an openly genuine way that allows Rory the psychological mobility to make her own choices and fashion her own identity. But Lorelai's parenting style has a complex and not altogether benign etiology. The fact that Lorelai is so clearly infantilized at Emily's dinner table—indeed, that she often announces how *hungry* she is at those dinners—implies that her permissiveness as a feeding mother is the direct result of maternal deprivation and Gilmore-style control.

To the degree that Lorelai and Rory seem to eat without consequence (without guilt, apology, weight gain, or routinely feeling sick), their flaunted proclivity for junk food is also a stand-in for sexuality. Lorelai's inability (or unwillingness) to control her reproductive body is, of course, the very premise of the show: everything proceeds from that originary moment. This point from the past is frequently reiterated, but whereas Lorelai's current relationships with men are central to each season, her actual sexual behavior is only obliquely mentioned. So too with Rory, who, despite her serial monogamy and frank discussions with Lane about the joys of sex, for the most part retains the innocent demeanor that is part of her character's charm. Like Lorelai, she is beautiful but not exactly sexy, sexually active but not erotic. Their reckless eating—uninhibited, unhealthy, and only occasionally overfilling—represents a more sanctioned gratification of appetite than the sexual behavior that so troubles Gilmore family propriety. For their part, the older Gilmores also work out problems of romance and fidelity through food. It is precisely the conflation of food and sex, for example, that incites Emily's jealous outrage when she discovers Richard has been secretly meeting old flame Pennilynn Lott at cozy lunches for years (though one might wonder what she expects, when she and Richard eat their own meals at opposite ends of a cartoonishly elongated dining room table).[1]

But food does, of course, get real women into serious trouble. For a program so smartly self-conscious in its exploration of the concerns of modern women, it is curious that so little mention is made of emotionally disordered eating. Even in a show in which irony is the dominant tonal register, occasional jokes about women's weight fluctuating because of problems with men seem more trivializing than thought provoking. There is no overt comment on the weight of the show's two heavy-set women, Sookie and Miss Patty. But because the one is both desexualized and professionally food obsessed,[2] and the other gratuitously oversexed and prone to licentious, "unlawful" dalliances

1. The Gilmores' dining arrangement may be an ironic homage to Charles Foster Kane and wife Susan in Orson Welles's *Citizen Kane* (1941). An especially comical exchange takes place between Emily and Richard when, after they have separated and Richard has moved into the pool house, he commits the heinous crime of entering the main house unannounced and uninvited. "What if I was sitting in the living room stark naked?" Emily screeches, to which Richard answers, in his stately and sober way, "You've never been in the living room stark naked. You've never been stark naked. We went skinny dipping one night, and you wore an overcoat" ("Written in the Stars" [5.03]).

2. Jackson and Sookie, for example, a down-to-earth couple in a very literal sense, conduct their courtship and marital romance almost entirely through the language of produce. In the early stages of their flirtation, for instance, Jackson accuses Sookie of "sneaking around behind [his] back" because she covets another man's strawberries and jealously barks at her, "You disgust me. . . . I hope you're happy together!" ("Kill Me Now" [1.03]). Later, Jackson's hydroponic tomatoes inspire this eroticized (and marital!) exchange in the Dragonfly Inn's kitchen: Jackson asks, "Do you want another piece?" and Sookie purrs throatily, "Do I," telling the assembled staff, "Leave us, please" ("Tippecanoe and Taylor, Too" [5.04]).

with food,[3] neither female character exactly represents *acceptance* of atypical weight or size.[4] In this context, Lorelai's and Rory's unabashed consumption plays out a fantasy of embodiment that is simultaneously greedy and self-contained. They are bodies managed without hardship, bodies magically disciplined from within, sisterly bodies invulnerable to parental restriction, self-policing bodies that defy the logic of calories or physiology. And this fantasy points in turn to a central conundrum in *Gilmore Girls:* to what extent is a woman's identity determined by her ability to properly manage desire?

Intersecting themes of food, sexuality, and familial disruption are established in the pilot episode of the series. In the first scene, Lorelai walks to Luke's Diner, where "FOOD" is prominently painted on the window; the episode then ends with Lorelai back at Luke's after dinner at her parents', flirting with him over coffee and chili fries and describing the "flagellation" she has received from the Gilmores. In conversation with Rory and Lane in this same episode, Mrs. Kim offers "muffins with no dairy, no sugar, no wheat" (delicacies so dry and hard they must be soaked in tea before they can be bitten into), and then asks whether any girls at school have gotten pregnant or dropped out—an oblique but obvious reference to the kind of "trouble" that issued in Rory's birth. Despite the quick transition from her unappetizing snack to her suspicion of teenage girls' promiscuity, Mrs. Kim exemplifies the fact that hunger for food is not to be understood as merely a substitute for sexual need, since in stripping a potentially moist and delectable muffin of anything palatable she underscores the dangers of physical pleasure of any sort. In her first exchange with Dean, Rory herself fixates on a different pastry: "Do you like cake?"

3. In "Cinnamon's Wake" (1.05), Miss Patty says that eating plums is "better than sex" and is reprimanded by Kirk for "put[ting] something in that mouth that doesn't belong there" when she samples the produce at Doose's Market.

4. It seems particularly ironic that when Rory has sex with a married Dean for the second time at the start of Season Five, it is at Miss Patty's studio ("Say Goodbye to Daisy Miller" [5.01]). This incident is the only representation in the series of adulterous (not just premarital) sex.

she asks him. "So, did I ask you if you like cake? 'Cause they have really good cake back there." In each of these interactions, food registers powerful anxieties about women's bodies and their propensity for behaving in unruly ways, and an equally potent determination to get what they want. "FOOD" is a literal but also symbolic sign of where things begin, in the oscillating tension between desire and denial.

Luke's Diner works here to frame the parameters of Lorelai's multivalent motion. She is propelled back and forth across a divide that separates her home of origin, with its vexed dining room, its rules and rigidity, from the town in which she can eat and flirt with whomever she likes. Her use of the word *flagellation* to illustrate her interaction with Emily and Richard makes an emphatic point about the consequences to her sense of self at her parents' house. To attend a dinner at the Gilmores' is to be not just emotionally but *corporeally* punished, and Lorelai must compensate in an immediate way by returning to Luke's for the specific brand of nurturance that he provides: home-style food of a particularly unwholesome sort, grouchily delivered in a safe, playful way, without pretense or caution ("Red meat can kill you. Enjoy," he is apt to growl). With Luke, Lorelai can seem to be "herself," a woman who determines what she will eat and with whom she will get frisky ("Luke, I need the largest cheeseburger in the world," she tells him in the aptly titled episode "Kill Me Now," and only partly suggestively, "Let's break a record, mister"). Getting the biggest cheeseburger in the world from a working-class man like Luke—or a burger poignantly shaped like Santa Clause to soothe Lorelai for having been disinvited to Christmas dinner at her parents' house ("Forgiveness and Stuff" [1.10])—stands in direct defiance of the paradox that is Emily's ostentatious restrictiveness where food is concerned. Food is a sexual metaphor, but it also articulates the intensity of Lorelai's need, physical and emotional, for caretaking.

Rory, too, employs a language of food both to mask and to manifest sexual desire, and through food she brings forth the needs and workings of her body. Her nervously repeated questions to Dean about cake indicate trepidation about revealing that she likes him, and of course at this early stage in the series, Rory is innocently virginal.

But at the same time, she cannot get Dean—or cake—off her mind. She likes cake, *wants* cake; she also wants to be able to want Dean, to authorize her interest in him. And she wants to ensure that he likes it—her—too. But cake, in this moment, does not exactly deflect attention away from the more provocative questions Rory might be asking about sex, since it inevitably calls to mind other appetites, and thus the consuming and even greedy fact of her body: she openly declares her desire for cake. Not surprisingly, this type of dialogue happens again and more overtly when Rory, now romantically involved with Dean, tries to resist both food and flirtation from Jess. "I've seen you eat," Jess says when she complains that a box of food he has brought her is "too much," as if to imply that she has already demonstrated her availability to him, that he knows just how "far" she will go. Then, when she offers him as many fries as he wants but balks as he starts to remove his coat, he retorts, "You told me to have all I wanted. That sounded invitation-like" ("There's the Rub" [2.16]). Food *is* an invitation—into the home, into the body—and so it is not at all a screen when Dean, interrupting them, seems most perturbed not that Rory and Jess are headed for a romantic liaison but rather that they have eaten so much.

Eating is both a literal act of consumption and a symbolic, metonymic gesture toward the problematic of women's (sexual) appetites and bodies. It is a real mechanism of nourishment and an expression of longing to be cared for, desired, and simply understood. To eat food, to want it, order it, enjoy it, and convey it to others, is to activate the body, put it on display, make known its urges and its independence. As a narrative device, it also places the issue of control over self and others in acutely high relief. If such characters as Mrs. Kim and Emily Gilmore imply that overindulgence is to be strenuously avoided as unhealthy or unseemly, respectively (with no less than moral collapse and the breakdown of social propriety at stake for those mothers, in terms of what their daughters eat), then Lorelai and Rory do make good on a central feminist tenet about self-determination and the shirking of rules aimed at keeping women's unruly bodies in line. They do not capitulate in any obvious or unquestioning way to cultural codes that govern women's appearances or sexual activity. To the contrary, they eat with abandon, and their romantic relationships are similarly unencumbered by excessive indulgence or restraint. Lorelai may be fraught with confusion and indecision where men are concerned, but her three primary relationships (with Max Medina, Luke Danes, and Christopher Hayden) each result in proposals of marriage.[5] Rory too has "normal" and monogamous sex compared to Lane, who returns from her honeymoon full of disgust for it, and even to Logan, who spends their brief hiatus apart sleeping with each of his sister's best friends.

One significant feature of the self-possessed quality of the Gilmore girls' appetites is the performative way in which they eat in front of men, particularly given the fact that neither of them cooks: food is brought *to* them, prepared for them by others. Indeed, most of their men friends seem to understand that the way to a Gilmore heart is through her stomach.[6] An important reversal is at work, one that brings women out of the kitchen and allows them to show off the fact of their hungry bodies. Men look on admiringly as Lorelai and Rory indulge, often in deliberately ungenteel and even gluttonous ways, eschewing fancy napkin holders or place settings for food straight from the take-out box or serving dish. Eating this way seems at once childish, lusty, and impolite, thus troubling the gendered and class norms that define (and confine) Gilmore women, and overtly spotlighting the erotic appeal of such resistance. But what do we make of the fact

5. Lorelai also has a brief romance with Jason "Digger" Stiles, who cooks breakfast for her and with whom she grocery shops in one of the few scenes set in a food store not owned by Taylor ("Ted Koppel's Big Night Out" [4.09]).

6. Lindsay cooks Dean a roast to get him back in "Say Goodbye to Daisy Miller," but her agitated attempt to get it right (we see her at the butcher shop demanding instructions for the third time) suggests both how futile that effort is (no perfect roast has ever cured marital woes) and also how problematic a position it is for women to be in when they orient themselves around catering to husbands' whims in denial of obvious strife and strain. On the history of promoting cooking to facilitate good marital relations, especially sexual ones, see Neuhaus 2001.

that so much eating is so infrequently observed, that there is always something *off* about it—off-camera, out of sync (with hunger, with others), out of open-lid boxes? Early in her relationship with Max, for example, Lorelai goes to his house for dinner but starts eating in earnest only after the meal is over; at the table, she takes "two, maybe three bites of this amazing dinner" Max has prepared for her, but as he cleans up, she sits on the kitchen counter voraciously eating food out of the pot, even food scraped into the pot from their dirty plates ("Paris Is Burning" [1.11]). The romantic "candles and flowers and plates and knives and cloth napkins" Max has laid out do not seem to inspire Lorelai's appetite, but "watching someone work makes [her] hungry," and though Max is clearly confounded by this behavior, he is also helplessly drawn to it.

Luke also cooks for Lorelai, both inside and outside his diner, and he does so in a way that is both remarkably sophisticated and comically profuse. After a night together, Lorelai descends the staircase to find Luke making breakfast in her kitchen—enough for the entire diner—using pans and utensils she does not recognize ("Tippecanoe and Taylor, Too"). It is a touching gesture, but Lorelai does not want to eat at home: she claims to want food from Luke only *at* Luke's, as if cooking in her kitchen is not just invasive but sacrilegious, no matter who does it; as if her kitchen were not an appropriately intimate space or, paradoxically, perhaps *too* intimate, so that she must hold him at bay. Or perhaps intimacy is something Lorelai performs only in public, where her eating can be witnessed and put into a social context. Later, Luke proves himself the "perfect man" by fixing Lorelai a dinner of "lamb and artichoke stew, penne with pesto and potatoes, roasted garlic with rosemary focaccia, tomatoes stuffed with bread crumbs and goat cheese, and ricotta cheesecake with amaretto cookies to go with [her] coffee" ("The Party's Over" [5.08]).

Here, "perfection" is defined by an ironic contrast that suits Lorelai's contrary personality: the diner owner and short-order cook has expensive culinary tastes, the elegant meal will be eaten using cutlery "pilfered" from the diner downstairs, and coffee is the only thing Lorelai regularly asks of Luke, so it becomes the base upon which his other expressions of desire are built. Luke's perfection in this instance lies precisely in his difference from Emily Gilmore: the panoply of choices is offered in a heartfelt rather than emotionally withholding way. Nonetheless, the exaggerated demonstration of skill and display of so much food seems motivated by nervousness as much as delighting in the bounty of food. If Lorelai is so hungry, it makes sense that Luke might feel compelled to serve up such an array of dishes in order to appease her hunger. The fact that their dinner is never "consummated" (it is interrupted by Luke's obnoxious brother-in-law T. J., so that we do not see them eat) merely reinforces the idea that something about desire and consumption must be deflected. Food is *there,* but it will be eaten later, elsewhere, already.

Lorelai's distaste for the act of cooking, her refusal to root herself in the gender-coded space of the kitchen, is clearly a feature of her resistance to a conventional domestic or maternal role, the kind of archetypal femininity personified by Donna Reed. Unlike Emily, she does not cook in part because she works; more than an issue of time constraints or the pressures of single motherhood, *not* cooking coincides with an identity rigorously forged around economic independence and professional stature. Emily, on the other hand, does not cook precisely because she *can:* it is one of the most tangible markers of her class status that she can afford to hire domestics to handle the prosaic matters of food preparation, while opulent displays of food secure her position in that social hierarchy.[7] Not cooking is also an expression of Emily's habit of deflecting caretaking functions onto other people, especially paid female servants whom she bullies. Again, to do so is part of her assumed class prerogative, but more subtly, servants also threaten the transparency of her predominance: hired cooks do not just bungle her orders; they prove her inability to wholly command her environment. Like Emily, Lorelai also procures food from

7. Think of the absurd, nearly grotesque amount of food laid out in the pool house on Rory's first morning as the older Gilmores' new resident ("The New and Improved Lorelai Gilmore" [6.01]). On the class connotations of certain types of food, see LeBesco 2001.

others, and is waited on, but her position within a network of food providers differs from Emily's in large part because Lorelai considers herself an equal rather than a superior. She respects people with skills that she does not have and uses food not to control but to please, to satiate, to inspire trust and even playfulness. Not cooking is effectively equivalent, for Lorelai, to loving.

If food registers the quality of women's relationships to their bodies, their needs, their lovers and family members, contradictions and complications around the act of eating seem inevitable in the context of mother-daughter dynamics. At first glance, Emily Gilmore and Mrs. Kim seem to represent diametrically opposed versions of how mothers restrict their daughters' freedom of self-expression. The extravagance of the one is countered by the sobriety of the other; whole grains and tofurky do not go down easy with opulent displays of imported cheese or Swiss chocolate. But the parodic nature of Mrs. Kim's single-minded brand of Korean Christianity is not so different from the fun poked at Emily's WASPish notion of dignity, insofar as each woman is depicted as holding fast to a set of behavioral rules that promise to keep emotional and corporeal chaos at bay. Both seem, in their comically hysterical ways, desperate for protection from being exposed, from taking their "clothes" off (as Lorelai has done literally and Lorelai and Rory have each done figuratively by "choos[ing] her own path in life" ["The Party's Over"]). Given that both Emily and Mrs. Kim use food to keep their daughters in line, *Gilmore Girls* suggests that it is not so much the particular *style* of caretaking that matters but rather the *intent.* Emily's well-bred and well-fed pretensions offer no more emotional nourishment than Mrs. Kim's prudish and calorically sensible rice cakes, whereas Lorelai's freely proffered goodies dramatize the openness of her affections, her willingness to support people just as they are (think of her ordering samples from all the local eateries for the kids in Rory's Yale dorm, feeding the new, the lonely, the socially inept ("The Lorelais' First Day at Yale" [4.02]).

For Lorelai, the fact that eating manifests physical hunger as well as psychological desire (thereby asserting individuality and thus difference from, perhaps defiance of, others) means that her dietary habits are inextricably bound up with her vexed relationship with her mother down to the level of food choice. This situation is obvious throughout the series, but it becomes evident to Lorelai herself only after her breakup with Luke at the start of the final season. In "Lorelai's First Cotillion" (7.03), her parents' reaction—or, to put this more accurately, the fact that "the absence of their reaction was worse than any freak-out they could have had"—reveals to Lorelai just how determined her actions have been by a desire to contradict her parents. "What if I don't like what I like because I like it," she asks Rory poignantly, "but because my mother doesn't like it, and doesn't want me to like it?" Music, movies, clothes, men, but also, elaborately, food:

> I can remember the first time I had a Pop-Tart. It was at my friend Erica Catcha's house, and she said, "Do you want a Pop-Tart?" and I knew that my mother would recoil at the very idea of me. I could just picture her—a *Pop-Tart*? And so I had one. And I opened the little silver wrapper, and I took a bite, and I thought nothing had ever tasted so good. I thought it tasted like . . . freedom. It tasted like I was my own person. The Pop-Tart tasted like freedom and rebellion and independence.

It is not just the idea of eating a Pop-Tart that Lorelai imagines will shock her mother but "the very idea *of me*." Indeed, Emily does "recoil" at Lorelai's essence, her ontology. Lorelai's desiring, ingesting, willful body becomes a source of disgust.

It is hardly surprising, then, that dinners with her mother might trigger Lorelai's adolescent resentment of Emily's controlling and insensitive ways, or that questions about how best to mother—again, about origin, nurturance, and identity—would surface so keenly in those moments when Lorelai is being fed by her mother. In a scene from "Driving Miss Gilmore" (6.21), Lorelai's immature behavior demonstrates how fully she reverts to the role of child under the sway of matriarchal predominance. Acting like a little girl is a gesture of defiance, surely intended to raise Emily's hackles, but it is also one of helplessness, stemming from what seems a defensively ironic sadness about the absence of maternal affection. In the scene, Lorelai and Rory are debating the relative merits of Ashlee Simpson's and Jessica Simpson's brown and blond hair. As she speaks, Lorelai brandishes a meatball, speared on her fork, for emphasis, while Emily looks on like a dog tracking a tennis ball, getting increasingly agitated:

> EMILY: All right, that's it. No more spaghetti and meatballs. . . . Every time we have spaghetti and meatballs, you fight.
> LORELAI: No, we're not fighting, we're just bonding.
> RORY: Grandma, I'm starving!
> EMILY: No! Spaghetti and meatballs is just too much excitement.
> RICHARD: They always fight when we have spaghetti and meatballs.
> EMILY: Can we please talk about something besides food?
> LORELAI: Starvation. Scurvy. The Donner party.

Like *flagellation,* words like *starving* and *starvation* dramatically insist that nothing salubrious ever occurs in this venue. On the contrary, a visit to the Gilmores is physically perilous, a dangerous high-seas voyage without adequate nutrition, a trek through the mountains so disastrous that Lorelai and Rory might resort to cannibalism to assuage their desperate hunger; indeed, they do consume one another, after a fashion, volleying accusations at each other ("You're nuts!" "You're double nuts!") in a way that prolongs, because it impels Emily to clear their plates, rather than offsets their hunger.

For her part, Emily does not simply withhold food; she is like a force of nature that traps the hapless Donner party in a blizzard, or *she* is the cannibalizing mother who annihilates her young to ensure her own survival. Though it is Lorelai who craves most severely a certain kind of maternal provision, *starving* is Rory's term, and her use of it invokes the dangerous possibility that the legacy of Gilmore withholding will be carried on despite Lorelai's efforts to protect Rory—using herself almost as a bodily shield—from her grandparents' emotional deficiencies.[8] That Lorelai might construe "fighting" with Rory at her mother's table as "bonding" (and that Emily would in turn misunderstand bonding as fighting) further suggests how fully Lorelai and Emily experience anything that happens in each other's company as antagonistic. Friday-night dinners are not just disappointing; they are toxic.

What might get overlooked in this exchange is that by serving spaghetti and meatballs, comfort food rather than haute cuisine, Emily has to the best of her capacity attempted to act lovingly. Miscommunication cuts two ways. When Richard reminds Emily that Lorelai and Rory "always fight when we have spaghetti and meatballs," he suggests that the younger Gilmore girls can be just as resistant to Emily's offerings as she is often stingy about making them. In the tense, delicate negotiation of risk and desire that is familial love, food is a sign of hope and a mechanism of hurt. Emily and Lorelai want fiercely to be loved by one another, but they have no adequate means of conveying that need or imparting its resolution. Serving spaghetti, awkward as it may be and inflected by Richard's defeatist pronouncement that any expression of care on their part results inevitably in failure, is nonetheless a legitimate gesture: Emily has tried to speak Lorelai's culinary language. But the claim that spaghetti and meatballs inspire too much "excitement" suggests that any attempt to cross boundaries gets scary. The risk of intimacy is too great, so that Lorelai must retreat into a defensive immaturity that holds Emily at bay, and the latter must in turn respond with a critical, disciplinarian, and ultimately jealous interruption of pleasure.

8. For a show so preoccupied with food, the concept of starvation occurs unusually often. In "Paris Is Burning," Max Medina chastises Lorelai for being "starving" after they have already eaten dinner. In "Let the Games Begin" (3.08), Lorelai announces that she is "starved" when a Friday-night dinner gets stalled because the soon-to-be-fired cook has put walnuts in the salad against Emily's wishes. In "The Party's Over," Lane complains to her mother's Korean exchange student, "You came to me starving, and I gave you fries," when she learns that Kyon has ratted her out to Mrs. Kim about hugging Zach.

Food is thus a prime weapon in the Gilmore family arsenal; if it soothes, it also punishes. A triangulated meal during Emily and Richard's separation shows both mothers and daughters using food in ways that ignore physical and emotional signals, seek to coerce, and impose meaning onto recalcitrant bodies. The Gilmore parents have agreed that Lorelai and Rory will have Friday-night drinks with Richard and dinner with Emily, but Emily, sniffing a trick, catches them eating skewers of beef on the patio and warns the girls, "You two better be hungry when you get inside, or else." In the next scene, at the dining room table, she accuses them both of not eating and complains about her husband, "He can't stick to a simple agreement. . . . He was trying to upstage me. He was trying to make his part of the evening the fun part. He's a child. A spoiled four year old. I should take his dump truck away and send him to bed without supper, or as he calls it: appetizers."

> LORELAI: Mom, seriously, we are starving. Look, *mmm*, wow, [to Rory] eat some carrots, eat some carrots.
> RORY: Carrots, delicious.
> EMILY: Well, if you're both that hungry, you must want more. [To the maid:] Olga, good timing. The girls are famished. Load 'em up.

In this exchange, Emily literally deploys hunger as a threat, not simply using Lorelai's and Rory's hunger as a symbolic pawn in her fight with Richard but also, more egregiously, forcing them into adversarial positions vis-à-vis their own bodies. Either they deprive themselves of their desire for barbecued beef in order to maintain hunger for Emily (thereby disappointing Richard), or they override feeling full in order to eat something else they might want as well as to avoid Emily's wrath. In the event, of course, they achieve neither, and eating becomes emptied of either need or satisfaction; eating is problematically inverted, a desperate act performed to pacify the angry parent rather than an expression of responsible or even just autonomous self-care. *Starving* and *famished* cease to have any physical significance, and the terms are used here in full awareness of how exaggerated they are as indications of anyone's hunger in this scene. Indeed, hyperbole around hunger is the Gilmore way, and here the only available choice concerning food is really no choice at all: to be force-fed or (what is not after all so very different) to be denigrated as a "spoiled four year old." Eating in opposition to one's own desire (eating too much or not eating at all) is required if the parents are to be appeased—but someone will always end up hurt or angry.

In the midst of this excruciating meal, Rory gets a cell phone call from Dean; he is still married to Lindsay, but they have reignited their romance behind his wife's back. Lorelai tries to protect Rory's privacy against Emily's intrusive questions about the caller, but when Rory returns to the table, she nonchalantly (and to Lorelai's confusion and dismay) reveals to Emily that she is seeing Dean again. When the dinner is over, Lorelai and Rory stagger, nearly drunk on food, into the Gilmore driveway, and the following spat ensues:

> LORELAI: Why'd you tell my mother about Dean?
> RORY: I'm not going to lie to Grandma about Dean. Why should I?
> LORELAI: 'Cause she's her.
> RORY: Mom, I am with Dean.
> LORELAI: All right, fine. [heavy sigh] You know, I'm actually hungry.

The proprietary question, "Why'd you tell *my mother*?" reveals just how complicated this triangulation is for Lorelai; in this moment, Emily can be neither Rory's grandmother nor someone with whom Lorelai and Rory share a relationship. And what pithier rendering of all that troubles Lorelai about Emily than "'cause she's her"—a statement that perfectly articulates Emily's maddening, suffocating, incalculably overbearing effect? Yet Lorelai must acknowledge that Rory is not on her side in this argument, and her final remark—"I'm actually hungry"—brilliantly captures the loneliness of that realization. To the extent that Rory's affair with Dean initially worried her sense of integrity, Lorelai has already had to face Rory's independence from her, an uncomfortable truth she again confronts when Rory pays Emily the respect of an honest disclosure. Rory is, in effect, acting like Lorelai, being her own person, making her own decisions, acting on her own desires. "Actually hungry" thus seems inflected in two ways, implying not just that Lorelai could eat after having already consumed two meals but also, more painfully, that she is not getting what she wants *even from Rory.*

If we imagine that "I'm actually hungry" calls to mind Lorelai's habit of leaving Gilmore dinners to go eat some more at Luke's, then her previous claim that "if it flew, swam, or crawled on this earth, we just ate it" suggests just how obviously and emphatically eating is prompted by psychological distress. *Gilmore Girls* persistently stages this kind of emotional eating, but it tackles in no direct way either the causes or the consequences of eating disorders. More curiously, the show minimizes the actual display of the *comfort* the protagonists seek through food. In a scene from "Concert Interruptus" (1.13), Lorelai asks, "Who wants cheese?" after she has agreed, reluctantly, to give up some old clothes for a rummage sale. The relinquishing of clothes—clearly an extension of self for a clotheshorse like Lorelai—provokes an obvious separation anxiety that she immediately seeks to assuage through food, but the scene cuts away before we see her actually eating any cheese.

In another early episode, titled "The Deer Hunters" (1.04), a despondent Rory demands chocolate (she has gotten a bad grade in Mr. Medina's English class). However, though she is soon thereafter shown clutching an entire bowlful of chocolate chunks, she merely nibbles at a single piece, more daintily than in a needy or greedy way. Later in the same episode, Rory and Lorelai ease a study session with potato chips, Rolos, Kentucky Fried Chicken, and Fritos, but we understand this frantic eating only through its aftermath; the bags and boxes are empty. Such leaps, from *wanting* to *having had,* are pervasive throughout the show's seven seasons, and they work to elide the material reality of eating too much food or consuming it to alleviate self-doubt. As we have been arguing, there is something self-actualized about the Gilmore girls' robust appetites, about their demands for food when they need it. But by suppressing their on-screen intake, the series undercuts that more positive message, seeming to deny its protagonists the very pleasure they seek through food, and thereby implying that there may indeed be something shameful about eating to soothe frazzled nerves or hurt feelings. The emotional and physiological ramifications of a binge are simply ignored.

If *Gilmore Girls* tends to underplay the thornier questions of women's disordered relationships to food by simply swerving around scenes of excessive eating, the show has on occasion referred to a woman's weight in an explicit and surprisingly uncritical manner. In the episode "We've Got Magic to Do" (6.05), Rory has organized an event for Emily's Daughters of the American Revolution club at which Logan's spectacularly wealthy parents unexpectedly appear. When Richard reveals to Emily what Mitchum Huntzberger has just confirmed for him in the men's room—Sheera's contempt for Rory as a suitable girlfriend for her son Logan and his dismissal of her journalistic skills—Emily launches her own searing attack of Sheera:

> Let me tell you this, Sheera. We are just as good as you are. . . . [L]et's talk about your money. You were a two-bit gold-digger, fresh off the bus from Hicksville when you met Mitchum at whatever bar you happened to stumble into. And what made Mitchum decide to choose you to marry amongst the *pack* of women he was bedding at the time I'll never know, but hats off to you for bagging him. He's still a playboy, you know. Well, of course you know. That would explain why your weight goes up and down thirty pounds every other month, but that's your cross to bear. But these are ugly realities. No one needs to talk about them.

We have come to expect all manner of tactlessness from Emily, but her comment about Sheera's weight, the connection it makes between overeating and the emotional distress of an unfaithful relationship, seems especially insulting. Perhaps what surprises most about the remark is the very fact that it does use weight fluctuation as an insult.

The implication here is that weight gain is repugnant, a sign of weakness or a character flaw. Denigrating associations between fatness and laziness, narcissism, and asexuality are, of course, firmly entrenched in American culture, but it seems unworthy of *Gilmore Girls* to repeat such an uncritical and stereotyped slippage. When Emily defends Rory's worth by exposing Sheera as "trash," the class outrage is unremarkable on her part; she and Richard perpetrate the very same elitism on Lorelai and Rory herself when they condemn Luke and Dean as working class and thus "not good enough" prospects for Gilmore women (see "The Party's Over"). But where the series allows the younger generation to contest that kind of class pretension, Emily's gendered slam on Sheera's weight problems goes uncorrected.

A similar avoidance of the "ugly realities" of disordered eating happens when Emily asks Rory, earlier in Season Six, if she is bulimic. "You look skinny," she says. "Are you bulimic?" ("Let Me Hear Your Balalaikas Ringing Out" [6.08]). Coming from Emily, "skinny" and "bulimic" sound just as critical as a comment about weight gain. Overeating, like undereating and purging, is simply a failure to regulate—an irrationality, so to speak, of appetite[9]—where Gilmore respectability depends on correctness, a properly balanced whole.[10] At the same time, *bulimic* is a word without meaning in Emily's blunt use of it, something she may know affects young women but does not understand, a concept she can summon to startle Rory into some kind of admission. Emily is characteristically obtuse; if Rory were underweight or bulimic, what could Emily possibly offer by way of intervention? The more complicated aspect of this moment is that its comic potential depends on viewers' understanding that Rory is surely *not* bulimic: we know how much she loves food, how "healthily" she indulges her desire for and pleasure in it (so much so that Kirk, struggling to peddle Rory and Lorelai as passengers in his new pedicab, jokes about the "freshmen fifteen" in the opening scene of "Girls

9. For an elaboration of the notion that appetite has been framed as irrational, see Brumberg 1997.

10. Emily is hardly a bastion of temperance. When she and Richard separate, she goes on shopping binges (as in "Scene in a Mall" [4.15]).

in Bikinis, Boys Doin' the Twist" [4.17]). That it makes no sense, in effect, to consider the possibility of Rory as bulimic reiterates the problematic aspect of how bingeing is represented in *Gilmore Girls.* For most women, a physique like Rory's would simply not coincide with the kind of eating she engages in with Lorelai.

Something else is implied by *skinny,* a word both Emily and Rory employ. In the spaghetti-and-meatballs scene, the repetition of *starving* and *starvation* signals how entanglements of food and intimacy circulate in the Gilmore family, closely tied to Emily's caretaking habits as matriarch. Thus, when Rory tells Lorelai, speaking for the first time since their estrangement, "You look skinny" ("Twenty-one Is the Loneliest Number" [6.07]), she raises the specter of a dangerous family legacy, quite different from the wealth and social status that Emily wields in her argument with Sheera Huntzberger. Both instances of *skinny*—Emily to Rory, and Rory to Lorelai—carry a kind of reproach, and both reveal the degree of emotional distance between observer and observed. In one way, to notice that Lorelai "look[s] skinny" simply shows that Rory has not seen her in some time, but since they do not typically engage in a stereotypically superficial discussion of their bodies, the phrase also smacks of awkwardness; it is a symptom of the stiffness between them.

The remark further implies, and in a more direct way than is usual for the show, that Lorelai's approach to food has an emotional basis. Like Emily's use of *skinny,* Rory's seems scornfully or perhaps grudgingly to hint at imbalance—Lorelai has been off-kilter, and the physical evidence of it is discomfiting. At the same time, of course, *skinny* has a very different valence than *fat.* Lorelai's eating might be out of whack because of psychical pain, but she does not, as does Sheera Huntzberger, *over*eat. Or to put this another way, because we see no visible consequences to her consumption, she only ever eats, does not overindulge. She is, in this problematic respect, still a Gilmore.

Ultimately, of course, neither Rory nor Lorelai is to be equated with Emily. "You look skinny" is also Rory's guarded way of acknowledging to Lorelai that the rift between them has been hard on them both, that she recognizes Lorelai's grief over their situation in its physical manifestation. Focusing on Lorelai's bodily condition in this moment allows Rory to deflect attention away from the emotional pain of their estrangement, but it also, in an exactly opposite manner, measures the intensity of Rory's regret about that situation, since to be "skinny" is presumably to have lost weight and thus not to be eating in the definitive Gilmore-girl fashion. Though prior episodes offer no evidence that Lorelai has stopped eating, bingeing *is* something she and Rory do together, a mark of their unique bond as well as their unique similarity to each other. Rory's comment, which in its way is distinctly maternal, gauges some part of what Lorelai has lost through their separation. We can hear in "You look skinny" a worry that Lorelai is no longer Lorelai: "You look *different,*" Rory might have said, no longer like the mother who indulges herself and me in defiance of her own mother, the mother with whom eating is fun ("too much excitement") and from whom food guarantees love rather than self- (or other-) restricting denial. It is thus utterly fitting that when the two eventually reconcile, Lorelai dashes off to Luke's for a cache of food—donuts, burgers, onion rings—with which to secure the reunion. "Don't skimp on the fries!" she cries to Luke. "We don't want to lose her again." Food may serve as a weapon in the fight for social dominance or emotional control, but it is also a means of establishing community and solidifying emotional bonds.[11]

We have been suggesting that *Gilmore Girls* tends to minimize examination of disordered eating as something that primarily women do, and do alone, beset by shame. But the show also makes a provocative link between eating and intellect that mitigates biases against women's eating as inherently guilty or out of control. To some extent, the display of unashamed and excessive eating brings food out of the closet, making it possible and even admirable for women to eat, as Lorelai and Rory do, plentifully. As Dean says to Rory very early on, "Wow, you can eat. . . . [M]ost girls don't eat" ("Kiss and Tell" [1.07]).

11. Bonding, of course, can become binding. Lorelai does, according to her own rhythms, control Rory through food.

More unexpectedly, eating is related to the fact of both women's considerable intelligence. When, for instance, Rory says in "The Deer Hunters" episode, "I don't think the fries and the horseradish sauce was the best idea we ever had," she implies that she and Lorelai binge almost as an act of creativity: food may be physically enjoyable, but it is also an *idea*. It is not just (or even) that the Gilmore girls eat despite their smarts, or when in doubt about their smarts; in some way, they eat *because* they are smart. Nourishing the self, gratifying the body, sharing pleasure with others: these are the acts of independent, intelligent women who are not, finally, afraid to assert their desires or admit their mistakes. If fries and horseradish do not make for the tastiest combination, we can have no doubt that the Girls will come up with something better—or equally unexpected—the next time.

14

"Nigella's Deep-Frying a Snickers Bar!"

Addiction as a Social Construct in Gilmore Girls

JOYCE GOGGIN

From his seat at the counter of Luke's Diner in the episode "I'm a Kayak, Hear Me Roar" (7.15), Kirk calls to Luke to "check it out"; he has been published.[1] As Kirk waxes poetic about being catapulted into the distinguished company of "published authors," Luke quickly learns that Kirk's masterpiece is really an advertisement to sell his mother's dinette set. When Luke, with characteristic sarcasm, asks if he is in fact referring to a want ad in the *Stars Hollow Gazette,* Kirk replies that it is "a powerful feeling seeing yourself immortalized in print. Sure, it's only newsprint. It rips easily, it comes off on your fingers, and the next day, people use it to wrap fish, but, hey, it's how Dickens got started."

As with all such brief exchanges in *Gilmore Girls,* this seemingly insignificant moment leads into a larger plotline, in this case one involving Luke's life-changing decision to sell his boat. In turn, this thread subtends the episode's more central theme of Lane's baby shower, but avid viewers of *Gilmore Girls* know just how much weight to give the segment and how to assess its role and importance with respect to the rest of the show. Fans know, for example, that phatic, embedded micromoments such as Luke and Kirk's dialogue

1. I am grateful to the Goggin girls—Linda, Kathie, Vanessa, Emma, and Amelia—for their help with the research for this article.

occur virtually nonstop in every episode and are intended to establish character and situation. At the same time, fans relish these segments because they are chock-full of the kind of intertextual references to literary texts, TV shows, films, and popular music for which the series is famous. Hence, these short but meaningful dialogues have a secondary function as fodder for faithful fans who delight in ferreting out sometimes-obscure references and speculating on possible meanings. Doubtless, then, somewhere on one of the many *Gilmore Girls* fan sites or Web logs (blogs) viewers have attempted to explain Kirk's reference to Dickens in this segment, thereby performing a task not unlike the one I have set for myself in this chapter.

My own viewer exegesis of the series will take Luke and Kirk's banter in this episode as a prime example, or perhaps symptom, of the critical points I want to develop. Delivered in rapid-fire fashion, over the ever-present cup of coffee, their dialogue unites the notion of commercial writing and serialized fiction with Charles Dickens, one of the genre's most famous practitioners. Moreover, it implicitly brings together particular forms of at least two cultural activities that play a central role in contemporary living, and got their start in the seventeenth century, along with the shift toward industrial modernity in the West. These activities—namely, coffee drinking and the consuming of serialized fiction (in forms such as novels and TV shows)—are potentially (and demonstrably) *addictive* and are, therefore, linked to essential aspects of modern living and being.

What at first may seem to be an unlikely point of entry into a screwball comedy series (with dramatic undertones) like *Gilmore Girls,* addiction proves to be particularly useful as a means for elucidating the series' appeal among fans. Addiction is one of the primary forces behind contemporary market-driven cultural production, of which the show is very consciously a part, and the good people of Stars Hollow provide a colorful rendition of consumer culture on a microeconomic scale. Characters like Emily, Lorelai, and Rory supply the demands that fuel the market, through a persistent drive to consume in the hopes of satisfying repetitive, insistent needs and compensating for the inevitable disappointments and growing pains faced by women of their class. This cycle of endless craving and conspicuous consumption forms the substance of the show's serialized narrative, which viewers addictively follow, and is mirrored by the "cute," compulsive behaviors to which fans aspire.[2] And although the yearnings and needs that drive the denizens of Stars Hollow may come from a variety of sources, shopping and consuming are presented on *Gilmore Girls* as the panacea. Hence, at www.tv.com we read that, after Rory becomes "anxiety-ridden over her future" as she graduates from Yale, "Lorelai tries to cheer her up with a day of *eating and shopping*."[3]

Moreover, while the above exchange between Luke and Kirk obviously takes place between two men, I will also discuss the role that has been historically assigned to women as consumers and purveyors of addictive foodstuffs, such as the coffee that the girls guzzle from queen-size cups at Luke's Diner. Because the widespread addiction to coffee and chocolate in particular, and junk food more generally, became exacerbated with the emergence of the modern market economy, I shall attempt to link Lorelai and Rory to a particular socio-economic tradition of female food "junkies." In so doing I will have occasion to draw on the historical conditions that groomed women as consumers whose role it was to drive the rising industrialized capitalist

2. Suffice it to say that www.gilmoregirls.org hosts eighty-four Web pages with the heading "You Know You're Obsessed with *Gilmore Girls* When . . ." On these pages fans record their own adorable compulsive behaviors related to the show, as, for example, "unconsciously . . . linking the weirddest [*sic*] stuff to GG," "almost everything you own has to do with GG or says something about GG on it," "instead of counting sheep to fall asleep you recite entire scenes from GG," "you plan your week around Gilmore Girl night and you SO cannot wait till tuesday nights," "you cannot pull yourself away from the computer when all you want to do is stay on gg.org even after you tell yourself over and over 'i'm gonna b so tired tomorrow,'" "you dream yourself into an episode of GG, and it fits perfectly," "you made yourself like caffee [*sic*] cause the girls do," or "people tell you that your GG addiction sounds sick and you agree with them but you don't care." See http://www.gilmoregirls.org/forum/index.php?topic=7781.msg348693#msg348693.

3. See http://www.tv.com/gilmore-girls/lorelai-lorelai/episode/962067/summary.html (emphasis added).

market of the eighteenth century, a market that profited immensely from the importation of coffee, cacao, sugar, and tea. Women, in their socially defined role as family shoppers, were conveniently centered in the home where caffeinated beverages such as tea became part of an important ritual, which necessitated increasingly expensive, imported goods. This historical backdrop may appear to recede into the distance behind a female protagonist—Lorelai Gilmore—who food shops by calling for take-out and serves her daughter by unwrapping Pop-Tarts, but, as I will show, it is certainly no coincidence that so much of the show's serialized narrative revolves around the procuring and consumption of addictive domestic foodstuffs.

With this background in mind, my analysis of *Gilmore Girls* will focus on a number of episodes from the show's fourth season. These episodes, originally broadcast in 2003 and 2004, present stellar examples of binge-eating, ravenous shopping, and excessive caffeine consumption, yet they also express a number of economic anxieties and ideological assumptions that were very much in the air in a post-9/11 United States. In moving toward this essay's conclusion, then, I will call on the historical tableau developed in the opening sections in the service of a closer analysis of various episodes from Season Four. In this way, I hope to show how a long-standing economic tradition that shaped women as consumers is endlessly reiterated through popular, addictive serialized narratives to serve political ends and to encourage particular patterns of consumption at key historical junctures.

Serialized Fiction, Consumption, and Modernity

> I'm Cathy Coffee, the bastard offspring of Mrs. Folger and Juan Valdez.
>
> —LORELAI to Luke in "Dead Uncles and Vegetables" (2.17)

According to Deborah Wynne, serialized fiction was already available to select consumers in England in the late seventeenth century

(2001, 11). This fact is somewhat remarkable given the limited literacy of the general populace at that time, as well as the price of paper, and the relative difficulty involved in producing printed text in volume. However, this early demand for compelling stories, parceled out into segments and sustained over a period of time, suggests a link with an emerging capitalist market that was beginning to manufacture products, sold in measured portions, for customers who came to expect such things. Hence, although I do not wish to reduce the complex web of influences through which the modern market grew to a simple question of causality, it does seem clear that at this early juncture the market was already exerting pressure on authors to produce fiction for modern consumers, whose leisure time was scarce and came in regular daily installments, perfectly suited to reading serialized publications.

In the eighteenth century, this trend of serialization gathered momentum as the reading population increased and the industrial means of producing affordable print improved. This period, therefore, was the century that saw the birth of papers such as the *Spectator*, which "was published daily, in single sheets printed on both sides in double columns, so reading it soon became a habit like having *tea or coffee*."[4] The publishers hoped to cultivate a reading public with a habit—a public that would look to a serial publication for the satiation of that habit. This century also marked the beginnings of a variety of other sensational periodicals such as the *London Spy* and the *Tattler* (1709) that fueled early celebrity culture and helped to drive the economy, while nurturing the public's interest in literary essays and entertaining popular fiction.

In the English tradition, it was also the century of the novel, a literary form that critics like Ian Watt and Terry Eagleton associate with burgeoning capitalism, both in terms of industrial advances in printing that made rises in production possible and in terms of plot details

4. See http://www.copernico-pv.it/Files/Didattica/Intell_potere/giornal_moder.htm (emphasis added).

and development (Watt 1987, 35–60; Eagleton 2005, 18–21). From the very beginning of the genre, novels have often involved subjects whose financial struggles and triumphs inform the narrative structure, hence the expression "from rags to riches."

Perhaps the most obvious example of a novel that relies on the theme of economy for its storyline is Daniel Defoe's *Robinson Crusoe* (1719), a text generally cited as the first true example of the novel. What delighted readers so thoroughly in this tale was its account of a middle-class *Homo economicus* who successfully applies his talents to developing a microeconomy on the island where he is shipwrecked. It would appear, in fact, that although Defoe remains true to his interests as the economist who authored *The Complete English Tradesman*, readers were unbothered by the endless balance sheets that record the history of Robinson Crusoe, a true modern fiscal hero, and simply took his nervous reckonings as an integral part of the narrative (Watt 1987, 63–68, 89–92).

As the novel form became firmly established in English culture later in the eighteenth century, it also became associated with women—in particular, female authors such as Fanny Burney and Jane Austen, who wrote novels, and female characters such as Cecilia Beverly and Elizabeth Bennet, who populated novels and met husbands at crucial narrative moments. Novels were also associated with the women who read them, and who were obliged to sell themselves on the same marriage market for which fictional heroines—with whom female readers identified deeply and emotionally—honed their cultivated tastes and applied their charming accomplishments. Moreover, although the novel's division into chapters—linked segments that could be consumed in one sitting—catered to female readers with limited leisure time, the satisfyingly symmetrical structure of plots by a "master" of the genre like Jane Austen came together with highly pleasurable resolutions that kept women reading (and wanting to read) (ibid., 44–45). In the case of Austen's work, each chapter contributed to an entire volume of juicy, gossipy narrative redeemed by intertextual and cultural references to other writers of the English canon as well as to theories of painting and landscape gardening, so that women of some culture could amuse themselves with the flattering assurance that they recognized the sources.[5]

As the novel continued to develop in the nineteenth century, popular authors like Dickens experimented with more openly market-based strategies to move their literary commodities. Ever the savvy businessman, Dickens learned to establish himself as a much sought-after brand through careful cover designs that served as tie-ins for previous novels and portraits of himself on the title page to ensure reader identification with the brand (Curtis 1995, 232–40). Dickens's aggressive marketing strategy also included exploiting the concept of serialization developed in the eighteenth century, as an inexpensive means of mass distribution for his novels, which were then sold as readily affordable segments in literary magazines like Dickens's own *All the Year Round.* Customers' impatience to purchase their next narrative installments was heightened by carefully planning episodes to coincide with seasonal changes and events, a practice that can be seen as a forerunner of the Thanksgiving and Christmas episodes in the classic TV tradition (Patten 1995, 128). Notably, such publications also included advertisements placed to whet readers' appetite for upcoming novels penned by Dickens, as well as for the ones composed by his own stable of writers, which Dickens established to produce even more commercially viable narrative entertainment. More important still, Dickens pioneered product placement in his novels for such addictive commodities as Negro Head tobacco, so that readers commonly enjoyed a nicotine high as they greedily tore through yet one more thrilling episode to be shared with family and friends, who had assuredly also read the last episode.[6]

5. Any annotated edition of a text such as *Pride and Prejudice* will yield countless examples, which include Austen's frequent references to William Gilpin's *Observations, Relative Chiefly to Picturesque Beauty, Made in the Year 1772,* when the topic of landscape gardening or attractive groupings of people at public and private occasions arises.

6. Along with the products that Dickens "placed," any number of spin-off products from his novels were marketed, including Pickwick cigars, Captain Cuttle

Yet another precursor of *Gilmore Girls* in serialized narrative fiction was the so-called sensation novel, a genre that cornered a ravenous readership in the nineteenth century. These serials in text form tended to the murder-mystery and the family drama and were intended to provoke the audience's appetite, "through tantalizing portions," in such a way as to have been spoken about by critic and author alike "in terms of the consumption of food" (Wynne 2001, 4).[7] Thackeray himself aligned serialized fiction with sumptuous foods such as "raspberry tarts," which he thought "especially suited to the 'mental palates' of women and young people" (ibid., 5). Indeed, each installment served as a heavy dose of highly emotional and enervating fiction and left a largely female readership hungering for the next episode by way of a cliffhanger, which acted as the teaser for the next installment.[8]

However, the metaphoric cluster around serialized fiction and compulsive eating also raised the possibility of its logical extension, and critics eschewed publishers' and writers' purposive nurturing of readers' constant craving for new "addictive, even poisonous" narrative installments (ibid.). This critique was heightened by the suspicion that consumption was sustained by keeping readers nervous, which was accomplished through "breathless rapidity of movement; whether the movement be absurd or not matter[ed] little, the essential thing [was] to keep moving" (G. H. Lewes quoted in ibid., 40–41). More

tobacco, umbrellas, aprons, pens, clothing, and fabric by the yard that depicted Dickensian scenes. See Steinlight 2006, 142. On the topic of domestic readership and social sharing of serialized fiction, see Wynne 2001, 12.

7. Note that in "The Fundamental Things Apply" (4.05), Rory makes this connection when she asks Trevor, a potential date, "[Do you] know what else I like to do besides talk about a really good book? Eat. Isn't that weird? And, actually, for me, they're linked. It's true. When I talk about a book, I get really hungry—starving."

8. Trollope, famous for being the most prolific writer of this kind of fiction in the nineteenth century, himself claimed to *write* compulsively under "hot pressure" that would reward him with "extreme delight." As Christina Crosby (1994) has shown, Trollope's compulsive writing cycle never left him satisfied but always with a taste for more, and this cycle, therefore, amounted to a very tenacious addiction.

important, sensation novels also represented frequent, nerve-racking accidents, reinforced with excessive emotionality, which, in turn, drove the characters in the narrative to compulsive behaviors, with the idea of inciting readers to increased consumption.[9]

As one fan of *Gilmore Girls* has written, you know you are obsessed with the show "when you feel proud when someone comments that you talk too fast, 'cause the Girls do too."[10] The signature nervousness and "shopaholic" need to consume that partially characterize *Gilmore Girls,* along with the breakneck speed of verbal delivery, connect the show to the long line of serialized fiction from which it descended and, in particular, to the sensation novel. In North America, this inheritance fueled the romance novel industry, whose best-known publishers are Harlequin and Avon, as well as the soap opera form that began with radio and eventually moved to TV. Hence, although *Gilmore Girls* is generally described as a comedy-drama (or "dramedy") series, it shares a number of traits with sensation and romance novels as well as with soap operas. For example, like the novelistic tradition from which the show descends, *Gilmore Girls* tends to focus on the processes that feed serialization by capitalizing on seduction rather than its consummation and providing multiple plotlines that help to sustain continuous episodes. Moreover, like both romances and soap operas, *Gilmore Girls* is constructed around excessive verbiage and high emotionality, focusing on long-term, sustainable pleasure rather than climax-directed satisfaction and resolution (Fiske 1987, 179–80). The show also cultivates strong viewer identification through the extensive use of close-ups and shot–reverse shot sequences in which the camera lingers over the characters' reactions. This practice leaves "a residue of

9. In the nineteenth century in the United States, this same tradition in fiction took the form of the romance, for which publishers hoped to induce a need that would guarantee "continuous buying" through "continuous feeding" of their audience. By 1971 W. Lawrence Heisey, of Canadian romance publisher Harlequin, openly sought to deliver a "carefully standardized product, which he also assumed created reader addiction" (Radway 1984, 22, 40).

10. See http://www.gilmoregirls.org/forum/index.php?topic=7781.15.

emotional intensity just prior to a scene change or commercial break," which serves to keep the viewer connected (Feuer 1984, 10–11).

"I'm Totally Addicted to This Show!": Addiction, Consumption, and TV

In the above paragraphs, I have endeavored to establish a connection between *Gilmore Girls,* the tradition of serialized fiction from which it descended, and the relationship of that tradition to consumption and the modern market. In what follows, I will bring these arguments concerning the commodification of fictional narrative since the seventeenth century together with the historical gendering of consumption and the popularization and socialization of addiction.

The heading for this section was taken from a comment posted on www.gilmoregirls.org, a Web site where items are bulleted with tiny coffee pots and fans have names like "TheHumanCoffeePot." But of course, the current fascination with and near veneration of addiction is hardly limited to *Gilmore Girls.* Addiction seems to crop up in just about all mainstream television series, and recent examples abound, such as Fanny's advice to Will of *Will & Grace* (NBC, 1998–2006) to get "something real to focus on like a dog or a plant or an addiction" ("Hocus Focus" [4.23]). Addiction, as I will argue, has become normalized in contemporary capitalist society as a logical response to the economy that drives Western culture and hails us as subjects. Significantly, the economy to which I refer has maintained a long and highly profitable relationship with addictive psychoactive substances such as caffeine, alcohol, and nicotine, so that being addicted to something now amounts to participating in the economy.[11] In the context of *Gilmore Girls,* the salient question is how we got this way, and

11. Although the history of alcohol and nicotine is fascinating, I wish to focus here on caffeine and cocoa as they are most frequently represented on *Gilmore Girls.* And although the present essay will not discuss alcohol, it would be interesting to investigate Rory's and Logan's binge drinking in relation to Emily's and Richard's genteel, yet habitual, cocktail consumption.

answering it will involve briefly returning to the historical juncture at which serialized fiction began: late in the second half of the seventeenth century.[12]

At that time, several European nations were moving toward full-scale colonial expansion, which would be underwritten by trade. A substantial quantity of colonial trade and import was in new luxury products such as silks, porcelain, carpets, and especially spices and foodstuffs that contained psychoactive stimulants like caffeine. Although the import of these substances was highly lucrative, it also had an enormous impact on national character and cultural definition. Consider tea, for example, a drink containing caffeine, which has come to define Englishness while providing a pretext for an afternoon ritual. Similarly, as coffee and cacao flooded Europe in the eighteenth century, they played a role in defining national character and cultural practices in northern European countries such as the Netherlands. In *The Protestant Ethic and the Spirit of Capitalism*, Weber argued that this wave of imported caffeine was related to the rise of capitalism in the Calvinist countries of the North because hot drinks like coffee and cocoa were sobering stimulants, making them conducive to the physically taxing work ethic that accompanied the growing capitalist market. Similarly, coffee in the United States came to play a nation-defining role, as by 1770 "tea [had become] a symbol of British taxes and tyranny," and by drinking coffee one avoided the tax (Courtwright 2002, 21). In the United States, therefore, the consumption of coffee became identified with both patriotism and sober business practice.

It was also in the eighteenth century that the word *consumer* was first used in the economic sense, purportedly in conjunction with the importation of coffee and tea into western Europe.[13] According to

12. David T. Courtwright situates this moment earlier. According to him, this development is a "signal event of world history" that "had its roots in the transoceanic commerce and empire building of the early modern period—that is the years from about 1500 to 1789" (2002, 2).

13. According to the *Oxford On-line English Dictionary*, the first recorded use occurred in 1745 in Defoe's *Complete English Tradesman*.

Elizabeth Kowaleski-Wallace, this semantic gain grew out of "the first experiences of many modern consumers [that] began with products that were quite literally addictive—coffee, tea, and tobacco" (1997, 147). She goes so far as to suggest that the concept of the specialized shop, as well as shopping as an activity, began with the quest for coffee, tea, tobacco, and sugar, which were not readily available in public markets. Restricted availability compelled consumers to scour shops outside of city centers until, with time, "luxurious commodities became a familiar habit" and "stimulated the mercantile community to set up country shops" (ibid., 77). Following the movement of psychoactive stimulants from the specialized country store to the familiarization of the modern subject with the idea of "shopping," Kowaleski-Wallace and others subscribe to the notion that shopping has always been intimately related to addiction.[14] It is allegedly owing to the twin emergence of shopping and the habitual use of psychoactives such as tea and coffee that we still understand consumption as being grounded in bodily need and compulsion.

The word *shop* became a verb in the eighteenth century, and some fourteen years after it was coined, the expression "we've been a shopping" appeared in Fanny Burney's first novel, *Evelina* (1778) (ibid., 91). In part, the verb's coinage is attributable to the emergence of the shop in the seventeenth century as an enclosed structure, detached from family dwellings and dedicated to the purpose of sale, which in turn stimulated the development of browsing and shopping as a cultural practice. Yet before the verb had formally entered the English language, procuring coveted imported goods and the consumption of luxury products had became a political issue about supporting the empire, colonial expansion, and national economic gain. In Joseph Addison's "Royal Exchange," published in the *Spectator* in 1711, the consumption of imported luxury goods made possible by colonial trade is described in terms of abundance, nobility, and patriotism:

14. Kowaleski-Wallace's argument here is based on the work of Shammas (1990) and Brewer and Porter (1993).

"Our ships are laden with the fruits of every climate; our tables are stored with spices and oils and wines; our rooms are filled with Pyramids of China and adorned with the workmanship of Japan; our morning's draught comes to us from all the remotest corners of the earth; we repair our bodies with the drugs from America and repose ourselves under Indian canopies . . . Trade, without enlarging the British territories, has given us a kind of additional empire" (Addison and Steele 1986, 2480–81). The importance of supporting this "additional empire" through the domestic consumption of "spices," a "morning draught," and "the drugs from America" is clear. The subject of this consumption is, however, intriguingly absent. Although underrepresented, the absent subject of the passage is, of course, the woman who will serve all of this imported bounty in the ritual of teatime, selecting tableware from "Pyramids of China . . . adorned with the workmanship of Japan."

Far from being mere ornaments, china teacups played a prominent role in the ideological enabling of the modern economy, while women's association with china helped to construct them as a specific type of consumer. Decorated with Oriental scenes, china vases and tableware began as exotic imports and were later domestically produced, while maintaining their economic aura as fine, rare objects to be addictively collected in sets. As such, china served multiple semiotic functions: as an object it signaled the domestication of the Orient as something that could be sampled, bought, and enjoyed. As a decorative theme in ever-popular china patterns such as Blue Willow, porcelain made exotic otherness an affordable commodity and a routine part of one's own daily diet. The foreign that was made domestic in this way, and proffered by female hands, also "testified to the status of . . . famil[ies] who participated in" England's mercantile expansion (Kowaleski-Wallace 1997, 60).

At roughly the same time, women's role began shifting to family shopper, as women were persistently positioned as domestic consumers in an emerging modern market. Yet while women were essential to the market, they were also associated with the kind of disastrous economic excesses for which the eighteenth century is well known.

Hence, although women were cast as nurturing domestic consumers who stimulated and supported foreign trade, they were also derided for their supposed compulsive need for luxury goods such as fashions that required vast quantities of expensive silks and superfluous collections of objects such as china.[15] Such associations, moreover, would form the basis of a long, ingrained tradition that continues to write women off as compulsive shoppers beset by seemingly irrational cravings for "things."

In the nineteenth century, American sociologist Thorstein Veblen wrote extensively on the role of women in consumer culture in his *Theory of the Leisure Class*. According to Veblen, along with their role as shoppers, women were also socially and economically "trained" to act as vehicles of display for their husbands' wealth. More specifically, Veblen writes, women's role in the moneyed classes is to serve as an "index of pecuniary culture" by spending enormous sums on sartorial enhancements that serve no purpose but cost a great deal of money (1925, 167). By mobilizing such domestic accoutrements as fine draperies and porcelain, and wearing lavish gowns and jewelry, women have served as the favored method of consuming conspicuously.[16] By the time Veblen was writing, then, women's roles had enlarged to accommodate ravenous consumption. Women then became identified with enormous appetite and showy superficiality, qualities essential to growing the economy and subject to scathing criticism.

This tradition has its legacy in contemporary popular fictions such as *Bridget Jones's Diary* and *Shopaholic* that portray women as addicted shoppers, and TV programs like *Gilmore Girls* that treat viewers to comic portrayals of women jonesing for another cup of coffee as they

15. As Addison writes rather sarcastically, "The single dress of a woman of quality is often the product of a hundred climates. The muff and fan come together from different ends of the earth. The scarf is sent from the torrid zone and the tippet from beneath the pole. The brocade petticoat rises out of the mines of Peru and the diamond necklace out of the bowels of Indostan" (Addision and Steele 1986, 2480).

16. According to Veblen, the suitable upper-class wife was "the chief ornament . . . perform[ing] conspicuous leisure and consumption" for her partner (1925, 180).

tear up the mall and buy too many pairs of shoes. As the beneficiaries of centuries of novels that portray women as being possessed of a voracious appetite, and decades of film and television that present women as the centerpiece of emotional and economic excess, viewers of *Gilmore Girls* know without thinking how to read addiction and excess in the show, and equally know why it is supposed to be funny.[17]

Entertainment, Ideology, and Identity

In his work on cinematic reflexivity, Robert Stam has argued that for a "passive consumer of entertainment . . . most television is as narcotic and culinary as the bourgeois theatre that Brecht denounced" (1985, 17). What is missing from narcotic, culinary visual culture, according to Stam, is the Brechtian *Verfremdungseffekt,* whose hopeful purpose was to incite audiences to think critically about what they were viewing. It is at this moment of estrangement [*Verfremdung*] that viewers are permitted to see through the fourth wall and by extension through theatrical illusion. The audience is thereby prompted to realize its own complicity in what is being represented, as well as the artificiality and theatricality of the situation. For Stam, such moments elicit the kind of "authentic reflexivity" that characterizes the "active thinking spectator" (ibid.). Stam's indictment of television as addictive, passive viewer culture has obvious implications for the analysis of a show like *Gilmore Girls* that is highly addictive, as blogs, Web sites, and, in my case, personal experience might lead one to believe.[18]

17. On the subject of "women as excess" in film and television (particularly in the genre of film noir, which is distinguished by plotlines motivated by the need to contain and punish that excess), see Doane 2000.

18. See viewer comments at http://www.gilmoregirls.org/: "I feel so loved here. It's the only place where I can feed my GG addiction and talk to cool peeps at the same time," "Well, I'm Still On & I'm Eating . . . lol. I'm Gonna To Get Into Trouble, I Just Know It But I Can't Sleep & I Can't Get Off On Here. Grr . . . lol," "I got hooked up by GG really bad, I'm like addicted," "I think this addiction of mine is becoming unhealthy! O-well . . . I'm addicted . . . I *need* this show."

In a similar vein, John Fiske argues that the middle-class ideology that informs most television programming seeks always to "recuperate contradictory signs back into [its] dominant system, and to smooth over any contradictions that might disrupt the ideological homogeneity of the narrative" (1987, 12). In other words, popular TV is able to maintain a pleasurable illusion of a homogenous (upper-) middle-class "reality" rather than startling the viewer with an uncomfortable, reflexive self-image. Yet, according to Fiske, another "essential characteristic of television is its polysemy, or multiplicity of meanings" that, he maintains, comes into play in the viewing, at which point TV becomes a text with multiple points of entry (ibid., 15). In this account, television's characteristic polysemy invites viewers to read their favorite shows in idiosyncratic ways, and the availability of many interpretant positions gives the viewer a sense of empowerment and the feeling of having asserted one's "social identity in resistance to, in independence of, or in negotiation with, the structure of domination" implicit in any TV show. If television is so popular, claims Fiske, it is because the medium offers "a variety of pleasures to such a heterogeneity of viewers," involving them in "active participation," that is, in the process of making sense and participating in their culture (ibid., 19).

Following Fiske, one could argue that *Gilmore Girls* is "all about" culture and interpretation. After all, doesn't Rory go to Yale, the alma mater of her wealthy and highly cultivated grandfather? Doesn't every DVD box set come with product tie-ins such as booklets that highlight quotable "*Gilmore*-isms" and explain recondite cultural references? Surely, it is participatory rather than passive viewing. Fiske also argues that television helps to empower popular audiences by providing culture that is outside of, and questions, the kind of class-based notion of culture that associates it with "forms, which a society considers to be 'high,' for example, classical music, fine art, literature, or ballet," that coincide with the "discriminating tastes" of those individuals with social power (ibid., 18). Interestingly, part of the polysemy of *Gilmore Girls* hinges precisely on the interplay between so-called low and high cultures.

However, high and low are by no means opposed in Stars Hollow, and virtually none of the characters is a member of the working class. All seem to live very comfortably on harebrained schemes and quirky identities in a population that is, with few exceptions (Michel and the Kims, for example), ethnically homogenous and white. By aligning much of the show's visual pleasure with the sumptuousness of the elder Gilmores' salon and the Velázquez in the Huntzbergers' entrance hall, as well as the perfectly manicured historical homes of Stars Hollow, *Gilmore Girls* consistently portrays the empowered classes in a favorable light. Yet at the same time, the show also flirts with the romance of the arguably rebel character of Lorelai, or less arguably in the character of Jess, who goes to Philadelphia to write Beat poetry and has a nonconformist uncle who bans cell phones from his diner. In other words, the show seems to embrace a dichotomous stance on culture, which is able to contain and neutralize both the high and the low. My point in analyzing various episodes from Season Four of *Gilmore Girls* is to ask what this admixture of class and cultural artifacts accomplishes. From there I hope to show what happens when late capitalism, consumption, and addiction come together with the political crisis ideology specific to the year the episodes originally aired.

"I Am Counting Down Each Minute. I Am Trying to Decide What Snack I Want"

Gilmore Girls' fourth season opens with Lorelai and Rory's return from a European vacation.[19] In keeping with their propensity to slum rebelliously, the girls have spent the summer in youth hostels. Lorelai expounds at some length on how glad she is not to have encountered youth hostels in her twenties or teens when she would "have been naive enough to think that [they] were exotic and romantic." Now

19. The quote in the subheading comes from http://www.gilmoregirls.org/forum/index.php?topic=6645.msg289299#msg289299.

safely in her thirties, Lorelai has "lived enough to know that [hostels are] gross and should be avoided at all costs." Like the rest of the show, the opening sequence depends on this kind of tension between "high" and "low" culture, between hotel and hostel. Typically, however, the verdict comes down in favor of sleeping in hotels in the future and avoiding hostels, where all "pillows smell like feet." Now, safely back at home, with Rory's departure for Yale looming, the girls decide to spend their remaining time together eating and hitting the mall.

In *Window Shopping*, Anne Friedberg has shown how the development of the shop window, facilitated by the industrial production of plate glass in the eighteenth century, gave rise to the addictive visual pleasure of the ambulatory urban shopping experience and led to "the organization of the look in the service of consumption" (1993, 3). The glass of the shop window, displaying endless scenes of consumable goods, became gender coded as the viewing apparatus for a particular kind of urban tourism. The mobile urban gaze, exercised in shopping streets, department stores, and arcades, would later evolve into "a primary component of contemporary cinematic and televisual spectatorship" so that, according to Friedberg, "from the middle of the nineteenth century . . . the shop window was displaced and incorporated by the cinema screen" (ibid., 7, 66). Early cinema treated viewers to the visual pleasure of "the travelling experience as a commodity," creating a sort of readily available, sedentary tourism, with the effect that this kind of cinematic spectatorship led to "a further instrumentalization of [the] consumer gaze" (ibid., 66, 59).

Similarly, Lorelai and Rory's trip to Europe provides viewers with this kind of commodity-experience, described in terms of shopping and eating, hence Sookie's litany of questions on their arrival: "I wanna hear about everything you did and everything you *ate*. . . . How was Barcelona? Did you see the Gaudi apartments? Ooh, did you see a bullfight? Did you see Anne Frank's house? Did you cry? Was Steven Spielberg there, huh? . . . Are you *hungry*? Do you want *anything* to eat? *I've got quiche*" (emphasis added). The implication here is obviously that Europe is a packaged deal filled with visual highlights and consumables, the story of which is best recounted over quiche.

What is more, by asking if Spielberg was at Anne Frank's house, Sookie implies that Europe is always already experienced vicariously and cinematically, mediated through the culture of blockbuster film and familiar narratives.

This episode also sets a precedent for the politics of Season Four, which aired from September 2003 to May 2004, commencing some six months after the first U.S. strikes on Baghdad. The season opened about six months after Representatives Robert W. Ney (R-WV) and Walter B. Jones Jr. (R-NC) declared that all references to french fries and french toast on the menus of restaurants and snack bars run by the House of Representatives would be removed. This decision was in response to France's criticism of the Iraq war and its refusal to support the United States, which disqualified France as a friend of America and established a trend in euphemistic food names such as "freedom fries" and "freedom toast."

Appropriately, then, one of the establishing hooks of "Ballrooms and Biscotti" (4.01) concerns a number of worried phone calls made by Babette to European consulates looking for Rory and Lorelai. In a subsequent scene, the camera finds Lorelai on the phone with the Belgian consulate, coquettishly explaining that they "just loved [the] fries." On hanging up, she reports that "Belgium's done, Lisbon's calling me back, Berlin had no idea what I was talking about, and Paris is pissed." When Rory asks with whom, Lorelai quickly replies, "Ugh, who knows?" thus framing France as stereotypically irrational and irascible. This thread will be picked up in the following episode ("The Lorelais' First Day at Yale" [4.02]), when Lorelai and Rory reinvent themselves as "those dirty, filthy, almost-French Stars Hollow girls" who "cast sidelong glances that are vague but slightly threatening," thereby listing a string of stereotypical images of the French that circulate in the United States, harking back to the time of World War I.[20]

20. Similarly, in "Chicken or Beef?" (4.04), Michel complains that he has to stand next to someone with "unforgivable B.O.," to which Lorelai quips, "Michel, you're French. How can you even tell?"

The relationship between international travel and threats to home security is skillfully picked up later in a conversation that, on the surface, appears to address Jackson's unwillingness to be informed as to the sex of his unborn child. The writers weave an intertextual thread through Ricky Ricardo to Dick Van Dyke, and back to 1954, at which point Rory quips, "So, you hear about that whole Sputnik thing?" to which Jackson replies, "Oh, Eisenhower's on top of it." In other words, in one rapid dialogue passage, which relates the show to its televisual tradition, we are reminded of the cold war—another time at which the United States believed itself under the threat of foreign attack.

Likewise, later in the episode when Rory wants Lorelai to spring her from a long night at her grandmother's, she explains, "This is Iran in '79, and you are Jimmy Carter. What do we do?" Moreover, when Rory arrives at Yale the paranoia of foreign attack is reaffirmed by her campus guide who tells all incoming freshmen that "it's a post-9/11 world, so your IDs are important. You'll be asked for it a lot, so always have it, always, always." As the day winds down and Lorelai prepares to leave Rory alone in her residence room, the latter laments her childlike anxieties, saying, "I can vote; I can fight for my country. I mean, I'm an adult." She goes on to project a scenario in which "it [will] to be very hard to be Christiane Amanpour broadcasting live from a foxhole in Tehran with my mommy." Although most of these comments invite the viewer to share the fear of foreign invasion and terrorist attack, this last comment constructs the war as a televisual event and viewers as safe, sedentary TV tourists to the war.

The United States is also, however, seen as a world imperial power, a notion expressed, not surprisingly, through the language of food and consumption in *Gilmore Girls.* In an attempt to help both herself and Rory to adjust to the major milestone of her leaving home for Yale, Lorelai decides to throw a residence party, which requires enormous quantities of various ethnic take-out foods. As she enters she asks:

LORELAI: I've got Balinese. Where does Bali go?

PARIS: Were still putting everything in geographic order. East to west.

LORELAI: That's the system. Where is Bali?

RORY: Indonesia.

PARIS: Is Indonesia east or west of the Philippines?

TANNA: East.

RORY: No, west.

LORELAI: Near Singapore? We've got Singapore here somewhere.

TANNA: Find Sri Lanka, it's a bit over from that.

LORELAI: But there's no Sri Lankan food.

RORY: Just put it by Vietnam.

PARIS: Is Vietnam east or west of the Philippines?

LORELAI: Ooh, boy, you guys really need to go to college.

RORY: We ordered too much food.

RORY: Where's the phone?

PARIS: Uh, under Mexico.

LORELAI: I bet it's the pizza. Come help.

TANNA: Germany fell on China.

LORELAI: Well, that's Germany for ya.

Although this dialogue is glib and obviously meant to be humorous, it constructs the United States as a place where hysterical food consumption can and does go on, and, in fact, the party is interrupted by the delivery of nine jumbo pizzas. At the same time, this dialogue is very much in the tradition of the Addison essay that I referred to earlier, in which he praises the wealth of an empire that calls "the vineyards of France [its] gardens; the Spice-Islands [its] hot-beds; the Persians [its] silk-weavers; and the Chinese [its] potters" (Addison and Steele 1986, 2480). The use of food as a synecdoche for countries and their politics ("that's Germany for ya") renders the sort of imperial expansion of which the United States is frequently accused both anodyne and comedic.

In a similar gesture, Kyle returns from Iraq in "We Got Us a Pippi Virgin" (5.05) sporting a prosthetic arm that rockets him to instant popularity with the young women of Stars Hollow. In fact, on seeing him for the first time since his hand has been replaced with a prosthetic claw, Rory tells him, "You look good. How you been doing?" As he explains, the "navy's been fantastic. Bitchin' rehab. . . . I can drive, type sixty words a minute. . . . This thing is a real chick magnet. . . . It's the Captain Hook thing. . . . Everybody loves the Bionic Man." Not only do these lines erase the horrors of the war, reference 1970s TV, and make it sound sexy and fun to lose a limb, but the notion that the navy offers "bitchin' rehab" would have helped to allay what were then growing suspicions that the U.S. government was not adequately treating veterans of the war on Iraq. But perhaps this kind of patriotism—losing one's arm for the empire and enjoying it—is to be expected only in Stars Hollow, a town where "George Washington ate, slept, or blew his nose all over the damn place" ("Chicken or Beef?").

Ravenous consumerism is also sometimes interpreted as a form of patriotism, particularly in 2003 when consumerism had slowed down but was essential to the progress of the hugely expensive war in Iraq.[21] Although there is a remarkable amount of shopping and consuming in the entire series, "The Lorelais' First Day at Yale" is notable for opening with Rory complaining that she has "too much stuff," which she blames on Lorelai, saying, "It's your fault. You inculcated into me a tolerance for rampant consumerism." And consume they do, but not before they pursue a charming dialogue about how they have no tote bags, although "every woman who's ever purchased seventy-five dollars' worth of Clinique products has some tote bags." This dialogue ends with Lorelai suggesting that because they do not have the proper shopping accoutrements, they will be identified as "the quirky backpack ladies." Although this remark positions the girls as being outside the standard consumer ethic, the rest of the episode follows a pattern of purchases and features a rather spectacular scene in which Sookie, ever the domestic goddess, shows Lorelai a shed that is full to overflowing with gender-coded blue merchandise that she has purchased for the baby she is expecting.[22]

21. For more on this topic, see Spigel 2004, 238.

22. This plotline will be pursued through "Will You Be My Lorelai Gilmore?" (7.16), in which Sookie buys an enormous pile of baby gifts for Lane since her own pregnancy has created a need for new goods.

Interestingly enough, when politics does come up, the threat posed to snappy dialogue is quickly diffused. In "Chicken or Beef?" when Rory's classmate Heather reads Hemingway's *Sun Also Rises* as an indictment of "a society which exploited its underclass to fight in the trenches of the First World War," Rory is quick to read the text outside of politics, countering that it is really about a "generation's loss of faith in love." Trevor, another classmate with a romantic interest in Rory, joins in, arguing that "the book's about a guy who can't sleep with the woman he loves," and as they leave the room, Rory and Trevor concur that Heather's problem is wanting the "workers of the world [to] unite" and that they have never met anyone "who likes the word *bourgeois* so much." Clearly, the romantic reading wins out over the political.

Later in the same episode the camera pans across a party scene as one character asks another if she wants "the guy that pumps your gas voting," to which she replies, "That is what America is about," thereby espousing the kind of easygoing liberalism with which the show is commonly identified. Yet it is not without political bias, hence a conversation in the same episode in which Lorelai refers to taking too many aspirins as "a major Marilyn moment" from which she has awoken with an urge to "sleep with a Kennedy," thus subscribing to the popular conspiracy theory that Marilyn Monroe was murdered for her affair with JFK. When Rory counters that she has heard that "Kerry's available," a link is effectively, if elliptically, forged between a former liberal president who kept the United States out of war to Kerry, whose criticism of the Iraq war earned him the title of "the French Kerry" on the FOX Network.

Although many viewers' impressions of *Gilmore Girls* would come close to Fiske's concept of televisual polysemy, whereby audience members are offered multiple points of entry and identification, the preceding examples suggest that this theory may not be entirely the case. For example, although Lorelai and Rory are critical of the upper class, they are also part of it and benefit fully, if reluctantly, in times of crisis and need. Hence, when the Huntzbergers decide that Rory is not a suitable match for their son Logan, she indignantly exclaims, "But I'm a

Gilmore," and Emily springs to her defense at the World War II–themed Daughters of the American Revolution benefit that Rory has organized ("We've Got Magic to Do" [6.05]). In other words, if the girls are critical about the upper classes, they manage to put their criticism aside long enough for Rory to graduate from Chilton and earn a degree from one of the world's most expensive universities, while money and influence guarantee her a future, possibly with someone even wealthier.

By supplying a subject position that claims to be critical while being comfortably complicit, *Gilmore Girls* effectively forwards a critique of class and then invites viewers to identify with upper-class characters and enjoy the spectacle of wealth and power. At the same time, the frenetic pace of the show, which is both pleasurable and nervous making, contributes to the creation of a text that can carry a great deal of political commentary passed off so rapidly that viewers have little or no time to apprehend or criticize it. Thus, when Lorelai tells a little girl at a birthday party—designed as product placement for the *Lord of the Rings* franchise—that she can do dangerous things like having a "Brazilian bikini wax" and that when girls go on adventures "they go in heels," it passes more or less unnoticed among the excess verbiage of the episode ("The Hobbit, the Sofa, and Digger Stiles" [4.03]). So although the show appears to engage serious political and social issues, it goes to great lengths to reinforce class structure, to support the American war effort, and to propagate conservative American ideology. Viewers are constantly, if subliminally, reminded that—for the most part—only well-off, self-satisfied white people can live in Stars Hollow, unless they speak with an adorable accent or aspire to the upper classes.

◆

As one blogger has written, "Fans like myself complain that the show is totally inane but they can't get enough. . . . [A]side from that, i'm totally addicted to this show!!!"[23] This is a very apt description of my

23. See http://www.gilmoregirls.org/forum/index.php?topic=864.msg152964#msg152964.

own relationship to *Gilmore Girls,* and herein, I believe, lays the danger. My purpose in studying the show as one of many forms of contemporary serialized addiction was to shed light on the cultural and historical developments that have given us this form of entertainment. I also wanted to investigate what consuming this kind of narrative fiction means in terms of subjecthood and why, for example, viewers might become addicted to droll patter punctuated by cultural references. In other words, I wanted to examine what it is about *Gilmore Girls* that keeps me—and millions like me—coming back.

In so doing, I hope to have shown how *Gilmore Girls* and its potential to addict is related to a number of social practices that began in the eighteenth century alongside the production of the novel and the consumption of psychoactive drugs like caffeine, chocolate, and tobacco. The show also belongs to the history of sensation culture and the marketing of leisure, including the sensation novel, the romance novel, and the soap opera. And although no one smokes on *Gilmore Girls,* products are placed and caffeine is consumed in astounding quantities along with junk food and cute clothes, all of which inform a social context that favors, and depends on, compulsive, addicted predominately female consumers.

Along the way, however, I also argued that *Gilmore Girls* presents itself as a postmodern, hybrid, polysemic comedy-drama that allows for a plethora of subject positions and interpretations. My conclusion, however, is that the show complicitly participates in privileging the upper classes and American expansionist politics, despite antiauthoritarian statements and occasionally bracing comments about the ruling elite (as in "I Solemnly Swear" [3.11], when Lorelai states, "That Francie [the leader of the Puffs at Chilton High] is so evil, she'll probably be president"). Hence, although Lorelai might make smug comments about women who spend seventy-five dollars on Clinique products, her comment effectively does the work of product placement. And in the same episode much is made of a segment in which she buys forty dollars' worth of alternative moisturizers from Kirk. The message here is clear: consume alternative, no-brand products if you must, but do not stop consuming.

Thus, although I am frequently offended by the politics touted on the show as well as its complicity with class structure, I greedily watch and rewatch every episode while reaching for a Snickers bar in much the same way as I consume Victorian fiction. And as is the case with Jane Austen's novels, if it is the gossip, great clothes, and female-focalized melodrama that got me hooked in the first place, it is perhaps the show's inheritance of intertextual pop cultural references and the hermeneutic cat-and-mouse game of pinning them down, as well as the show's relationship to canonical narrative strategies, that keep me coming back.

15

Java Junkies Versus Balcony Buddies

Gilmore Girls, *"Shipping," and Contemporary Sexuality*

A. ROCHELLE MABRY

When Lorelai Gilmore broke her engagement to fiancé Luke Danes and ended up sleeping with and later marrying old flame (and father of her daughter) Christopher Hayden toward the end of *Gilmore Girls'* seven-season broadcast history, fan reaction was explosive and immediate. In online communities such as TelevisionWithoutPity.com, those who had spent six seasons waiting for Luke and Lorelai to make it to the altar expressed outrage, disgust, and grief as the relationship appeared to implode, with hopes for the couple's indefinitely deferred happy ending being challenged, if not dashed altogether. The passionate fan responses to the Lorelai-Luke and Lorelai-Christopher relationships raise a number of questions about "shipping," a term used to denote a fan's investment in the romantic relationships among characters in pop culture texts. How do fans interact with and read the romances found in popular texts? More important, in what ways do the desires and anxieties expressed by shippers about their favorite couples reflect concerns about gender, sexuality, and romance in the larger contemporary culture? These and other interrelated questions will be explored in the following pages.

A comparison of the fan responses to the Lorelai-Luke romance (whose fans are known as "Java Junkies") as well as the Lorelai-Christopher relationship (whose fans are often dubbed "Balcony Buddies") as expressed in the Internet forums TelevisionWithoutPity.com (or TWoP) and the fan fiction sites Black & White & Red (www.gilmore-fiction.net) and FanFiction.net is instructive, as they each put forth distinct fantasies that are particularly potent in the contemporary moment. The Luke-Lorelai pairing offers the vision of an independent woman being loved by the equally independent man who "gets" her (that is, he understands where her familial and professional priorities lie while keeping pace with her breakneck babble). This match is particularly complex, insofar as it casts light on aspects of masculinity and femininity that could be read both conservatively and progressively. The Lorelai-Christopher relationship, on the other hand, offers the potential for the nuclear family to be reunited—a fantasy that would no doubt be compelling in an era of rising divorce rates and increasing single-parent households. However, this pairing too is complicated by a less obvious discourse on the connections between class and romance. As they interact with these fantasies in online discussions and fan fiction, as they respond to a televisual text with an equal measure of adoration and frustration, "shippers" create their own texts that reveal how effectively *Gilmore Girls* addresses viewers' desires and anxieties about contemporary sexuality and relationships.

A "Town Meeting" for the New Millennium: Participatory Fandom and the Internet

The ways in which fans interact with their favorite pop culture texts and the degree of "control" these devoted consumers have over their meanings have been concerns of critical reception studies for nearly two decades. Critics like Henry Jenkins and Nancy K. Baym have argued for a model of participatory fandom in which fans actively use a given television show as a springboard for their own creative efforts and furthermore engage in debates over that show's meanings (although, as Jenkins has shown with the fandom surrounding *Beauty and the Beast* [CBS, 1987–90], the potential for true control over meanings or resistance to an underlying ideology is limited at best) (Jenkins 1992, 129–30; Baym 2000, 31–32). With the advent of the Internet, opportunities for fans' interaction with and sense of ownership over pop culture texts have increased exponentially. Although there is some debate over the power of these more visible and numerous online fan communities (see Simone Murray's slightly pessimistic take on Internet *Lord of the Rings* fandom [2004]), critics like Denise D. Bielby, Lee Harrington, and William T. Bielby (1999) have argued persuasively that Internet fan communities provide valuable spaces for textual analysis and criticism.

One area of fandom that reveals the complex interactions of viewers with their favorite shows is that of "shipping," or the practice of maintaining a deep and prolonged intellectual or emotional investment (or both) in a romance between characters in a work of fiction. Although the practice predates its name, the growth of Internet fan communities over the past decade has allowed for an increase not only in the number of spaces where fans can discuss their favorite "ships" but also in the intensity of their responses to them. Online fan sites such as TelevisionWithoutPity.com feature dozens of threads in which shippers can talk about, analyze, and speculate about the romantic couples on their favorite shows. The TWoP *Gilmore Girls* forums, for example, contain separate threads for the Lorelai and Luke, Lorelai and Christopher, Rory and Logan, and Rory and Jess couplings. Shipper threads are spaces where fans can celebrate (or "squee" over) their favorite fictional couples, commiserate during tough times (when romances hit the rocks), or speculate about forthcoming developments in the characters' stories. Through their discussion and analysis, fans often engage with and sometimes contest the show's dominant ideology, particularly regarding issues of gender and sexuality, with varying degrees of success. As we will see in the case of *Gilmore Girls* fandom, these responses reflect more than just the fans' wishes or frustrations about their favorite couples' storylines. Read symptomatically, they also reveal the ways viewers use television romances to work through their own ideas about contemporary male-female relationships.

Reader engagement with romances has long been understood as a complex interaction that provides moments of both resistance and constraint. Both Janice Radway and Tania Modleski have argued that romance reading offers women a way to question the assumptions that underlie our traditional ideas about romance, marriage, and women's place in society (Radway 1984, 214–15)—even if, as Modleski argues, the novels often end up reaffirming these traditional ideas (Modleski 1998, 113). In the same light, Christine Scodari examines the conflicting messages embedded within prime-time romantic comedies of the 1980s and 1990s, like *Cheers* (NBC, 1982–93) and *Northern Exposure* (CBS, 1990–96), which are supposedly modeled after the more "egalitarian" screwball romantic comedies of the 1930s and 1940s. Although these shows may nod toward the older model of the spirited romance among equals, Scodari argues that they often fall prey to masculine assumptions about what makes a good TV romance (such as the chase being more interesting than the catch, or violence being an entertaining component of romance), and therefore end up undercutting any attempts to present a more progressive image of relationships (1995, 23). The question of whether—and how effectively—readers or viewers can resist the ideologies of pop culture texts has been debated for decades, with compelling arguments on both sides of the political spectrum. Perhaps at this point a more interesting and more illuminating question is not how fandom acts as a site of resistance or submission but how, through their interactions with television shows, books, or movies, fans are actually responding to issues circulating in the larger culture.

Neither the various productions that collectively constitute popular culture nor the fan responses to those texts are produced in a vacuum, and many critics stress the importance of taking cultural and historical contexts into account when examining particular fandoms. One genre that is particularly responsive to changes in the culture is the romance. Because they deal with fundamental issues of gender and sexuality, while focusing on relationships between the sexes, popular romances have an especially symbiotic connection to the larger culture. Frank Krutnik argues that the romance genre is a site where accepted ideas about (heterosexual) romance and marriage are expressed and reinforced, but over time the ideas put forth in these texts must adjust to "the shifting cultural environment" (1990, 62). Romance texts—whether in the form of novels or as the many subplots driving televisual narrative—must be responsive to larger cultural changes in order to maintain widespread appeal and credibility as their audiences change. In navigating these changes, producers of romance texts often attempt to address the anxieties and desires that contemporary audiences may be feeling about sexualized relationships. Reading romances within their larger context can provide insights into the often conflicting discourses on sexual relationships that may characterize a given era, but such hermeneutic pursuits provide at best theoretical or hypothetical scenarios of viewer response. Examining actual fan responses to these texts, however, can shed light on how consumers of these texts respond to the romances the texts portray—and perhaps to the ideology that underlies them.

The very idea of fan response, of course, brings us to a critical intersection, a long-standing debate between the advocates of textual analysis and those scholars who pursue empirical audience research. One way to bridge this division is to look at the forum postings and fan fiction produced by *Gilmore Girls* fans in response to the show's romances as a set of texts to be read and analyzed within the larger framework of contemporary ideas about heterosexual relationships. This approach seems particularly well suited to examining Internet fan activity. It allows for the analysis of particular responses rather than decontextualized, ahistorical analysis, but it also avoids some issues associated with ethnographic studies such as the power dynamics between researcher and subject and the accuracy of responses by fans in prewritten surveys or research-directed interviews. Posts on Internet forums are made in response to the show, not to questions asked by a researcher; as such, they are arguably more spontaneous and less compromised than responses to surveys or interview questions. It is true that such responses may be shaped by the centrifugal force of the overall tone or position of a particular community (as people with similar interests and attitudes are more likely to engage in conversations with each other)—or, in the case of TWoP, by rules enforced by forum moderators. It is also true that Internet fan communities most likely represent a small hyperinvolved segment of a show's audience (posters on *Gilmore Girls* forums at both TWoP and FanForum had adopted the moniker "CIP," an abbreviated reference to the name given by *Gilmore* star Lauren Graham to the show's overinvolved online fans: "crazy Internet people." Still, these postings approximate an unmediated, spontaneous response to a show's issues—in this case, responses to *Gilmore Girls*' discourses on romance and sexual politics. As such, they provide insights into how viewers respond to these discourses and how those responses grow out of cultural anxieties and personal desires about modern relationships.

Love, Coffee, and Chuppahs: Luke, Lorelai, and Contemporary Sexuality

One relationship that has generated a large volume of online responses among *Gilmore Girls* fans is that between Lorelai and Luke. Although the relationship between Lorelai and her daughter, Rory, effectively functions as the show's narrative armature, and is acknowledged by most fans to be the most important part of the show, the Luke-Lorelai romance far outstrips any other element of the show in terms of the sheer number of fan postings on most online forums. As of March 2008 the "Lorelai and Luke" thread at TWoP has more than 1,590 pages with more than 23,800 posts, compared to the 117 pages and just over 1,700 responses in the "Lorelai and Christopher," "Lorelai and Rory," and "Lorelai and Emily" threads combined. Fans cover a wide range of topics in these forums, from analyzing "anvils" (a term used to denote heavy-handed hints about future plotlines) related to Luke and Lorelai's romance to reliving their favorite Luke-Lorelai moments from earlier seasons (which was particularly comforting throughout the dark days of the summer of 2006, when the sixth season left Luke-Lorelai shippers with the image of the female protagonist in Christopher's bed and with little hope that she and the scruffy diner owner would get back together). Yet, as they speculate on what it means that Luke's flannel shirt coordinates with Lorelai's dress in a particular scene, or share their favorite pre–"Raincoats and Recipes" (the episode in which Luke and Lorelai first kiss [4.22]) moments, Java Junkies also reveal, sometimes unwittingly, the ways that they *use* the romance as a way to deal with the ins and outs of modern sexual relationships. On occasion, their responses to the more traditional aspects of the Luke-Lorelai romance seem to evoke a longing for a time when ideas about gender and sexuality were more clear-cut.

In many ways, the Luke-Lorelai romance operates quite conventionally, even in its uses of generic elements. Beginning with the first two episodes, Luke and Lorelai are established as the show's "will-they-or-won't-they?" couple, in the tradition of the prime-time romances featured in shows like *Cheers, Moonlighting* (ABC, 1985–89), and *Northern Exposure.* The attraction between the two is first foregrounded in the first two episodes of Season One, both of which feature scenes with close-up shots of Luke and Lorelai exchanging meaningful (and perhaps longing) glances. Viewers familiar with the "will-they-or-won't-they" conventions of television romance at once understand that Luke and Lorelai are going to be the show's central couple, but also know that they will have to wait a while for them to get together (in the case of *Gilmore Girls,* viewers had to wait four seasons). Indeed, the progression of the Luke and Lorelai story follows the conventions of television romance throughout its development, including the use of "near-miss" moments, such as the "almost kiss" in the first season's "That Damn Donna Reed" (1.14), and Lorelai being interrupted just as she appears ready to confess her feelings for Luke in the Season Four episode "In the Clamor and the Clangor" (4.11). The series also includes the expected romantic roadblocks and tangents in the form of reappearing exes and relationships with other characters, including the return of Luke's old flame Rachel in the first season and Lorelai's engagement to Max Medina, Rory's teacher, in the second season. An even bigger stumbling block is the recurring presence of Christopher, Lorelai's first love and Rory's father, who is established as a complicating factor from his first appearance in Season One and will continue to act as such throughout the run of the show—much to the dismay of many Java Junkies. In its adherence to these conventions, the Luke-Lorelai romance is practically a case study in how to both establish a prime-time couple and maintain the dramatic tension involved in getting them together.

At least two moments in the early seasons—before their romance takes flight—clearly signal that Luke and Lorelai are not only meant to be but headed for marriage and children. In "Red Light on the Wedding Night" (2.03), Luke brings Lorelai a chuppah he has made for her upcoming marriage to Max. The two have a subtext-laden conversation about what it means to be married and share a meaningful look when talking about marrying the right person. Significantly, this emphasis on the "right person" is a motivic focus of classic screwball comedies, which typically invert traditional gender dynamics (by showing women chasing men) yet fall back on romantic notions of what an ideal romantic partner is. What *Gilmore Girls* and other long-running TV series or serial narratives are well suited for, though, is the complicating of that ideal of a "true pairing," a process that has the potential to update or "modernize" the more conservative characteristics of 1930s and 1940s romantic comedies.

The above-mentioned scene in "Red Light on the Wedding Night" ends with a lengthy shot of Luke and Lorelai standing side by side with their backs to the camera and silently, under the chuppah, looking very much like a casually dressed bride and groom. It is this image that many fans claim as evidence of Luke and Lorelai's matrimonial destiny. Similarly, the third season opens with what a number of viewers have taken as foreshadowing that Luke and Lorelai will not only be married but also have children. In the teaser to the season's first episode, "Those Lazy-Hazy-Crazy Days," Lorelai dreams that she is happily married to Luke and pregnant with twins. In the dream, we see the two behaving as a typical TV married couple, bantering over her coffee intake and possible names for their unborn twins, discussing what they need from the drugstore, and kissing each other goodbye as they leave to start their days. Although both of these scenes are open to multiple interpretations, they do appear to confirm that the show's creators intended for Luke and Lorelai to end up married and possibly expecting children—and they have certainly been interpreted by many of the show's fans as evidence that the two are heading for (or were supposed to be heading for) such a future.

Many viewers have embraced these textual cues as evidence that Luke and Lorelai are meant to be headed for a traditional happy ending, and Internet forums and fan fiction have become spaces for them to analyze anvils that foreshadow this happy ending, speculate about how Luke and Lorelai will achieve it, and fantasize about what their future might look like. "I think the show created a self-fulfilling prophecy by having that brief shot of [Luke and Lorelai] under the chuppah in RLOAWN," asserts one fan. "It's things like that (and Lorelai's happily-ever-after-dream) that makes [*sic*] me more certain that TPTB [the powers that be] will get them together" ("Lorelai and Luke," January 29, 2004). Fantasies of Luke and Lorelai's "happily ever after" are explored in depth through multichapter fan fiction stories that envision the couple's courtship and married life. The two-part, nearly ninety-chapter "It's Right There" and "It's Still There," for example, is a "classic" fanfic written before Luke and Lorelai got together on the show, one that follows them from the beginning of their romance through their wedding (under the chuppah) through their first months with their first child (not twins in this case, but a boy named Joshua). The strength of fan expectations that Lorelai and Luke would be married by the end of the series is even more pronounced in posts made after the announcement that the seventh season would be the show's last. As only two episodes remained in the season at the time of the announcement and Luke and Lorelai had not yet reconciled romantically, it became clear that the long-expected Luke-Lorelai wedding would not manifest. Fan responses reflect their disappointment and outrage at having their hopes of seeing Luke and Lorelai's "middle" (a term Lorelai uses in Season Five to describe a lifelong committed relationship as opposed to only getting a happy ending) dashed:

> This just . . . sucks! I'm so SMAD right now. Sad because we'll never see their middle and mad at ASP [show creator Amy Sherman-Palladino] and DR [seventh-season executive producer David Rosenthal] for spending so much time on the destruction of the Ls and the EiF

> ["Exercise in Futility," the fan moniker for Lorelai's relationship with Christopher in the seventh season]. (ibid., May 3, 2007)

> I can't believe I won't see the chuppah getting used. I can't believe . . . any of this. 2 more episodes??? (ibid.)

> So, now that the show is winding down towards its last 2 episodes, are LL fans realistically supposed to be happy that our 'ship will someday get married and have kids, yet we won't get to witness it? . . . And I agree with everyone who's argued about all the anvils, symbolism, and not-so-subtle hints about a marriage for Luke and Lorelai. I really do feel cheated/used/sucker-punched, etc. (ibid., May 4, 2007)

Although there is some variance among forum posters on whether they want to see a full-blown season (or series) finale capped by a wedding or pregnancy storyline (or both), many fans seemed to want—and expect—to see Luke and Lorelai married and settled by the show's end.

Clearly, whatever the intentions of the show runners, a number of fans believe that the only satisfactory way to end the Luke-Lorelai romance is with a wedding under a chuppah and the arrival of flannel-clad twins a year later. It may seem that, in expressing their desires to see Luke and Lorelai married and playing with their babies, and in using forum postings and fan fiction to play out various scenarios of the couple's happily married future, at least some viewers are merely buying into the more conservative message of nearly all popular romances: a love story only ends "happily ever after" if the hero and heroine are united in matrimony. A strong argument can be made for this view, and a number of posters mention having bought into what they saw as the idealized (at least until the end of Season Six) romance between Luke and Lorelai. Yet, when framed in a different light, the need to see Luke and Lorelai married and raising a family on-screen can also be interpreted as a way to deal with the changes and uncertainties that followed the women's liberation movement and the sexual revolution of the 1960s, which continue to inform modern relationships.

In the decades following these paradigm shifts in the popular understanding of gender roles, long-held ideas about marriage, family, and sexual relationships were constantly being interrogated and transformed, leaving many participants and onlookers unsure about how men and women were supposed to relate to one another or what place women were to take in their sexual relationships and within society. Ruth Rosen writes that by the 1970s marriage had been "battered by growing divorce rates, the values of the counterculture, and new ideas about sexual freedom" (2000, 314). Nancy F. Cott reports that "the divorce rate rose . . . furiously" from the 1970s to the 1990s, and that the number of unmarried couples living together increased tenfold between 1960 and 1998 (2000, 203). It was not only marriage, however, that was affected by the cultural shifts of the last decades of the twentieth century. Rosen points out that, in the wake of the sexual revolution and the women's rights movement, "men were confused and no longer knew how to behave around women. Women were confused as well" (2000, 187). More important, she argues that the generation of women that followed was left confused about its place in Western culture and whether the goals of the women's movement were even desirable, let alone feasible (ibid., 275).

Popular television shows often act as immersive spaces in which audiences can work through issues circulating in the larger culture, and in *Gilmore Girls* fans' responses to the Luke-Lorelai romance we can see an attempt (though not always an overt one) to come to terms with contradictions and confusions of contemporary sexual relationships. For some, Lorelai's relationship with Luke offers a scenario in which women can experience at least some of the gains of feminism and the sexual revolution without threatening the status quo. In the Luke-Lorelai romance (and through their possible marriage), some fans see an independent woman who has raised her daughter on her own and started a successful business but who eventually subordinates that independence to finding "true" (heterosexual, monogamous) love and taking her rightful place as a wife and mother. "The only woman who has expressed repeatedly that 'married with children' is her ultimate dream is Lorelai, and I can live with that, because she has shown us time and time again how great she can do on her own," argues one poster at TWoP, adding, "She achieved everything that you can achieve on your own. I can understand that after all that, she has the desire for something else" ("One Is the Loneliest Number," May 17, 2006). Another fan sees Lorelai as one of a number of women who are "ambitious and driven and all that, but . . . as soon as family becomes a viable choice, they happily back away from ambition and buy minivans" ("Lorelai and Luke," May 18, 2005). This reading resonates with certain (postfeminist) discourses that encourage women to rethink their place in the post–women's movement culture and renew their focus on marriage and motherhood. Further, it offers a comforting vision of contemporary romance between men and women. In this scenario, the gains of Second Wave feminism and the sexual revolution allow for pleasant diversions for women making their way to assuming real grown-up roles in patriarchal society. Women's economic and personal freedoms are not threatening, and new ideas about sexual relationships are not troubling, because women ultimately leave them aside to take their culturally accepted place next to men as wives and mothers. In the end, everything returns to the status quo, and anxieties over shifting definitions of sex, romance, and marriage are avoided because such categories have remained intact.

The fantasies that some Luke-Lorelai fans concoct may seem to reaffirm traditional ideas about marriage and gender, but other postings show that the Luke-Lorelai romance also offers a model based on balance and equality that is more in line with contemporary ideas about gender and sexuality. One aspect of Lorelai's relationship with Luke that a number of fans apparently appreciate is the way the two have always supported each other and the fact that their opposing qualities complement each other. "He allows her to take a breath because he'll pick up the slack and she'll do the same thing," writes one poster. "She makes his life interesting and bright, he grounds her and lets her put her guard down" (ibid., July 21, 2006). For some fans, the balance and complementary qualities Lorelai and Luke bring to their relationship make their romance a story of "two independent people . . . meshing their lives together" (ibid., May 18, 2005). "What I like about [Luke and Lorelai] as a couple is that they really have remained true to themselves, all the while making some adjustments so that they can be together," observes one fan of Luke and Lorelai's relationship in Season Five. "These adjustments haven't been things that are out of character for them, it's more about making accommodations in the independent lives they have built" (ibid., March 7, 2005).

It is particularly important for some fans that Lorelai's relationship with Luke allows her to maintain a degree of autonomy. "Lorelai is one of the most independent people on the face of the earth," writes one fan, adding that "Luke knows this. He completely understands her" (ibid., May 18, 2005). Rather than having to give up her hard-won autonomy to achieve romantic fulfillment, Lorelai gets to maintain her independence and be loved by a ruggedly good-looking man who not only gets her need for independence but supports it. This reading of the Luke-Lorelai romance, particularly with its emphasis on (female) independence, allows viewers to envision a model of romance that does not need to dismiss the changes in relationships between the sexes or in women's position in our culture that have taken place over the past forty years. In performing this reading, some Java Junkies offer a model of contemporary relationships in which neither love nor the woman's autonomy has to be sacrificed—a model that is no doubt appealing to viewers who do not expect to forgo their own goals or accomplishments in order to find love.

Making Dan Quayle Proud: Lorelai, Christopher, and the (Reconstructed) Nuclear Family

Just as the Luke-Lorelai romance allows viewers the opportunity to work through issues related to traditional gender roles, the Lorelai-Christopher pairing (finally realized in Season Seven) offers a means of negotiating anxieties plaguing contemporary society: the perceived decline in the nuclear family and the growth in the number of children living in single-parent homes. An article published nearly ten years ago in the *Journal of Marriage and the Family* states that, between births to unmarried mothers and changes in parental living arrangements, "nearly 50% of White children and two-thirds of African American children are likely to spend at least part of their childhood in a single-parent family" (Teachman 2000, 1239). Concerns over the problems of children living in single-parent homes, from a lack of emotional stability to economic hardship, have become an accepted part of our popular consciousness, raising anxieties among many. As succeeding generations experience the reality of living in single-parent homes (whether as caregivers or children), popular culture continues to provide spaces in which to deal with anxieties over the changing American family. In the case of *Gilmore Girls* and the romance between Lorelai and Christopher, it offers the fantasy of a reunited two-parent family.

Lorelai refused to marry Christopher when she became pregnant with Rory at sixteen, but the show has always held out the idea of Christopher, Lorelai, and Rory coming together, one that could conceivably fulfill the fantasy of bringing the nuclear family together. The desire for these three to fulfill their destiny as a traditional family is expressed by a number of characters through the course of the show's run. In the pilot episode, Emily, Lorelai's tougher-than-nails mother, reiterates her argument that Lorelai should have done the right thing by marrying Christopher and giving Rory a family (even though it is sixteen years after the fact), insisting that "when you get pregnant, you get married." This argument is later repeated in the sixth season episode "Friday Night's Alright for Fighting" (6.13). Although Lorelai balked at marrying Christopher simply because she was pregnant, for much of the show's run she does appear to hold on to the fantasy that she, Christopher, and Rory may someday form a "real" family. "I always thought if [Christopher] could just get it together, grow up-maybe we could do it," Lorelai confesses to Luke near the end of the third season opener. "Maybe we could really be a family, in the stupid, traditional 'Dan Quayle, golden retriever, grow old together, wear matching jogging suits' kind of way."

More important for the purposes of this chapter, Rory also expresses a desire to see her family members (re)united. Although Rory always supports her mother in her various romantic entanglements and is never shown hatching *Parent Trap*–style plans to get Lorelai and Christopher together, the series presents a number of moments that exhibit her wish to form a family with both her parents. In "Christopher Returns" (1.15), Rory is delighted when her father visits Stars Hollow, and she takes several opportunities to try to convince Lorelai that Christopher is finally getting his act together and is ready to make a full-time family with them. Rory's fantasy of having her parents married goes underground and remains dormant after Christopher leaves his daughter and Lorelai to return to his pregnant girlfriend, Sherry, at the end of the second season. She even warns Christopher to stay away from Lorelai at several points in Season Five, but reverts back to her earlier fantasy when Lorelai and Christopher do get together and marry in the seventh season. Though she is wary at first, she eventually encourages their relationship, and even reacts with delight when her parents elope (after initially expressing dismay at being left out of the event), telling Lorelai that it is "every kid's dream" ("Introducing Lorelai Planetarium" [7.08]). As we shall see, this fantasy of the (re)united parents is powerful for viewers who have come of age in a society of increasing single-parent homes.

For *Gilmore Girls* fans who are Lorelai-Christopher shippers, the fact that the two share a child is often cited as a reason that they should end up together. "Lorelai and Christopher should get married, and the series should end [with] them being the family they always should have been," asserts one poster ("One Is the Loneliest Number," September 15, 2006). "[Christopher] is not only Lorelai's first love and oldest friend, he's also Rory's father," writes another fan ("Christopher," September 6, 2006). Much of the Lorelai-Christopher fan fiction also focuses on their relationship as parents. In "Helping Rory," for example, Lorelai rediscovers her love for Christopher as they work together to get Rory through the stealing-a-yacht-and-dropping-out-of-Yale crisis of the show's fifth and sixth seasons. (This fantasy is especially telling, as Christopher does not actually appear on the show during any of the aforementioned crises.) In fact, in a number of the stories in which Lorelai and Christopher are together, such as "Honk If You're in the Hartford Elite" or "And

Then He Smiled at Me," they are not the romantic focus of the story; rather, they are the loving, united (and decidedly upper-class) parental backdrop for Rory's story.

The promise of Lorelai and Christopher finally forming a family with their daughter explains why some fans support the pairing, but it also shows us how this storyline can foreground the anxieties caused by changes in the modern family structure. In the face of these changes, a romance in which the uniting of two people also brings together a two-parent family can be both potent and comforting, as we see in this post by a Lorelai-Christopher shipper: "Despite their flaws, people love and forgive their fathers, hoping for another chance at being a complete family. Rory wants her dad in her life and, just like all children, would love to see her parents together. Lor wants the same thing. If Christopher makes her happy and they are able to be together, ultimately it's the best solution to a problem that has dragged on for Rory's whole life. Who here would not like to see their real parents together and working things out?" This same poster later comments that "it's a shame some fans don't want to see the family unite" ("Christopher," October 26, 2006). An unspoken implication in the above posts is that Christopher-Lorelai appeals to a generation of viewers who, as the data above suggest, have grown up in an age of growing divorce rates and may have either lived with a single parent or raised kids on their own (or both). These viewers could achieve some vicarious satisfaction from watching Christopher and Lorelai marry and form a family with their daughter.

Ironically, other viewers claim the ideal of the nuclear family as a reason to dislike—or at least dismiss—Christopher and Christopher-Lorelai. "But there is no nuclear family to unite because there never was one in the first place," writes one poster in response to the argument that Christopher and Lorelai should be together to unite their family. "It was Lorelai and Rory who have been a family and Christopher who has always been an occasional participant in their family life" (ibid.). In fact, numerous posts cite Christopher's shortcomings as a father (he is arguably portrayed as having been marginally involved at best in Rory's early life, and he is absent from her life for long stretches of the show's run). The same poster who argues that Lorelai, Rory, and Christopher have never been a family sums up the arguments for Christopher as an emotional and financial "deadbeat dad":

> It was in Season 2—when Rory was already seventeen—that Christopher had any regular contact with her through their weekly telephone calls and occasional visits. . . . Season 2 was also the one and only time Christopher attended a major event in Rory's life—the debutante ball. And that was it. That was the extent of his fathering role. No child support, no helping with Chilton fees, and no offer of college funding. He never offered financial aid for the care of his elder daughter until he was a rich man and such an expense would be no burden to him at all. (ibid., June 9, 2006)

For some fans, Christopher's negligence of his daughter is reason enough that he should not "win" Lorelai at the end of the series. "If Chris shaped up tomorrow, with everything that has happened in the past, I would say he is still undeserving of Lorelai," argues one TWoP poster. "This is especially true in regards to how he has treated Rory. . . . I tend to think his relationship with Lorelai should be affected by how he has treated their daughter myself" (ibid., September 19, 2006). Another poster expresses concern over what "messages" a (potential) Christopher-Lorelai pairing sends about "deadbeat" parenting in our culture. "I hate the L/C pairing because of the message it send out to viewers. . . . [I]f *GG* somehow rewards Chris with Lorelai & Rory after having been a complete non-event for Rory's entire lifetime, and without having matured or made amends to any serious extent, then it is a disaster IMO [in my opinion]" ("Lorelai and Christopher," June 20, 2006). The argument that Christopher is a deadbeat dad is a common (and perhaps not altogether unbiased) reason some fans do not want to see Lorelai with him, but the term also ties fans' responses to the character to larger issues circulating in American society. The problem of the deadbeat dad has become part of the popular discourse over the past two decades, as states and localities explore ways to compel delinquent fathers to pay child support, and television shows from *Family*

Matters (ABC, 1989–97) to *Grey's Anatomy* (ABC, 2005–) portray the lasting effects of absent or negligent fathers on adult children. Applying the deadbeat-dad label to Christopher turns him into an object of scorn through which viewers can express their outrage over a growing problem in contemporary culture.

Oy! with the Couples, Already: Fantasies of Female Independence

Of course, not every *Gilmore Girls* fan cares about the show's romances—or even wants to see Lorelai end up with Luke or Christopher. "I'd *love* to see a show that doesn't define a 'happy ending' as every main character riding off into the sunset with the man of their dreams," argues one TWoPer on behalf of an "I choose me" ending for Lorelai. "I think it fits with Lorelai's character and the themes of the show for her to end the series single, happy about it, and excited about other opportunities and even curveballs life might have in store" ("One Is the Loneliest Number," October 28, 2006). Another poster ties Lorelai's story more closely to feminist ideology: "The only thing I find anti-feminist . . . is Lorelai's and L/L's fans obsessions with her getting her *whole package* and being pregnant with Luke's kid. *That* is anti-feminist. There is no other prescription for Lorelai to be happy. No other avenue open to her. . . . If that's what will make her happy, that's great. But to think that is the only way she can be happy seems [ridiculously] narrow minded, to me" (ibid., February 16, 2007). Although this seems to be a minority opinion among TWoP *Gilmore* fans, it does indicate that some are willing to resist long-standing conventional wisdom about popular romances (the couple always gets together in the end), even if it means dismissing one of the show's main storylines. More important, however, these responses illustrate that the show provides a space in which to oppose (still dominant) traditional ideas about what women are supposed to desire. In this vision of a *Gilmore Girls* ending with the quirky, independent heroine happily sans hero, a romantic relationship with a man becomes but one option available to a woman. Such a vision upholds ideals of women's autonomy, but also gives viewers who have or would choose lives outside of marriage and children—even in the face of continuing pressure to follow the traditional path—validation of those choices.

Whether they want Lorelai to end up with Luke or Christopher or to simply be content to be on her own, the posts and fiction written by many *Gilmore Girls* fans illustrate the ways the show has become source material for their own exploration of contemporary sexuality and gender roles. On Web sites like TelevisionWithoutPity.com and FanFiction.net, fan-authored texts become laboratories for testing what romantic and sexual relationships can or should be after decades of questioning and redefining such concepts. Some of these texts reaffirm cultural norms in the midst of large-scale social and political change, while others offer more progressive views of gender and sexuality in the face of traditional ideology. Whatever scenario they envision, the responses of *Gilmore Girls* fans illustrate the power of popular culture as a tool for working through larger issues and concerns. Perhaps more important, an analysis of these responses might provide a model for a critical hermeneutics that synthesizes textual analysis, cultural context, viewer response, and peer-to-peer engagement.

16

"But Luke and Lorelai Belong Together!"

Relationships, Social Control, and Gilmore Girls

JIMMIE MANNING

It is not uncommon to hear individuals discussing someone else's romantic relationship—offering advice, praise, and sometimes even critiques. These social interjections, regardless of whether they are supportive or critical, tend to continue throughout the duration of most relationships. Friends, family members, and even complete strangers will make direct and indirect comments assessing and scrutinizing the new directions relationships have taken, who is really at fault when one of the individuals in the relationship screws something up, or—in the aftermath of a breakup—what has led to the relationship's disintegration. In short, when relationships exist, people have opinions. These opinions can be helpful, hurtful, or both, and, despite the best efforts of those actually *in* the relationship, they can sometimes cause turmoil or strife even when the comments or concerns come from uninformed or uninvolved parties.

Imagine, then, how television characters would feel if they could hear the curious comments made about their relationships. Those relationships adored by audiences would be required to uphold almost unreasonable expectations: "The whole world is cheering you on! You have no choice but to make it!" Similarly, those relationships detested by audiences would be cursed, for, even if two people were "meant to be together," all of the negativity aimed at that relationship would likely cause it to fail, since such external critiques often bring added insecurities and relational doubt.

This scenario is especially intriguing in the case of *Gilmore Girls,* a television series in which many of the romantic relationships divide audience members in terms of support. For Rory it has arguably happened four times: first as the centerpiece in a love triangle involving Tristan and Dean; then on another occasion with the dueling suitors Dean and Jess; then in a different kind of triangle that hinged on Dean's infidelity to his wife, Lindsay; and finally (on a much smaller scale) one involving college students Logan and Marty. As for Lorelai, although many fans of *Gilmore Girls* have pined for her to be with Luke ever since she dated a variety of men during the series' early days, she has been part of only one true love triangle—the one between her, Luke, and Christopher.

These love triangles collectively pose an intriguing question: what is the underlying nature of the show's romantic relationships in which Rory and Lorelai are situated opposite different partners? Answering this question offers insight into the world of *Gilmore Girls* as well as the world of the fans who steadfastly followed it from its first season to its last. To this end, we will first revisit the love triangles of Rory and Lorelai to provide a reminder of the relationships presented throughout the program and the reception of these relationships among fans. Next we will explore interpersonal relationship theory, through which we will analyze what Rory and Lorelai seem to be craving most in their romantic partnerships with men. Next, we will look at fan reactions to what is probably the show's most enduring romantic triangle, that of Lorelai, Luke, and Christopher. Finally, I conclude with suggestions of how fan reactions to *Gilmore Girls* are indicative of the ways in which particular Western cultures handle relationships. Ultimately, I hope that the reader will begin to reconsider his or her stance on not only the romantic dealings of Rory and Lorelai but also the relationships in his or her own life.

Triangles, Triangles, Triangles

Based on the fan buzz from Internet message boards, each of the abovementioned triangles emerged with its own unique set of discursive characteristics.[1] The discussions surrounding Rory's relationships often became more mature with the introduction of each new triangle. Talk about Dean versus Tristan often concerned who was better looking and whether Rory needed a "good" boy or a "bad" boy. When good-boy Dean won out, the newly introduced bad boy, Jess, became an object of scorn for many fans who failed to understand what Rory could see in this rebellious young man (while others expressed appreciation for their shared love of music and culture). Although Jess eventually won Rory's heart to close out this triangle, our indecisive heroine soon returned her affections toward Dean after Jess flaked out and skipped town. Since Dean was married at this point, many viewers criticized the fact that Rory lost her virginity to him (although many reported enjoying this darker side of the character, who was finally beginning to shed her good-girl image). After her romantic fling with Dean crumbled once again, Rory met Marty and Logan, two students at Yale. Although Logan seemed to have Rory's heart from day one, many fans longed for her to be with Marty.

Although Lorelai was a participant in only one triangle over the course of the series, it proved to be a particularly intense one. After she finally began dating Luke, Christopher reentered Lorelai's life—first as a result of Richard and Emily's interference, then as a refuge for a crumbling relationship between her and Luke once the diner owner's teenage daughter, April, descended on Stars Hollow. Despite its somewhat soapy nature, hinging on hokey plot twists (like a long-lost daughter emerging from the woodwork), the triangle proved to be a dramatically rich one, layered with the tensions between the support offered by Luke to Lorelai as she initially left the comforts of

1. To protect message-board participants (and in accordance with human-subject regulations), neither specific message-board names nor participant names are included. All message boards were located via a Google search. Thirteen different message boards and 152 threads were explored for this study. All data presented as quotations are left in their original, unedited state in order to preserve the tone of each message. Thus, names and words may be misspelled, facts may be incorrect, and grammar and punctuation may be incorrect.

her wealthy family to make it on her own and the long-standing history Lorelai shared with Christopher, the father of her only child. Interestingly, besides Christopher, no other suitors for Lorelai's affections really registered as the third point of a triangle involving her and Luke. When Lorelai was engaged to Max Medina, Luke's affections were only the slightest of flirtations, and many viewers wondered if anything would ever come of their boisterous banter. The other men Lorelai dated, such as the tellingly named Alex Lesman during Season Three (a coffee connoisseur who took her fishing and was so inconsequential that he disappeared from the show with no explanation) and Jason "Digger" Stiles (a character deemed "pathetic" and "disgusting" by fans posting comments on *GG* message boards), seemed to be momentary stopgaps, temporary guys to pass the time before the constitution of the show's "real" romance—the one between Lorelai and Luke. For many, it seemed that Christopher was the only true challenge to Luke for Lorelai's affections, at least judging from message-board contributions.

Rory and Her Suitors: Uncertainty Reduction and Social Exchange

In analyzing Rory's romantic possibilities, two interpersonal communication theories help in illuminating the nature of her dating relationships. The first is uncertainty-reduction theory. Developed largely by communication social scientist Charles Berger (1988), uncertainty-reduction theory looks at how, in the face of meeting new people, individuals attempt to reduce uncertainty about each other and make decisions based on these relational assessments. As originally proposed, Berger's theory contains many axioms (or rules) about how uncertainty reduction works. For the purposes of this chapter, however, the portion of his theory exploring the natural curiosities one person may have about another person proves to be particularly useful.

To be certain, Rory experiences uncertainty beyond the scope of this interpersonal theory. From the beginning of the series, she longs to be a world-famous journalist, and inherent within that dream is a curiosity to discover new and exciting things. This curiosity carries over to Rory's potential romantic partners, too. Whereas this curiosity seems pleasant and polite in her relationships with Dean and Marty (if what she had with the latter individual could even be considered a relationship), it pales in comparison to her interest in the first of what many fans have deemed Rory's "bad" boys, Tristan. With his confrontational nature and rebel stance, Tristan (a fellow student at Chilton) proves to be a clear challenge to Rory. Although she avoids him on many occasions and is ultimately able to resist his romantic advances (giving him only one kiss, something she expresses as regretting later in the program), it is clear that she is intrigued by what makes Tristan tick and hopes to find a bright mind behind his standoffish demeanor and teenage sneer.

This desire is later realized more fully once the show's second bad boy, Jess, has been introduced. As the nephew of the rugged but gentlemanly diner owner, Jess presents a somewhat shocking (and, to many, widely disdained) presence.[2] In the short time that he resides in Stars Hollow, he manages to steal Lorelai's beer, sass his uncle, and (gasp!) talk disrespectfully to the townspeople. He is instantly framed as a foil to Dean, dichotomizing their good boy–bad boy roles, his curt nature toward Rory balanced by what he could bring to the table (an understanding of punk music and contemporary art plus a certain sex appeal). It is already evident from this cursory exploration that Jess's identity and ability to enliven Rory's curiosity set him apart from the less complex Dean. In other words, Dean, as initially presented, is a remarkably easy character to read: he is kind, considerate, and earnest, and the parts seem to equal the whole. The same could not be said for Jess. For every wrong thing that he does, he also does something right. Additionally, Rory appears to be the only person to realize what Jess has to offer. Precisely because he is complex and multilayered, some might say contradictory, Rory is drawn inquisitively toward Jess, unsure of what she might encounter.

2. To be fair, Jess had many fans as well. In fact, many of the Internet message forums consulted for the purposes of writing this chapter are filled with the musings of fans who fantasize that Rory will one day cross paths with Jess again.

Of course, Dean's character evolves as the series progresses, particularly after he marries Lindsay. During the couple's courtship, it is evident that Rory is experiencing difficulty in letting Dean go. This fact can be chalked up as a common relational occurrence, given that many people, even after dissolving relationships they perceive as wholly negative, have a hard time letting go of their relational identity and sometimes need time to process the fact that those relationships have fully ended. Dean flirts with Rory well after he marries Lindsay, however, and viewers might question whether Rory is returning these flirtatious cues simply because she longs for the simplicity of the past (especially in the aftermath of her breakup with Jess). Or does she seek the complexity of uncertainty, the danger she faces in pursuing a relationship with a married man? One could logically think the former, for after Rory loses her virginity to the married Dean she defends the action to her mother by saying that he belonged to her and that things are the way they are "supposed to be." In many ways it is apparent that Dean likewise wishes to restore his memories of the recent past through Rory.

The above scenario speaks to another interpersonal theory relevant to any romantic relationship, but particularly highlighted in Rory's relationships: the theory of social exchange. Developed by Harold H. Kelley and John W. Thibaut (1978), social exchange theory provides an almost economic model of how the costs of being in a relationship compare to the rewards. Individuals will often stay in relationships when the perceived costs seem to outweigh the perceived rewards. In other words, people stick with their partners because they *need* something (or, at least, they perceive that they do). When Rory and Dean enter into an adulterous affair, they do so based on the needs they get from the relationship. Even though both have to pay dearly for this relationship, these costs—at least for a short time—are worth it for the emotional rewards they both receive. This notion of social exchange should not be confused with complementary or supplementary elements of relationships; it does not examine how each individual's personal traits work in conjunction with each other in a relationship. Social exchange deals more with what the individuals in a relationship need, how they find a partner who can fulfill that need, and then deciding whether it is worth the price in terms of what has to be sacrificed in order to maintain the relationship.

In comparing Dean and Jess, the elements being socially exchanged are quite apparent. In her initial relationship with Dean, Rory seems to be seeking the genuine joys of first love. The same likewise appears to be what Dean is searching for, as the two of them play into a stereotypically sweet and wholesome relationship where each person respects the other. Tristan is there only as a contrasting image, to remind Rory of what she most wants: someone good, simple, and caring (all things that the Chilton student seems not to be). Tristan's presence in the series does, however, illustrate Rory's desire to do "bad" things from time to time. Even though she will later balk at the kiss she shares with Tristan, it is evident that she enjoyed the brief encounter. It is later quite difficult for Dean to understand why Rory would want someone like Jess, but to fans of *Gilmore Girls*—even to those viewers who cannot stand the rebellious figure—it is apparent that she needs to tap into someone who can bring out her "wild" side. Jess shares Rory's love for music and literature, but also exhibits an aggressive sexuality, evident in their occasional public displays of affection. Although Jess does not always treat Rory with respect, she is willing to overlook such things because of what he can offer her. Still, this element of their relationship has left many fans disliking Jess and befuddled by Rory's choices.

From these brief analyses, it appears that Logan may have been a good fit for Rory even though they were not together when the series ended. In analyzing Rory's need for uncertainty and the type of qualities she seeks in the social exchange process, it is apparent that Logan offers both, and it seems that they are offered in a balanced, reasonably respectful (if not realistically flawed) way. The relationship between Rory and Logan is complicated to say the least, which is to be expected given the complexity of the two individuals. After their initial meeting, Rory becomes increasingly interested in Logan because he is the exact kind of guy from which her mother shielded her. More than a boring socialite, though, Logan exhibits intellectual curiosity as well as the bad-boy qualities that have always intrigued Rory—only this time with a sophisticated charm and educated worldliness. Logan's emergence offers a new world to be discovered, albeit one permeated with the negativity that results from his difficult relationship with his father, Mitchum. The uncertainty associated with Logan gives Rory the chance to again indulge her curiosities in the relationship process.

Reciprocally, Logan also finds much about Rory to be stimulating. As the show establishes early on, Logan was not the type to settle down until meeting Rory, a defiant, brilliant young woman very different from his previous partners. This difference results in an uncertainty that fits into what each person needs and gets from the relationship in terms of social exchange. Again, uncertainty highlights the elements of exchange as Rory becomes charmed by Logan's irreverent surprises (pulling a stunt in her class, taking her to secret society events, and so on) and his sophisticated demeanor. Perhaps Logan is simply offering Rory something that Lorelai denied her (as she at one point acknowledges in a fight with her mother): the right to make her own decisions about her life. Logan acknowledges Rory's will to tackle life on her terms—although not a strong, direct force of nature, she is someone who has a backbone. If Rory craves sophistication and a sense of adventure from Logan, it is also obvious that he yearns for her defiant yet gentle nature. The fact that the relationship disturbs the parents of both Rory and Logan is just part of the exchange: both partners know the cost of their parents' being upset, yet both decide that the reward of each other's companionship is worth it. As romantic as this idea is, it also leads to a significant amount of interpersonal deception as the two of them try to understand the other's world. And, in an interesting turnabout (one that capsizes the upper-class tradition of women deferring to the men), Logan is ready to follow Rory.

Lorelai, Christopher, and Luke: Relational Dialectics

Even if Lorelai is not shown entering into as many romantic pairings as Rory, it is evident that this thirtysomething woman values being in stimulating relationships. To be certain, the partnerships between

Lorelai and her two main love interests are sometimes overly complex to the point of testing fans' patience. As one message-board user put it, "It's almost like they're wracking their brains trying to come up with ways to keep them apart. I mean really, a long-lost daughter he [Luke] finds at the science fair?" Before fully exploring those reactions it is important to consider the tensions present in Lorelai's primary relationships. As one message-board user put it after Lorelai had accepted Christopher's proposal, "I guess I can understand why Lorelai thinks Christopher is the right choice. We can see that he isn't, but in many ways it is about her needs and who she thinks can provide for those needs. I think she needs comfort, something she's never had, and she doesn't see that with Luke and his new daughter and thinks Christopher is the way to go."

This comment reflects in many ways some of the underlying tenets of what Leslie A. Baxter and Barbara Montgomery (1996) refer to as relational-dialectical theory. Based largely on the writings of Mikhail Bakhtin, relational-dialectical theory explores how relationships are filled with contradictory tendencies representative of the complexities of one's needs. As communication scholar Em Griffin notes, "Quality relationships are constituted through dialogue, which is an aesthetic accomplishment that produces fleeting moments of unity through a profound respect for the disparate voices" (2008, 488). That is, relationships are filled with needs that pull one's identity in two different directions. In a romantic relationship, one often longs for integration with a romantic partner, yet, at the same time, she or he also yearns for a sense of independence. One often desires a relationship to be stable and reliable, yet at the same time one also often wants the relationship to continuously evolve and change. These tensions and others test not only the individuals in a relationship but also the relationship itself.

Three chief dialectical tensions affect almost every close relationship: integration-separation, stability-change, and expression-nonexpression (Baxter and Montgomery 1996). They play out both internally (within the relationship) and externally (between the couple and a community). These dialectics can be applied here to analyze Lorelai's respective relationships with Luke and Christopher, and in order to assess the apparent comforts and conflicts found within the tensions. In considering the first of these three primary tensions, integration-separation, Baxter notes, "No relationship can exist by definition unless the parties sacrifice some individual autonomy. However, too much connection paradoxically destroys the relationship because the individual identities become lost" (1988, 259). In other words, if one side loses in the tug-of-war for independence, then the relationship is doomed.

In considering Lorelai's individual identity, it is quite clear that both of the men being considered in this essay allow her the freedom to be the person she wants to be, and both are willing to let her identity thrive. In both relationships, when Lorelai wants to stay in her house the men are accommodating, with Luke building onto the abode to make it more comfortable and Christopher leaving his own lavish home to join the community of Stars Hollow. What is more, the men also cater to Lorelai's eccentricities, attending screenings of *Pippi Longstocking* (1969), celebrating Christmas after the holiday has past, and tolerating (if not always embracing) her unique culinary habits, pop culture interests, and behavioral quirks. With these men being so accepting of Lorelai, one might question whether they are expected to give up *too much* of their own personal identities.

In the case of Christopher, it is fair to ask whether Lorelai has asked him to relinquish too much of his individuality and personal identity. He obviously does not fit in with the quirky characters populating Stars Hollow, people like Babette and Miss Patty who have difficulty warming up to him. In moving in, he is also teased for many of the luxuries that he previously enjoyed, like his large-screen TV. Of course, a similar thing happened earlier with Luke (particularly in the case of the ugly bed he tries to move into Lorelai's house), but whereas he makes concessions in moving in with Lorelai he still has his diner and retains his identity in the town. Although Luke navigates this dialectical tension well in terms of physical negotiation, he exhibits serious shortcomings (or, in sticking with the tug-of-war metaphor, he tugs too hard) when it comes to his newfound daughter, April. Clearly, he is not ready to integrate *all* aspects of his life with Lorelai's, which proves to be hurtful to her. Soon, an external force comes into play: April's mother, Anna, does not want Lorelai in Luke's life, but even so, relational tensions do not exist in a vacuum. As many fans of *Gilmore Girls* have remarked online, Luke makes a serious mistake in closing himself off from Lorelai.

The issues coming into play with April also speak to the second chief tension of stability—change. This notion is similar to the concept of uncertainty reduction, but it is different in that it refers to the negotiations made by couples composed of individuals who want to feel like they know each other while avoiding the sense of the relationship becoming too routine or predictable. On a different level, the dialectic also highlights how well relationships adapt to change. Although no significant change comes into play during Lorelai and Christopher's relationship (with the exception of their taking Gigi—the young daughter of Christopher and Sherry—to Paris), it is clear that, together, Luke and Lorelai do not handle change well. Again, the April incident allows insight into how Luke is not ready to deal with integrating his daughter into the relationship. Of course, it could be argued that Luke is afraid that he might lose the right to see his daughter if he allows Lorelai into her life, but at the same time, even before Anna's threats, he had kept April hidden from Lorelai, both in the sense that he did not tell Lorelai about his daughter at first and then, after telling her, made sure that Lorelai and April did not see each other often.

Questions of openness and reticence in a relationship are often explored in the relational dialectic of expression-nonexpression. As the phrase implies, this dialectic draws attention to how open people tend to behave in a relationship and how they negotiate their conflicting needs to have some semblance of privacy while still remaining sensitive enough to keep a relational partner satisfied. Although many may envision the ideal relationship as one in which each partner is candid and open, it is perhaps more realistic to acknowledge the value placed on privacy between relational partners. To again borrow the tug-of-war metaphor, it is when the pull for privacy or the pull for openness is too hard that the relationship may be in trouble, and, to again look at the April situation, it is obvious that openness is a problem for both

Luke and Lorelai. As noted earlier, Luke is not forthright about his daughter, and Lorelai is not open about her confusion regarding the wedding. In fact, she reveals her concerns about being married in a drunken speech at Lane's wedding before she brings the issues up with Luke. This closed-off approach to one's emotions does not reflect the same healthy pattern of exchange occurring between Lorelai and Chris. In fact, it seems that, more than any other person (even Rory), Lorelai can be open with Chris. He is her touchstone, the one to whom she can reveal almost anything. As one fan sums up nicely in a post to an Internet message board:

> I loved Chris and Lorelai together. I was sad when they broke up. I like Luke, but Luke shuts down too much and Lorelai is a communicator and so is Chris. If you noticed when Chris and Lorelai fought they talked about it right away after a cool off. When Luke and Lorelai fought Luke took off and wouldn't talk to her for a day or two. That drove her crazy. Luke and Lorelai are cute and i like them, but if they were a real couple i don't think it would last because of the two ways of different communications. It would make an unhappy relationship in the long run. Chris and Lorelai just seem to communicate well. When he didn't show up at the hospital and turned off his phone, that is not the usual Christopher they write, so that didn't make sense. Anyways, i am with you about Chris. I also read that Lauren actually thought Chris was better for her character.

Social Support, Social Control, and a Sense of the "Real"

The above analysis may not sit well with many *Gilmore Girls* fans. Actually, gathering from what most fans have reported via online message boards, it is not so much the *April situation* but, rather, the *Christopher situation* that proves most to be frustrating. That is, while many audience members are not happy with the storyline involving Luke's long-lost daughter, the expressed dissatisfaction in that regard pales in comparison to the anger expressed toward Lorelai's sleeping with Christopher after breaking off her engagement with Luke. Many fans complain that it makes no sense: why would Lorelai do it? Yet when one takes into consideration the show's relational dialectics, it makes sense that she would run to Christopher. Her mounting frustrations with an increasingly closed-off Luke stem from the uncertainty between them. In many ways, it makes *perfect* sense that she would go to the person with whom she feels most open, someone with whom she shared an ongoing, respectful relationship.

With a long-running television series like *Gilmore Girls,* where viewers are heavily invested in the characters and eagerly follow the developing plots with fierce loyalty, it is natural that the characters begin to take on a life of their own, with fans actually worrying about their welfare. Indeed, the above analysis treats the characters as if they *are* real individuals. Just as I am doing here, fans analyze the show's relationships on a regular basis, although—given their investment in the characters—it should not be surprising that their analysis frequently becomes emotional. People cannot help but become involved in others' relationships and quickly form opinions on whether other people should be together.[3] In many ways, a relationship can be burdened with the rhetoric of what others expect it to be. This outsider's view of relationships illustrates how audience members have come to terms with the relationships of the titular characters.

Because the data that I have encountered online best support these relationships, we will return briefly to the previously discussed triangle of Lorelai-Christopher-Luke and to the relationship between Rory and Logan. The discourses apparent on online message boards dedicated to *Gilmore Girls* will be analyzed with representative samples used to demonstrate how, exactly, fans wish for (and sometimes demand) changes to be made to the program regarding romantic pairings. Before examining what message-board members have to say, though, it is important to consider how discourses concerning relationships often function as a means of asserting social support or control. Simply defined, social

3. For a variety of essays dealing with relational intrusion, see Spitzberg and Cupach 1998.

support refers to the emotional, physical, or tangible reinforcements provided by friends, family members, coworkers, and other close associates.[4] Social control, on the other hand, denotes the ways in which members of a community regulate individual or group behavior.[5] In many ways, the two work in conjunction with one other. Whereas the former is often framed by social scientists as a set of specific actions, it can be argued that the perhaps more amorphous notion of social control is often accompanied by the rhetoric of support. Moreover, social control measures actually support those individuals who are following the rules that others are breaking.

When exploring a fan's posting on a message board, it is sometimes immediately evident how social support or social control comes into play. For instance, consider the following message: "Lorelai is a slut and doesn't deserve to be with anyone. So if she and Luke get back together and then have a fight, who can she run off and sleep with?" Although this message-board user probably does not believe that a fictional character—Lorelai—will actually see this posting and make changes in her life, it is evident that the writer is asserting what is good and bad in a relationship. While Lorelai cannot receive the message and adjust accordingly, others reading the harsh words are confronted with what this one person expects of the relationship and can gain an understanding of relational rhetoric. In this case, the message-board user is suggesting two things: women who do what Lorelai has done cannot be trusted, and they will likely do it again. Beyond that thought, these messages combine into a larger appeal, one that urges others not to replicate Lorelai's behavior if they wish to be seen as a credible participant in a relationship.

Before diving too deeply into Lorelai's complex relationships with Luke and Christopher, it is important to point out that the postings on online message boards betray an investment in other relationships as well. For example, the relationship between Logan and Rory, which

4. For more on social support and relationships, see Walen and Lachman 2000.

5. For more on social control and relationships, see Indvik and Fitzpatrick 1986.

terminates in the penultimate episode of the series, illustrates how viewers interact with one another in hopes of making sense of plot developments and character arcs. When people talk via online message boards about the characters of a television program, they often do so in a way that conflates the fictional and the "real." This point can be demonstrated through excerpts of fan postings culled from online conversations, especially character-directed comments such as "rory!! what are you thinking!! logans perfect for you!! he has really mellowed out, hes sweet too!! *And he loves you!!*" Talk *about* the characters can also assume a gossiplike quality, too. For instance, one posting reads: "Rory treats all her bfs like nothing when you really think about it. She gets her way then leaves them in the dust. She treats all men like that, she's a little heartbreaker . . . Dean, Tristan, Jess, Marty, Logan." These last two comments dig into the heart of viewer frustrations, with Rory's rejection of Logan's proposal a source of disappointment for many—though not all—fans. As one such audience member notes, "There was a debate about who Rory should end up with. And since everyone has their own preference . . . the only possible way not to piss someone off one way or another . . . is to have her be alone in the end." As pointed out earlier, only one true triangle emerges for Lorelai; with Rory, there are more options available both to her and to the fans of the series. Although several of these options are kept at bay for years (or, in the case of Jess, are only intimated in his occasional guest spots), fans still clamor for their return. One fan even takes the writing of the show into her own hands: "With Logan something would happen with his work and he ends up drinking and drinking and becomes a alcoholic and Rory gives up on him and cries and is like 'i thought you loved me . . . ' and logans like 'i do but this will always be the way i am'. (Not a logan fan obviously. . . .). At least . . . that would have been a good reason for them to break up." In the case of this particular online message, it is evident that the fans sometimes *support* and sometimes *wish to control* relationships with a sense of heightened drama. It is not enough that Rory and Logan end things; he must also become an alcoholic to offer a clear justification of why they should not be together. While many viewers support these types of fantasies and enjoy concocting their own storylines for the show (even if they make the characters act in sometimes ridiculous ways), these same fans will often chastise the writers and producers for putting characters in similar—and sometimes more believable—predicaments.

Of course, I do not mean to suggest that fans of the program always (or even mostly) act unreasonably with regard to these fictional relationships. In fact, many fans tend to give a reasoned account of their opinions, as the following illustrates: "As far as Rory and Logan, Rory was stupid to turn down Logan's offer. Logan really loves her and went through all that trouble and was even nice enough to ask Lorelai for her permission. Logan is like a one in a million find because he is sweet and really cares, that only problem is Rory didn't want him and thought that having no future plans was a better idea. . . . How stupid." Notice the difference between this poster's response to the situation and the reaction of this viewer: "i guess you can see that im quite agitated by this horrible, no tragic turn of events. they are perfect together and it would have ended the season off nicely. end of rant." Succinct and certainly more melodramatic, this message (like the ones before it) offers an assessment—a statement of support and control, if you will—of what a relationship should be and how it should develop. Of course, the possibility of Rory's not ending up with Logan does not pack as much of an emotional wallop as the prospect of Lorelai's not ending up with Luke. After all, many fans contend that the Luke and Lorelai pairing had been in the works since the first season. It is interesting to consider, then, how fans have reacted to the Season Seven storyline involving the end of Luke and Lorelai's relationship, her marriage and divorce from Christopher, and the eventual reuniting of Luke and Lorelai in the show's final episode.

Viewer ~~Opinions~~ Demands: Supporting and Controlling Relationships

It is evident from the many message-board conversations regarding the Luke-Lorelai-Christopher triangle (more than 150 different threads regarding this topic were examined for this analysis) that emotions play heavily into the equation. For instance: "I am so MAD! Do they not read these boards? Do they not understand us? They have totally ruined Lorelai! She's done. She can't bounce back from this. She and Luke are so perfect together. Why would she do this? I want to smack her and Amy and everyone at the WB. Thanks but no thanks. If this is how Lorelai is going to act then I'm not watching anymore. How can we like her now?" An interesting element of this message and others like it is that the author talks about Lorelai as if she were an actual person, someone she wishes to "smack," and thus as "real" as the show's creator and writer, Amy Sherman-Palladino. Beyond that point, a clear assessment of both Lorelai and her relationship choices is offered, in addition to sanctions against Lorelai (the author says she is not going to watch her anymore), the producers (she will not watch their show), and, inherently, the way relationships are written.

This particular message also highlights a feature of many other postings regarding the triangle, in that it lists vague terms for why Luke and Lorelai are such a good fit: they are "so perfect" or "they just make sense." It is perhaps unfair to pass judgments about message-board contributors, but it would appear that the heightened rhetoric that characterizes their writing reflects a latent desire for a fantasy world. Playing into this desire for true love, another message from a different user states, "Luke and Lorelai are destined to be together. It is fate. Christopher is a drunk idiot with a retarded daughter. He can wag off!" This particular author offers an assessment of why Chris is bad, referring to his problems with alcohol, and uses pejorative terms to insult the character's daughter. One might question why the "retarded daughter" comment is even made. With the "He can wag off!" at the end of the message, the writer breaks the wall between reality and fiction and appears to be upset with Chris as a *real person.*

Disdain for Christopher was rampant when Lorelai slept with him after she and Luke broke off the engagement. As one author writes, "Why would anyone like Chris? Especially when Luke is around. Everyone should cut off Lorelai and tell her that they don't want her in Stars Hollow if she's going to be an idiot. Does she not know what she's throwing away? Luke will take care of her[,] something she needs.

We women want a good man and she has one and does this. Get her Patty and Babette!" The implications latent within any form of social control are frighteningly exhibited here. In terms of social support, it is significant that the poster does not suggest that Lorelai's friends and family reach out to her to see what is going on and why she made a bad decision. Instead, the author of the message calls for her to be shunned by her whole town and asks for Patty and Babette to confront her. The scenarios would almost be comical if it did not match the reality of how many people would likely handle similar situations.

These reactions, though seemingly extreme, are the normative backdrop against which *Gilmore Girls*' fandom is articulated online. My analysis is not meant to scold fans who have taken their love of the show to great lengths. Longtime viewers obviously care for Lorelai and have simply grown upset with her actions. I do wish to argue, however, that these messages and similar ones demonstrate a need for caution and consideration in volatile, emotional situations, such as the ones exhibited in the show. It is quite possible that people in everyday interactions may exhibit the same knee-jerk reactions when support may be needed. Of course, many message-board users inject a great deal of sensitivity into their online postings. Although unable to include many of them in this chapter, such messages represent a rich array of viewer opinions and offer honest, well-thought-out assessments of Lorelai's desire to be with Luke. Even if she and Christopher represent an excellent blend of relational dialectical tensions, is it enough to outweigh the passion she feels for Luke? And, turning that question on its head, is the passion that these latter individuals feel for each other enough to overcome their obvious communicative issues in the relationship?

Many implications regarding relationships can be assumed from this chapter, in terms of how cultures and societies define them and expect them to be. It is evident that many fans of *Gilmore Girls* treat the characters as living, breathing creatures. It does not mean, though, that fans are delusional, but rather that they immerse themselves wholly in the world created by the producers. Much like friends do in other social situations, *Gilmore Girls* fans gather online to discuss the relationships of their other "friends"—the fictional characters who have resonated so deeply in their lives. This point reminds us that relationships are judged and that, based on these judgments, punishments or rewards are suggested.

The online discourses presented in this study are only a small part of the many sanctions suggested by fans, with regards to Rory's and Lorelai's relational decisions. But these sanctions are indicative of how larger communities react to other relationships as well, since many people looking in on others' relationships feel as if they have a stake in them. Interestingly, on several occasions the characters in the *Gilmore*verse are scrutinized for the same behaviors described in this essay. Viewers curse Emily for interfering with Lorelai's relationship and may feel frustrated with Lorelai for not understanding Rory's relationship with Logan. For better or worse, it seems inevitable that when a relationship is seen, it is appraised for all of its glory or failure. Unfortunately, research suggests that people are more apt to see the potential for failure than they are to acknowledge the potential for success (Antonucci, Akiyama, and Lansford 1998).

One has to wonder how the writers and producers of *Gilmore Girls* might respond to these assessments. Would they, in adopting the relational-theory line and thinking that Christopher is a good fit for Lorelai, still have written a divorce into the show and then have Lorelai return to Luke? Or, if the online fan culture were more accepting of the former relationship, would it have continued to thrive? The answers to these questions may never be known, since the viewers as well as the producers of *Gilmore Girls* ultimately chose a romantic notion of true love for their main characters. They appear to have believed that, despite their differences and interpersonal obstacles, Luke and Lorelai's love would endure. And in the fertile minds of the viewers—the only place where Luke and Lorelai's story will completely be told—it probably has.

17

What a Girl Wants

Men and Masculinity in Gilmore Girls

LAURA NATHAN

> EMILY: I want to go on a date.
> LORELAI: With a man?
> EMILY: No, a weasel. Of course with a man!
> —"Emily Says Hello" (5.09)

> LORELAI: I'm attracted to pie. It doesn't mean I feel the need to date pie.
> —"Cinnamon's Wake" (1.05)

We live in a time when masculinity and femininity can no longer be easily defined. This point is evident in the earliest episodes of *Gilmore Girls,* as we meet characters like Michel Gerard, a metrosexual (perhaps queer) male who is obsessed with Celine Dion, his chow dogs, and his fastidiously maintained appearance; Kirk Gleason, the quirky Stars Hollow resident who lives with his mother and has a different job each week; and Luke Danes, the local diner owner whose uniform of choice is a flannel shirt and a baseball cap worn backward. Through these varied representations of masculinity, the audience gets a sense that—at least in the fictional universe created by Amy Sherman-Palladino and her husband, Daniel Palladino—one need not be the primary breadwinner, married (or heterosexual), strong and stoic, or a father to be considered a "man."

As easy as it is to say that there is nothing wrong with men opting for adventure over financial security, for careers over family, or for other men over women as objects of romantic or sexual desire, the seven seasons of *Gilmore Girls* teach us that, even in a postmodern world where gender identities are fractured and destabilized, not just any man will suffice as a life partner. Not Kirk, whom Lorelai—the show's thirtysomething leading lady who gave birth to Rory when she was sixteen—dismisses as too odd after he asks her to dinner (in "Haunted Leg" [3.02], the same episode in which we learn that he has a "dyspeptic parrot problem"). Not Max Medina, Rory's charming high school English teacher with whom Lorelai ends her engagement without explanation. Not Dean, Rory's first boyfriend who makes her a bracelet, builds her a car, and puts the Gilmore prodigy on a pedestal. And, for a while, not even Lorelai's well-read, career-oriented father, Richard, from whom Lorelai's mother, Emily, temporarily separates after nearly forty years during the series' fifth season. If these men are not good enough for the Gilmore ladies, who is? With fans, the show's characters, and even the Palladinos (plus their heir apparent, David S. Rosenthal, the final season's show runner) all debating that question, *Gilmore Girls* invites an exploration of masculinity and the ways that each potential or eventual paramour struggles to be both himself and the man the Gilmore women desire.

Regular viewers of the series have likely noticed that, flings aside, every Gilmore ex has returned to the narrative fold at some juncture, desperate for his beloved Gilmore girl to take him back. This trend may be partly explained by the fact that, with the exception of Luke (to whom Lorelai is romantically linked off and on for the show's final three seasons), neither main character's love interests are permanent fixtures of the series, leaving their presence and the continuity of their on-screen romantic relationships dependent on both the writers' whims and the actors' other commitments. Viewers are not supposed to stop and ponder this notion, of course, for Lorelai's and Rory's narratives gloss over the realities of show business to provide viewers a "caffeinated" narrative that might resemble their own lives: men coming and going, attempting to change their behavior based on what the Gilmore women desire. The male characters' on-screen struggles are also complicated by their own self-interests and the gender expectations of previous generations. Gender identities, after all, are never ahistorical or without sociopolitical context, explains Judith Butler, a renowned feminist literary critic whose book *Gender Trouble* Rory must purchase for a class that she and her roommate Paris are enrolled in during Season Seven. If a man can describe his gender identity as "masculine" (or "feminine"), it is only because the behaviors or characteristics that have enabled him to do so mimic or correspond in some way to his predecessors' own gender-coded practices and the definitions generally agreed upon by the culture at large (Butler 1993, 226–27).

Further complicating matters is the fact that the various manifestations and forms of masculinity—at least in this rarefied "*Gilmore*verse"—are shaped by the desires and expectations of those Gilmore girls linked to the *past* (Emily as well as Richard's mother, Gran) and the *present* (Rory and Lorelai). Thus, because masculinities, and heterosexual masculinities in particular, cannot be fully understood in the absence of a critical inquiry into the role that femininity plays in the cultural at large, I will consider the negotiation of these different strands in terms of their desirability among the Gilmore women: Do Lorelai and Rory—and even we viewers, who so often root for one guy over another, knowing that, on some level, our desires are bound up with the desires of these fictional characters—really want men who hark back to the "Donna Reed" era, a period in American cultural life linked to Richard's early manhood and comically commented upon in "That Damn Donna Reed" (1.14)? Or do the show's leading ladies click best with men produced by the twentieth century's feminist and postfeminist movements?

Whereas males who came of age before the 1960s were believed to know how to be "men" (May 1988, 116, 128), anyone who might desire either half of this mother-daughter duo must grapple with issues related to family and parenting, friendship, wealth and career, physical and emotional intimacy, grooming, "handiness," and the presence of other men who might be perceived as "threats" or "competition." Uncertain of the "proper" way to articulate their manhood, suitors occasionally appear vulnerable, wounded, or threatened by other men or even Rory and Lorelai. During these moments it becomes evident that the *Gilmore* men live in the midst of a masculinity crisis, one that sometimes inspires uncharacteristic acts of anger in hopes of restoring the power that has historically been associated with manhood (Cohan 1997, xi).

With its final seasons focusing less on Stars Hollow, the fictional Connecticut wonderland that Lorelai and Rory call home, and more on Rory and Lorelai finding "the ones" (as Rory calls them in "A Vineyard Valentine" [6.15]), *Gilmore Girls* plays out as a significant struggle among three generations—those individuals born during the Depression era and World War II (Emily's contemporaries), those characters of Generation X (Lorelai's suitors), and the ones composing Generation Y (Rory's peers). This struggle invites viewers to ponder whether Lorelai and Rory are really the independent women they purport to be, and whether they seek something other than the postmodern man, perhaps someone who exhibits the qualities of masculinity embodied by Richard and other men born in the midst of World War II.

The final two seasons raise many other questions: Will Lorelai and Rory end up alone, or will they find love and happiness? Will the generations in which each girl has been classified by the show's creators prove prescriptive, or merely descriptive? Are such concerns complicated by the elder Gilmores' attempts to play both Geppetto and Yenta throughout the series? It is obvious that Richard and Emily want to see Rory and Lorelai marry men like the Gilmore patriarch, men who will carry on his formidable legacy of wealth and means. Masculinity, at least in the *Gilmore*verse, cannot be understood, then, without considering gender's intersections with class. Manliness, in the elder Gilmores' book, is defined through gentility and the ability to be a breadwinner, someone who will ensure a comfortable existence for his wife and children. This measurement becomes evident during the Season Five episode "The Party's Over" (5.08), when Lorelai's parents fete their Yale alumni friends who, conveniently, have only their sons in tow. Because Rory is again dating Dean, whom Richard describes as "a very nice young man, but . . . certainly not good enough for Rory," the elder Gilmores have taken it upon themselves to find their granddaughter a beau who will carry on the family tradition of New England nobility while lavishing Rory with the love and material comforts befitting a young woman of her background. After all, as Emily boasts to her invited guests, the girl is going to be a journalist, a profession that will put her talents and education to good use, no doubt, but one that also necessitates a wealthy husband.

For Lorelai, Emily and Richard want the same, as we learn during the first of many tense Friday-night dinners at the Gilmores' Hartford home. Mentioning the Internet company that Lorelai's high school sweetheart and Rory's father, Christopher, is launching, Richard says, "Very talented man, your father. He always was a smart man. You must take after him" (1.01). Christopher, the ensuing argument between Lorelai and Emily reveals, epitomizes what Emily and Richard have always wanted for their daughter: a smart, successful man who could have given her a "lovely life," an existence free of financial burden that would have allowed her to live among people like her parents, a life in which she would not have *had* to work, certainly not at an inn, as she does throughout the series (first at the aptly named Independence, then at the Dragonfly).

Although the three generations of Gilmores rarely share the same professional goals and personal desires, Richard is the progenitor character who connects them all. Without him, there would be no Gilmore girls. The series' first four seasons have Gran (Richard's mother) to remind us that Emily was not the first of the strong-willed Gilmore women. But Richard is positioned as the Gilmores' "Adam," the man against whom every potential Gilmore spouse must be measured. During Seasons Five and Six there are moments—Emily kicking Richard out of the house; Emily trying to buy an airplane—when Lorelai's mother seems to embrace the independence made available to her daughter's generation by the feminist movement. But her emotional breakdown during Richard's hospitalization in Season Seven reassures us that Emily remains wedded to her traditional brand of femininity and the type of man it necessitates she desire. And so Richard remains the reference point—at least from Emily's perspective—for what a man should be, for what the Gilmore girls seek in men. A product of the gender expectations of his generation and the men who preceded him, Richard has been married to Emily—whom he began dating in college—for forty years as of the fifth season, enabling us to deduce that he was probably born during World War II. The Gilmore patriarch came of age, then, during the 1950s, when men were expected to be stoic breadwinners dressed in gray flannel suits and whose wives would coordinate the other details of their lives—children, meals, home decorating, clothing, parties, gifts. Rarely taking a break from work, Richard typifies this type of man, with an aristocratic twist. As Emily reminds Lorelai during Season Seven, Richard provides for his family financially but needs someone to manage life's other details. While the Gilmore patriarch would "get his hair cut at the butcher's" if his wife would let him (as she explains in "I'd Rather Be in Philadelphia" [7.13]), Emily's characterization of Richard as helpless seems to be grounded in her imagination, her own desire to be needed, as much as the generation that spawned him.

Given the extent of *Gilmore Girls*' cultural reach—ranging from message-board discussions about whom Lorelai and Rory should end up with to the show's frequent references to both pop and high culture—this examination of the series' depiction of gender roles is necessarily concerned with the extent to which popular culture informs "real-life" conceptions of masculinity and femininity, as well as the degree to which mainstream culture informs media representations of men and women. In a media-saturated culture heavily influenced by what we see on television and in the pages of *Us Weekly* and *People,* such an investigation should help us gauge how far men and women have come since World War II and how far we must go before fulfilling the promises of the feminist and postfeminist movements of the twentieth and twenty-first centuries.

For Love or Money: Crisis and Conflict for Lorelai's Suitors

Born in the late 1960s, the staunchly defiant Lorelai represents the first generation of Gilmore women who does not intend for her life to revolve around a man. Seemingly produced by Second Wave feminism, she gave birth during the 1980s when single motherhood and deadbeat dads were subject to intense political criticism, coming to a head in the 1992 "Murphy Brown"–Dan Quayle debate. Lorelai's suitors, then, are dealt the challenge of dating a single mother who juggles family and career between requisite coffee breaks. Given the progression of Lorelai's relationships over the show's seven seasons, it is not coincidental that her first significant relationship is with Max, who, without a violent or competitive bone in him, is the least stereotypically "masculine" of the series' men. Then again, it takes someone unconcerned with proving his manhood to teach literature, particularly at Chilton, a school that caters to rich families, most of which share traditional understandings of gender roles. It also takes someone more focused on nurturing than on being the breadwinner. For a single mother like Lorelai, Max's concern for his students is quite attractive. It helps that Max cares about Rory in particular, going so far as to convince the school's headmaster to allow to her do extra-credit work after a deer runs into her mother's Jeep on the way to school, causing her to miss a test.

When Lorelai breaks off her engagement with Max just days before their wedding, the bride-to-have-been cryptically tells her best friend, Sookie, "It's a long story. I don't really wanna go into all the whats and whys and gory details right now. . . . To figure out exactly what happened, you'd have to dig up Freud himself and have him work on me full-time" ("The Road Trip to Harvard" [2.04]). Lorelai's Freud reference is telling. No matter how much he tries to dissociate himself from Chilton's rigidity and elitism, Max, who is typically clad in a suit, button-down shirt, and tie, bears a striking likeness to Lorelai's father. By aligning himself with the school's headmaster (a friend of Lorelai's parents) and refusing to allow Rory to take a test for which she is late, Max becomes associated with the rigidity of the elder Gilmores and Chilton, or what Lorelai, in "The Deer Hunters" (1.04), calls a "rotten, stodgy rat hole." As Max tells Lorelai in the subsequent episode, "I was doing my job when I didn't let Rory take that test. I didn't like it, but I had to do it. . . . And I'd do it again" ("Cinnamon's Wake").

Like Richard, Max is something of a stickler, too capable—at least for Lorelai's taste—of separating his professional life from his personal life, as he does when he and Lorelai (by then his ex-fiancée) serve on a PTA committee together.

Further complicating matters is the fact that Max, like Rory, shares Richard's love of books. When Lorelai suggests that they let their relationship simmer, Max convinces her otherwise by loaning her the Marcel Proust classic *Swann's Way* (1913). But Lorelai, despite having the wits to run a successful business and having been the smartest girl in her class before dropping out of school, is intimidated. Although Max respects Lorelai's intelligence, the show's ongoing dialogue about this unread copy of Proust's nearly impenetrable novel suggests that she cannot be with someone so erudite. As Rory says in "Paris Is Burning" (1.11), "You know what it means when a man loans you a book, don't you?" Lorelai's response: "That he's already read it?" to which Rory replies, "Yep." If Lorelai's failure to get past the first page is any indication, she seems unsettled by Max's intelligence, as if he and Proust are reminders of the person she might have been had she not gotten pregnant at sixteen. Lorelai does not take instruction well, and marrying a teacher might compromise her identity, which revolves around independence, assertiveness, and an ability to overcome seemingly insurmountable odds.

That Lorelai never introduces her parents to Max and does not tell them about their engagement suggests this charming man is something to hide. Max, despite teaching at an elite private school, does not earn as much as the people whose children (or, in the Gilmores' case, grandchildren) he teaches. In some respects, he is their servant, working to secure their futures, preserve their legacies. Max is, in other words, the type of man who is capable of caring deeply about Lorelai and Rory but cannot necessarily provide for them, financially or physically (if the fact that we never see him working with his hands is any indication). Situated somewhere between Luke, with his flannel work shirts and toolbox, and Richard, with his expensive suits and lucrative insurance business, Max simply is not "man enough" for Lorelai.

Given these paradoxical intimations that Lorelai needs someone both a little *more* and a little *less* reminiscent of her father, it seems fitting that Jason, Lorelai's next boyfriend, who appears in several episodes, comes "from [her] world," and is thus a reminder of the life she fled when she moved to Stars Hollow. Viewers unversed in the Gilmores' ways might suspect that Lorelai dates Jason to appease her parents, but in fact she begins dating Richard's business rival–turned-partner to spite Emily, who has never been a fan of Jason and is suspicious of his sudden desire to go into business with her husband. More than mere "mom issues" dictate Lorelai's decision, for it is Jason's ability to keep pace with her witty retorts that gets the pair past their first date. As Jason replies when Lorelai asks why he is buying Sno Balls: "You wouldn't be curious about pink marshmallow coconut balls? Who makes these? How did the decision to dye the coconut pink occur? Why are they shaped like a chest? Is there any dessert on the face of the planet that could stimulate this much debate?" ("Ted Koppel's Big Night Out" [4.09]). It also helps that Jason has a posh but comfortable townhouse, makes Lorelai breakfast, and is a walking book of compliments—all but the latter being powerful enough to seduce Lorelai, a rebel who lives to mock rich people and their neuroses.

Initially, Lorelai is charmed by Jason's knack for manipulation, which enables her to get her way even more than usual. But although Jason might appear to be a gentleman, a fierce competitiveness underlies his negotiating abilities, as we see in his desire to "piss off" his father by going into business with Richard ("The Hobbit, the Sofa, and Digger Stiles" [4.03]), as well as his eventual decision to sue Richard despite his relationship with Lorelai. With his subtle and physically nonviolent *American Psycho* streak, Jason is reminiscent of the 1980s stockbroker who is driven by profit and material possessions, by deals that enable him to accumulate more things. Money can be seductive, and it takes Jason's decision to sue Richard to make Lorelai realize just how opposed their priorities are. The clues to their incompatibility had been there all along, of course: though cordial to Rory, Jason shows no interest in getting to know her. And why should he? He has neither the time nor the emotional capacity to be a father, much less "do funerals," not even Lorelai's grandmother's ("The Reigning Lorelai" [4.16]).

Given that the Bangles-loving Lorelai is a child and mother of the 1980s, it seems appropriate that Christopher, with whom Lorelai shares unresolved feelings throughout the show's first six seasons, resembles one of that decade's male prototypes: the deadbeat dad. Though willing to marry Lorelai after getting her pregnant, Chris all but disappears from her and Rory's lives, popping in and out at his convenience. Not only does he miss Rory's high school graduation (not to mention her valedictory speech), Chris, as Luke reminds him at the elder Gilmores' vow renewal in "Wedding Bell Blues" (5.13), was not there when Rory had the chicken pox. In fact, Chris did not visit Stars Hollow until after his daughter had turned sixteen. Initially immature and prone to flight, Christopher lacks Richard's stability. Until he receives a sizable inheritance during Rory's junior year of college (Season Six), Chris never supports his first child financially, though he can afford a new Volvo as early as Season Two ("Presenting Lorelai Gilmore" [2.06]).

Christopher's choice to buy himself toys before financially supporting Rory reflects not merely his selfishness but also his deficiencies as a caretaker and provider. This fact becomes increasingly evident after Chris's wife, Sherry, leaves him and their daughter, Gigi. Christopher can barely care for the toddler, relying on nannies and—after they quit out of frustration—Lorelai to do most of the work. And if Christopher's lack of parenting skills were not enough, he does not seem particularly handy, at least until Season Seven, when his character was modified in the wake of the Palladinos' departure. Though Chris is suddenly handy under David Rosenthal's reign, he reveals this quality only when it suits him. Why else would he put up a plasma-screen TV in Lorelai's house, *their* house, to "watch Reggie Bush score touchdowns"? Lorelai, we know from her ironic response ("Which one of the Bush twins is that?") and her lack of interest in or knowledge of contemporary television technology, does not care ("To Whom It May Concern" [7.12]).

There are moments when Chris's shortcomings cannot keep Lorelai from finding him attractive, but they are mere reminders of the past or insinuations that her former boyfriend is getting his life in order, becoming someone other than the boy she loved as a teenager. Rory puts it best when she warns her father against reuniting with Lorelai: "You'll mess everything up! Because every time you come back, it always ends up the same way. Mom's crying and you're not . . . there" ("Norman Mailer, I'm Pregnant!" [5.06]). Although Christopher usually tries to right his wrongs, his need to prove himself to Lorelai and Rory is actually part of the problem. As Lorelai's relationship with Christopher transforms from a one-night stand during the last episode of Season Six (the final episode penned by the Palladinos) into impromptu marriage early in Season Seven (the first episodes written by Rosenthal), both characters act uncharacteristically needy and infuriating. But although the show's writers change and Rosenthal's apparent uncertainty over who these characters really are might be to blame, the way in which Christopher seduces Lorelai into marriage during a trip to Paris plays into the Palladinos' well-established narrative concerning the clash between generations and genders: Lorelai's "old world," as personified by Christopher, seduces her with a fantasy world rich with the perks of the elder Gilmores' lives but lacking the stodginess, rules, and incessant bickering. As Chris tells Lorelai in "French Twist" (7.07), something has changed since they first planned to visit Paris together in high school: "This time I'm loaded."

Indeed, it seems that money has bought Lorelai's happiness and made her forget about Chris's immaturity. Why else would she say, "I love you," for the first time in the series as they look out on the Eiffel Tower from a restaurant that Chris has paid to open at five in the morning? Though Christopher says their union has been twenty-five years in the making, their marriage signals the arrival of a "new Christopher," one who is suddenly more romantic than the old one, thanks to his inheritance. That we are led to believe that Paris and wealth have effectively wooed Lorelai—someone who has never really acted impulsively when getting into a relationship (*getting out* is another story, however)—suggests that she associates Christopher with her parents' tendency to buy people off.

And rightly so. Just one episode earlier ("Go, Bulldogs!" [7.06]), Christopher—trying to make up for missing out on his firstborn's childhood—takes Rory and her *Yale Daily News* staff to an expensive French restaurant and gets them drunk. Add to this scene the subsequent Paris dinner with five waiters tending to the couple's every need, and Chris's inclination toward overcompensation for his failed manhood becomes apparent. Illuminating the untenable nature of this deception of both himself and others, Chris feels threatened by Luke once the newlyweds return to Stars Hollow to start their life together. We see it when Luke introduces Lorelai to his newborn niece and when Chris discovers Lorelai's character reference for her former fiancé. Instead of reassuring his new wife with sweet talk and expensive meals, Chris attempts to reassert his manhood with physical power, by attempting to beat up Luke. He then performs the old deadbeat-dad, passive-aggressive disappearing act when Richard is hospitalized. In the process, Chris proves that his money was a red herring, that he remains irresponsible, unstable, unreliable, and self-centered, and thus, he can be nothing more than a "wonderful possibility," the one Lorelai "want[s] to want" ("Farewell, My Pet" [7.14]).

After seeing the Christopher fantasy in her own home, its mystique cleared away, Lorelai realizes that she must compromise to hook a man with her father's stability, maturity, stoicism, and business smarts, as well as her fierce sense of loyalty and parenting skills. That man is, of course, Luke, the diner owner to whom Lorelai is engaged before her reunion with Christopher and with whom she is again romantically linked when the series ends. Like his nephew and Rory's second boyfriend, Jess, Luke tends to be stoic and resists discussing his problems, even after learning that he has a twelve-year-old daughter. When his manhood is wounded and in need of resurrection, Luke fights, as he does when he drives from Connecticut to Boston to punch Christopher after learning that he slept with Lorelai the night she broke off their engagement. Lorelai, whose other suitors—Chris excepted—rarely flex their muscles, accepts

Luke's insecurities, partly because he is not likely to get into another fight once he wins her for good, and partly because the diner owner's inclination toward fighting reveals his fatherly side. (He offers to protect Rory by beating up her suitors.) Mostly, though, Lorelai accepts Luke's occasional masculinity crisis because he allows her to be herself. We see it in Luke's reaction to Miss Patty and Babette's speculation that Lorelai has humiliated Luke by proposing to him and usurping his manly "responsibility" ("The New and Improved Lorelai" [6.01]). Unfazed by their reaction, Luke likes that Lorelai has taken the lead, doing what he had not yet gotten up the nerve to do. As Lorelai tells Sookie after she proposes, "I saw this guy in front of me who was a *real man*. He was solid, and he was strong. He would protect me, but he *got me*. I knew all these things when we started dating, but in that moment when I realized how much he cared for Rory . . . all of a sudden I was ready."

All of a sudden, as if viewers had not yet realized it, after seeing Luke frequently appear on Lorelai's doorstep with his toolbox or watching him accompany her to the hospital when Richard got sick during the series' first season. We could mark it up to chemistry, but Lorelai and Max had sparks, too, as did Lorelai and Chris when the Palladinos were writing their dialogue and pairing them up only at the most inopportune times.

What is it, then, that makes Luke—a curmudgeon who is painfully predictable and less gregarious than Lorelai—"the one"? Lorelai can count on him to show up, whether for a date or a family illness or an awkward Friday-night dinner–turn-interrogation with Lorelai's parents. He is a caretaker who cooks and can fix anything. If it were the 1950s, he might be accused of having a gender identity disorder. But it proves to be perfect for Lorelai, who can cook little more than Pop-Tarts and wants an equal for a partner, someone who will listen to her and be there for Rory, someone she does not associate with the privileges of her parents' world. At the same time, Luke's appeal for Lorelai stems from his need to be reined in and her ability—and desire—to take on this "project," this man whose worldliness, wardrobe, and liveliness could stand some improvements. In this sense,

Luke is someone around whom Lorelai will always be the more colorful, dynamic, and vivacious character.

Their pairing is also aided by Luke's and Lorelai's mutual refusals to be forced into anyone's mold. Like Lorelai (at least once she has opened her own inn), he has money, but lives modestly and mocks ostentatious rich folk, around whom his discomfort is palpable. Luke has business smarts and, as sarcastic and curmudgeonly as he seems, is down to earth and family oriented. In this sense, Luke is Lorelai's match. He embodies what might be the least-disdained, most entrenched aspects of traditional masculinity: physical strength, handiness, a rugged appearance. Yet these characteristics are modified in light of the emergence of Second Wave feminism, giving way to a respect for women, a willingness to let them take the lead, and an eagerness to take responsibility for child care and cooking. He embodies a compromise between an "emasculated" subject and the strength (of body, mind, and character) associated with Richard's generation. And, lest we forget, *compromise,* as Emily tells Lorelai when her marriage to Christopher shows signs of trouble, is what one does to make a marriage work ("Merry Fisticuffs" [7.10]).

"I'm So Tired of Fighting": Rory's Suitors Strike Back

Perhaps it is reasonable that Emily and Richard seem preoccupied with Rory, who was born in 1984 and comes of age with the rise of Third Wave feminism. Although Rory, like her grandmother before her, becomes a member of the Daughters of the American Revolution (DAR), she has yet to mention a desire to bear children and continue the Gilmore legacy. Instead, she talks of becoming a journalist, the next Christiane Amanpour.

In *Gilmore Girls*' earliest episodes, Rory gets to know both Dean (her first boyfriend) and Richard, the grandfather she barely knew throughout her first sixteen years thanks to Lorelai's estrangement from her parents. Both men win over Rory with the aid of literature, Richard calling to say that he has found an H. L. Mencken book she wants (in "Kill Me Now" [1.03]) and Dean asking about *Moby*

Dick and mentioning that he saw Rory reading *Madame Bovary*. But it immediately becomes apparent that the Chicago-born Dean, a Stars Hollow newcomer who likes indie rocker Liz Phair and old flicks like *Rosemary's Baby* (1968), is not driven by intellectual pursuits like Rory and Richard are. When Rory, in the pilot episode, says that she is enjoying *Moby Dick* and that it is her "first Melville," Dean responds succinctly: "Cool." No discussion of the novel's plot or symbolism or the author's writing style ensues. In fact, Dean does not really read; he just happens to notice what Rory peruses. But because being attentive, loyal, and respectful counts for plenty in most relationships (and because many would say that men do not notice the little details in women's lives, such as new hairstyles, the books they are reading, and the clothes they are wearing), Dean's chivalry keeps Rory happy for most of the couple's first two go-rounds. After all, she is accustomed to being put on a pedestal, to being the best. By enabling this trend's continuation, Dean is an obvious first love. It certainly does not hurt that, as a polite boy whom Donna Reed would have loved seeing her daughter bring home, Dean neither judges nor interferes with Lorelai and Rory's close, unconventional relationship. Instead, he sits silently as they eat junk food while talking through movies.

Later, in "Tick, Tick, Tick, Boom!" (4.18), when Dean, eighteen and married, drops out of college so that he can work another job and buy his wife, Lindsay, a condominium, Rory second-guesses his behavior: he had such promise, she tells her best friend, Lane, and Lindsay is making him throw it away. But Dean's potential has always been hindered by his role as Rory's "yes-man." Even after dating and marrying Lindsay, Dean has not changed from the guy Rory rejected for Jess a year earlier. After entering the series with an air of urbanity, Dean seems remarkable only in his ability to remain mundane in the presence of Rory and Stars Hollow's other denizens. Like a working-class man of the 1950s and 1960s who relies on his hands and raw strength rather than his brains to earn income, Dean works at Doose's Market, builds a car for Rory, and later works on a construction team, helping to build Lorelai's Dragonfly Inn. But unlike many working-class people who find outlets in books, music, social networking, or political organizing, Dean has only Rory. That this point is problematic becomes evident in "The Party's Over," when Rory asks for his opinion of an article she wrote for the *Yale Daily News:*

> DEAN: I like everything you write.
> RORY: Do you think I painted the picture interestingly enough? Because I tried to be objective, to a certain extent, but it is a feature piece, so I wanted to have some human spark, you know?
> DEAN: I thought it was good.
> RORY: Nothing specific, though?
> DEAN: Hey, you're the writer. I can't critique these things. I just read it, and I was interested.

Dean, as this exchange reveals, is not the man for the Yale-educated Rory who, as it turns out, yearns for something more than a cheerleader and a handyman. As Rory tells Headmaster Charleston in "The Lorelais' First Day at Chilton" (1.02), she wants to be like CNN's Christiane Amanpour so she can "travel . . . see the world up close, report on what's really going on, be a part of something big." In this statement, our first glimpse at what Rory wants, it becomes evident that Lorelai's daughter seeks a life that will take her places far beyond the somewhat sequestered world of Stars Hollow, a life with someone who, like her grandfather, travels for business and pleasure. Although Rory imparts this information during the series' second episode, it takes five seasons—and seeing Rory, clad in a tiara and diamonds, with her soon-to-be beau Logan and his wealthy friends—before Dean begins to understand. Recognizing the similarities between Lorelai and Rory and their relationships with Stars Hollow men, Dean, after he walks away from Rory for good, tells Luke, "They want more than this. Don't you see that? This town, it's all you are, and it's not enough. She's going to get bored, and you can't take her anywhere. You're here forever" ("To Live and Let Diorama" [5.18]).

When *Gilmore* fans compare Dean and Jess, Rory's first and second loves are typically cast as opposites: Dean is the chivalrous "good boyfriend," while Jess is the "bad boy" not just from another place but from another time. With his leather biker jacket, dark hair, close-fitting shirts, and a temper that flares up any time he sees Dean, Jess has more Stanley Kowalski or Jim Stark in him than anyone in Stars Hollow before or since. But Jess is more a product of the 1960s than the 1950s. He comes from New York City, hangs out in Washington Square Park, proclaims himself to be as cool as "Frank at the Sands," and annotates Rory's copy of Allen Ginsberg's *Howl.* More stoic and secretive than Dean, Jess epitomizes the 1960s rebel who relies on his relationships, and competition, with other men to assert his manhood. In Season Two, Jess reveals his cultural literacy, remarking, in "The Ins and Outs of Inns" (2.08), "You actually went to that bizarro town meeting? Those things are so *To Kill a Mockingbird.*" He discusses Ayn Rand and Ernest Hemingway with Rory, and in doing so proves to be something of a 1960s response to men like Richard: an intellectual and rebel who, at the age of eighteen, shows no interest in living in a small town, much less settling down.

Contrary to the WB's previews and the message-board debates over whether Rory should be with Dean or Jess, her first two boyfriends share more than a desire for the youngest Gilmore. In keeping with traditional notions of masculinity, both reveal a machismo streak at times. From his first meeting with Jess, Dean feels threatened—and justifiably so: Rory is falling for Luke's nephew. To reassert his control over Rory, Dean erupts into yelling fits, if not physical violence, whenever he so much as hears Jess's name. Even when Dean has moved on to Lindsay and Rory is with Jess, Dean feels the need to prove his manliness and protect his ex-girlfriend. In this sense, Dean's chivalry revolves around the woman's honor; he can be kind and gentle or, conversely, brutally violent. That he can be so aggressive attests to a larger crisis in masculinity that is unique to the contemporary moment, to the postmodern milieu: if kindness and chivalry are not enough to win Rory's love, more testosterone must be the answer.

Not that Jess is any better. He has simply mastered his impersonation of the 1960s man, particularly the young Turks of the Beat generation who, like *On the Road*'s Dean and Sal (based on Neal Cassady and Jack Kerouac, respectively), struggled to maintain healthy emotional relationships with women. As Rory tells Lorelai once her relationship with Jess nears its end, "I'm so tired of fighting. Or not even fighting because he won't fight. He just gets mad and disappears and then comes back, and I don't like how I feel and I don't like what I do" ("Say Goodnight, Gracie" [3.20]). Despite outward appearances, Jess's own masculinity crisis is spurred less by Dean and more by a world of people who expect certain things of him—his mother, Luke, Lorelai, Rory, and even the principal at Stars Hollow High, where he is flunking out. By threatening to restrain Jess, to keep him from being the person he wants to be, these men and women cause him to raise his voice, fight, deceive, and disappear. His crisis speaks to the larger cultural constraints of the first decade of the twenty-first century, to the fact that contemporary American life can be characterized by a *lack* of freedom and openness—the very things extolled in the Beat poetry and fiction of the 1960s.

A combination of age, success, freedom, and self-confidence enables Jess to redeem himself when, during the show's sixth season, he returns to remind Rory of her potential and "save" her from the mess she is making of her life by dropping out of Yale and working for the DAR. When Jess shows Rory the novel he has written (in "Let Me Hear Your Balalaikas Ringing Out" [6.08]), he appears, for the first time, to be content and in control of his life. That we can say the same for Dean after he finally abandons a diamond-clad Rory in the aforementioned "The Party's Over" suggests something peculiarly unpostmodern: there *can* be closure to men's stories, or at least a marking off of a "before" and "after" in their life journeys; they *can* move on to new phases of their lives, to more progressive ways of articulating their masculinity.

Then there are men like Marty, who, if Season Seven is any indication, never move on. Marty is Rory's study buddy, the first male friend she makes in college. He is taciturn and appears to be a wallflower, standing alone at a dormwide party. Marty appreciates the trustworthiness Rory exudes when she finds him passed out in the hall naked, gives him her robe, and promises not to tell anyone about the embarrassing incident. But in mistaking her kindness for romantic interest, Marty reveals his naïveté. Still, by bringing Rory leftovers from the fancy parties he works, by studying and watching movies with her, Marty is, during the fourth and fifth seasons, the guy who seems destined to become her next beau. Yet like Dean, Marty pales in the presence of someone more exotic, more daring, more flippant. When Rory finally rejects Marty's advances, she rebuffs a man with her grandfather's disposition but without his worldliness and self-assuredness.

Marty, despite taking Rory's rejection more gracefully than Dean, seems to become neither wiser nor more mature for it. Sure, Marty, as (re)written by David Rosenthal in Season Seven, styles his hair better and wears hip clothes. But Rory's old friend remains socially stunted, pretending not to know her when they find themselves in the same room among mutual friends ("French Twist"). By ignoring Rory, Marty—in a manner reminiscent of the old Dean and Jess—tries to preserve his masculinity, to protect himself as well as Lucy (his girlfriend and Rory's new pal whom he has neglected to inform of his friendship with Rory). Underscoring his image as the wounded man trying to salvage his manhood, Marty apparently came to be with Lucy by stalking her, attending her theater performances night after night. In this sense, Marty is Dean's brainy, passive-aggressive alter ego, something of a 1990s man—a bit old-fashioned and considerate, until his ego is crushed. Perhaps this facet, along with the fact that Wayne Wilcox (the actor who played Marty) was not available for many episodes at the time, while Matt Czuchry (who played Logan) was, helps explain why Rory rejects Marty after her breakup with Dean. More important, though, she has had enough of this kind of guy and needs to move on to someone different.

Rory's choice—Logan, who becomes her on-again, off-again beau until the series' penultimate episode—is at first perplexing. When the attraction begins, the wealthy Logan spends his weekends jumping off hundred-foot platforms with the elitist Life and Death Brigade. He rarely works and presumably got into Yale thanks to his father's money and legacy. A "player" who relies on his good looks and charm to get girls, Logan—at least in his first two seasons on the show—harks back ever so slightly to the 1960s rebel, the guy who asserts his masculinity through a lack of emotional attachment and his knack for wooing any girl he wants. But Logan is also a mix of the twenty-first-century metrosexual who puts considerable thought into his appearance and the trust-fund baby in need of motherly taming. What distinguishes him from Jess, the other guy Rory tries to rein in, is his unwavering confidence. Even when the couple fights, as they do when Rory writes an article criticizing the people at the launch party for Logan's Internet company, he remains poised. Yet unlike Dean, Marty, and Jess (when the latter was dating Rory), Logan will admit when he is wrong. Occasionally, he feels threatened by other men, as he does when, in "Merry Fisticuffs," he tells Lucy that Marty and Rory know each other and when Rory invites him to have dinner with her and Jess. But these moments become increasingly rare as their relationship progresses. True love instills people with trust, as we discover when Logan dismisses Rory's confession that she has a crush on her economics teaching assistant, admitting he has had crushes on other women, "of course," but does not act on them.

All of this talk of men changing, becoming more mature, begs a question: if both the older Jess and Logan exhibit confidence and an ability to, after some introspection and retrospection, admit their mistakes, why does Rory stick with Logan instead of opting for the new-and-improved Jess? It is, after all, Jess who helps Rory snap out of her DAR-induced coma by reminding her, "This isn't you! . . . You going out with this jerk, with the Porsche! We made fun of guys like this." There are a couple of easy answers: the actor who played Jess, Milo Ventimiglia, was preparing for roles in *The Bedford Diaries* (WB, 2006), *Heroes* (NBC, 2006–), and the big screen's *Rocky Balboa* (2006). Again, viewers are not invited to ponder such extratextual details influencing the *Gilmore Girls'* production and are lured to believe that Rory chose Logan for other reasons. Perhaps Rory resents Jess's judgment of her relationship with Logan, of his belittling her love life when he does not have a great record in that department. Perhaps she opts for a slightly more stable history, for someone she believes will make her happy.

For as odd a match as Rory and Logan initially appear to be, the couple eventually clicks because he is, for Rory, a balance of the old and the new. He offers financial security, but unlike her grandfather, Logan the romantic partner is not an economic anchor first and foremost. Logan is eager to help when Paris kicks Rory out of their apartment and when Richard has a heart attack. Logan likes that Rory is independent, determined, and talented, and—as suggested by the second-semester senior care package he sends her—he is her cheerleader. But unlike Dean, Logan has his own life, his own business dealings, his own mind. He is not exactly like Rory and does not pretend to be. Instead, the closer they become, the more he seems to complement her, not just emotionally but physically, if his wardrobe and appearance are any indication. And as complicated as Logan's brand of masculinity might be, it seems to facilitate the promises of feminism and postfeminism, women's independence, sexual freedom, and the end of a world in which men are expected to be breadwinners and women their homemakers. But, to Logan's detriment, this promise of freedom can also create a wanting for more of the same.

Logan, in the end, cannot rein in Rory and convince her to marry him. For this young man of privilege, happiness ultimately seems to be tied up in finding the perfect woman. But is the same true of the twenty-first-century woman he desires? As he tells a distraught Rory just days before he proposes, she will be happy soon ("Lorelai? Lorelai?" [7.20]). But does Rory's happiness—or any woman's happiness, for that matter—depend on a man alone? Logan may have changed enough to fall in love and convince Rory that he was worth committing to for the duration of college, but he could not change her mind enough to convince the aspiring journalist to settle down at twenty-two, to limit herself to San Francisco (where Logan, at the series' end, has landed a job) instead of entertaining the many job and travel opportunities sure to come her way. Perhaps what Rory needs or wants is a man not entirely unlike Logan, someone with his brains, good looks, financial stability, humor, and confidence, but with a willingness to put Rory's career first rather than making her feel like she must choose between marriage and career. What Rory needs is someone who does not see marriage and relationships as "all or nothing," as she tells Logan during their parting (in "Unto the Breach" [7.21]). Unlike Emily, who sees Logan's proposal as "an opportunity" that "doesn't come along very often," Rory does not consider marriage her main goal in life, at least not at this juncture. She needs someone who will allow her to continue to grow, to discover herself, to navigate what to many young feminists seems to be the tension between marriage and career. It seems that she needs someone like her arch nemesis–turned–college friend Paris's beau, Doyle, who—after Paris broke up with him to ensure he would not sway her decision about where to attend law school or medical school—taught the two young women that one need not choose between love and career, so long as the man is willing to sacrifice *his* career.

"Lost and Found"

Regardless of how many years have elapsed since *Gilmore Girls* ended its celebrated run in the spring of 2007, the show will remain an important cultural artifact, one that will tell us much about twenty-first-century gender expectations. As an indicator that American cultural attitudes have changed in both radical and subtle ways since the 1950s, and have embraced the idea of the independent woman, *Gilmore Girls*—despite featuring a single mother who got pregnant at sixteen—has been widely hailed as a noteworthy show by the Family Friendly Programming Forum, which funded the pilot episode, and ABC Family, which continues to air the show in syndication.

With Rory choosing career and freedom over marriage at the show's conclusion, it is also apparent that Rosenthal, like the Palladinos, recognized that neither *Gilmore Girls* nor the "real-world" fans of the program (in particular, Rory's Generation Y contemporaries) quite correspond to the values put forth in a Victorian novel. Although some college women marry upon graduation, many others are less certain about whether they want a husband or children or both. This realization owes a debt of gratitude to Lorelai's Generation X, which brought forth not just the working woman's joys (being able to decide how money gets spent, feelings of self-worth and empowerment) but also the inevitable challenges of romantic partnerships and the compromises that such relationships may require.

Yet, at the same time, both Lorelai's and Rory's desires for progress, the right to choose career over family and the option to propose marriage, bespeak a degree of nostalgia for the men of old, for brands of masculinity that predate the twenty-first century. Is it any wonder, then, that so many of the *Gilmore* men, like our real-life suitors who try to adapt to our preferences in this Darwinian ritual we call dating (and, for some, mating), seem to find themselves in the midst of a masculinity crisis?

Coda

Postnetwork Television and Netflix's *Gilmore Girls: A Year in the Life*

HYE SEUNG CHUNG AND DAVID SCOTT DIFFRIENT

On November 25, 2016, nine years after the final episode of *Gilmore Girls* (2000–2007) aired on the CW, Netflix revived the series as a four-episode online miniseries titled *Gilmore Girls: A Year in the Life.* Although the DVD-by-mail and video-on-demand (VOD) giant, which currently has nearly 100 million worldwide subscribers, had already resuscitated several canceled network and cable shows, including *Arrested Development* (Fox, 2003–6), *The Killing* (AMC, 2011–13), and *Longmire* (A&E, 2012–14), its relaunch of *Gilmore Girls* was a media event of a different sort. Netflix's release was particularly well-timed, as it had started streaming all seven seasons of *Gilmore Girls* in October 2014, rekindling the show's cult fandom and recruiting a new legion of viewers who had missed the series during its original broadcast. Eight months later, on June 6, 2015, the fourth annual ATX Television Festival in Austin featured a closing-night reunion panel in which series creator Amy Sherman-Palladino was joined by several cast members, including the two lead stars, Lauren Graham and Alexis Bledel. Scott Patterson, the actor who plays Luke, praised the event, reporting that "fans were lined up around that venue all day in 100-degree heat. ATX really drove it home to all parties involved that [the revival] could work" (Stanhope 2016a). To borrow the words of one critic, when Netflix green-lighted the project after months of speculation and ordered new episodes of *Gilmore*

Girls (then tentatively titled *Gilmore Girls: Seasons*) in October 2015, "the internet—to put it lightly—lost its mind" (Yahr 2017).

The reaction was particularly enthusiastic because many fans were still recalling their disappointment upon completing the show's final season, which had been produced without the creative input of show runner Amy Sherman-Palladino and executive producer Dan Palladino after a contract dispute with Warner Bros. For this power couple, Netflix looked to be a perfect outlet to relaunch their project, as its subscription-based revenue model—in contrast to network TV's traditional reliance on commercial advertising—allowed greater creative freedom for producers of original content. The husband-wife team could serve as the sole writers, directors, and executive producers for Netflix's four, roughly 90-minute installments, bearing the seasonal titles "Winter," "Spring," "Summer," and "Fall" (a nod to the lyrics of Carole King's 1971 song "You've Got a Friend"). This meant that Sherman-Palladino would get the much-anticipated dream ending that she always intended for the show's original final episode—a cliff-hanger that reveals Rory's out-of-wedlock pregnancy, symmetrically repeating Lorelai's path of single motherhood. She was initially resistant to Netflix's instant release of the entire miniseries because she was worried that some viewers might skip to the ending and spoil it before other binge-watchers had made it to the final scene. The show runner ultimately endorsed the new media platform, stating that "the good outweighs the bad in the sense that it is a wonderful place to be able to create things and do things in a different way." Dan Palladino echoed his wife's sentiment when he said that "I don't think we would have wanted to bring back anything that resumed the traditional series. Netflix was really open to a new format" (Stanhope 2016a).

Televisual Reformatting and the "Netflix Effect"

Three months prior to Netflix's November 2016 release of *Gilmore Girls: A Year in the Life*, Kevin McDonald and Daniel Smith-Rowsey edited a collection of academic essays concerning the online content provider and producer. *The Netflix Effect: Technology and*

Entertainment in the 21st Century casts a wide net over this recent trend in media convergence, covering a range of topics—from the website's data collection techniques and the "algorithmic logic of predictive personalization" to individual case studies such as *Orange Is the New Black* (2013–) that reveal Netflix's brand-making, risk-taking approach to adult subject matter. In their introduction to this volume, McDonald and Smith-Rowsey define what they and other commentators refer to as the "Netflix effect" (2016, 1–13). Put simply, this expression denotes the online video store-turned-streaming service's disruptive and "creatively destructive" impact on a constantly evolving media industry, one in which companies that once relied on traditional transactional encounters between producers, vendors, audiences, and advertisers (e.g., video tape/disc rental company Blockbuster and premium pay cable channel HBO) have, as the economist Mark Perry points out, either been driven to extinction or been forced to adapt to significant changes in audiences' consumption patterns (Perry 2015).

That "effect" gives Netflix the ability to alter its own business model rapidly and to challenge outdated notions of distribution and exhibition in a volatile marketplace where "virtual" content is quickly replacing material culture (DVDs, Blu-rays, etc.). It has achieved those two goals through a user-friendly approach that ostensibly puts power into the hands of American consumers, many of whom in recent years have chosen *not* to watch broadcast television and/or currently reside in households without a cable TV subscription (Lindsey 2016, 173). However, as Sarah Arnold reminds us, Netflix's user-friendly interface "maintains the perception of choice but also directs the viewer toward content more likely to keep them engaged and subscribed" (2016, 51). By broadening consumer choices (either in truth or in appearance) and by providing access to individuated or tailored programming for subscribers, Netflix is indeed influencing how its chief competitors in the field of streaming entertainment (including Hulu and Amazon) adapt to an increasingly atomized, microsegmented yet conglomerate-controlled media environment. One way that Netflix, Amazon, and Hulu are doing so is by expanding their focus beyond being content *providers* to become content *producers*.

By the time that *Gilmore Girls: A Year in the Life* debuted on the online streaming service in November 2016, Netflix, under the forward-thinking leadership of CEO Reed Hastings and chief content officer Ted Sarandos, had increased its production of original programs from one (*House of Cards*) in February 2013 to over 100. As Sherman-Palladino states in an interview with *The Hollywood Reporter* around the time of her program's release, "There was no Netflix for years and years and years. Without a Netflix, it wouldn't have happened. . . . So it was the right time, it was the right place . . . the right outlet to do something different . . . with our characters" (Stanhope 2016b). Although Netflix, launched in 1997, did exist during the show's original run on the WB (2000–2006) and the CW (2006–7), its recent shift into the role of content producer did not happen until three years prior to the streaming release of new *Gilmore Girls* episodes. The original series was rerun on ABC Family (now FreeForm) after its original broadcasting, but Netflix's revival helped to rebrand and reformat the show as an edgy example of "quality TV" (rather than middlebrow family fare), one that was designed to be consumed in longer programming blocks (88–120 minutes rather than 42–44 minutes).

As Mareike Jenner states in her article "Is This TVIV? On Netflix, TVIII and Binge-Watching," the online platform, "often hyped as a 'new HBO' . . . actually offers a different kind of TV revolution than previously associated with the premium cable channel: Netflix is simply not TV" (2016, 261). Like HBO, which promoted itself as "not being [ordinary] TV" but rather a premium producer of quality programs, Netflix differentiates its original programming from network and cable channel offerings by giving "creative and budgetary freedom to television auteurs like Mitch Hurwitz and Jenji Kohan" (ibid., 263), who are allowed "to develop riskier and more demanding shows" (Sim 2016, 188). In other words, Sherman-Palladino's *Gilmore Girls*, which on the surface is not a particularly "risky" undertaking (especially when compared to Netflix originals like *Narcos* [2015–] and *Hot Girls Wanted: Turned On* [2017]), is a perfect fit for their new business model. In addition to enabling the "Netflixication" of quality TV (something equivalent to what the filmmaker Kevin Smith has called the "Miramaxization" of independent cinema of the 1990s), the streaming platform, which is not littered with linear television's commercial interruptions (Arnold 2016, 51) and is not structured around week-long waiting periods for episodic and serial installments, encourages a particular type of viewing—namely, binge-watching—which both results from and produces a particularly devoted form of fandom. *Gilmore Girls* certainly meets this criterion, as evidenced by fan tweets in reaction to Netflix's September 11, 2014, announcement of the entire show's streaming release (which debuted the following month). One fan tweeted, "*Gilmore Girls* on @Netflix??? Time to start using those vacation and personal/sick days! #gilmoregirls." Another tweet read, "Oh man, Netflix is going to have the entire run of *Gilmore Girls*? This isn't going to be good for my productivity. Or my hygiene. Or my life." Yet another fan tweeted, "I'm just preparing myself to fail out of college in October due to the fact that Netflix is getting *Gilmore Girls*. My life is made." Likewise, another Twitter user wrote, "*Gilmore Girls* is coming to Netflix. Please don't speak to me after October 1st, I'm v busy (indefinitely)" (Harris 2014). These short bursts of fannish discourse attest to the cult show's compatibility with the binge-watching mode, which Netflix's business model has helped to normalize. Defined as sustained engagement with a televisual text over several episodes viewed back to back, binge-watching has been likened to a form of spectatorial "addiction" that, if one is to take the above tweets seriously (and thus think of Netflix as a way to get one's "netfix"), apparently comes at the expense of professional productivity and one's social life.

The Netflix imprimatur, which promised the kind of creative autonomy and flexibility that Amy Sherman-Palladino and Dan Palladino found so conducive to their artistic aspirations, has also been a source for discontent among certain fans and cultural critics. For example, in her blog for *The Verge*, Kaitlyn Tiffany complains:

> Netflix has a reputation for giving its content creators complete freedom, so it's retroactively clear that the family-friendly constraints

> of *Gilmore Girls*' primetime network days actually helped the team rein in some gaudier impulses. Aesthetic restrictions may have made the Palladinos double down on wit and sparkle in their writing—something they all but abandoned in the revival. And while the original scripts could be a bit prudish, at least they weren't hostile and misogynistic in their dealings with sex (2016).

In particular, Tiffany faults the Netflix miniseries for being a "story about female ambition cut off at the knees" whose younger heroine is "a jobless person [living] off of a trust fund [with] a terrible, self-aggrandizing idea" of writing a memoir (ibid.). When the audience last saw Rory at the end of the original series finale, she was a recent Yale graduate who had just accepted an offer to follow then–Senator Barack Obama's presidential campaign as a fledgling political reporter. At the end of *Gilmore Girls: A Year in the Life*, 32-year-old Rory is without a job, has no spouse, and is virtually homeless. To make matters worse (or, at least, more interesting), she is pregnant with a baby whose father's identity remains undisclosed (although it is assumed to be Logan, her rich boyfriend-turned–occasional lover who is engaged to another woman). The blogger responds to these developments with cynicism, writing, "And of course the four-part movie ends on November 5, 2016, just before the election that gave us President-Elect Trump. It's a sparkly, sinister message-in-a-bottle from the final days before female ambition was excoriated on the grandest scale imaginable" (ibid.). Similarly, writing for the *New York Times*, Margaret Lyons shares an opinion with which many fans likely agree:

> There's one way to look at Rory's miserable flailing, which is to see it as a cautionary tale about raising an overly-indulged child, one who was always praised for her intelligence not her effort, and who has therefore never actually developed skills pertaining to hard work or diligence. But I doubt strongly that Amy Sherman-Palladino . . . views things that way—just look at how the show mocks the "30-something gang," even though presumably these are people Rory would have gone to school with for most of her life (2016).

It is understandable that fans might feel frustrated to see their beloved Rory, a smart overachiever with an Ivy League degree, fail miserably in terms of securing a steady and fulfilling professional career. However, some socially conscious viewers might find Netflix's nostalgia-filled but relatively more "realistic" Stars Hollow refreshing in its portrayal of the harsh realities of unemployment among millennials who are forced to move back with their parents in order to save money. As of 2016, the unemployment rate among millennials was 12.8 percent, more than twice that of the national average of 4.9 percent (Alton 2016). According to a Pew Research Center study, "In 2014, for the first time in more than 130 years, adults ages 18 to 34 were slightly more likely to be living in their parents' home [32.1 percent] than they were to be living with a spouse or partner in their own household [31.6 percent]" (Fry 2016). As a casualty of the economic recession and downsizing of the journalism market, Rory, like many of her millennial peers, temporarily moves back with her mother in the "Summer" episode. Audiences learn quickly that, during her absence, Stars Hollow gained a new fixture in town, the so-called "30-something gang," a group of "kids" whom Rory's next-door neighbor Babette introduces as being "all about your age." "They've been to college and then out in the real world," Babette says, before continuing, "It spit them out like a stale piece of gum and now they're all back in their old rooms. Like you."

In a blog for the college women's lifestyle website *Her Campus*, Sydnee Lyons defends Sherman-Palladino's 30-something joke, telling its detractors (who found the gang to be "an offensive and demeaning depiction of hardworking, debt-riddled college graduates"):

> This group does exist. They are not lazy or entitled, nor are they unrealistic or pathetic . . . They do spend hours tweaking their résumés, offering their professional services free of charge . . . They do not return home downtrodden . . . because they have, over the years, developed some irrational, inflated sense of self. I believe their goals are noble; their desires to contribute something great to the future of the world are less narcissistic than is often suggested . . . If

> we stray from the problematic case of Rory Gilmore . . . and think of more realistic Gang members—ourselves and friends and former school colleagues—I think we may find we relate more closely than we thought (2017).

Despite some fans' disappointment, one can argue that the narrative premise of *Gilmore Girls* matured and became more socially conscious in the show's Netflix reboot precisely because it refused to offer a fantasy solution to a serious problem like millennial unemployment. Lorelai's wedding aside, the miniseries' surprise ending, which concludes with two words most fans were *not* expecting to hear (Rory's "I'm pregnant"), is decisively downbeat compared to the Season Seven finale in which the whole town gathers to send the young woman off with a euphoric celebration of her professional success. This realistic progression is a hallmark of quality television, which rejects most traditional network programs' formulaic narratives, contrived resolutions, and obligatory happy endings.

In Memory of Edward Herrmann

In the aforementioned *Hollywood Reporter* interview, Amy Sherman-Palladino explains her authorial intent behind the new Netflix episodes, saying,

> We did go into it . . . with the purpose of, we want it to be for the fans, so there were certain things we had to honor for the fans . . . But we really wanted this to also be something that if you hadn't seen *Gilmore Girls* and you sat down to watch it, you were still going to be drawn in by the characters, what they're going through, the universal themes of where is my life, fork-in-the-road, three generations of women who lost the patriarch and what does that do to them? (Stanhope 2016b)

Notably, the offscreen death of Rory's grandfather, Richard Gilmore, who succumbed to a heart attack four months prior to the beginning of the "Winter" episode of the Netflix miniseries, is treated as a narrative device that serves both newcomers and devoted fans. On a diegetic level, Lorelai's inability to share a single inspiring or personally moving story about her dead father at the funeral, a painful scene presented in flashback, further strains her already rocky relationship with her mother, Emily, and intensifies the drama of witnessing a dysfunctional family melt down even more. Like the oversized portrait of Emily's late husband decorating her living room, the specter of Richard haunts and looms over all four episodes of *Gilmore Girls: A Year in the Life* as three generations of women cope with their bereavement and grief. On an extradiegetic level, the passing of actor Edward Herrmann, who died of brain cancer on December 31, 2014, adds poignancy to the plotline for fans and cast members.

In a way, the revival functioned as a curative form of group therapy for the creators and acting staff of *Gilmore Girls* by commemorating Herrmann's life and career through televisual storytelling. As Sherman-Palladino puts it, "Ed Herrmann's passing was very fresh in our minds and we were all pretty crushed by it and it felt like a way to honor him and what he meant to us" (Stanhope 2016b). Lauren Graham opines that the death of Richard/Herrmann made the show a more "grown up" version of its previous self by adding "depth and emotional complexity" and by portraying her character Lorelai's difficult road to recovery from that loss (Stanhope 2016a). Herrmann's television spouse Kelly Bishop, who plays Emily, even felt a kind of communion with the dead on the set of the Warner Bros. lot, stating, "I said, 'Ed was that you?' . . . I just feel like he's here. Besides the script and the way we all feel about him, the giant portrait is all calling him to come to the set" (Shaw 2016). Perhaps Scott Patterson sums it best when he muses in his *Entertainment Weekly* interview, "[Herrmann's death] left a big void, but Amy honored it beautifully. He's throughout . . . these stories. It's a wonderful homage to him as a person and to his character as well. It's nice to have him around" (ibid.).

Like the storyline about the 30-something gang and millennial unemployment, the mourning for Richard/Herrmann's passing is another indication that the Netflix miniseries casts a shadow over the perhaps "too-perfect" fictional world of Stars Hollow with references to the real world (where, to be blunt, bright young people are unemployed and sick old people die). Like a grown-up, disillusioned Rory, who faces the brutal reality of the job market (the only offers she gets are her high school principal's charity post and an unpaid editorial position for the town's rinky-dink newspaper), fans catch glimpses of the darker side of their favorite town and characters, demonstrating how far the show has come since it left the air in 2007 and was subsequently revived as a more mature, more bracing Netflix miniseries.

Appendix

Works Cited

Index

Appendix

Complete Episode List

Season One

1.01: "Pilot" (October 5, 2000)
1.02: "The Lorelais' First Day at Chilton" (October 12, 2000)
1.03: "Kill Me Now" (October 19, 2000)
1.04: "The Deer Hunters" (October 26, 2000)
1.05: "Cinnamon's Wake" (November 2, 2000)
1.06: "Rory's Birthday Parties" (November 9, 2000)
1.07: "Kiss and Tell" (November 16, 2000)
1.08: "Love and War and Snow" (December 14, 2000)
1.09: "Rory's Dance" (December 20, 2000)
1.10: "Forgiveness and Stuff" (December 21, 2000)
1.11: "Paris Is Burning" (January 11, 2001)
1.12: "Double Date" (January 18, 2001)
1.13: "Concert Interruptus" (February 15, 2001)
1.14: "That Damn Donna Reed" (February 22, 2001)
1.15: "Christopher Returns" (March 1, 2001)
1.16: "Star-Crossed Lovers and Other Strangers" (March 8, 2001)
1.17: "The Breakup: Part 2" (March 15, 2001)
1.18: "The Third Lorelai" (March 22, 2001)
1.19: "Emily in Wonderland" (April 26, 2001)
1.20: "P.S. I Lo . . ." (May 3, 2001)
1.21: "Love, Daisies, and Troubadours" (May 10, 2001)

Season Two

2.01: "Sadie, Sadie" (October 9, 2001)
2.02: "Hammers and Veils" (October 9, 2001)
2.03: "Red Light on the Wedding Night" (October 16, 2001)
2.04: "The Road Trip to Harvard" (October 23, 2001)
2.05: "Nick & Nora/Sid & Nancy" (October 30, 2001)
2.06: "Presenting Lorelai Gilmore" (November 6, 2001)
2.07: "Like Mother, Like Daughter" (November 13, 2001)
2.08: "The Ins and Outs of Inns" (November 20, 2001)
2.09: "Run Away, Little Boy" (November 27, 2001)
2.10: "The Bracebridge Dinner" (December 11, 2001)
2.11: "Secrets and Loans" (January 22, 2002)
2.12: "Richard in Stars Hollow" (January 29, 2002)
2.13: "A-Tisket, a-Tasket" (February 5, 2002)
2.14: "It Should've Been Lorelai" (February 12, 2002)
2.15: "Lost and Found" (February 26, 2002)
2.16: "There's the Rub" (April 9, 2002)
2.17: "Dead Uncles and Vegetables" (April 16, 2002)
2.18: "Back in the Saddle Again" (April 23, 2002)
2.19: "Teach Me Tonight" (April 30, 2002)
2.20: "Help Wanted" (May 7, 2002)
2.21: "Lorelai's Graduation Day" (May 14, 2002)
2.22: "I Can't Get Started" (May 21, 2002)

Season Three

3.01: "Those Lazy-Hazy-Crazy Days" (September 24, 2002)
3.02: "Haunted Leg" (October 1, 2002)
3.03: "Application Anxiety" (October 8, 2002)
3.04: "One's Got Class and the Other One Dyes" (October 15, 2002)
3.05: "Eight O'Clock at the Oasis" (October 22, 2002)
3.06: "Take the Deviled Eggs . . ." (November 5, 2002)
3.07: "They Shoot Gilmores, Don't They?" (November 12, 2002)

3.08: "Let the Games Begin" (November 19, 2002)
3.09: "A Deep-Fried Korean Thanksgiving" (November 26, 2002)
3.10: "That'll Do, Pig" (January 14, 2003)
3.11: "I Solemnly Swear" (January 21, 2003)
3.12: "Lorelai Out of Water" (January 28, 2003)
3.13: "Dear Emily and Richard" (February 4, 2003)
3.14: "Swan Song" (February 11, 2003)
3.15: "Face-Off" (February 18, 2003)
3.16: "The Big One" (February 25, 2003)
3.17: "A Tale of Poes and Fire" (April 15, 2003)
3.18: "Happy Birthday, Baby" (April 22, 2003)
3.19: "Keg! Max!" (April 29, 2003)
3.20: "Say Goodnight, Gracie" (May 6, 2003)
3.21: "Here Comes the Son" (May 13, 2003)
3.22: "Those Are Strings, Pinocchio" (May 20, 2003)

Season Four

4.01: "Ballrooms and Biscotti" (September 23, 2003)
4.02: "The Lorelais' First Day at Yale" (September 30, 2003)
4.03: "The Hobbit, the Sofa, and Digger Stiles" (October 7, 2003)
4.04: "Chicken or Beef?" (October 14, 2003)
4.05: "The Fundamental Things Apply" (October 21, 2003)
4.06: "An Affair to Remember" (October 28, 2003)
4.07: "The Festival of Living Art" (November 4, 2003)
4.08: "Die, Jerk" (November 11, 2003)
4.09: "Ted Koppel's Big Night Out" (November 18, 2003)
4.10: "The Nanny and the Professor" (January 20, 2004)
4.11: "In the Clamor and the Clangor" (January 27, 2004)
4.12: "A Family Matter" (February 3, 2004)
4.13: "Nag Hammadi Is Where They Found the Gnostic Gospels" (February 10, 2004)
4.14: "The Incredible Shrinking Lorelais" (February 17, 2004)
4.15: "Scene in a Mall" (February 24, 2004)
4.16: "The Reigning Lorelai" (March 2, 2004)

4.17: "Girls in Bikinis, Boys Doin' the Twist" (April 13, 2004)
4.18: "Tick, Tick, Tick, Boom!" (April 20, 2004)
4.19: "Afterboom" (April 27, 2004)
4.20: "Luke Can See Her Face" (May 4, 2004)
4.21: "Last Week Fights, This Week Tights" (May 11, 2004)
4.22: "Raincoats and Recipes" (May 18, 2004)

Season Five

5.01: "Say Goodbye to Daisy Miller" (September 21, 2004)
5.02: "A Messenger, Nothing More" (September 28, 2004)
5.03: "Written in the Stars" (October 5, 2004)
5.04: "Tippecanoe and Taylor, Too" (October 12, 2004)
5.05: "We Got Us a Pippi Virgin" (October 19, 2004)
5.06: "Norman Mailer, I'm Pregnant!" (October 26, 2004)
5.07: "You Jump, I Jump, Jack" (November 2, 2004)
5.08: "The Party's Over" (November 9, 2004)
5.09: "Emily Says Hello" (November 16, 2004)
5.10: "But Not as Cute as Pushkin" (November 30, 2004)
5.11: "Women of Questionable Morals" (January 25, 2005)
5.12: "Come Home" (February 1, 2005)
5.13: "Wedding Bell Blues" (February 8, 2005)
5.14: "Say Something" (February 15, 2005)
5.15: "Jews and Chinese Food" (February 22, 2005)
5.16: "So . . . Good Talk" (March 1, 2005)
5.17: "Pulp Friction" (March 8, 2005)
5.18: "To Live and Let Diorama" (April 19, 2005)
5.19: "But I'm a Gilmore!" (April 26, 2005)
5.20: "How Many Kropogs to Cape Cod?" (May 3, 2005)
5.21: "Blame Booze and Melville" (May 10, 2005)
5.22: "A House Is Not a Home" (May 17, 2005)

Season Six

6.01: "The New and Improved Lorelai Gilmore" (September 13, 2005)

6.02: "Fight Face" (September 20, 2005)
6.03: "The UnGraduate" (September 27, 2005)
6.04: "Always a Godmother, Never a God" (October 4, 2005)
6.05: "We've Got Magic to Do" (October 11, 2005)
6.06: "Welcome to the Dollhouse" (October 18, 2005)
6.07: "Twenty-one Is the Loneliest Number" (October 25, 2005)
6.08: "Let Me Hear Your Balalaikas Ringing Out" (November 8, 2005)
6.09: "The Prodigal Daughter Returns" (November 15, 2005)
6.10: "He's Slippin' 'Em Bread . . . Dig?" (November 22, 2005)
6.11: "The Perfect Dress" (January 10, 2006)
6.12: "Just Like Gwen and Gavin" (January 17, 2006)
6.13: "Friday Night's Alright for Fighting" (January 31, 2006)
6.14: "You've Been Gilmored" (February 7, 2006)
6.15: "A Vineyard Valentine" (February 14, 2006)
6.16: "Bridesmaids Revisited" (February 28, 2006)
6.17: "I'm OK, You're OK" (April 4, 2006)
6.18: "The Real Paul Anka" (April 11, 2006)
6.19: "I Get a Sidekick Out of You" (April 18, 2006)
6.20: "Super Cool Party People" (April 25, 2006)
6.21: "Driving Miss Gilmore" (May 2, 2006)
6.22: "Partings" (May 9, 2006)

Season Seven

7.01: "The Long Morrow" (September 26, 2006)
7.02: "That's What You Get, Folks, for Makin' Whoopee" (October 3, 2006)
7.03: "Lorelai's First Cotillion" (October 10, 2006)
7.04: "'S Wonderful, 'S Marvelous" (October 17, 2006)
7.05: "The Great Stink" (October 24, 2006)
7.06: "Go, Bulldogs!" (November 7, 2006)
7.07: "French Twist" (November 14, 2006)
7.08: "Introducing Lorelai Planetarium" (November 21, 2006)
7.09: "Knit, People, Knit!" (November 28, 2006)

7.10: "Merry Fisticuffs" (December 5, 2006)
7.11: "Santa's Secret Stuff" (January 23, 2007)
7.12: "To Whom It May Concern" (January 30, 2007)
7.13: "I'd Rather Be in Philadelphia" (February 6, 2007)
7.14: "Farewell, My Pet" (February 13, 2007)
7.15: "I'm a Kayak, Hear Me Roar" (February 20, 2007)
7.16: "Will You Be My Lorelai Gilmore?" (February 27, 2007)
7.17: "Gilmore Girls Only" (March 6, 2007)
7.18: "Hay Bale Maze" (April 17, 2007)
7.19: "It's Just Like Riding a Bike" (April 24, 2007)
7.20: "Lorelai? Lorelai?" (May 1, 2007)
7.21: "Unto the Breach" (May 8, 2007)
7.22: "Bon Voyage" (May 15, 2007)

Works Cited

Books, Chapters, and Articles

Adams, Elizabeth Kemper. 1921. *Women Professional Workers*. New York: Macmillan.

Addison, Joseph, and Sir Richard Steele. 1986. "The Royal Exchange." In *Norton Anthology of English Literature,* edited by M. H. Abrams, 1:2478–81. New York: Norton.

Altman, Rick. 1987. *The American Film Musical*. Bloomington: Indiana Univ. Press.

Alton, Larry. 2016. "Millennials Are Struggling to Get Jobs—Here's Why, and What to Do about It." *Forbes*, Dec. 22. https://www.forbes.com/sites/larryalton/2016/12/22/millennials-are-struggling-to-get-jobs-heres-why-and-what-to-do-about-it/.

Amesley, Cassandra. 1989. "How to Watch *Star Trek*." *Cultural Studies* 3, no. 3: 323–39.

Anderson, Benedict. 2006. *Imagined Communities: Reflections on the Origin and Spread of Nationalism*. Rev. ed. London: Verso.

Anderson, Christopher. 2005. "Television Networks and the Uses of Drama." In *Thinking Outside the Box: A Contemporary Television Genre Reader*, edited by Gary R. Edgerton and Brian G. Rose, 65–87. Lexington: Univ. Press of Kentucky.

Antonucci, Toni C., Hiroko Akiyama, and Jennifer E. Lansford. 1998. "Negative Effects of Close Social Relations." *Family Relations* 47: 379–84.

Argabrite, Angie, and Dawnie Walton. 2003. "Love Is in the Air: Who's TV's Hottest Couple?" *Entertainment Weekly,* Jan. 27.

Arnold, Sarah. 2016. "Netflix and the Myth of Choice/Participation/Autonomy." In *The Netflix Effect: Technology and Entertainment in the*

21st Century, edited by Kevin McDonald and Daniel Smith-Rowsey, 49–62. New York: Bloomsbury Academic.

Amesley, Cassandra. 1989. "How to Watch *Star Trek*." *Cultural Studies* 3, no. 3: 323–39.

Anderson, Benedict. 2006. *Imagined Communities: Reflections on the Origin and Spread of Nationalism*. Rev. ed. London: Verso.

Anderson, Christopher. 2005. "Television Networks and the Uses of Drama." In *Thinking Outside the Box: A Contemporary Television Genre Reader*, edited by Gary R. Edgerton and Brian G. Rose, 65–87. Lexington: Univ. Press of Kentucky.

Antonucci, Toni C., Hiroko Akiyama, and Jennifer E. Lansford. 1998. "Negative Effects of Close Social Relations." *Family Relations* 47: 379–84.

Argabrite, Angie, and Dawnie Walton. 2003. "Love Is in the Air: Who's TV's Hottest Couple?" *Entertainment Weekly*, Jan. 27.

Bakhtin, Mikhail. 1981. *Four Essays by M. M. Bakhtin*. Edited by M. Holquist. Translated by C. Emerson and M. Holquist. Austin: Univ. of Texas Press.

Baldwin, Kristen. 2000. "*Gilmore Girls:* Auto Pilot." *Entertainment Weekly*, June 19.

Baxter, Leslie A. 1988. "A Dialectical Perspective on Communication Strategies in Relationship Development." In *A Handbook of Personal Relationships*, edited by Steve Duck. New York: John Wiley and Sons.

Baxter, Leslie A., and Barbara Montgomery. 1996. *Relating: Dialogues and Dialectics*. New York: Guilford.

Baym, Nancy K. 2000. *Tune in, Log on: Soaps, Fandom, and Online Community*. Thousand Oaks, Calif.: Sage.

Berger, Charles. 1988. "Uncertainty and Information Exchange in Developing Relationships." In *A Handbook of Personal Relationships*, edited by Steve Duck. New York: John Wiley and Sons.

Bergman, Anne. 2000. "Age of Reason: The Over-40 Crowd Could Be Taking Back TV." *Variety*, June 13.

Berkshire, Geoffrey. 2002. "Gilmore Goes Laffer Route on Ballots: Skein Walks Comedy-Drama Line as Crix Argue Genre." *Variety*, June 13.

Bernstein, Paula. 2001. "Hot Spots Dot Racy Shows: Advertisers Resist Temptation." *Variety*, Feb. 21.

Bielby, Denise D., Lee Harrington, and William T. Bielby. 1999. "Whose Stories Are They? Fans' Engagement with Soap Opera Narratives in

Three Sites of Fan Activity." *Journal of Broadcasting & Electronic Media* 43, no. 1: 35–51.

Bordwell, David. 1985. *Narration in the Fiction Film.* London: Routledge.

Bordwell, David, Janet Staiger, and Kristin Thompson. 2002. *The Classical Hollywood Cinema.* London: Routledge.

Bourdieu, Pierre. 1984. *Distinction: A Social Critique of the Judgment of Taste.* Translated by Richard Nice. 1979. Reprint, Cambridge: Harvard Univ. Press.

Brewer, John, and Roy Porter, eds. 1993. *Consumption and the World of Goods: Consumption and Culture in 17th and 18th Centuries.* New York: Routledge.

Browne, Nick. 1996. "The Undoing of the Other Woman: Madam Butterfly in the Discourse of American Orientalism." In *The Birth of Whiteness: Race and the Emergence of U.S. Cinema,* edited by Daniel Bernardi, 226–56. New Brunswick: Rutgers Univ. Press.

Brumberg, Joan Jacobs. 1997. "The Appetite as Voice." In *Food and Culture,* edited by Carole Counihan and Penny Van Esterik, 159–79. New York: Routledge.

Brunsdon, Charlotte. 1991. "Crossroads: Notes on a Soap Opera." In *Imitations of Life: A Reader on Film and Television Melodrama,* edited by Marcia Landy, 466–71. Detroit: Wayne State Univ. Press.

Bryan, Frank M. 2004. *Real Democracy: The New England Town Meeting and How It Works.* Chicago: Univ. of Chicago Press.

Butler, Judith. 1993. *Bodies That Matter: On the Discursive Limits of "Sex."* New York: Routledge.

Caldwell, John T. 2000. "Excessive Style: The Crisis of Network Television." In *Television: The Critical View,* edited by Horace Newcomb, 649–86. 6th ed. New York: Oxford Univ. Press.

Clarke, Kelly. 2005. "Bite Club: Touched by the Frosting; Saint Cupcake Blesses Northwest Portland." *Willamette Week,* Dec. 14.

Cohan, Steven. 1997. *Masked Men: Masculinity and the Movies in the 1950s.* Bloomington: Indiana Univ. Press.

Costello, Matthew. 1999. "The Pilgrimage and Progress of George Bailey: Puritanism, *It's a Wonderful Life,* and the Language of Community in America." *American Studies* 40, no. 3: 31–52.

Cott, Nancy F. 2000. *Public Vows: A History of Marriage and the Nation.* Cambridge: Harvard Univ. Press.

Courtwright, David T. 2002. *Forces of Habit: Drugs and the Making of the Modern World*. Cambridge: Harvard Univ. Press.

Cresswell, Tim. 2004. *Place: A Short Introduction*. Malden, Mass.: Blackwell.

Crosby, Christina. 1994. "A Taste for More." Unpublished paper, presented at "New Economic Criticism," Case Western Reserve Univ., Cleveland, Oct. 22.

Cullen, Jim. 2003. *The American Dream: A Short History of an Idea That Shaped a Nation*. London: Oxford Univ. Press.

Curtis, Gerard. 1995. "Dickens in the Visual Market." In *Literature in the Marketplace: Nineteenth-Century British Publishing and Reading Practices,* edited by John O. Jordan and Robert L. Patten, 213–49. Cambridge: Cambridge Univ. Press.

Defoe, Daniel. 1994. *Robinson Crusoe*. Edited by Michael Shinagel. New York: W. W. Norton.

Dempsey, John. 2004. "True Invites Gastineau Duo to Reality TV Party: Mother/Daughter Partygoers Become Celebs." *Variety,* Aug. 29.

Doane, Mary Ann. 2000. "Women's Stake: Filming the Female Body." In *Feminism and Film,* edited by E. Ann Kaplan, 86–99. Oxford: Oxford Univ. Press.

Dyer, Richard. 2003. *Heavenly Bodies: Film Stars and Society*. 2nd ed. London: Routledge.

Eagleton, Terry. 2005. *The English Novel: An Introduction*. London: Blackwell Press.

Echart, Pablo. 2005. *La comedia romántica del Hollywood de los años 30 y 40*. Madrid: Cátedra.

Ferguson, Andrew. 1998. "Ye Olde Town Gimmick." *Time,* Mar. 2.

Feuer, Jane. 1984. "Melodrama, Serial Form, and Television Today." *Screen* 25, no. 1: 4–16.

Fiske, John. 1987. *Television Culture*. London: Routledge.

Freeman, Michael. 2003. "Dramedy Makers Need to Choose Sides: *Ed, Sex, Gilmore* Tough to Categorize." *Variety,* June 10.

Fretts, Bruce. 2000a. "*Gilmore Girls:* Happy Gilmore." *Entertainment Weekly,* Sept. 29.

———. 2000b. "*Gilmore Girls:* Whirled Series." *Entertainment Weekly,* Nov. 14.

———. 2001. "*Gilmore Girls:* Ballot Boxing." *Entertainment Weekly,* June 14.

Friedberg, Anne. 1993. *Window Shopping: Cinema and the Postmodern.* Berkeley and Los Angeles: Univ. of California Press.

Frost, Bill. 2002. "Dirtnap Central: Your Favorite TV Shows Have Been Canceled, but Just Look at the New Crap a-Comin'!" *Salt Lake City Weekly,* May 23.

Friedberg, Anne. 1993. *Window Shopping: Cinema and the Postmodern.* Berkeley and Los Angeles: Univ. of California Press.

Frost, Bill. 2002. "Dirtnap Central: Your Favorite TV Shows Have Been Canceled, but Just Look at the New Crap a-Comin'!" *Salt Lake City Weekly,* May 23.

Fry, Richard. 2016. "For First Time in Modern Era, Living with Parents Edges Out Other Living Arrangements for 18- to 34-Year-Olds." *Pew Research Center*, May 24. http://www.pewsocialtrends.org/2016/05/24/for-first-time-in-modern-era-living-with-parents-edges-out-other-living-arrangements-for-18-to-34-year-olds/.

Frye, Northrop. 1991. *Anatomía de la crítica*. Caracas: Monte Avila.

Gehring, Wes D. 2004. "Screwball of the Silver Screen." *USA Today Magazine,* Mar., 62–65.

Graser, Marc. 2002. "H'wood Looking to Land Brands: BMW, Ford Pioneering Ad Appeal." *Variety,* Nov. 14.

Grasso, Aldo, and Massimo Scaglioni. 2003. *Che cos'è la televisione.* Milan: Garzanti.

Grego, Melissa. 2003. "Girls Going to ABC Family: Agreement a First: Multi-year Run to Debut Fall 2004." *Variety,* Jan. 22.

Griffin, Em. 2008. *A First Look at Communication Theory.* 7th ed. Boston: McGraw-Hill.

Gruber, Howard E. 1985. "Which Way Is Up? A Developmental Question." In *Adult Cognitive Development,* edited by R. A. Mines and K. S. Kitchener, 112–33. New York: Praeger.

Hall, Stuart. 1980. "Encoding/Decoding." In *Culture, Media, Language,* edited by Stuart Hall et al. London: Routledge.

Hanson, Christopher. 1996. "Where Have All the Heroes Gone?" *Columbia Journalism Review* 34, no. 6: 45–48.

Harris, Kristin. 2014. "The Best Twitter Reactions to *Gilmore Girls* Coming to Netflix." *BuzzFeed*, Sept. 11. https://www.buzzfeed.com/kristinharris/the-best-twitter-reactions-to-gilmore-girls-coming-to-netfli?utm_term=.klQM4W3Qn#.ot3d1N8wg.

Heffernan, Virginia. 2005. "The Gilmore Noodge." *New York Times,* Jan. 23.

———. 2006. "A Series Changes Horses, and the Ride Gets Bumpy." *New York Times,* Nov. 7, E1.

Hewlett, Sylvia Ann. 2002. *Creating a Life: Professional Women and the Quest for Children.* New York: Hyperion/Miramax.

Hills, Matt. 2004. "Defining Cult TV: Texts, Inter-texts, and Fan Audiences." In *The Television Studies Reader,* edited by Robert C. Allen and Annette Hill, 509–23. New York: Routledge.

Indvik, Julie, and Mary Anne Fitzpatrick. 1986. "Perceptions of Inclusion, Affiliation, and Control in Five Interpersonal Relationships." *Communication Quarterly* 34: 1–13.

Jacobsen, Craig. 2006. "How TV Met Narrative Sophistication." *FlowTV: A Critical Forum on Television and Media Culture* 5, no. 1. Available at http://www.flowtv.org.

James, Caryn. 2001. "Home Sweet Home, but Not Saccharine." *New York Times,* Feb. 25, TE4.

Jameson, Fredric. 1991. *Postmodernism; or, The Cultural Logic of Late Capitalism.* London: Verso.

Jancovich, Mark, and James Lyons. 2003. Introduction to *Quality Popular Television: Cult TV, Fans, and the Industry,* edited by Mark Jancovich and James Lyons. London: British Film Institute.

Jenkins, Henry. 1992. *Textual Poachers: Television Fans and Participatory Culture.* New York: Routledge.

———. 2002. "Interactive Audiences? The 'Collective Intelligence' of Media Fans." In *The New Media Book,* edited by Dan Harries, 157–70. London: British Film Institute.

———. 2006. *Convergence Culture: Where Old and New Media Collide.* New York: New York Univ. Press.

Jenkins, Henry, and John Tulloch. 1995. *Science Fiction Audiences: Watching "Doctor Who" and "Star Trek."* London: Routledge.

Jenner, Mareike. 2016. "Is This TVIV? On Netflix, TVIII and Binge-Watching." *New Media & Society* 18 (2): 257–73.

Jewel, Dan. 2002. "*Gilmore Girls* w/o the Suds, Please." *Media Life Magazine,* Nov. 11.

"Journalism Must Be Carefully Integrated." 2005. *Yale Daily News,* Nov. 16. http://www.yaledailynews.com/articles/view/15724.

Kelley, Harold H., and John W. Thibaut. 1978. *Interpersonal Relationships.* New York: John Wiley and Sons.

Kibria, Nazli. 2002. *Becoming Asian American: Second-Generation Chinese and Korean American Identities.* Baltimore: John Hopkins Univ. Press.

Kowaleski-Wallace, Elizabeth. 1997. *Consuming Subjects: Women, Shopping, and Business in the Eighteenth Century.* New York: Columbia Univ. Press.

Kozloff, Sarah. 1992. "Narrative Theory and Television." In *Channels of Discourse Reassembled: Television and Contemporary Criticism,* edited by Robert C. Allen, 67–100. London: Routledge.

Krutnik, Frank. 1990. "The Faint Aroma of Performing Seals: The 'Nervous' Romance and the Comedy of the Sexes." *Velvet Light Trap* (Fall): 57–73.

LeBesco, Kathleen. 2001. "There's Always Room for Resistance: Jell-O, Gender, and Social Class." In *Cooking Lessons: The Politics of Gender and Food,* edited by Sherrie A. Inness, 129–49. Lanham, Md.: Rowman and Littlefield.

Lindsey, Cameron. 2016. "Questioning Netflix's Revolutionary Impact: Changes in the Business and Consumption of Television." In *The Netflix Effect: Technology and Entertainment in the 21st Century*, edited by Kevin McDonald and Daniel Smith-Rowsey, 173–84. New York: Bloomsbury Academic.

Lotz, Amanda. 2004. "Textual (Im)possibilities in the U.S. Post-network Era: Negotiating Production and Promotion Practices on Lifetime's Any Day Now." *Critical Studies in Media Communication* 21, no. 1: 22–43.

———. 2006. *Redesigning Women: Television after the Network Era.* Urbana: Univ. of Illinois Press.

———. 2007. *The Television Will Be Revolutionized.* New York: New York Univ. Press.

Lynch, Moira. 2006. "The Gilmore Girls Stay Girly Enough." *Columbia Daily Spectator,* Oct. 31.

Lyons, Margaret. 2016. "Watched All of the *Gilmore Girls* Revival? Let's Talk about It." *New York Times*, Nov. 29. https://www.nytimes.com/2016/11/29/arts/television/gilmore-girls-netflix-revival-recap.html.

Lyons, Sydnee. 2017. "The 30-Something Gang on *Gilmore Girls* Hits Way Too Close to Home." *Her Campus*, Jan. 11. http://www.hercampus.com/entertainment/30-something-gang-gilmore-girls-hits-way-too-close-home.

Mackey, Margaret. 2003. "Television and the Teenage Literate: Discourses of *Felicity*." *College English* 65, no. 4: 389–411.

Mackin, Anne. 2006. *Americans and Their Land: The House Built on Abundance*. Ann Arbor: Univ. of Michigan Press.

Martin, Denise. 2005. "*Gilmore Girls:* The Definitive WB." *Variety*, Jan. 20.

May, Elaine Tyler. 1988. *Homeward Bound: American Families in the Cold War Era*. New York: Perseus.

Maynard, Kevin. 2002. "Indie Helmers Zoom in on Cable Gigs: Newfound Freedom in P'gramming Pulling Pic Directors." *Variety*, June 14.

McDonald, Kevin, and Daniel Smith-Rowsey, eds. 2016. *The Netflix Effect: Technology and Entertainment in the 21st Century*. New York: Bloomsbury Academic.

Melville, Herman. 2007. *Moby Dick; or, The White Whale*. Charleston: Bibliobazaar.

"Mencken's Chrestomathy." 2004. *Your Guide to "Gilmore"-isms: The 411 of the Show's Witty and Memorable Wordplays and Pop Culture References*. Los Angeles: Warner Bros. Entertainment.

Metz, Christian. 1974. *Film Language: A Semiotics of the Cinema*. Translated by Michael Taylor. New York: Oxford Univ. Press.

Mittell, Jason. 2004. *Genre and Television: From Cop Shows to Cartoons in American Culture*. New York: Routledge.

———. 2006. "Narrative Complexity in Contemporary American Television." *Velvet Light Trap* 58 (Fall): 29–40.

Modleski, Tania. 1998. "My Life as a Romance Writer." In *Old Wives' Tales and Other Women's Stories*. New York: New York Univ. Press.

Morrison, Sara. 2007. "Your Guide to the Real Stars Hollow Business World." In *Coffee at Luke's: An Unauthorized "Gilmore Girls" Gabfest*, edited by Jennifer Crusie. Dallas: BenBella Books.

Murray, Simone. 2004. "'Celebrating the Story the Way It Is': Cultural Studies, Corporate Media, and the Contested Utility of Fandom." *Continuum: Journal of Media and Cultural Studies* 18, no. 1: 7-25.

Neale, Steve, and Krutnik, Frank. 1995. *Popular Film and Television Comedy*. London: Routledge.

Neuhaus, Jessamyn. 2001. "Women and Cooking in Marital Sex Manuals." In *Kitchen Culture in America: Popular Representations of Food, Gender, and Race*, edited by Sherrie A. Inness, 95–117. Philadelphia: Univ. of Pennsylvania Press.

O'Brien, Geoffrey. 2007. "A Northern New Jersey of the Mind." *New York Review of Books,* Aug. 16.

Parks, Lisa. 2003. "Brave New *Buffy:* Rethinking 'TV Violence.'" In *Quality Popular Television: Cult TV, Fans, and the Industry,* edited by Mark Jancovich and James Lyons. London: British Film Institute.

Patten, Robert L. 1995. "Serialized Retrospection in *The Pickwick Papers.*" In *Literature in the Marketplace: Nineteenth-Century British Publishing and Reading Practices,* edited by John O. Jordan and Robert L. Patten, 122–42. Cambridge: Cambridge Univ. Press.

Perry, Mark J. 2015. "The 'Netflix Effect': An Excellent Example of 'Creative Destruction.'" AEIdeas, Aug. 6. http://www.aei.org/publication/the-netflix-effect-is-an-excellent-example-of-creative-destruction/.

Press, Joy. 2004. "TV Review: *Gilmore Girls.*" *Village Voice,* Oct. 27.

Priggé, Steven. 2005. *Created by . . . : Inside the Minds of TV's Top Show Creators.* Los Angeles: Silman-James Press.

PR Newswire. 2003. "TV Review: *The O.C.*" *Village Voice,* Aug. 20, 49.

———. 2004. "TV Review: *Weeds.*" *Village Voice,* Oct. 27, 52.

———. 2006. "American Eagle Outfitters and the CW Television Network Announce Groundbreaking Partnership for Tuesday Nights: 'aerie Tuesdays on the CW' to Feature Real-Life aerie Customers in Unscripted Chat Sessions Appearing During *Gilmore Girls* and *Veronica Mars.*" *Television Week*, Sept. 14.

Radway, Janice. 1984. *Reading the Romance: Women, Patriarchy, and Popular Literature.* Chapel Hill: Univ. of North Carolina Press.

Ricchiardi, Sherry, and Virginia Young. 1991. *Women on Deadline.* Iowa: Iowa State Univ. Press.

Robinson, Tasha. 2002. "Joss Whedon." In *The Tenacity of the Cockroach: Conversations with Entertainment's Most Enduring Outsiders*, edited by Stephen Thompson, 369–77. New York: Three Rivers Press.

Rosen, Ruth. 2000. *The World Split Open: How the Modern Women's Movement Changed America.* New York: Penguin Books.

Rowe, Stephanie. 2007. "It's Not Luke's Stubble." In *Coffee at Luke's: An Unauthorized "Gilmore Girls" Gabfest,* edited by Jennifer Crusie, 107–18. Dallas: BenBella Books.

Said, Edward. 1979. *Orientalism.* New York: Vintage Book.

Saltzman, Joe. 2002. "Frank Capra and the Image of Journalists in American Film." *USA Today Magazine,* Nov., 54–56.

Schatz, Thomas. 1981. *Hollywood Genres: Formulas, Filmmaking, and the Studio System*. Austin: Univ. of Texas Press.

Schneider, Michael. 2000. "Frog Leaps Ahead with New Laffers: WB Decides to Skip over Repeats for Some Skeins." *Variety*, Sept. 8.

———. 2005. "Irked Competish Asks: Is *Desperate* a Laffer? Net Enters Dark Hourlong in Comedy Category." *Variety*, June 14.

Scodari, Christine. 1995. "Possession, Attraction, and the Thrill of the Chase: Gendered Myth-Making in Film and the Television Comedy of the Sexes." *Critical Studies in Mass Communication* 12: 23–39.

Shames, Laurence. 2005. "The More Factor." In *Signs of Life in the U.S.A.: Readings on Popular Culture for Writers*, edited by Sonia Maasik and Jack Solomon, 55–61. 5th ed. Boston: Bedford/St. Martin's.

Shammas, Carole. 1990. *The Pre-industrial Consumer in England and America*. New York: Oxford Univ. Press.

Shaw, Jessica. 2016. "*Gilmore Girls* Revival: Edward Herrmann's Death to Be Paid Tribute." *Entertainment Weekly*, Apr. 8.

Sim, Gerald. 2016. "Individual Disruptors and Economic Gamechangers: Netflix, New Media, and Neoliberalism." In *The Netflix Effect: Technology and Entertainment in the 21st Century*, edited by Kevin McDonald and Daniel Smith-Rowsey, 185–202. New York: Bloomsbury Academic.

Simpson, John Warfield. 1999. *Visions of Paradise: Glimpses of Our Landscape's Legacy*. Berkeley and Los Angeles: Univ. of California Press.

Smith, Greg M. 1995. "Plotting a Show about Nothing: Patterns of Narration in *Seinfeld*." *Creative Screenwriting* 2, no. 1: 82–90.

Speier, Michael. 2002. "TV Review: *Everwood*." *Variety*, Sept. 10.

Spigel, Lynn. 2004. "Entertainment Wars: Television Culture after 9/11." *American Quarterly* 56, no. 2: 235–70.

Spitzberg, Brian H., and William R. Cupach, eds. 1998. *The Dark Side of Close Relationships*. Boston: Lawrence Erlbaum.

Stam, Robert. 1985. *Reflexivity in Film and Literature: From Don Quixote to Jean-Luc Godard*. Ann Arbor: Univ. of Michigan Press.

Stanhope, Kate. 2016a. "*Gilmore Girls* Team Open Up about Netflix Revival and 'Journey' to Those Final Four Words." *The Hollywood Reporter*, July 27. http://www.hollywoodreporter.com/live-feed/gilmore-girls-netflix-revival-preview-915022.

———. 2016b. "*Gilmore Girls* Bosses on How Edward Herrmann's Death Inspired the Revival and the Series' Future." *The Hollywood Reporter*,

Nov. 17. http://www.hollywoodreporter.com/live-feed/gilmore-girls-creator-netflix-revival-948258

Steinlight, Emily. 2006. "Anti-break House: Advertising and the Victorian Novel." *Narrative* 14, no. 2: 132–62.

Taggi, Paolo. 1997. *Un programma di: Scrivere per la television.* Milan: Pratiche Editrice.

Tasker, Yvonne. 2000. *Working Girls.* London: Routledge.

Teachman, Jay D., Lucky M. Tedrow, and Kyle D. Crowder. 2000. "The Changing Demography of America's Families." *Journal of Marriage and the Family* 62, no. 4: 1234–46.

"Television: Wholesome Goodness." 2000. *American Demographics* (Aug.).

Thompson, Robert J. 1996. "Television's Second Golden Age: The Quality Shows." *Television Quarterly* 28, no. 3: 75–81.

Tiffany, Kaitlyn. 2016. "The New *Gilmore Girls* Is Weirdly Hostile toward Fans, Women, and Storytelling in General." *The Verge*, Nov. 28. https://www.theverge.com/2016/11/28/13765088/gilmore-girls-year-in-the-life-review-netflix.

Tobias, Scott. 2005. "Interview with Amy Sherman-Palladino." *Onion AV Club.* http://www.avclub.com/content/node/23372/print/2.

Tseng, Ada. 2006. "You Break, You Buy: The Indelible Mark of *Gilmore Girls.*" *Asian Pacific Arts,* a biweekly Web magazine, Aug. 23. Los Angeles: UCLA Asia Institute http://www.asiaarts.ucla.edu.

Tuan, Yi-Fu. 2001. *Space and Place: The Perspective of Experience.* Minneapolis: Univ. of Minnesota Press.

Tucker, Ken. 2000. "*Gilmore Girls:* Hits and Messes." *Entertainment Weekly,* Oct. 3.

Veblen, Thorstein. 1925. *The Theory of the Leisure Class.* 1899. Reprint, New York: Huebsch.

Walen, Heather R., and Margie E. Lachman. 2000. "Social Support and Strain from Partner, Family, and Friends: Costs and Benefits for Men and Women in Adulthood." *Journal of Social and Personal Relationships* 17: 5–30.

Watt, Ian. 1987. *The Rise of the Novel: Studies in Defoe, Richardson, and Fielding.* London: Hogarth Press.

Weber, Max. 2000. *The Protestant Ethic and the Spirit of Capitalism.* Translated by Talcott Parsons. London: Routledge.

Weiner, Allison Hope. 2002. "The Story Behind the Hit Show *Gilmore Girls.*" *Entertainment Weekly,* Mar. 19.

Weinman, Jaime. 2006. "How to Make Fans Very, Very Angry." *Macleans* (Aug. 21): 88.

"Welcome to the *Gilmore Girls*." 2004. Making-of Documentary. Season One DVD. Los Angeles: Warner Bros.

Westbrook, Perry. 1982. *The New England Town in Fact and Fiction*. Madison, N.J.: Fairleigh Dickinson Univ. Press.

Whedon, Joss. 2003. "An Interview with Joss Whedon: The *Buffy the Vampire Slayer* Creator Discusses His Career." *Film Force*. http://filmforce.ign.com/articles/425/425492p1.html.

Wilonsky, Robert. 2003. "Me and My Beaver; Plus: Where's Newy?" *Dallas Observer*, Apr. 10.

Winters, Jill. 2007. "Happiness under Glass: The Truth about Lorelai and Life in Stars Hollow." In *Coffee at Luke's: An Unauthorized "Gilmore Girls" Gabfest*, edited by Jennifer Crusie, 97–106. Dallas: BenBella Books.

Winthrop, John. 2003. "A Model of Christian Charity." In *Norton Anthology of American Literature*, edited by Nina Baym, 95–105. 6th ed. New York: Norton.

Wynne, Deborah. 2001. *The Sensational Novel and the Victorian Family Magazine*. New York: Palgrave.

"Yale Launches Journalism Initiative." 2006. Press release, Jan. 25. http://www.yale.edu/opa/newsr/06-01-25-04.all.html.

Yahr, Emily. 2017. "More *Gilmore Girls*? Actually, Netflix, We're Good." *Washington Post*, Mar. 8. https://www.washingtonpost.com/news/arts-and-entertainment/wp/2017/03/08/more-gilmore-girls-actually-netflix-were-good/.

Zahed, Ramin. 2002. "Laughter, Tears Merge in Dramedy: Genre Mimics Life Better than Sitcoms, Dramas, Sez *Ed* Scribe." *Variety*, Sept. 2.

Zukin, Sharon. 1995. *The Cultures of Cities*. Malden, Mass.: Blackwell.

Miscellaneous Web Sources

"American Women: Women and the New Business." n.d. http://memory.loc.gov/ammem/awhhtml/awser2/women_in.html.

"And Then He Smiled at Me." n.d. *FanFiction.Net*. http://www.fanfiction.net/s/3281921/1/.

"Bob Woodward: About the Author." n.d. http://www.bobwoodward.com/About/.

"Christiane Amanpour." n.d. http://edition.cnn.com/CNN/anchors_reporters/amanpour.christiane.html.

"Christopher." n.d. *Television Without Pity*. http://forums.televisionwithoutpity.com/index.php?showtopic=3118377&st=0.

"Family Guide to Prime Time Television: *Gilmore Girls*." n.d. *Parents Television Council: Family TV Guide Show*. http://www.parentstv.org/.

"Family Guide to Prime Time Television: *The O.C.*" n.d. *Parents Television Council: Family TV Guide Show*. http://www.parentstv.org/.

Gregorybnyc. 2004. "A Chick Series Even Boys Could Love." *Internet Movie Database,* May 26. http://www.imdb.com/title/tt0238784/.

Harvard Extension School: Journalism and Publishing. n.d. http://www.extension.harvard.edu/journalism/.

"Helping Rory." n.d. *FanFiction.Net*. http://www.fanfiction.net/s/2585223/1/.

"Honk If You're in the Hartford Elite." n.d. *FanFiction.Net*. http://www.fanfiction.net/s/3049794/1/.

"Ida Tarbell: Life and Works." n.d. http://tarbell.allegheny.edu/biobib.html.

"It's Right There." n.d. *Black & White & Red: "Gilmore Girls" Fanfic Archive*. http://www.gilmore-fiction.net/viewstory.php?sid=353&warning=Adult.

"It's Still There." n.d. *Black & White & Red: "Gilmore Girls" Fanfic Archive*. http://www.gilmore-fiction.net/viewstory.php?sid=505.

"Lorelai." n.d. *Television Without Pity*. http://forums.televisionwithoutpity.com/index.php?showtopic=1194825&st=0.

"Lorelai and Christopher." n.d. *Television Without Pity*. http://forums.televisionwithoutpity.com/index.php?showtopic=3138720&st=0.

"Lorelai and Emily." n.d. *Television Without Pity*. http://forums.televisionwithoutpity.com/index.php?showtopic=3118502&st=0.

"Lorelai and Luke." n.d. *Television Without Pity*. http://forums.televisionwithoutpity.com/index.php?showtopic=2583896&st=0.

"Lorelai and Rory." n.d. *Television Without Pity*. http://forums.televisionwithoutpity.com/index.php?showtopic=3118418&st=0.

Mercy Bell. 2002. "Life (Caffeinated, with Some Lemon Juice Please)." *Internet Movie Database*, Aug. 16. http://www.imdb.com/title/tt0238 784/.

Natan62. 2003. "Modern Day Jane Austen." *Internet Movie Database,* Feb. 26. http://www.imdb.com/title/tt0238784/.

"Nieman Foundation for Journalism at Harvard." n.d. http://www.nieman.harvard.edu.

"One Is the Loneliest Number: The Unpopular Opinions Thread." n.d. *Television Without Pity*. http://forums.televisionwithoutpity.com/index.php?showtopic=3145192&st=0.

"Pilot: Trivia & Quotes." n.d. TV.com. http://www.tv.com/gilmore-girls/pilot/episode/2800/trivia.html#quotes.

Stillbits12. 2004. "Fast Paced, Intelligent Show." Internet Movie Database, Aug. 19. http://www.imdb.com/title/tt0238784/.

"Tom Wolfe." n.d. http://www.tomwolfe.com/bio.html.

"Women's History." n.d. *About.com*. http://womenshistory.about.com/library/prm/blcommunications.htm.

"Yale Journalism Initiative." n.d. http://www.yale.edu/writing/journalism.

"Yale Launches Journalism Initiative." n.d. http://www.yale.edu/opa/newsr/06-01-25-04.all.html.

Index